"Scriptural, searching, haunting, humbling, challenging, energizing, down-to-earth, up-to-the-minute—all this and more is true of *Being the Body*, a radical update of Colson's blockbuster of a decade ago, now even more powerful than it was before. Here is visionary dynamite. Read it thoughtfully, and it will mark you for life."

—J. I. PACKER, Professor and best-selling
author of *Knowing God*

"No one can match Colson's unique blend of story-telling, contemporary insight and prophetic vision."

—PHILLIP YANCEY, best-selling
author of *Soul Survivor*

"Chuck Colson and Ellen Vaughn have once again given us a compelling and humbling testament to how God's grace and truth are best embodied when the church truly lives *Coram Deo*—before the eyes of God. Through numerous stories from the earliest days of Christianity to the present . . . your heart will be touched and your mind challenged."

—RAVI ZACHARIAS, best-selling
author of *Jesus Among Other Gods*

"Chuck Colson is a national treasure—not only that, he is a light for the universal church. The church, as Dr. Colson teaches us again: that embodied presence of Christ active in the world, today as yesterday."

—MICHAEL NOVAK, George Frederick Jewett Chair in
Religion, Philosophy, and Public Policy,
American Enterprise Institute

"I am profoundly challenged and encouraged. Truly, there has never been a more vital time in history than now for the Body of Christ as individuals and as a community to understand and respond to our high calling, and I'm thankful for this book that sounds that calling loud and clear."

—STEVEN CURTIS CHAPMAN, multi-platinum, Grammy and Dove Award-Wining Artist

"This passionate and piercing book made me want to stand and cheer! The church must not ignore its clarion call."

—LEE STROBEL, best-selling author of *The Case for Christ*

"It is not surprising that the world tries to squeeze the church into its own mold. That the church cooperates so readily is the true cause for alarm. In *Being the Body,* Colson and Vaughn have given us a clear picture of the way God would mold the church in the image of His Son. Read it and be challenged."

—DAVID NEFF, editor, *Christianity Today* magazine

"As America faces a difficult and uncertain future, we all must wonder—is the church able to meet the challenge of being a light for God's love and holiness in a world of growing darkness? Chuck Colson once again proves himself one of our great God and Savior's most influential agents of change as he exhorts the body of Christ to live up to its calling and its destiny."

—BILL BRIGHT, Campus Crusade for Christ

BEING
THE
BODY

CHARLES COLSON
ELLEN VAUGHN

W Publishing Group™

www.wpublishinggroup.com

A Division of Thomas Nelson, Inc.
www.ThomasNelson.com

BEING THE BODY

Published by W Publishing Group, A Division of Thomas Nelson, Inc., P. O. Box 141000, Nashville, Tennessee, 37214.

Unless otherwise indicated, Scripture quotations used in this book are from the *New King James Version,* copyright © 1979, 1980, 1982, Thomas Nelson, Inc., Publishers.

Other Scripture quotations are taken from *The Holy Bible, New International Version* (NIV), copyright © 1973, 1978, 1984 by International Bible Society. Used by permission of Zondervan Publishing House.

The King James Version of the Bible (KJV).

Study Guide prepared by T. M. Moore.

ISBN 0-8499-1752-2

Printed in the United States of America
03 04 05 06 BVG 9 8 7 6 5 4 3 2 1

Soli Deo Gloria

CONTENTS

Contents

WITH GRATITUDE

MOST WRITERS DO NOT RETREAT to solitary cloisters to ponder great thoughts and then, in glorious moments of illumination, compose timeless prose. No, at least from our perspective, books are the product of a process.

They begin with what we read and study and think about; they are influenced by thinkers and mentors, as well as the trials and joys of personal experience. Gradually, ideas begin to emerge. Some ripen into convictions. And at some point in the process, we even dare to think, *This could be a book . . .*

But even at that point, writers don't have the luxury of retreating into solitude. Books get written in the midst of living. Even as you are writing about the church, you walk into a prison cell and meet a man who reflects the true fear of the Lord. *This is what we all need,* you think. Then there are conversations with all sorts of people, more books read, ideas maturing, drafts written, consultation with theologians, and visits to churches, from South Central Los Angeles to Timisoara, Romania.

And then, most precious of all, are those moments when you sense the power and guidance of the Holy Spirit in forming convictions—and then articulating them.

We spent almost three years in that process for the first release of this book and the better part of a year on this revised edition. And it has indeed been collaborative, not only between the two of us, who have worked together for twenty-three years on *many* different writing projects, but also with Prison Fellowship colleagues, friends, pastors, and teachers.

There are so many to whom we are much indebted.

The dedication expresses the first order of gratitude. We have sensed over and over God's anointing on this work, and so we can do no other than to first consecrate this work to Him for His glory.

Then we must thank the group of scholars who contributed to the first inspirations for this work. Foremost among them is Dr. Carl F. H. Henry, Chuck's friend and teacher since the earliest days of his Christian life. Carl has taught us through the wealth of his prodigious theological, historical, and sociological knowledge, as well as through the authentic model of his own personal life. His lectures on the church, given to the Prison Fellowship staff, formed a foundation of sorts for this work; his meticulous reading and editing of the manuscript were crucially important. As we write, Carl is in a nursing home, facing severe health challenges—but because of the vitality of his writing and teaching, he remains a powerful influence on modern evangelicalism.

Next is the late Dr. Francis Schaeffer. Schaeffer's writings have profoundly affected so many evangelicals. and his writings on truth informed our theme here regarding the church as a pillar of truth in a lost culture.

Father Richard John Neuhaus has also been a tremendous inspiration. He has one of the keenest minds we've ever known. He writes with weight and gritty substance and profound insight. His book *Freedom for Ministry* was one of our richest sources. We deeply appreciate his help in reviewing portions of this manuscript, and for his contributions in our understanding of the unity of the Body.

In addition, we are indebted to Rev. T. M. Moore, pastor of teaching ministries, Cedar Springs Presbyterian Church in Knoxville, Tennessee, and theological consultant to the Wilberforce Forum and Prison Fellowship. T. M. helped formulate the earliest ideas at this book's conception and was of immense help throughout its gestation. We consider T. M. one of the bright lights in evangelical circles.

Father Tom Weinandy also reviewed and critiqued the entire original manuscript of *The Body*. This was particularly gracious since he was teaching at Oxford University at the time. Weinandy is a classical scholar, a powerful thinker, and as is apparent to all who are privileged to know him, a loving and holy man.

Dr. J. Daryl Charles, formerly of Prison Fellowship's staff, now teaching at Taylor University, provided invaluable research for the first edition of this work. We are deeply grateful to Kim Robbins of the Wilberforce Forum, who did the painstaking background research and fact checking for this edition.

We are profoundly thankful as well for Dr. Timothy George, dean of Beeson Divinity School, a member of Prison Fellowship's board of directors, and one of the most influential theologians in the evangelical world. Timothy gave generously of his counsel and advice in this anniversary edition of the book.

As always, we would not have survived or produced this book without the matchless skill of Judith Markham. Judith's editorial and conceptual expertise make her not only the best editor in the business, but the nicest as well.

In addition, we are grateful for the many pastors and laypeople in the United States who made their time available for interviews and who shared insights and experiences with us. It was a privilege to be part—even briefly—of so many tremendous and committed congregations across the country. And we will never forget the valiant brothers and sisters of Eastern Europe who so graciously opened their hearts and homes to us. Thanks also to Margaret Shannon for her special interest in Poland and World War II and for her help in accessing Library of Congress resources.

Particular thanks are in order for Rev. Bob Russell, whose taped sermons Chuck listens to faithfully each week, and Rev. John Aker, for reviewing and critiquing sections of the manuscript. Thanks also for their hospitality in opening their churches to us.

We give thanks as well to our wonderful colleagues at Prison Fellowship who managed the paper flow: first, Chuck's faithful and longtime assistants, Nancy Niemeyer, Diane Longenecker, and Val Merrill. Thanks as well to John Dawson for guarding Chuck's schedule, and for his work with our friends at W Publishing, for whom we are also most grateful.

We owe a special debt to our home church pastors, who have given us a firsthand experience of what the local Body should be: Neal Jones of Columbia Baptist in Northern Virginia was Chuck's friend and pastor for many years, and we have valued his counsel, as well as that of Dr. Hayes

Wicker of the First Baptist Church of Naples, Florida, who has been Chuck's pastor for the past ten years. We are grateful as well to John Hutchinson, senior pastor of McLean Presbyterian Church, friend to both of us and pastor to Ellen.

And finally, our thanks to the real heroes of every effort like this: our spouses, who put up with many a late night and more than a few sleepless ones.

Patty Colson has suffered through twenty books now, and through each one she has demonstrated the remarkable fortitude, generosity of spirit, and loving support that helps keep Chuck sane and continuously grateful to God for her.

And thanks to Lee Vaughn, who has maintained great grace and enthusiasm through both the challenges and the fun of Ellen's writing life, as well as Vaughn children Emily, Haley, and Walker, who have learned to be quite flexible when they see Uncle Chuck coming.

As we have stressed throughout this book, the Christian life is a corporate undertaking. Even as we acknowledge and thank those who have contributed so kindly to the completion of this project, we see that fact made clear to us yet again. We thank God for His grace in bringing us to Himself—and then knitting us into the wonderful fellowship of His Body.

—CHARLES W. COLSON
—ELLEN SANTILLI VAUGHN
December 10, 2002

PROLOGUE: CATASTROPHE

Catastrophe: *Function:* noun *Etymology: Greek* katastrophé, *from* katastrephein *to overturn, from* kata- + strephein *to turn*
1: *the final event of the dramatic action especially of a tragedy*
2: *a momentous tragic event ranging from extreme misfortune to utter overthrow or ruin*
3: *a violent and sudden change in a feature of the earth*

JOHN FELT LUCKY THAT MORNING. His nephew always said there are exactly eleven beautiful days in New York. That's all. This was one of the eleven. It was crisp, clear, the sky an endless blue—and he was heading to a breakfast meeting at the top of the World Trade Center, where the views went on forever.

The PATH train from New Jersey pulled into the station beneath the Twin Towers. He'd been commuting like this for years, but it still amazed him to see the huge river of humanity that flooded the station. Thousands of men and women all hustling toward some destination, moving toward some appointment, hurrying along one by one yet part of the whole, like some vast ant colony.

Usually John went from there to his brokerage firm three blocks away, but today he rode up the big escalator toward the lobby in Tower One. Just as he was getting off, the woman behind him stumbled and fell.

John turned to help her. Her narrow heel had gotten stuck and thrown her off balance. Now she was sitting awkwardly on the floor at the top of the escalator, dazed, the offending shoe in her hand. Her leather portfolio had fallen, and files littered the floor. Meanwhile, a swarm of people scuttled past her, stepping on her papers.

John stooped beside her. "Are you okay?" he asked. She nodded, embarrassed. "Let me help you," he said. He gathered up the files and papers and memos and helped her over to a bench. She leaned on him, limping a little, still carrying her high-heeled shoe.

"I'm okay," she said as she sat down. "Thanks. You go ahead. I don't want to make you late!"

"Okay," he said. "Take care."

As soon as he was out of her sight, he looked at his watch. His brief but unplanned encounter *was* going to make him late. Maybe he wasn't so lucky after all. His meeting was at Windows on the World, the glass-sided restaurant on the 107th floor, and it would take a few minutes to get up to the top.

As John waited for an elevator, throngs of people were still milling around in the lobby, lingering in the warm light of the serene September day, just for a while, before they went to work. John checked his watch again and cursed. He had told a colleague he'd meet him at 8:40 in the restaurant. And now it was almost 8:46.

WHEN ARCHITECT MINORU YAMASAKI designed the Twin Towers in the mid-1960s, his challenge was to devise twelve million square feet of floor area. He reasoned that if he laid in floors and controlled the bearing weight at the middle and edges, he could build the tallest buildings in the world. His towers would sustain 60 percent of their supporting weight at the center, with the rest on the outside walls. As a result, 75 percent of each floor's acreage could be leased for occupancy, as opposed to the usual 50 percent at the time.

"World trade means world peace," Yamasaki said famously—and, as time would show, ironically—"and consequently the World Trade Center . . . [becomes] a living representation of man's belief in humanity . . . his belief in the cooperation of men, and through this cooperation his ability to find greatness."[1]

Three thousand five hundred construction workers labored to make Yamasaki's great dream come true. They poured more than 425,000 cubic yards of concrete. They erected 200,000 tons of steel. They installed the world's largest air conditioning system. The north tower soared 1,368 feet, crowned with a 360-foot television antenna that pierced the sky. From the observation decks one could see 45 miles in any direction. On any given day, 50,000 people passed in and out of each building, using 103 elevators that could travel 27 feet per second.[2]

As John waited for one of those elevators, he tapped his foot impatiently. When the car arrived at the lobby level and the doors opened, he hustled inside.

"Let's go!" he said to the operator. But the man held the doors for a man and a woman who were approaching. The seconds lagged.

AT THE SAME TIME, up on the 106th floor in one of the gleaming kitchens of Windows on the World, Eliezer—or Junior, as his family and friends called him—whistled as he chopped scallions, red peppers, and cilantro. He had been on vacation and wasn't supposed to come back to the restaurant until tomorrow, September 12. But he had asked to come back early so he could get paid for an entire week's work.

Usually he had the radio on, tuned to Latin salsa or sometimes the news, but today he was making his own music. *Seguire soñando.* He had sung it as a solo in church recently, and the words kept echoing in his mind.

The thought of himself as a church soloist would have been absolutely inconceivable a year ago. But things were different now. He'd quit drinking and staying out all night, and he was bringing his whole paycheck home to Rosa and the children. He had always thought Christianity was just a religious layer that made you guilty, an old coat he'd outgrown from his childhood in Puerto Rico. But here he was, thirty-eight years old, and his faith was brand-new. And it wasn't about guilt. In fact, Junior had never felt so free.

He chopped the scallions on the cutting board, his big knife marking the measures of the music in his mind:

seguire soñando . . .
el soñar con un mundo de la alegría . . .

Prologue: Catastrophe

"I'm dreaming . . .
dreaming of a world of joy . . .
dreaming of planting my feet on God's heavenly shore . . .
dreaming of heaven . . .
and waking up in His arms one day."

GLENN SAT IN HIS BLUE CONVERTIBLE on the West Side Highway. He was general manager of Windows on the World, and this morning he had a 9:00 meeting in his office on the 106th floor. He had wanted to get there early, but already he knew that was not going to happen.

Glenn usually took his sons, Taylor and Spencer, to school before he went to work in the city. It gave them time together, just the guys. So today when eleven-year-old Taylor had seen Glenn getting ready to go out the door early, alone, he had stopped him.

"Wait, Dad!" he had yelled. "I'm going with you!"

"Your mom can take you today," Glenn had said. "I have to be at work early."

But Taylor had bugged him so much that Glenn finally agreed. "If you can be ready in about two minutes I'll take you," he said. Taylor had shoved his breakfast in one side of his mouth, hopping as he pushed his legs into his pants, buttoning his shirt as he scrambled out the door. So Glenn had taken him to school. And now, unless there was a small miracle, he was going to be late getting to the World Trade Center.

No miracle. Traffic was clogged, as usual, and Glenn was listening to the radio and sitting, just sitting, in a long line of cars heading south into the city. It didn't bother him though. It was such a gorgeous day. He leaned his head back and looked into the blue sky.

Glenn loved his work. Windows on the World was the top-grossing restaurant in the United States. It employed five hundred people and served customers from all over the world. The two-acre complex on the 106th and 107th floors of Tower One included the main restaurant, offices, kitchens, banquet space for eighteen hundred people, a bistro called Wild Blue, and The Greatest Bar on Earth, where people could stare at the skyline and sip specialty drinks like Lady Libertinis and the highest Manhattans in

Manhattan. The wine cellar stocked fifty thousand bottles. The food was extraordinary. Gleaming silver and fine linens graced the tables.

Glenn was proud of the Windows operation. And he loved the people who worked there. They all worked long hours, and many days they ate most of their meals together, like a family. A diverse family, since the employees were from two dozen countries and spoke twenty languages. And although Glenn didn't interact with every one of them, certain individuals stuck out. Like Junior.

Glenn had sat with Junior in the employee cafeteria for lunch one day just recently. Junior was a sous-chef, but he had the potential to go far. He was full of energy, always smiling, whistling, shaking hands with people in the hallways. He moved with quick efficiency, always upbeat. A sharp, fun guy who worked hard for his family. He would do well.

"Prisa, GENESIS! HURRY!" Rosa called to her daughter. "We have to hurry!" Genesis was eight years old and due for a checkup at the dentist this morning. Rosa didn't have the address, and she wasn't sure which subway stop to exit. She picked up the phone to call her husband. Junior would know.

Junior answered on the third ring, cradling the phone on his shoulder as he wiped his hands with the white towel at his waist. *"¿Que pasa?"* he said eagerly. Rosa smiled in spite of her hurry. They had just celebrated their sixteenth wedding anniversary on the last day of August. Now that God had answered her prayers and Junior had given his life to Christ, they were like newlyweds again. But much better. They had gone on a church retreat the weekend before, and her girlfriends had given her a hard time. "Oh, we see," they had told her, laughing, "now that your husband is part of the church, you just don't have time for us anymore. You two are inseparable!"

Rosa had teased Junior about it. "I told you Jesus would double your love," she had told him last night. But he hadn't smiled. "I'm serious," he had told her. "This is so different. I feel like I'm a new person."

He acted like a new person. Instead of leaving the children's concerns to her to handle, he was supportive. "Okay," he was saying now on the phone, "to get to the dentist, you need to take the subway to—"

PROLOGUE: CATASTROPHE

AT THAT MOMENT American Airlines Flight 11, a Boeing 767 jumbo jet weighing 400,000 pounds, 156 feet from wingtip to wingtip, loaded with 24,000 gallons of jet fuel, smashed into the north tower of the World Trade Center at 500 miles per hour, with a force of 25 million pounds. Seismometers 30 miles away recorded the velocity of the ground vibration like the waves of an earthquake, their needles tracing violent black peaks across the rolling graph paper.

The tower had been designed to withstand the known terrors of its day: hurricanes, earthquakes, conventional explosives, even a direct hit from a 124-ton Boeing 707. But it was not equipped to resist the unthinkable inferno created by the 767's two tanker trucks' worth of burning jet fuel spilling down the elevator shafts, incinerating human beings, unchecked by the sprinkler systems, blazing at 2,200 degrees Fahrenheit. The tower's mammoth supporting columns, bearing the weight of each acre-sized floor, were made of steel. And steel melts at 1,500 degrees.

ON THE PHONE WITH HIS WIFE, Junior heard a huge boom and felt the immense building sway like a long spoon stuck into a jar of honey.

He stopped abruptly. "Hold on," he said. People were running around the kitchen, unsure of what had happened. Ladles and colanders were swinging on their hooks on the wall. "I'm going to hang up," Junior told Rosa. "There's been an explosion or something. I'll call you back."

ONE HUNDRED AND SIX STORIES BELOW, on the elevator, John had watched as the doors started to slide smoothly shut. Then there was a boom, then the sharp explosions of shattering glass. "What the . . .?" the elevator operator sputtered. The building rocked. The elevator bounced into the air and down again like a yo-yo on a string. The door was stuck half-open. John froze, wondering what had happened. Maybe a bomb?

PROLOGUE: CATASTROPHE

EVEN AS ROSA STOOD BY THE PHONE, not knowing what to think, it rang. Junior sounded uncharacteristically calm. "They're saying an airplane hit the building," he told her. "Maybe a prop plane or something. Turn on the TV and see if there's anything about it on the news."

THE ELEVATOR WAS STILL ROCKING. John shakily stepped out into the lobby, his chest constricted and his heart pumping fast. Smoke was already filling the huge atrium. Pieces of concrete were falling like hail. Through the smoke he could see a walkway. It was covered with shoes. High heels. Loafers. Business shoes. Then he saw bodies, and parts of bodies. Arms. Legs. Torsos. People were jumping. At first John couldn't tell they were real human beings. In movies, people fell from great heights in slow motion. These were falling faster than he could follow, their arms and legs flailing helplessly as they plunged to the ground. The noise when they hit was horrific.

Something landed with a crash right next to John. He ran the other way. He came to a man covered with white ash, barely breathing, leaning against a pillar. He looked like a bloody ghost. John stopped. The man took two breaths and died.

AS CAR RADIOS UP AND DOWN THE LANES OF STALLED TRAFFIC blared the disaster, Glenn stared at the black smoke rising over lower Manhattan, trying to reconcile what he was hearing with what he was seeing. He called his wife. "Oh, Glenn! It's Tower One," Merry Anne wept into the phone. "The plane hit right below Windows!"

Police officers had stopped traffic heading into the city. And now, in the opposite lanes of the West Side Highway, which were usually north-bound heading out of Manhattan, emergency vehicles shrieked south, sirens blaring, speeding toward the disaster.

"I've got to get there," Glenn told Merry Anne. "I've got to see what I can do to help." He motioned to an officer and showed him the Port Authority authorization card he kept in his wallet. It allowed him emergency access to the Trade Center at any time. The officer waved him through. His mind numb, Glenn raced toward the Twin Towers, the only civilian car in a screaming parade of police vehicles, fire engines, and ambulances.

Glenn got a block from the WTC and could drive no farther. In shock, he carefully locked the car and paused a moment, numbly wondering if he should put on his tie.

Crunching through broken glass, he tried to call Merry Anne but couldn't get through. At Tower One, the windows and doors at the entrance were broken; through the holes he could see that the fire chiefs had set up a command center in the lobby. Dozens of firemen were waiting for instructions, their faces tense.

Still outside, Glenn looked up to where his office and his friends were. He felt absolutely helpless; he couldn't get to them. All he could do was stare. The building was so high that he had to put his head all the way back, his face parallel to the sky. High, high above he could see tiny squares of white waving out of the broken windows of the restaurant. His friends were waving kitchen towels and table linens. He couldn't hear them. He could only see the white flags fluttering in the thick black smoke. *Here we are. Help us!*

Then, off the southwest corner of the tower a massive piece of metal pulled away and tumbled through the air, falling with a huge crash about fifty yards from Glenn. It jolted him out of his daze. He started to move away from the buildings. The air was still and strangely silent.

And then the bodies began to fall.

ROSA STARED AT THE TELEVISION, her palm cupped over her mouth, praying without any words. Flames and smoke were consuming the side of the great tower.

She had forgotten little Genesis, who crept up behind her, staring too.

"My daddy's in there!" she screamed. "My daddy's in there!" Rosa ran to the set and clicked it off, scooping her daughter into her arms.

Impossibly, the phone rang again. "It's filling up with smoke, *Mamita*," Junior whispered tenderly to Rosa. "We've got wet towels; we're going to try to get out—"

The line went dead.

"Oh, God!" Rosa prayed. Her thoughts flitted like ashes scattering in a strong wind. She fell to the floor. "Oh, God!" An image came to her mind: Shadrach, Meshach, and Abednego, bound in the flames of the fiery furnace. God had saved them. Beyond all hope, God had saved them! She shook and she wept and she prayed for Junior. God could save him too.

DOWN IN THE LOBBY, John ran through the smoke to get outside. People were screaming, crying, covered with ash, staring into the chaos in disbelief. He kept running . . . but then he slowed down and turned. Even in the thunderous hail of death, he could hear a plane flying low. A big plane. He looked up, and just then a plane smashed into the south tower.

Debris hailed down on the plaza as the upper floors of Tower Two ingested the exploding airliner. There were people everywhere, and smoke, and screaming, and shoes on the pavement where their owners had run right out of them, and terrible masses of blood and body parts. John saw a man running, then flattened like an ant by a piece of concrete the size of a refrigerator. John's brain shut down.

Next thing he knew, he found himself in a little park behind an apartment building. Another building stood between him and Tower Two, and somehow the grass and the trees made him feel safer than the concrete jumble he had left behind. He could see the upper half of Tower Two, burning, burning.

Then the tower started to collapse, liquefied, pouring down like a decreasing waterfall. John thought of the time twenty years earlier when he'd been on the *Maid of the Mist*, the sightseeing boat at the base of Niagara Falls, the enormous, uncontrollable thunder of the falls . . .

Then the choking, thundering wave of black smoke moved out like a thousand freight trains, and John ran for his life.

GLENN SLOWED HIS ASH-COVERED CAR and pulled into his driveway. Though it was only a forty-five-minute drive from the city, it seemed like it had taken him hours to get home. He hadn't been able to get through on the phone to let Merry Anne know he was okay.

The front door opened, and his wife flew down the steps and rushed to his arms. "I thought you were dead!" she sobbed, shaking and weeping uncontrollably.

She wiped her eyes with a wadded tissue. "Did Christine get through to you on the phone?" she asked.

Christine was Glenn's assistant. They shared an office. She supervised the morning staff and had overseen the remodeling and redecoration of the dining rooms. She was the one everyone went to with questions. She was the person who cheerfully wore a fireman's hat and coordinated the regular fire drills.

"No," Glenn said.

Merry Anne looked at the ground. "She called here at five after nine," she said. "She told me everyone was together. They hadn't heard from fire command. They didn't know which escape route they were supposed to use. She was in control, like always, but her voice was shaking. She said part of the ceiling had caved in and smoke was everywhere and it was getting very difficult to breathe. She said she just didn't know what to do."

AN HOUR OR SO AFTER BOTH TOWERS HAD COLLAPSED, John was still alive. He had made his way six blocks north. The nuclear winter around him obscured almost everything. But at a little building on the corner of Lafayette and White he saw people outside, calling to the shell-shocked wave of survivors who were staggering up the street like zombies.

"Come on in," an elderly man called to John. John stumbled up the steps, trying to get his bearings, dimly taking in the front desk, the plaques on the walls. It was a homeless shelter. And these were Bible verses on the walls. He read the one nearest him: "Come to Me, all you who are weary and burdened, and I will give you rest."

Someone pointed John to a chair and he collapsed onto it, his head on his knees. He'd heard of that Bible verse before, but it had always sounded so quaint. Irrelevant. Now, with the black clouds, the white ash, and the millions of sheets of paper that had been thousands of financial transactions, floating down on the streets like reams of shredded ticker tape, all he was now was one broken broker.

A young African-American man with a missing tooth stood before him. He looked like one of those born-again street people. He handed John a bottle of cold water. "Come on," he said gently. "We've got showers upstairs. You can get that stuff off you."

For the first time John looked at himself. The white ash was all over him. He had lost his jacket. His shirt was torn, and there was blood down one sleeve, a dried red river right down to the monogram on his starched cuff. He looked at the young man. "That would be great," John said slowly. "But I don't have another shirt, and this one's ruined."

The man nodded. "That's okay," he said. "You can have one of mine. I have two."

ROSA DID NOT KNOW WHAT TO DO. For three days she did not sleep. Her pastor and his wife prayed with her and her mother and father-in-law; her girlfriends from church brought meals. They watched the endless news reports. They waited by the phone. Nothing.

Then, very early in the morning of the third day, Rosa slept. She tumbled into a deep dream, and there was Junior. When she woke, she somehow had peace. She could hear Junior singing his song that had come true.

> *seguire soñando* . . .
> *el soñar con un mundo de la alegría* . . .
> "I'm dreaming . . .
> dreaming of a world of joy . . .
> dreaming of planting my feet on God's heavenly shore . . .
> dreaming of heaven . . .
> and waking up in His arms one day."

ON THE SUNDAY AFTER September 11, Glenn hugged his two sons hard. "If you ever want to talk about what happened, if you have any questions or if something is bothering you, let me know," he said. "You don't have to hold it inside."

Taylor looked at him, holding on to Glenn's shoulder. "Dad," he said. "Not to sound like we don't care about other people, but we got over this the minute we heard you were okay."

That morning Glenn sat in the worship service at his church, Redeemer Presbyterian in Manhattan. The valiant silver notes of a solitary trumpet filled the auditorium. Thousands of people sat with their heads bent, wadded tissues in their hands, arms around one another. Many had not been to a church service in years, some never before in their lives. For Glenn, the music and words of the service washed over him like waves breaking on the shore of his grief:

"Peace I leave with you. Peace I give unto you. Not as the world gives, give I unto you . . . "

"That soul, though all hell shall endeavor to shake, I'll never, no never, no never, forsake . . ."

"We grieve, but not as those without hope . . ."

Pastor Tim Keller's voice broke as he prayed. "Oh, Lord! Others can rebuild buildings, but only You can heal broken hearts. . . . We pray for the churches of our city. Make us wise! Make us useful to our neighbors. Help us to be Christian communities for the good of the city. Protect us with Your power, nurture us with the sense of Your presence, fill us with Your peace . . . so we can be like Jesus, who came not to be served, but to serve."

What can I do? Glenn thought. *How can I serve?*

His son's words came back to his mind. *Dad, we got over this the minute we heard you were okay.*

How wonderful it is that children can be so myopic, Glenn thought. As long as *their* dad, *their* mom, *their* home, *their* lives, were okay, then the enormity of the suffering eluded them. Their world was still intact. Mayor Guilliani had said that there were thousands of children who had lost a dad or a mom in the terrorist attacks. Or both. What were *those* kids going to do? Their parents were not okay. There was no getting over it.

"Oh, God," Glenn prayed. "Help me help!"

People started giving Glenn checks. Signed checks with the amounts filled in but the recipient's name left open. "These are for widows and children," they said.

Glenn and others created a fund called Windows of Hope to benefit the families of Windows on the World employees who were killed. Help poured in from across the country. Christians of every denominational background worked together alongside other agencies, distributing water, Bibles, blankets, clothes, food, providing shelter. Everything. Anything.

For its part, Redeemer Presbyterian opened the doors of its counseling center free of charge and gave out more than two million dollars to people in need, many of whom did not qualify for other aid.

Glenn called Junior's widow. He had never met Rosa, but he had heard that she, too, was a Christian. He gave her a big check that a friend had given him. He told her—and many other widows—about Redeemer, so they could get more help.

ROSA WAS WORRIED ABOUT MORE THAN MONEY; she was concerned for her children. They could not understand the loss of their father. She brought Genesis and Jonathan to meet with Lois, a therapist at Redeemer's counseling center. Lois, fluent in several languages, probed the children gently.

As they gradually warmed to her, chatting in Spanish, they drew pictures to illustrate their feelings. Lois drew right along with them.

Burning towers. Airplanes. A thornbush: the heart of a terrorist, spiked with hate. The cross of Christ. Blood. Love flowing down from a crown of thorns. A child: a slender young tree crushed in a September storm. A choice: Will it grow again? Will it bear bitter thorns? Or good fruit? The love of that cross can reach it. Love can make the tree grow strong and bear sweet fruit.

One day when young Jonathan was drawing such things, there was a knock on Lois's office door. It was Glenn. Jonathan's eyes grew big as he realized this tall, gentle man was the boss of his dad's boss's boss's boss.

"Jonathan," Glenn said, "I knew your dad. I knew that he loved to cook. I knew he loved to sing. I knew he *loved* the Yankees.

"But you know what else? Your dad was so proud of you. He talked about you all the time. Even more than baseball! He worked so hard for you, your sister, and your mom. *Your father loved you.* And you will see him again one day."

A few months later, on Junior's birthday, his little family ate a small breakfast before heading out to school and work. Genesis was quiet, staring into space and dreaming a little. Finally she wiped her mouth with a napkin and turned toward Rosa. "Well," she said in a matter-of-fact way, "it's Daddy's first birthday with Jesus!"

A FEW MONTHS AFTER HIS OWN CATASTROPHE of September 11, John, too, made his peace with God.[3] He had been a skeptic about religion for years. It seemed so irrelevant. He figured that when he got older, maybe when he retired early, he'd decide what kind of spirituality worked for him. Any time he wondered, vaguely, just what he was really knocking himself out to achieve in the business world, he'd tuck such questions under a cultivated crust of cynicism.

Then came the tragedies, and cynicism rang hollow when people died.

Nor, in the wake of such sorrow, does Christianity offer easy answers. But after the toothless Jesus person gave John his shirt at the homeless shelter, John couldn't stop thinking about the writing on the wall: "Come to Me, all you who are weary and burdened, and I will give you rest."

The shelter's director told John about a church in Manhattan. John went to the overflow service at Redeemer Presbyterian on September 16—and then he kept coming back, Sunday after Sunday. Everything about Redeemer defied his expectations about church and church people. There was no grand building, no begging for money, no pious grandstanding. The people around him came from every ethnic background, every economic strata, every political perspective. And as Tim Keller opened the Scriptures and articulated the truths of the Bible with a quiet, joyful irony that John appreciated, he heard a quiet affirmation of truth that struck a chord somewhere deep in his soul.

But it wasn't just intellectual. To his own shock, John actually joined a small group from the church that met every Wednesday night. It was open to anyone, even pagans and skeptics. Especially pagans and skeptics. They'd gather in somebody's apartment after work, have dinner, talk, and consider a section of the Bible. It was like a book discussion group, but much better.

As John would get off the elevator and stride down the narrow hallway to his friends' front door, he'd smell the fragrance of pasta with fresh basil and hear the sounds of someone strumming a guitar, others laughing and talking, and he realized it was the first time, really, that he felt like he was coming home.

It brought a funny image into his mind. It was like one of those car rental parking lots at the airport. When you return your rental car and drive into the lot, there are jagged barriers on springs that gently roll forward under the weight of your car, allowing you to drive right in. But if you try to leave the lot the same way, those same sharp devices would shred your tires. It's a one-way lot.

With the group, he could, of course, leave at any time. But as he became part of these people, he realized that if he left, he'd shred himself in the process.

The group had two married couples, but the rest were single professionals in their late twenties and early thirties. Eventually one of the younger women hit a crisis. She was a new Christian, and she found out she was pregnant. Her parents were far away, the father of the baby was no longer part of the picture, and she was frantic. She told the group. They held her hand when she cried. They prayed for her. Week after week, they helped her make plans, they gave her a little money here and there, they supported her in every way they could, whether it was convenient or not. They were her family—all the way through to the birth and her gutsy choice to place the baby for adoption.

John's intellect had been satisfied by Tim Keller's persuasive presentation of the Bible. But in that little group, John *saw* that Christianity was real. It wasn't just reasonable ideas and ideals. It could be lived out by real people in the mess of real life, mixed together with the rich fragrance of tomato sauce simmering on the stove, friends sitting cross-legged on the floor as another poured out her heart. Eventually one of them was her birth coach in the labor room; the others celebrated with flowers and balloons when the baby was born.

John laughed at the outrageous wonder of it all, prayed to receive Jesus, and he, too, was born. Again.

EARLY IN THE MORNING on the third day after the terrorist attacks, while it was still dark, a construction worker named Frank Silecchia was working in the tomb that had been the World Trade Center. He had just helped to remove three bodies from the smoking wreckage. He wiped his face with the back of his sleeve and bent over, hands on his knees. When he stood up . . . there, in the midst of the chaos, he saw the cross. A perfectly straight, twenty-foot cross made of cast-iron beams. Silecchia knelt in the ash and wept.

The cross, it turns out, was not simply two cross beams remaining from one of the buildings. It was formed out of girders from Tower One that crashed into Building Six, shattering in the collapse to create a symmetrical sign in the midst of utter ruin.

In the weeks and months that followed, the cross at Ground Zero became a potent symbol of hope. Hard-hats prayed under it. Victims' families laid flowers at its base. In a ceremony soon after its discovery, it was blessed with holy water; priests, nuns, pastors, and construction workers sang "God Bless America" and fire department bagpipes played "Amazing Grace." In a land where crosses usually dangle from fine gold chains or atop the lovely churches of landscaped suburbs, this cross was different. It was a sign of contradiction, of defiance, of paradox, of hope in the horrific remains of devastation and death.

And in that it had much in common with the bloodstained cross of Golgotha.

"When I first saw it, it took my heart," Frank Silecchia said of his discovery of the cross at Ground Zero. "It helped heal the burden of my despair and gave me closure on the whole catastrophe."

For many, Ground Zero is still a raw and open wound. But in every such wound, in every catastrophe that has followed September 11, small and large, national and individual, the question is, *Where is the good?*

Where was God on September 11?

Certainly the "wild truth," as G. K. Chesterton called Christian theology, can address such questions persuasively, for those who have ears to hear.

But as it was for John, the presence of Christ in a broken world is best demonstrated by deeds rather than words. And the challenge for today's church is not so much convincing skeptics of the truth of the gospel as it is really believing it ourselves. Believing it in the radical way that compels us to be the Body of Christ, undeniably alive in the midst of death and destruction.

That is the improbable plan Christ put in place two thousand years ago, leaving the evidence of His continuing presence in the world in the hands of a motley crew of flawed human beings.

"What about you?" Jesus asked them. "Who do you say I am?"

Simon Peter answered, "You are the Christ, the Son of the living God."

Jesus replied, "Blessed are you, Simon, Bar-Jonah, for for flesh and blood has not revealed this to you, but My Father who is in heaven. And I also say to you that you are Peter, and on this rock I will build my church, and the gates of Hades shall not prevail against it."

Are not these days of the early twenty-first century a season of urgency, shattered complacency, hellish loss . . . and unprecedented opportunity? If freedom is at war with fear, if catastrophe can turn from death to resurrection, if hope can triumph over despair . . . if there was ever a time for the church to be the church, it is *now*.

PART I
WHAT IS THE CHURCH?

1

CHALLENGE

All earthly cities are vulnerable. Men build them and men destroy them.
At the same time there is the City of God which men did not build and cannot
destroy and which is everlasting.

—AUGUSTINE, A.Ð. 410
upon receiving the news that
Rome had been sacked[1]

SEPTEMBER 11. No matter how much time goes by or what has happened since, it still seems unbelievable. A dividing line in all our lives. Before and after.

Whether we watched it unfold on television from far, far away, or knelt in the ash-strewn streets of Manhattan, or lost someone we loved in the fireball at the Pentagon or in the field in Pennsylvania, it is a universal touchstone of horror and violation. *Catastrophe.*

C. S. Lewis said that in every human story, as in divine history, there are two catastrophes. The first is utter ruin: the catastrophe of disintegration and undoing, the end of life as we know it, light extinguished and death's dark triumph. The crucifixion.

The second is the good catastrophe: the reintegrating and remaking, new hope rising out of the ashes—the good that would otherwise not be. The resurrection.

Both catastrophes dwell in the unsought stories of September 11. We cannot begin to do them justice. We cannot capture the horror of evil's fiery day.

Nor can we adequately portray the triumph of hope: every candle lit in a nation whose heart was broken, every selfless act of service to those who were hurt and bereaved, every pint of blood given, every fragile tie of community restored where it once was not.

Like the unity of the heroes of Flight 93, who made sure their plane plunged into a Pennsylvania field rather than through the White House or the Capitol dome. They said farewell to their families on the phones. They prayed the Lord's Prayer and the Twenty-third Psalm, their hoarse voices rising together in the shadow of death. And then they took a last deep breath and rushed the plane's long aisle to the end—in order to save others.

Just as we cannot do justice to September 11, we could not begin to detail all the ways that churches across our nation lived their faith in its wake. In the darkest hour, so many of the people of God stood as His church, doing what the church does best: *being* the community that brings hope and comfort to brokenness and pain.

Think of that New York homeless shelter, a beacon for the weary and burdened, where cups of cool water were offered in Jesus' name. Or of the churches that helped widows and orphans in their distress . . . the essence of "true religion," as the book of James says. Or of the communities of believers gathering together in homes and churches across that great city—singing praises to God, bringing their pain to Jesus, and drawing their grieving neighbors to the love of Christ.

Think, too, of the service at Washington's National Cathedral a few days after the disaster. Government leaders, foreign dignitaries, and four ex-presidents gathered for an extraordinary service of remembrance.

Speaking with humility and power, Billy Graham laid out the gospel. "This cruel plot," he said, leads us to "confess our need for God. We've always needed God . . . many who died [in the attacks] are in heaven right now. They wouldn't *want* to come back. . . . Each of us must realize our own spiritual need. . . . The cross tells us that God understands our sin and suffering. He took it upon Himself. And from the cross, God declares, 'I love you!'"

Billy Graham went on to challenge Americans to use this terrible calamity as a wake-up call to focus on the reality of the hope of the gospel. Hope for the present, that this be a time of spiritual revival, and hope for the future—"not just for this life, but for heaven and the life to come."

In the weeks that followed, networks carried profoundly moving memorial services for those heroes—firefighters, police, and ordinary citizens—who died in the tragedy. Life as usual was no more, and millions of Americans went about their daily tasks with a thoughtful reverence born of brokenness.

Complacency—the greatest enemy of spiritual vigor in the West—had been shattered by the catastrophes of life and death, good and evil, hope and despair. Churches filled across our nation, as thousands of people realized—or subconsciously *sensed*—that the terrorist attacks of 2001 had actually changed everything.

IN 1992, the year *The Body* was originally published, professor of public policy Dr. Francis Fukyama published *The End of History and the Last Man.* It became a bestseller, voicing the exhilarating hope of the times: The Berlin Wall had fallen, the Iron Curtain had rusted away, the Soviet Union had crumbled, the Cold War was over. The world as we had known it had changed, and America, to its exuberant surprise, found itself the lone remaining superpower: King of the World.

The End of History became standard fodder for commentators and op-ed writers, its ideas trickling down to the masses. It was an irresistibly seductive notion: Western liberal democracy had won the great ideological struggle of the twentieth century. Communism and fascism had been vanquished. A new era of enlightenment had dawned. Defense budgets were slashed, fueling the great economic boom of the nineties. Nothing could now derail a future of peace and prosperity, with America and its ideas reigning throughout the planet.

Had human nature indeed been transformed and evil banished?

Any such utopian hopes collapsed the day the Twin Towers fell.

Perhaps a more prescient prophet of the twenty-first century was Harvard professor emeritus Samuel Huntington, who in 1996 wrote *The Clash of Civilizations.* Huntington's controversial book posited that the world is divided along the lines of the great religious civilizations: those states comprising the Eastern religions in one bloc, the Judeo-Christian West in another, and yet another being the scattered nations of Islam, which form a belt around the globe's girth from Nigeria in the west, eastward to Indonesia. The great confrontation, predicted Huntington, would be between the Muslim world and the West, a clash that Huntington said Islam *will* win.

While we challenge Huntington's ultimate conclusion, his analysis was prophetic. Many Christians did not see the coming confrontation between Islam and the West; we were distracted by the simmering culture wars between Judeo-Christian tradition and the aggressive forces of secular naturalism.

Then 9-11 jolted us to the reality of another, more chilling front in the war of world-views. While the culture war, for the most part, is conducted with clever words in Hollywood, on Capitol Hill, and in newspaper editorials, this new war of world-views is literal. It is waged with bombs and hijackings and murderous annihilation.

Islam is intrinsically a militant religion, which, if true to its own doctrine, expands by force. Some moderate Muslims say the term *jihad*, which literally means struggle, is used *figuratively* as a picture of the individual's struggle to achieve holiness. That is doubtless so for millions of Muslims. Yet it was during an intense time of local wars that Mohammed, seeking to unite his people against aggressors, wrote of jihads. Many scholars believe that he meant it quite literally; indeed, the new religion Mohammed founded soon vanquished its enemies by the sword.[2]

Some Muslims still follow that paradigm today, including terrorist cells scattered throughout the world. This is why those who have been privy to classified information, like former CIA Director Jim Woolsley, believe that we are in the middle of World War IV. (The Cold War was World War III.) That's a harsh thought; it pierces any complacent visions of the end of history.

Any who question the seriousness of the confrontation with radical Islam should examine the differences between its world-view and Christianity's.

First, consider their respective views of human nature. The Muslim believes that human beings are inherently good, that all that hinders paradise is the failure to advance Islam, and that once it is fulfilled (by whatever means), there will be peace and happiness.

What militant Muslims seek, therefore, is no different than what Hitler and the Marxists desired: Give us power and we will usher in the perfect state, the super race, or the workers' paradise. The greatest horrors of the twentieth century were perpetrated by utopians, who always suppress liberty (usually with bloodshed) because they will, by force if necessary, put their views of what is good ahead of your right to determine that for yourself.

The Judeo-Christian world-view believes that human beings are sinful people who need individual redemption and the continuing restraints of law and culture. (As G. K. Chesterton said, this doctrine of original sin is the only philosophy validated by thousands of years of recorded human history.) Paradise is not achieved by anything *we* can do—spiritually, politically, or otherwise—but by the gift of God.

Second, Islam is a theocracy. The Koran is the law, and under that law, those of other faiths cannot truly exercise full rights of citizenship. This is why Christians are not allowed to practice their faith, even in private, in Saudi Arabia—and why in most Islamic states, people other than Muslims cannot hold office and indeed in some places must pay extra taxes. There is intense persecution of Christians in many Muslim states like Sudan, Nigeria, Indonesia, and Pakistan.

While secular elites in the West carp about religious groups (usually meaning Christians) "imposing their view on others" (as if we could) or chipping away at the proverbial "wall of separation between church and state," nothing in our experience is even remotely close to theocracy.[3]

In reality, the democratic *ideal* of the West—one that is not understood by those who seek to banish religiously informed values from public life— is genuine pluralism. This is the religious freedom and healthy tolerance that respect people's unalienable rights—not just Christians'—to pursue and practice their religious beliefs. As for religious persecution, it is noteworthy that the West came to the aid of Bosnian Muslims against their Serb oppressors, who were largely Orthodox Christians in name.

Third, the Koran's view is that Allah rules by his will, with no assurance of ultimate redemption for his followers—unless a Muslim dies as a martyr in a jihad to repel the infidels. Hence the seemingly endless supply of suicide bombers. For most Muslims, any hope of redemption lies in being able after death to walk across the sword of judgment, being pronounced by his or her deeds as acceptable to Allah.

On the other hand, the God of the Bible is the deity of such supreme love that He sent His Son to die a substitutionary atoning death for all who believe. He *promises* heaven—not for good deeds, and surely not for the murders of opponents, but by the extravagant gift of His grace for those who put their trust in Him.

This leads to yet another major difference. Islam rejects the Trinity, saying it is the worship of three gods and is thus blasphemy to Allah. Muslim students on American campuses today are handing out tracts showing a diagram of three separate gods—Christianity's fundamental heresy, they say.

But for the Christian, difficult as the mystery of the Trinity may be, it goes to the heart of our belief. God the Father and Creator, Jesus the Redeemer and the Word become flesh, and the Holy Spirit the Sustainer are one essence. The same God who made us sacrificed Himself to save us and lives in us by His Spirit.

Finally, Islam advances inevitably by force as it achieves power in each state. This is why militant Muslims are fomenting unrest and violence around the globe. They must, if consistent with their own beliefs, seek political power. But the Christian gospel, by definition, advances in the world only as God's love is extended, people are redeemed by Christ, and by His Spirit believers perpetuate His good in the world around them.

This sketch is brief, but it highlights the fundamental differences between Islam and Christianity. No one who understands these distinctions can be sanguine about the clash of civilizations. Two immense belief systems are contending for influence and for the advancement of their beliefs—and their basic suppositions are fundamentally at odds.

Thus we cannot accept the mushy civic religious ecumenism that sprouted after September 11. In the many religious services that followed the tragedy, organizers scrupulously gave equal billing to all faith groups. The nation received a massive dose of politically correct sensitivity training—and it stuck. Polls showed that Americans' respect for Islam actually *increased* after September 11.[4]

President Bush, understandably anxious to reach out to moderate Muslim governments and to avoid a backlash against Arab Americans, hosted the first dinner ever held at the White House for Muslim clerics.[5]

Other politicians were equally sensitive; appropriately so, considering the volatile circumstances. After all, the politician's role is different from the pastor's.

But some pastors evidently didn't make that distinction. Muslim imams not only appeared at interfaith services, but also spoke from pulpits in some Christian churches. And incredibly, a poll showed that nearly 50 percent of highly committed evangelical Protestants agreed with the statement that many religions can lead to eternal life.[6]

It is important not to inflame a difficult situation or trigger a reaction against Muslims in this country, the overwhelming majority of whom are surely patriotic, peace-loving Americans. But it is also crucial for Christians not to blur the clear differences between our beliefs. How can we contend for Christian truth if we don't know the distinctives of our faith or why the truth claims of other world-views fall short? Our case must, of course, be made in a loving manner; that's a given. But being loving doesn't mean ignoring truth.

In fact, if we follow Jesus, we will love Muslims so much that sharing the love of Christ with them is the most natural thing we can do. This is more important now than ever, for thoughtful, peace-loving Muslims should find terrorist violence abhorrent. Is this, then, not a good time to introduce them to the love of the Christ, who died and was bodily raised from the dead, and to the promise that their sins can actually be forgiven and that they can have the *assurance* of paradise with Christ forever?

I have found that Muslims respond to this message, particularly the historicity of the resurrection. Once, during a trip to visit with Prison Fellowship India volunteers and workers, I was invited to address a Christian Businessmen's evangelistic luncheon in Bombay. It was a particularly sensitive time in India. Several missionaries had had their visas revoked, and a former Indian president had issued a public warning against Christians who were seeking political power.

Four hundred businessmen, about half in Western dress, the other in traditional Nehru jackets, gathered for the luncheon in one of the city's luxury hotels. I described my own conversion to them in detail. Then I talked about why my experiences in the White House and Watergate had convinced me of the historicity of the resurrection of Christ.[7]

Many decisions for Christ were made during that luncheon, and a long line of people waited to speak to me as I was leaving. One was a jovial, round-faced man. "Oh, Mr. Colson, that was wonderful," he said. "I believe in Jesus too." He proceeded to explain that he was president of the All-Islamic Conference of India. "We believe the same thing," he said in an obvious gesture of friendship.

As he stood there with an expectant expression, I hesitated, questioning what I should do. Should I just nod and be polite? There was a lot of ferment against Christians there and I could get in trouble. Besides, he was such a kind-looking man. Or should I . . . ? The answer came swiftly.

"I'm sorry, sir," I said, "but we do *not* believe the same thing. I believe Jesus was raised bodily from the dead—and as a Muslim, you don't." The man looked deflated.

But then he straightened and put one hand on my shoulder. "I know," he said slowly. "Today is the first time I have really understood that."

I beckoned to two of the host committee members, who escorted the Islamic leader to a quiet table where they could talk. Leaving the room moments later for a flight to south India, I glanced back over my shoulder to see the three men huddled together deep in conversation.

So even as we take stock of the mammoth struggle and unprecedented challenge of our times, we must remember what phrases like "the clash of civilizations" and "culture wars" sometimes obscure. As with that man in Bombay, we are dealing with *individual* men and women whose hearts can be lured to the love of Christ. Therefore we must stride forward with love and hope, even as we understand the extraordinary stakes of the big-picture spiritual war all around us.

As America and its allies wage war on terrorism, our nations have powerful tools at hand: elite special forces, sophisticated weaponry, economic sanctions, massive electronic intelligence, armies, navies, and air forces on alert. These are the tools of war in the kingdoms of this world.

But in the kingdom of God, the tools are different. We are armed with faith, hope, truth, love, and the good that overcomes evil. It's a great paradox: Bearing these weapons that seem so weak, the church is the one institution in society that can provide strong moral resolve and spiritual inspiration that feeds the soul, cares for the needy, and guides those who have lost their way. It is the church that creates the character that will carry us through the historic struggle of our times. It is the church that will endure forever, even as the kingdoms of this world topple and fall.

To do this, however, the church must recapture a core understanding of its biblical identity. What does it really mean to be the people Jesus called His own, against whom the gates of hell will not stand? As individuals and as a corporate entity, how do we understand our high calling as the Body of Christ?

There are no more crucial questions. And their challenge caused my longtime colleague, Ellen Vaughn, and I to write this book—well, actually to write it twice.

The first edition of this work, *The Body,* was published in 1992. It reflected our conviction that the church was infected with the most virulent virus of modern American life, what sociologist Robert Bellah called radical individualism, with many Christians consequently perceiving Christianity as "Jesus and me," a solitary belief system.

Energized by the conviction that, in fact, *there is no such thing as Christianity apart from the church,*we studied contemporary theologians like Francis Schaeffer, Christopher Dawson, Carl F. H. Henry, Richard Neuhaus, and Helmut Thielicke, as well as the classics, both Protestant and Catholic.

And then, as we began writing, the Berlin Wall came down, and out of Eastern Europe began coming extraordinary stories of the role the church had played in the defeat of communism. Ellen traveled to Romania, Hungary, and Poland for interviews with remarkable church leaders. I traveled to the Soviet Union, Czechoslovakia, and Hungary. Here at home, Ellen and I visited scores of local congregations, from the country's fastest growing megachurch to a tiny band of believers on death row.

The result was *The Body,* and to our delight, it struck a tremendous chord with readers. Thousands of church groups studied the book in tandem with its study guide and video program. The book won awards and sold hundreds of thousands of copies. There was a sense that *The Body's* stories and its focus on unity, truth, and being light in the darkness resonated powerfully with Christians from a cross-section of different denominations and church traditions.

But now, while the doctrines we believe about the church have not changed, our world circumstances have. So W Publishing urged Ellen and me to rewrite *The Body,* updating the stories, adding new ones, looking at the role of the church in light of today's new challenges.

So we did.

In the pages that follow we'll look at the church as it is commonly perceived, from the outside and inside. We'll address the biblical definition of the church and its characteristics, both the universal Body and the local confessing congregation.

Understanding the character and purpose of the church is absolutely vital. Many Christians are anxious to organize antipornography or anti-abortion campaigns, work for criminal justice reform, clean up inner-city neighborhoods, and defend religious liberty. All these are noble and worthy good works, but all are doomed to failure unless they proceed out of *who we are* as God's people.

For we cannot give what we do not have. We cannot *do* until we *are.* To *be* the church—our highest calling—depends on understanding the very character of the Body of Christ on earth. It's organic: As we draw our identity from Christ, the great Vine, we will, like healthy branches, produce fruit that nourishes the needy people around us.[8]

So what exactly is the church? In part 1 we'll consider that question. In part 2 we'll explore the great tension: the church against the world. In the battle for truth—the great issue of our times—how can the church be the custodian of *the* truth, the guardian of God-breathed holy Scripture?[9] In part 3 we'll examine how the church operates in the world, for the world. How should the church serve the world around it? And how might churches equip their people to do so?

But before we begin, a few caveats are in order.

First, this is not a book about churches. It is a book about *the church.*

Some readers may wonder why great churches (like the ones they belong to) are not discussed in detail; others will be looking for specifics on how to improve evangelistic efforts or expand prayer groups. They will be disappointed. Many helpful how-to books are already available on these subjects. Our desire here—however imperfectly realized—is to highlight the great doctrine of the church, inspire the grand vision of the church, and restore a high view of the church.

This hasn't been the trend. Over the last number of years, there has been a noticeable dearth of both scholarly and popular work in this regard, at least among evangelicals. Pastor Robert Patterson has cited this as evidence of the low view evangelicals have of the church. Evangelicals disregard baptism, the structure of ministry, and accountability, he says, putting emphasis chiefly on the individual's personal relationship to Christ. This is in part due to the entrepreneurial nature of the parachurch movement and the fierce independence of many evangelical churches. Some seminaries, in fact, do not even offer courses on the doctrine of the church.

In the course of our research we have discovered at least one of the reasons for this neglect: You cannot deal with the doctrine of the church without walking through doctrinal and denominational minefields—and setting off some explosives in the process.

Which brings us to the second warning. While we have attempted to address this subject from the most inclusive perspective possible, believing passionately that the church consists of God's people from every race and nation and confession, we are nonetheless aware that our own views will invariably color how we perceive the church. I am a Baptist with a thoroughly Reformed theology, Ellen is a Presbyterian (PCA, or Presbyterian Church in America), and we both have a catholic—small "c"—universal view of the church. The reader will have to take this into account. However, we have made every effort to write a book that is consistent with the great creeds and confessions of the church, the commitments orthodox believers have held through the ages, pledging ourselves in loyalty to "one holy catholic and apostolic church," as the Nicene Creed puts it.

But—and here is the third caveat—some readers may find this inclusiveness difficult to accept. Some cannot surrender the old prejudices that not only make them feel comfortable, but affirm that they are really right. Others genuinely believe that the fundamental differences within the church are irreconcilable. We understand that belief. But if it is true, we have a bigger problem than this book—because Jesus Himself called us to be *one*.

Of course there are doctrinal differences between sacerdotal and nonsacerdotal churches, between Arminians and Calvinists, between premillennialists and postmillennialists, between Catholic, Protestant, and Orthodox—and we should not attempt to gloss over these differences as some twentieth-century ecumenists have done. Differences do matter, and doctrinal disputes exist. And, as will be discussed later, some may even serve a healthy purpose.

Despite these differences, however, we need to come together around the great truths all believers have shared regarding Christ's teaching about His Body. It is a difficult line to walk, but walk it we must if the power of the church is to be felt in today's world.

As a fourth caveat, we would note that there are issues other than confessional differences that may offend some readers. For in the course of our work we found ourselves questioning some comfortable modern evangelical practices. Like the notion that evangelism is the only call of the church. Or hit-and-run witnessing. Or tried-and-true methodologies that are obsolete in today's post-Christian culture and thus guarantee that Christians end up talking only to themselves. Or the presumption that unless certain words are said, certain prayers repeated, one may not make it into the kingdom.

We didn't set out to be controversial. But some called the original version of *The Body* just that. Yet better to stir up healthy debate than simply be complacent and comfortable. At any rate, we have consulted with some of the best theological minds, whose help we later more fully acknowledge and for which we are profoundly grateful, and we can only hope that if this book spurs discussion, it will invigorate the church.

During a trip to the Midwest after the first publication of *The Body,* I encountered a young pastor who enthusiastically told me about the book's impact on his church. "We read *The Body* and took it seriously," he said. "The elders and I decided to see what would happen if we really incorporated its principles in our church.

"You've never seen such controversy," he went on. "At one point, the church was divided right down the middle and I was asked to leave. Dissident groups broke away. It was horrendous. But then it began to change. People got serious about being Christians—and today we're people on fire for God."

Finally, we want to point out that we've drawn many examples from prisons and from the oppressed church in other parts of the world. It is natural that we use the former since, through Prison Fellowship, we spend a great deal of time with the church behind prison walls. And we chose the latter because some of the greatest challenges for the comfortable church in the West come from our brothers and sisters living in much tougher places and situations around the world.

Some critics have asked, Why would Chuck Colson write on the church? What are his credentials? After all, he is a layman who never attended seminary [which happens to be one of my great personal regrets] and never pastored a local congregation [for which, I'm quick to confess, I would lack the patience].

Fair question. My answer is that I've been part of the universal church for thirty years, and as leader of Prison Fellowship for twenty-seven of those years, I have worked with and gathered insights from pastors and laypeople in thousands of vital congregations in the United States and around the world. I may be an "outsider" to the pastorate, but then again, that may not always be a disadvantage. As theologian Os Guinness has said, "If you want to know about water, the last one to ask is a fish."

During the Reformation, *Coram Deo* became a rallying cry for the Reformers. It meant "in the presence of God" or "before the eyes of God," and as theologian R. C. Sproul has written, nothing marked the Reformation more than an awe of the holy, majestic God who calls men and women to Himself.

Coram Deo. Filled with this holy fear and reverence, the early church changed the world. Recapturing the biblical vision for God's people in the world, the Reformers were used to transform the culture around them. And fearing God rather than man, the persecuted church in the former Soviet empire changed the maps of the world at the end of the twentieth century.

Today, in the early years of the twenty-first, what the church needs most desperately is holy awe: to understand that we live day by day in the presence of God; that, in truth, we live each instant not knowing whether in the next we will meet Him face to face.

The catastrophe of 9-11 served as a profound reminder of that truth. It also reminded us of a fact that applies every single ordinary day of our lives: *Life is a mess.* Any Christian who chirps platitudes to the contrary is deluded. From the beginnings of His church, Jesus made it clear that we would be the Body in the midst of a sinful, broken world.

Once we understand that severe challenge, it can set us free. For it is in the darkness that the light shines most brightly. It is in alienation that Christ's healing power is seen most clearly. It is in our weakness and brokenness that God's great strength is revealed. God did not design us to be robots in a sterile environment—"Stepford" Christians who are programmed to spout cheerful inanities and cannot handle any deviations from carefully constructed conventions.

No, as September 11 should remind us forever, we are to be the Body—the manifestation of God's hope—in the blood, dirt, dust, and tears of the battlefields of this world.

The question is, Are we ready for that challenge?

2
CRISIS?

I am my own church.

—RESPONDENT TO GALLUP POLL ON THE CHURCH

I didn't go to religion to make me happy.
I always knew a bottle of Port would do that.
If you want a religion to make you feel really comfortable,
I certainly don't recommend Christianity.

—C. S. LEWIS

AFTER THE CATASTROPHES OF SEPTEMBER 11, nonbelievers were asking fundamental questions about faith, suffering, the problem of evil, the meaning of life, life after death. Churches across America were full. For many of us, it seemed like an unprecedented time of opportunity.

But what happened? Certainly there were pockets of revival and many individual conversions to Christ. But as one critic put it, many churches missed the opportunity because they did not connect their new attendees with the unique truths of the gospel. "After 9-11 . . . all of a sudden, people were flocking to churches. All the denominations were giddy. But three months later, they are back out. People are looking for comfort and answers . . . . The reason people are leaving church now is they have serious questions as to where their dead daughter is or how the world is going to end. Churches offer musical productions and food, but they are not answering the questions."[1]

Barna polls taken a year after 9-11 showed that 41 percent of church-goers said that their congregations did nothing over the prior twelve months to address issues raised by the attacks. Only 16 percent said that

17

they had heard sermons or other teachings related to the serious questions the disasters raised.

Other polls showed that in spite of a rise in spirituality, Americans' view of basic moral truths and Christian teaching actually *declined.* By 64 to 22 percent, adults sampled in the wake of 9-11 said truth is always relative; among born-again respondents, only 32 percent believed truth is absolute, compared with 38 percent before September 11.[2]

George Barna observed: "Millions stay away, because they cannot make the value equation work. When they calculate the amount of time, money and energy they would have to invest in a church, they do not see a reasonable return on the investment. Most of the unchurched figure they've gotten along just fine without the church for a long time, and until someone gives them reason to feel otherwise, they will remain spiritually unattached."[3]

This disdain for corporate commitment is a fundamental, defining characteristic of our culture at large. It also seems to be one enduring reason that even the shock of 9-11 did not catapult more people into a lasting relationship with a local church.

THE REIGN OF INDIVIDUALISM

As we'll explore in more detail in later chapters, individualism's iron grip on today's culture actually goes back to the 1960s, when the ground rules of American life changed utterly. Through the 1950s American culture was largely Christianized. There was a common language of morality and common values that flowed from the Bible. A majority of Americans were part of a church community, which often formed the center of middle America's cultural life.

But the tumultuous 1960s upended cultural norms and questioned traditional structures of authority and tradition. With some exceptions in the Midwest and Bible Belt, the culture became more and more secularized, with a general loss of belief in absolute truth. Relativism set the ground rules—which meant there were no ground rules. Each person was to find his or her own concept of truth, whatever that might be. As a result, the focus of life moved from community to self.

In his landmark 1985 work, *Habits of the Heart,* sociologist Robert

Bellah called this "radical individualism." No authoritative creed or scripture or shared vision of the common good can bind a people whose primary commitment is to self. There is the law, of course, but in the absence of common social stigmas and ideals, law is only as strong as the ranks of the police that enforce it.

The 1970s became what social critic Tom Wolfe called the "me decade," with books like *Looking Out for Number One* becoming bestsellers. In the 1980s the "me" trend led to self-pilgrimages to discover your inner child, get in touch with yourself, be your own best friend, build your self-esteem, and enhance your self-image as you sat in a hot tub surrounded by aromatic candles, blissfully reading *Self* magazine.

Then, as the use of personal computers mainstreamed in the 1990s, the PC took individualism to a whole new level. (Robert Putnam of Harvard wrote of this new individualism in his insightful work, *Bowling Alone: The Collapse and Revival of American Community*.) Rather than connecting with one another in civic groups, volunteer organizations, churches, and synagogues, many Americans sat alone at their PCs, madly accessing the endless playground of the Internet and chatting on-line with faceless strangers using made-up names.

The self is now sovereign, and membership in institutions—that network of associations that historically characterized American civic life— has suffered. Membership in service groups like the PTA, League of Women Voters, Kiwanis, Shriners, and Jaycee's has been in a steady decline.[4]

The poster girl of Robert Bellah's study was a woman named Sheila who explained her faith as listening to "just my own little voice." "Sheilaism," as Bellah labeled it, means being your own God—the ultimate consequence of individualism.[5] "We can discern in the life of religious communities something that is going on in the society in general," concluded Bellah. "Participation is less about loyalty and a strong conviction of membership and more about *what one will get out of participating.*"[6]

As Bellah pointed out, the world's habitual individualism has shaped nonbelievers' expectations about religion and the church. It has also, both subtly and obviously, affected the thinking of many believers as well, creating an identity crisis in many local congregations.

Consider some examples of how the church, its character, and its role are often misunderstood in American life today.

The Church Is a Building

One of the most basic elements of confusion about the role of the church is apparent in how we use the word *church*. To both Christians and non-believers alike, it means, first, a building.

Who does not say, "I'm going to church"? We call the place where we worship, *the* church. And when we say we are "building a church," we mean we are constructing a facility, not that we are building men and women in spiritual maturity. In a thousand common expressions we refer to the church as a place.

Though it is usually said unconsciously, this is no harmless colloquialism. It both presupposes and conditions our view of the church, creating what some have aptly called the "edifice complex," wherein the importance and success of the church is directly measured by the size and grandeur of the structure itself.

It is interesting to note that Redeemer Presbyterian Church in New York, which has such a vibrant ministry, owns no building. The congregation has chosen to embark on "a deliberate strategy to reject the megachurch model." Instead of becoming a megachurch, they say, they "want to raise a whole new generation of leaders and churches. Instead of keeping our gifts to ourselves, we want to become a movement of churches and a servant of the whole Body of Christ in New York and beyond."[7] As we write, Redeemer has planted and funded twelve daughter churches in twelve years and is currently involved in the planting of twenty-two new "mission" churches. These new mission churches are both within, as well as outside, the denomination.

But if the church is perceived as simply a building, just a place one goes for weddings, funerals, or to drop in as it suits our fancy, it's just another beautiful building. Thus it's no surprise that 82 percent of the American people have said they can arrive at their own religious views without regard to a body of believers.[8]

The misperception of the church as a building is a symptom of a much deeper problem: a misunderstanding of its character and its biblical purpose and mission.

Sometimes Christians have trouble even defining what the church is. Is it a local congregation or a denomination? Is it all Christians worldwide or just those who are on membership rolls? What about those who watch services on television, those who are baptized as infants, those who have never been baptized?

And what is the church's mission? To worship? Evangelize? Grow? Feed the hungry, elect politicians, fight pornography? The list goes on and on. Just engage anyone, Christian or not, in a conversation about the church and you'll hear a variety of opinions—good, bad, indifferent.

It's no surprise that nonbelievers don't know much about the church's identity or mission. But when Christians are experiencing a widespread identity crisis, then we are in big trouble.

The Churchgoer Is a Consumer Looking for Therapy

Another significant misconception resulting from individualism's pervasive mind-set is that church attendance is all about consumerism. Aside from those hierarchical denominations that assign members to the parish in which they live (and many today ignore that), most American churchgoers are officially free to choose which church they will join or attend—and many choose on the basis of "what's in it for me?"

Ask people what they look for in a church and the number-one response is "fellowship." Other answers range from "good sermons" to "the music program" to "youth activities for the kids" to "it makes me feel good." People flit about in search of what suits their taste at the moment.

It's what some have called the "McChurch" mentality. Today it might be McDonald's for a Quarter Pounder; tomorrow it's Wendy's salad bar or perhaps the two-pickle chicken sandwiches at Chick-Fil-A. Thus the church becomes just another retail outlet, faith just another commodity. People change congregations, preachers, and denominations as readily as they change banks, grocery stores, or health clubs. The point is to go where you can come away feeling good about your investment.

We've encountered this mind-set over and over again, as in the case of two friends to whom Patty and I witnessed for years. One Sunday when we were in their city, they agreed to accompany us to church. On the way, the woman said, "Oh, I hope the pastor will cheer me up today. I'm so depressed. I found a dead bird at the back door this morning."

Another longtime acquaintance told me he was now attending a Unity church.

"Why?" I asked. "You are a Christian, and that is a cult."

"Really?" The man looked surprised.

"Of course it is," I said. "They don't believe in the resurrection or even one true God."

"But my wife and I love it," he said. "We always come away feeling better."

Even secular observers have noted how this demand for "feel-better" religion is affecting church life and practice. Ten years ago there was a dramatic religious resurgence among the nation's baby boomers, according to *Newsweek,* which reported that more than 80 percent considered themselves "religious and believe in life after death." But "unlike earlier religious revivals, the aim this time (apart from born-again traditionalists of all faiths) is support, not salvation, help rather than holiness, a circle of spiritual equals rather than an authoritative church or guide. A group affirmation of self is at the top of the agenda *which is why some of the least demanding churches are now in the greatest demand.*"[9]

In today's continuing consumer culture, what many are looking for is a spiritual social club, an institution that offers convivial relationships but does not make authentic demands as to what they believe or how they live. And whenever a church does assert a biblically orthodox position that might in some way restrict an individual's doing whatever he or she chooses, it is indignantly accused of being "out of touch"—as if its beliefs are to be determined by majority vote or market surveys.

As Terry Mattingly wrote in late 2002, "Ask Americans questions about how September 11 affected their religious feelings and the poll numbers will soar. Ask them questions about specific religious beliefs and practices and the numbers will plateau or even decline. The emerging consensus seems to be that vague, comforting spirituality is healthy, but that doctrinal, authoritative religions may even be dangerous."[10]

Spiritual consumers are interested not in what the church stands for, but in the fulfillment it can deliver. Thus the under-forty-five generation, 60 percent of whom define themselves as independent spiritual seekers, reject the notion that one should be limited to a single faith. The result is "an age of mix 'em, match 'em, salad bar spirituality."[11]

This consumer mentality, in turn, pressures churches to respond in kind. When the findings of a major foundation study revealed the sharp decline of several Protestant denominations, the chief researcher acknowledged with disarming candor: "The challenge, I tell ministers, is that they must ask themselves why people are in front of them on Sunday mornings instead of somewhere else. The church is in a competitive situation for people's leisure time."[12]

If people are looking at religion as a product, then the church reckons it must furnish a competitive one. It's not a conscious process. Few church boards sit down and decide to replace their orthodox doctrines with warm, soothing nostrums. But pastors feel the pressure to make the message as inviting as possible to draw people in. So the process is gradual: a little rationalizing here . . . a little rounding off there . . .

The spiritual odyssey of one evangelical church reveals how the process works and where it can lead.

Realizing that the median age in the church was rising—a grave danger sign, according to church growth experts—the pastor of this long-established Baptist congregation commissioned a market survey of upscale families in his area. The first discovery was that most of the potential market was put off by the term "Baptist."

"People don't like denominational tags anymore," the pastor told a reporter. "All they want to know is, 'What's in it for me?'"

The obvious solution? Rename the church.

Then, examining the next point on the market study—accessibility—the church picked a location right off a freeway and built a new building. Nothing that would scare anyone off, of course. The six-million-dollar building with beamed ceilings and huge stone fireplaces has no crosses or religious symbols; it looks like a dude ranch.

Some would argue that this congregation was simply striving to be "user-friendly," a computer term that has spilled over onto everything, including church planning. Unfortunately they didn't stop with names and architecture. They also decided to abandon standard theological terms.

"If we use the words *redemption* or *conversion*," the pastor explained, "they think we are talking about bonds." So he has banished all "hellfire and damnation" preaching and proudly displays a version of the Bible he personally produced, which is just right for the McChurch generation. All essential passages are in boldface and it can be read in thirty half-hour sittings.

Imagine it: God's knowledge, the mystery of the ages, consumed in just fifteen hours!

Not surprisingly, the congregation couldn't be more enthusiastic.

"There's a spirit of putting people over doctrine. The attitude is that they are for life, love, and liberty," one member enthused.

"The church totally accepts people as they are without any sort of don'ts and dos," says another. "When relatives visit, they wish they had a church like ours," she brags. Why not? What's not to like?

Churches across the country are responding to the McChurch consumer by disguising their identity. When one megachurch acquired an enormous new facility, it included no cross in the auditorium, or arena, where the pastor preaches to thousands every Saturday and Sunday. "I don't know why it's not there," said one attendee. "Maybe the cross is just, you know, too much of a downer."

Similarly, years ago Denver's Full Gospel Chapel changed its name to the Happy Church. "It draws people," said the pastor.[13] Apparently so. The church has thrived ever since, according to its Web site.

Hard to argue with success. Except that capitulating to consumerism has profound consequences for the church.

First, it dilutes and perverts the message. Some clergy have simply "airbrushed sin out of their language. Having substituted therapy for spiritual discernment, they appeal to a nurturing God who helps His (or Her) people cope. Heaven by this creed is never having to say no to yourself, and God is never having to say you're sorry."[14]

Certainly the church should provide comfort for the grieving, the suffering, and the needy. But ministering to the afflicted is entirely different from the therapeutic model that teaches us to look within ourselves to discover and heal our wounded psyche. As we will discuss later, self-realization and God-realization are diametrically opposed.

The gospel teaches that our hope is not in finding our true selves, but in losing ourselves. That which defiles us is what is in us, Christ said. When we honestly look inside at our sin, we are repulsed. We repent and die to ourselves so that Christ's atoning grace might cleanse us.

This is why the feel-good, restore-your-self-worth, therapeutic gospel is so dangerous. It is but a short step from therapy to the health-and-wealth, name-it-and-claim-it heresy, forms of which have been propagated in conservative churches as well as by some televangelists over the years. Therapy and the promise of material reward may lure people into our churches, but so might free packets of Prozac handed out during Communion. We need a cure that cuts far deeper than feeling good.

Second, and very similarly, responding to the market changes the essential goal of the church. What J. I. Packer calls "hot tub religion" seeks and embraces anything that makes us feel better about ourselves. So the Body is transformed from a worshiping community into a comforting haven from life's pressures. Rather than being a Body of people coming together to esteem and worship their one holy, eternal, Creator God, it becomes a spa for people to nurture and fondle their way to a comfortable sense of self-esteem.

Third, a market-driven church can turn worship into a spectator sport. Patty and I attended the services one weekend at one of the most "successful" megachurches in America. Volunteers guided us to our parking space; shuttles were waiting on the pathway near our car to whisk us to the main entrance. I was dazzled by the way in which several thousand people were efficiently guided into the church. Inside the sanctuary we all eased in and filled the neat pews in an orderly fashion.

The service was as efficient as the parking operation. The choir and soloist gave a stellar performance in exactly nineteen minutes. The pastor then gave a twenty-two minute sermon that was excellent, biblically rooted, powerfully delivered. Precisely fifty minutes from the time we sat down, ushers were guiding us out in the opposite direction from which we had entered, even as new worshipers were entering for the next service.

There was a warm, welcoming feel in the church; the message was good. But I confess that I felt oddly empty. Why?

There was no sense of participation. We were treated like spectators, or an audience who had come to watch a performance. The closest parallel experience I could relate to was when I was escorted with a team owner to an NBA game and sat in his box. I felt like I had been sitting in a box in that church service.

It's great to be well-organized and to strive for excellence, of course. But to me it had seemed all too orchestrated, too antiseptic, too precise— when in reality the church is a messy thing. It's an organic body made up of strange and broken people—dirty sinners who need to be cleansed, sweaty soldiers who need to be equipped for spiritual warfare. The church is not a club for perfect people; it's imperfect, sometimes unpredictable, a cross-section of life, and the Holy Spirit uses it to draw lost sheep home to the Father. But my tidy-church experience had the airtight precision of a television production, not the fresh breezes of the Holy Spirit.

Fourth, succumbing to consumerism strips the church of its authority. Providing peace through the feel-good gospel rather than pointing people to the truth of Christ and the reality of their own sin parallels and makes credible the New Age movement.

Millions of Americans find "born-again Christianity too tacky, Protestantism and Judaism too suburban and Catholicism too papal."[15] So instead of flocking to churches, they flee to New Age spas, spectator sports events, or the comforts of the *New York Times* Sunday crossword puzzle.

But when the church complies by trying to lure people by responding to market pressures, it forfeits its authority to proclaim truth and loses its ability to call its members to account. In other words, it can no longer disciple and discipline.

The task of the church is not to make men and women happy; it is to make them holy. *And when we seek solely to please them, we lose them anyway.* Consider the poll data in the decade since this book was first published. In 2001, almost 30 million Americans said they had no religion—more than double the number from 1990.[16] Gallup polls found the same trend, noting a drop from 54 percent who said they were religious in 1999 to 50 percent in 2002. People with no religion now account for 14 percent of the nation, up from 8 percent in 1990.[17] Another study reported in the *New York Times* reached almost identical conclusions: The number with no religious preference rose from 7 percent in 1990 to 14 percent by 2000.[18] George Barna found the same decline: 24 percent of adults were unchurched in 1991; today that number is 34 percent.[19]

Fifth, a self-directed church often loses its evangelistic thrust. Instead of being a "go and tell" community it becomes one of "come and see." We're to go and proclaim the gospel to all the nations, not wait for them to come knocking at our door; and if our focus is only meeting the needs of those who come to us, we will in due course lose our fervor to go to places of darkness and need.

Sixth, consumerism works against the unity of the church. By nature, a consumer mentality creates a competitive market environment where each producer of goods and services tries to outdo the others. So churches end up competing for "customers," and the mutual cooperation of the Body is destroyed. That means we lose our unity—which is, in fact, our greatest, driving evangelistic witness that Jesus is who He claimed to be.[20]

It is tragic, in these times of great challenge and opportunity, that the ongoing identity crisis within many modern American churches renders them impotent! Many Christians speak glibly about going to church (even though the church is not a place), in consumer-driven, user-friendly language, toward the goals of feeling good and being comfortable (absolutely the wrong objectives).

Growth for Growth's Sake

Then we compound those errors by measuring the church against the wrong standard: growth—and growth alone.

Over the years, I've conducted my own pastoral poll. "How are things going in your church?" I'll ask. With few exceptions, the answers are quantitative: "Membership up 20 percent . . . a hundred baptisms last year . . . starting a new building . . . going to three services . . ."

Cultural values have so captured the church that we equate success with size. It's a reflex reaction. If a church isn't growing, someone is doing something wrong. Maybe the pastor and the elders haven't analyzed the market well enough or invested in the right programs. This is why church growth has become the hottest business in the religious world today. If "the customer is king," then the church has to react as any organization does to consumer demand, which means finding the right marketing strategy.

According to one church growth movement leader, a minister's performance is measured not by faithfulness to the gospel, but by whether "the people keep coming and giving."[21] With the right strategy, there's no limit to growth; it's simply a matter of finding the right formula. To this end, many professional organizations furnish churches the same services commercial marketers or political campaign strategists subscribe to: polls, market studies, message analysis, image-making, advertising, and product labeling.

Church growth has not only become big business, but it also emulates big business. Church growth literature often speaks of products and services and investments: x amount of time and money invested in a particular project will yield y results. Believing that successful business principles can produce similar results for the church, one megachurch sent groups to study firms like IBM, Xerox, and Disney World.[22]

Another church approached the owner of a number of fast-food restaurants for marketing tie-in ideas for a musical performance. Parking attendants at some big churches are told to view people who drive onto the "campus" as "customers." Admittedly, such strategies sometimes draw people to hear about Jesus who would otherwise not come near a church. But when the goal is growth for growth's sake, such strategies can lose the distinction between service and sales.[23]

Conversely, some churches take pride in their *lack* of growth, as if dwindling numbers signify the doctrinal purity of the faithful—an equally distorted view. There is nothing wrong with church growth! Biblically faithful churches grow. Nor is there anything inherently wrong with using marketing strategies as *tools* to evangelize unchurched people. Ten years ago Willow Creek, the Chicago area megachurch phenomenon, served as a thriving model of that mind-set. Today the Willow Creek Association includes thousands of member churches that desire to grow by adding new converts, not simply shuffling Christians from one congregation to another. As we will discuss later, Willow Creek, though not without flaws, broke new ground in its beginnings, adapting its evangelism and outreach *techniques*—not its message—to the post-Christian mind-set of the people who lived in its area of influence.

Another church that does a good job is Southeast Christian in Louisville, Kentucky. I have visited there many times and have been enormously impressed that the church has grown not only in numbers, but in discipleship and community influence. I listen each week to Pastor Bob Russell's or Pastor Dave Stone's messages on tape, and they never vary from a solid, biblical content.

I've seen the same thing in my own home church, First Baptist of Naples, Florida, where Dr. Hayes Wicker preaches the hard truth of Scripture as well as its comfort. The church has steadily grown and now occupies a new site, with three weekend services attended by five to six thousand people. It's not the numbers, however, but the seriousness of the members that impresses me most.

The trouble comes when we confuse technique with truth, and when the mission or message is compromised. Many churches have found a great balance; behind their music and skits and gymnasiums and fanfare stands a solidly orthodox message that proclaims the lordship of Jesus Christ and rigorous discipleship.

Indeed, growth is often a sign of God's blessing. When Peter preached after Pentecost, people were convicted, repented, and were baptized—three thousand on the first day—and the Lord was "adding to their number day by day," with five thousand in one day alone.[24]

What matters is not whether a church uses contemporary music or squash courts. What matters is biblical fidelity. If a thoroughly orthodox church challenges people to live holy lives and is growing, it is being blessed by God. If a church continuously disguises its identity and preaches a message intended to keep everyone in a state of perpetual comfort, then its growth is man-made. "Growth for growth's sake, man-made growth can be spiritually deadening," says Richard Neuhaus. "Institutional growth is the last refuge of ministries that are spiritually sterile."[25]

The real pressure elders and church boards should be putting on their pastors is for growth all right—but spiritual growth, not numbers. The church has little to do with slick marketing or fancy facilities and everything to do with the people and the Spirit of God in their midst. What matters is the *character* of the community of faith.

One often sees that vision strongest in the oddest places. For me, the most profound pictures of the church being the Body was not in a successful megachurch, but in a gathering of society's losers. It was the first Easter of the new millennium, and I was in a cold, ugly prison. By morning's end, however, it was blazing with the flaming reality of the risen Christ.

3

COURAGE

I'VE SPENT THE LAST TWENTY-FIVE EASTERS IN PRISON—correctional institutions from Nebraska to Texas to Louisiana to New York and a lot of places in between. Frankly, it would be much easier to stay at home, skip the travel, the logistical hassles, the metal detectors, and the prison processing, and just get up on Easter morning and worship in my own home congregation of believers.

But I'll keep going back—taking as many people with me as I can—for as long as I can.

Why?

First, because I want to encourage Christian inmates and draw non-believers to Jesus. It's a great thing for people in prison to know that the Body of Christ outside the walls is with them, not just spiritually but physically, on the great day of Christ's liberation from the tomb.

Second, I go in an effort to remind myself and other Christians that we must be people who "go and tell" the good news. And that means going to places that are ugly, needy, or inconvenient, especially those places whose residents cannot come to us. After all, that's what Jesus did.

Third, I go to prison every Easter because it is the perfect paradox.

I have found that in these stifling places of iron bars, concrete walls, and razor wire, I experience the reality of Jesus Christ's bursting free from death and the grave far more powerfully than I would in the lily-scented comfort of the church outside.

That was certainly the case in Delaware on Easter 2000. It was a cold, windy morning, more like winter than the beginning of spring. We arrived at the Sussex Correctional Institution just as the day's first light was filtering through the morning clouds. There's always such a sense of drama about dawn on Easter morning. I invariably think about Christ's disciples hurrying to His tomb in the dark . . . the sorrow, the confusion, the angels, the incredulity, the absolute, stunning thunderbolt of joy . . . then the sun breaking through the dark clouds, the hearts on fire, and the cry that echoes down through the ages: "Christ is risen! He is risen indeed!"

This particular resurrection morning was the kickoff of Operation Starting Line, an intense cooperative evangelistic campaign sponsored by about a dozen different evangelical ministries, including Prison Fellowship. We had enthusiastic Christian volunteers from those different ministry groups, as well as a number of corrections officials from Delaware and the prison's own chaplain, Larry Lilly, a longtime friend and a real champion for Jesus in the prison.

The prison, a drab, low-slung series of buildings, was opened in 1931. It holds about eleven hundred maximum-, medium-, and minimum-security inmates, all men, as well as a boot camp with one hundred beds that houses ninety men and ten women.

Franklin Graham of the Billy Graham Association, Bruce Wilkinson of Walk Thru the Bible, and I were to lead the worship services. Before that, however, we visited inmates who could not come out to the main service because they were in segregation. We went from cell to cell in the segregation units, where sex offenders, vulnerable inmates, and those who were isolated for disciplinary reasons were held, as is necessary. The officers even allowed some of the prisoners to gather in a central seating area outside the cells.

We spoke gently to them, one by one, about the love of Christ. But there was little sense of recognition on their faces, no smiles, no joy. These, after all, are the most hopeless of the hopeless. Some are separated from the rest of the prison population because they are vulnerable targets for rape. Some are predators who would violate others. Some are sex offenders, the most despised and odious inmates of all, who would not be safe in the prison yard because they have violated children.

But as we prayed with these men, Christ's love broke through their sin and shame. Many prayed to receive Him, believing the Bible's open invitation: "Yet to all who received him, to those who believed in his name, he gave the right to become children of God—children born not of natural descent, nor of human decision . . . but born of God."[1]

Later in the morning, our team gathered in the center area of the outdoor prison compound. We were on a raised platform, with sound equipment for the musicians, our microphones, and other paraphernalia. It was a good setup, but I was distressed when I saw the rest of the arrangement. There was a big chain-link fence between the platform and the prisoners, and fences between each section of inmates. To my left as I faced the crowd I could see the minimum-security inmates. To their right, fenced off, were the medium-security men. Then another fence, and a section where the boot camp inmates stood military style, at parade rest, through the whole program. Then another fence, and to my far right were the maximum-security inmates. The volunteers and dignitaries were immediately in front of the platform—again, with a fence between them and the prisoners.

Though there were gates in the fencing so I could pass in and out of the different groups, I was disappointed. I knew there was a strong group of believers in this prison. They'd been having Bible studies for years, and Chaplain Lilly was a great shepherd to the flock. I had wanted for us all to be able to mingle together, volunteers and inmates alike, and to celebrate as one the joy of Christ's resurrection. But we were rigidly divided. I didn't blame the prison administration—certainly any event like this is a security risk. But it made us feel separate, rather than one.

To make it worse, it was getting colder. An icy northwest wind whipped through the prison yard. I had on a heavy, lined raincoat, and I was still chilled to the bone. My heart went out to the prisoners, who were standing in that wind with no jackets, just their thin, white, prison uniforms.

After music by Charlie Daniels and worship teams that warmed the men up as much as anything could, I told the inmates my own story: how the risen Christ had saved me. I spoke about Jesus, the prisoner, and about what had really happened at Calvary. I tried to put the story in terms that these inmates—mostly under thirty years of age—could relate to. I talked about how Jesus had been turned over to the authorities by one of His friends who turned on Him, how He'd been held in an isolation cell, strip-searched, beaten up. I talked about the guards who gambled for His clothes, the people who just stood by staring, watching the drama unfold, the officials who cared only about their own power . . . and then I talked about the prisoners who hung on the crosses on either side of Jesus. One mocked Him—like the other cynics in the crowd that day. The other recognized his own sin—and the fact that Jesus really was the Son of God. And he was promised eternal life.

At that I turned the service over to Franklin Graham, who, in his clear way, took the men through the plan of salvation in the Scriptures. He invited them to receive Christ and to indicate their decision by raising their hands. Many, many men did so. *What a great Easter morning,* I thought.

But it wasn't over.

Not wanting to leave out Bruce Wilkinson, I leaned over after Franklin finished and whispered to him, "Bruce, why don't you go up and say a word to the men, and then close the service with prayer?"

He nodded and got up. I prepared to bow my head for prayer.

Now, Bruce had never been in a prison before in his life. This was all new to him. He hadn't been through our eighteen-hour Prison Fellowship training in which we carefully counsel volunteers about what to do and say, and what to *never ever* do, and say, in prison.

If you've read Bruce's books, you already know that he is a guy who isn't exactly confined by normal conventions. He's an iconoclast. He's all about extending territory and breaking through boundaries. He just won't stay in a box—even if the box is a long, rectangular prison yard ringed with coils of razor wire, officers, guard towers, and about six hundred inmates standing in the freezing wind.

Bruce walked up to the microphone and looked at the inmates who were all crowded against the fence trying to get closer to the platform. They looked at him. He didn't introduce himself or give any warm opening remarks. He just said: "I want all of you men who are pushing up against the fences to move back about ten or twelve paces." No "please" or anything.

You should understand that the prison environment is very macho. Even though we were dealing with a crowd that included Christians, there were plenty of hostile inmates in that group as well. And in a setting like this, you just don't tell prisoners what to do, particularly if you haven't won the right to be heard, or don't have authority that they recognize.

When Bruce told the men to move back, nothing happened. There was a cold silence. I looked toward the correctional officers who were guarding the entrances, and they were suddenly on alert. You could feel the tension.

Bruce was not rattled at all. "Go ahead," he said to the inmates. "I want you to move back. All of you. Get back from the fence. Get back ten or twelve paces."

My stomach clenched a little. There was still a cold silence, and some of the men started to shuffle backward a little. I caught the eye of the commissioner of correction, and he looked worried, as did the chaplain. I muttered a little prayer under my breath. It wasn't theologically sophisticated: *Lord, help us here. I don't know what Bruce is doing. Please help us!*

Meanwhile Bruce stood, looking over the inmates, his hands on his hips. "Men, move back," he said again. "A few more steps back." Finally, the crowd of men had cleared a perimeter about twelve feet back from the fence that separated them from the podium.

"Okay," said Bruce. "Now I want all of the Christians, those of you who gave your lives to Christ today, those of you who have been believers for a while—I want all of you to walk forward to the fence."

I covered my eyes with my hands. *This is it,* I thought. *You just can't do this in prison. He's setting these guys up for trouble.*

But when I looked up, to my amazement, half a dozen guys walked to the fence without hesitation. Then five or six more. Then they just poured forward. About two hundred inmates walked up to the fence and stood there with a kind of quiet confidence—not fidgeting, just standing and waiting, looking at Bruce.

Bruce waited until it seemed that all the believers had stepped forward. Then he continued in a methodical, deliberate fashion, as if taking his cues from the Holy Spirit and then passing them on to the rest of us.

"All right," he said. "Good. Now, all you men who stepped forward . . . you have stepped forward as the people of God in this prison. You are the church here. And now I want you to turn around, with your backs to me. I want you to do an about-face and look at the rest of the prison population standing there."

At this point my heart was back in my mouth. The prison officials and corrections officers were shooting glances at one another, the officers watching certain inmates closely. Bruce seemed to be setting up a situation with two sets of inmates in confrontation; something like this could easily get out of hand.

But what happened was unbelievable. The Christian guys who had walked to the fence paused a moment. Then, almost as one, they turned around and stood looking straight into the eyes of the rest of the men.

Bruce kept pushing. "Now," he said, "I want you believers to get down on your knees. You're the church in here. I'm going to pray for you. I've asked you to turn so you're facing the rest of these guys because they are your mission field. Your job as Christians is to share the gospel with them. Love them. Serve them."

Talk about boldness! The Christian men got down on their knees, and then, without instruction, put their hands on one another's shoulders. It was such a beautiful, powerful paradox—a kneeling army of believers, arms around one another, in a posture of service before the rest of the tough, skeptical men in that institution.

My friend Dallen Peterson, who goes with me into prison every Easter, was in the crowd of inmates. (Dallen doesn't hang back; he just wades right into the action, and he'd been with the inmates for the entire program.) Dallen had been talking to two young African-American prisoners, both much taller than he, tough, hardened inmates. They had been laughing and mocking the program. One told Dallen that his grandmother had taken him to church and prayed for him when he was a little boy . . . and that was the last time anyone had really cared for him. But as an adult, he wasn't interested in Christianity. It was for wimps and losers.

As Dallen stood with these guys and Bruce started instructing the Christian inmates, these two prisoners got more and more rattled. They kept joking and jiving, but they were clearly thrown off by the whole thing.

And as the Christian inmates got down on their knees before the rest of the prison population, they shut up altogether.

Bruce looked over the sea of men with their arms around one another, kneeling before the stunned prison crowd. "All right," he said, his voice choking a little. "You're the church. You are one in Jesus Christ. Let me pray for you."

Bruce prayed, and a holy hush came over that cold prison yard. He prayed that the church might continue to be one in unity in that prison, that these men might boldly witness to the love of Christ, that they might be filled with the grace of God, and that He would use them to build His church, extend His kingdom, so that more and more inmates in that prison community would turn their hearts to give glory to God.

As Bruce prayed, Dallen looked at the two tough inmates next to him. Their heads were bowed. After Bruce ended his prayer, he asked if any more men would like to follow Jesus Christ. And both young men raised their hands, as did inmates all over that prison compound.

Those men were still in prison, but they were free indeed.

I will never forget that Easter morning in Delaware. I've been in great cathedrals and beautiful sanctuaries and seen wonderful demonstrations of believers affirming their faith. But I have never seen a clearer picture of the church than I did there, behind that chain-link fence, with the razor wire coiling above their heads and the guard towers at the edges of the yard.

In those prisoners I saw four key characteristics essential for the church in the world today. First of all, they demonstrated *humility*. They were literally on their knees, ready to serve those who stood before them—a pretty hostile crowd, at that. The church in the world today cannot be triumphal and arrogant. We must be *servants* to the unbelievers who are all around us.

Second, they had *courage*. It takes raw guts to do what those guys did in that prison that day. Yet so many of us, in contrast, are afraid to take risks, afraid to be inconvenienced or uncomfortable, timid rather than boldly ready to venture wherever God calls us in His name.

Third, they were *united*. I will never forget that wall of kneeling believers, their arms draped around each other's shoulders. So often we Christians spend all our time squabbling with other Christians. It's a sign of our complacency. But when you're surrounded on every side by a culture that ridicules and persecutes Christians, you *have* to stand together as one.

And fourth, precisely because they were one, they were *ready to evangelize*. Bruce commissioned them to win their fellow inmates to Christ by the demonstration of their daily lives. They were to *be* evangelists. Not to "do evangelism" as one little part or program in their Christian lives, but to demonstrate the reality of Jesus Christ's power by the fruit of their everyday lives in Him.

That Easter morning crystallizes the call to the church today.

How tragic that we get sidetracked by a thousand splintering distractions! How sad that we're lulled to sleep by the personal comfort of our own complacency! The world around us may well be cynical, uninterested, and even hostile . . . but no more so than that prison crowd. Can't we cleave to the holy identity commissioned by our Savior and be His Body in the world? If we follow Jesus' example, we, too, can be humble, courageous, united evangelists and servants.

The firm foundation to our identity, of course, goes back to another Easter, more than two thousand years ago. It goes back to the very beginnings of the church and the unchanging truths upon which Christ has built His body.

4
ON THIS ROCK

He cannot have God for his father
who does not have the church for his mother.

—AUGUSTINE

W HEN THE CHURCH IS THE CHURCH, the people of God moved by the Spirit of God do the work of God, and evil cannot stand against them. That is the incredible mandate Jesus put before His followers when they arrived in Caesarea Philippi, a town at the foot of Mount Hermon, source of the springs that feed the River Jordan.

Many believe this to be the pivotal moment in the great New Testament drama. Jesus had aroused controversy since His ministry became public, and now many dared to hope that He might be the long-awaited leader who would free them from their oppressors.

But Jesus did not speak or act according to people's expectations. He didn't placate the huge crowds that followed Him; instead, He spoke to them in mysterious parables and hard sayings. He annoyed and outraged those in power, even as He healed and helped the poorest of the poor. He was gentle yet strong, supremely confident yet humble. He spoke of a kingdom beyond this world.

Who was this man who provoked curious controversy in ancient Palestine?

That was the very question Jesus put to His followers that day in Caesarea Philippi: "Who do people say that I am?"

"Some say you are John the Baptist," the disciples replied. "Others say Elijah, and still others believe you are Jeremiah or one of the other prophets."

Then Jesus looked into the eyes of these men who had turned from their trades, even their families, to follow Him. "But what about you?" He asked. "Who do you say I am?"

To which the irrepressible Peter replied, "You are the Christ, the Son of the living God."

One can almost imagine a hush in heaven at that moment. The words had been spoken. Soon the whole world would know that the long-awaited day was here. The Messiah had come.

Such faith, Jesus said, could only come from God. "Blessed are you, Simon son of Jonah, for this was not revealed to you by man, but by my Father in heaven."

Jesus' next words, however, are critical for understanding the nature of the Christian faith. For in direct response to Peter's confession, Christ announced: "On this rock I will build my church."

And to that church He promised a vast grant of authority, which He called "the keys of the kingdom of heaven."

"Whatever you bind on earth will be bound in heaven," Jesus said, "and whatever you loose on earth will be loosed in heaven."[1] The church was to be His instrument on earth, and whatever was done in His will would have eternal significance and consequence.

Whether Jesus meant He would build His church upon Peter himself or upon Peter's confession of faith is a point about which Christian traditions disagree. But the critical historical fact remains: Jesus' response to Peter's confession was to announce that He would build His church. And from this declaration we learn four crucial lessons about the church.

First, the church is not a building. The church is people. Just looking at the original Greek text of this passage shatters one of the most widespread misconceptions about the church. *Ekklesia,* the Greek word translated "church" in the New Testament, never refers to a building or a structure. An *ekklesia* was a gathering of people.

Jesus' word choice was well understood by the people of Palestine. For the culture at large, *ekklesia* meant a public assembly of citizens. It was used when they were "called out" of the city to vote. But its Hebrew counterpart, *qalal,* also meant the congregation of Israel constituted at Sinai and assembled before the Lord. It meant those whom He brought together and called by His name. The people of God.

Nowhere in the New Testament does anyone say, "Let's go to church," nor is the church referred to as a building, except as a metaphor.[2] All references to the church, including the metaphorical "body" and "holy nation," refer to God's people. As the hymn writer put it:

> The church is not a building,
> The church is not a steeple,
> The church is not a resting place,
> The church is a people.[3]

Second, the church is more than simply a collection of people; it is a new community. Many modern Christians see the Christian faith primarily, if not exclusively, as the gospel of "Jesus and me." Christianity is simply a personal relationship with Jesus. Accept Christ into your life and you will be saved.

This is true, of course, but it falls short of the whole. We are justified through our individual faith. Yet Christianity is much more than a private transaction with Jesus.

When Peter made his confession, Jesus did not say, "Good, Peter. You are now saved and will have an abundant life. Be at peace." Instead, He announced the church and established a divinely ordained pattern. When we confess Christ, God's response is to bring us into His church; we become part of His called-out people. When we become followers of Christ, we become members of His church, and our commitment to the church is indistinguishable from our commitment to Him.

Radical words.

Many Christians say they are believers but are not members of a church. By that, some mean that they are not members of a local congregation. But many mean that they do not need the church in any sense.

Yet according to the Scripture, Christianity is corporate. This is why we speak of the body with its different parts, the community of the redeemed, the holy nation and royal priesthood—or, as Carl Henry calls it, "the new society of God's people, the new society of the twice-born."[4]

The church is no civic center, no social club or encounter group, no Sunday morning meeting place. It is a new society, created for the salvation of a lost world, pointing to the kingdom to come.

And if we properly understand the exchange between Peter and Jesus and the rest of Scripture, we come face to face with a truly staggering truth about the nature of this new society: It is so dear to our Lord that He purchased it with His own blood.[5]

If we really comprehend that awesome, terrifying fact, it will cause any petty divisions or self-centered focus to fall away. We should fall to our knees in gratitude.

For we are part of the Body for which Christ died![6]

Therefore, the church belongs to God. He bought it at the most extravagant and painful price. But how often have you heard a pastor or a board of elders or deacons say "my church" or "our church"?

For some, it's just a habit of speech. Others mean it. And most congregational squabbles arise over precisely this point: Who owns the church? Who has the authority? Whose church is it anyway?

Early in my Christian life I was invited to give the message, consisting of my testimony, at two Sunday services of a well-known church. The practice was to videotape both services, then choose the better and release it for broadcast the following week.

During the first service something happened that could only be explained as an anointing of the Holy Spirit. I lost all track of time, yet finished exactly as the cue card saying "stop" was raised in front of the camera. I wasn't sure what I had said, but as I closed in prayer, people, without an invitation, knelt in place, tears streaming down their faces. A holy hush came over the congregation.

Afterward, as we waited for the second service to begin, the pastor's assistant began coaching him. When I prayed at the conclusion in the next service, he urged, the pastor should move up beside me, put his arm around my shoulder, look at the camera, and beckon people forward.

The second service was nothing like the first. Aware of the carefully laid plans and the need to repeat "the performance," I was self-conscious, watching the clock. Then as I began my closing prayer, the pastor moved up next to me, slipped his arm around my shoulder, and made a great dramatic gesture toward the congregation . . . and the camera. Nothing happened.

After the service I asked the pastor's assistant to use the first service tape for the television broadcast that week. "No, no," he said, shaking his head. "The second was much better."

I pressed the point, but he kept shaking his head. Finally he put his hand up, palm outward like a police officer holding back the traffic. "You don't seem to understand, Mr. Colson," he said. "This is Dr. Showforth's church!"[7]

How easily we are impressed with ourselves and our own inflated importance, foolishly seeking our identity in our office or position in the church! Where were we when God created His church? We live and breathe and serve at His pleasure. How absurd to think of us being the instrument for making men and women holy . . . to think of the redemption of mankind in human hands.

"I will build My church," said Jesus. Those unequivocal words should be posted over the entrance of every church building on the planet.

By His power, the church will triumph. "The gates of hell will not prevail against it," Jesus promised. Ultimately, Christ's new community of called-out people will triumph over the forces of sin and evil.

But this also has to be taken as a commission. We can't sit back and wait for the final victory. This is a call for the people of God to be a holy people, to stand against evil, and to fulfill their Sovereign's demand for justice and righteousness in the world today. Right now, wherever we are.

When the people of God understand this commission, then the church becomes the church.

BUT THIS STILL LEAVES US WITH MANY QUESTIONS. How do we define this church? To most of us, the church means our own denomination or the congregation where we worship on a Sunday. So how does that relate to what we have just been talking about—this called-out community of God's people? What's the relationship between the worldwide church and the particular place where we worship? And is everyone sitting in the pews on Sunday morning part of the church?

The word *ekklesia* does not help us with these distinctions because in some places in the New Testament it refers to all of God's people in a particular region or city or worldwide, in others it designates a local congregation meeting in a private home, and in some cases it means a collection of representatives of local churches meeting to conduct common business.[8] No distinction is made in Scripture because, unlike modern Christians, the New Testament writers believed that to be part of the church in one aspect was to be part of the church in all aspects.

It is the loss of this New Testament understanding of the comprehensive character of the church in both its spiritual essence and visible manifestations that is at the heart of modern-day confusion. We need to see this character clearly and appreciate its interrelationship if we hope to recapture God's vision for His people.

THE CHURCH UNIVERSAL

In its essence the church is a spiritual entity, for it is created by God Himself as He works the reality of salvation in those whom He wills. Only God knows who is in this vast invisible cloud of witnesses passing across the ages. And it is universal since He calls men and women from all races, colors, backgrounds, and parts of the globe. For this reason, Christians, from the earliest creeds onward, have confessed to being part of "one holy, catholic, apostolic church." This is the Body of Christ, all true believers of every denomination and tradition.[9]

But only by belonging to a visible community of faith can individuals truly make visible the reality of the church.

From the beginning it was clearly God's plan that the Body would be made manifest to the world by gathering into confessing communities to fulfill His mission—that is, to administer the sacraments, preach the Word, and make disciples. Thus, immediately after Pentecost, He established the pattern: Individual believers were to gather into particular communities.

THE CHURCH PARTICULAR

When those moved by Peter's powerful Pentecost sermon asked what they should do, the apostle replied, "Repent and be baptized."[10] Then they would receive the gift of the Holy Spirit, he told them, and would be among those whom the Lord called to Himself—that is, the church. So "those who accepted his message were baptized," not only as a sign of the forgiveness of their sins, but also of their entry into the visible church, and then they gathered together for the apostles' teaching, fellowship, breaking of bread, and prayer.[11] This is the normative, biblical pattern by which those redeemed by the saving power of Christ become part of the visible, or how those in the universal become part of the particular.

When Christians in the early centuries gathered together, they became known as the *communio sanctorum,* meaning "the communion of saints."[12] And they were indeed that, bound together as only men and women could be who were surrounded by an angry, hostile society ready to feed them to the lions. But by being the church, they made visible the mystery of God's salvation, and their witness changed the world.

This is the process by which the visible church has fulfilled its mission and witness to the world through the centuries. It's not unlike an army, where men and women of all sizes and shapes sign up to serve. At the beginning these recruits are one big, disorganized mass of humanity, and only the Pentagon knows who they are. Until it is trained and organized, this army is useless. So men and women are assigned to training units to learn the skills and disciplines of soldiers. Then they are stationed into divisions and headquarters and honor guards and counterintelligence, all working together so the army can do its job. Only when it is fully uniformed and deployed can the world see the army at work.

So it is with the church. Its recruitment is universal, but it has to be broken down into visible fighting units. It may have command structures, such as denominations or episcopal government. And it may have special training forces to equip its fighting units: parachurch movements such as Prison Fellowship and Evangelism Explosion and others. These are visible structures we create to outfit God's army—the Body—to do the job it is called to do.

Where Do We Fit?

There is today a widespread belief that one can be a Christian and develop one's own faith system apart from the church. The proposition is ludicrous. Everyone regenerated by God is, by definition, a part of the universal church. It's not a matter of choice or membership. And following the pattern made normative in the book of Acts, each believer is to make his or her confession, be baptized, and become part of a local congregation with all of the accountability that implies.[13] Membership in a church particular is no more optional than membership in the church universal.

Unfortunately it is not uncommon for Christians to drift from congregation to congregation, usually where their friends lead them or where the pastor happens to give the most satisfying message or where the style of music appeals to them. Many have no sense of roots or responsibility, and some never even join a local church.

Yet membership in a confessing body is fundamental to the faithful Christian life. We are explicitly warned not to forsake "our assembling together."[14] His understanding of this prompted Martin Luther to say, "Apart from the church, salvation is impossible."[15] Not that the church provides salvation; God does. But because the "saved" one can't fulfill what it means to be a Christian apart from the church, membership becomes an indispensable mark of salvation.

"So highly does the Lord esteem the communion of His church," Calvin wrote, "that He considers everyone a traitor and apostate from religion who perversely withdraws himself from any Christian society which preserves the true ministry of the word and sacraments."[16]

Those are strong words. But if, as we will later argue, it is impossible to fulfill the Great Commission apart from the church particular, if apart from the church particular one cannot participate in the ordinances or sacraments, then one cannot claim to be a Christian and at the same time claim to be outside the church. To do so is at the least hypocrisy, and at the worst, blasphemy. And if the purpose of the church is to herald and point to the coming kingdom of God, as both Protestant scholars and Vatican Council II agree it is, then the Christian life must be rooted in community; for the kingdom to which it points is itself the ultimate community.

This is why writer Warren Wiersbe says he does not attend church to hear a sermon or to have fellowship, though he enjoys both, but "to bear witness that Jesus Christ is alive and worship Him."[17]

There is, as Richard Neuhaus puts it, "no Christianity apart from the historical community that bears its truth."[18] Therefore, our understanding of this community shapes our view of ministry, accountability, and Christian duty. Failure to understand this causes confusion in our understanding of our holy identity—and diffusion in our ability to serve and influence the world around us.

When a person is converted and thereby comes into the church universal, the first step of discipleship is membership in the church particular. Therefore, it is the duty of those who are involved with new converts to guide them not just into a Bible study or fellowship group, but into a local church where the Word is taught and the sacraments administered.

But the other side of the coin is equally important: The church particular must in every sense feel and behave as a part of the church universal. Often evangelicals fail to understand this reciprocal duty. Just look at the number of congregations that include "independent" in their name. Although they are signaling their independence from any denomination or ecclesiastical structure, the name also suggests that they are independent from the rest of the Body. And some actually come to see themselves that way as they jealously guard their own views on doctrine or practice.

Of course, as we will discuss later, believers and congregations should stand firmly for what they believe to be biblical truth and defend their view of liturgy or sacraments or eschatology or other matters upon which Christians honestly differ. And there may even be occasions when believers, to remain faithful to their confession, must separate themselves from those who renounce the truth or are clearly apostate.

The overarching fact, however, is that one cannot be part of a body God has created and at the same time declare that one is "independent" of that body. It is to deny what God Himself has ordained.

All Christians are in one Body—the church universal. These believers then become the visible church as they become part of local congregations—the church particular—which may be structurally independent or part of an episcopal government or denominational fellowship. The whole equals the sum of the parts. All neat and tidy. All clear and uncomplicated? Right?

Unfortunately, no. In practice it just doesn't work that way in the visible church. Look out over any local congregation on any Sunday morning—any church particular—and you will find lukewarm believers, cultural Christians (those who were born in America and, believing it to be a Christian country, go to church occasionally and thus call themselves Christian), and a sprinkling of New Agers and self-helpers who use God as their copilot. There will be seekers, reprobates, and those who with all their heart confess Christ—all mixed together. And we call it the church—although only God Himself knows those within it who are truly His.

THIS IS THE GREAT TENSION. On the one hand, there is the church God has created and intends for ultimate consummation as the bride of Christ. That church, said C. S. Lewis, is a spectacle that makes the boldest demons uneasy, for "she is spread out through all time and space and rooted in eternity, terrible as an army with banners."[19]

But that ultimate vision is far more glorious than the present reality we see around us every day in this fallen world: little congregations gathering in white wooden chapels and vast denominations meeting in grand cathedrals, street-corner preachers, megachurch pastors, Salvation Army bell-ringers, television orators, and traveling evangelists. Many of them spend much of the time either bickering with or ignoring each other. This church, the one the world sees, resembles nothing so much as a gigantic flea market with the vendors competing against one another, hawking their wares in a huge, discordant din.

Messy, ambiguous, imperfect? You bet. There is no perfect or model church. But we should not despair—for at least two reasons.

First, tensions allow for a variety of expressions which, often confounding human wisdom, reach people who might not otherwise be reached. There is richness in our diversity that strengthens the overall witness of the church. Different confessions, because of their own emphasis, make differing aspects of the spiritual reality visible. Historically, for example,

Protestants have done a better job of making visible the spiritual reality of the Word in preaching, while Catholics have done better at making visible the spiritual reality of worship.

But there's a second and even more important reason not to despair. The great scholar John Courtney Murray, who believed "religious pluralism is against the will of God," was forced to acknowledge that it is "the human condition; it is written into the script of history." The institutional church, like all other institutions, comes under the influence of the Fall. But as Murray and many others have recognized, this dynamic may well save us all from the one fate worse than chaos: triumphalism.[20] That is, the very real temptation to believe that we have all of the truth, thus confusing ourselves with the kingdom of God.

As has been said, the church is like Noah's ark: The stench inside would be unbearable if it weren't for the storm outside. It's true—sometimes we stink. And the world is stormy. But as imperfect as we are on this side of heaven, the miracle is that God in fact chooses to use His church—us—as His means of proclaiming love, truth, and hope.

Not always clearly; not always unequivocally. We all cringe when a church leader does some dreadful thing or when a layperson says something crazy into a television camera. But somehow, through all the muddle, the gospel goes forth. People often come to church for all the wrong reasons, but God draws them to Himself. Churches can thunder down all the wrong tracks, and then repent and be renewed.

Admittedly, the pettiness and failures, the division and discord, can be disheartening at times. What a sorry mess we mortals often make of things in the name of the church! But our comfort comes from God's miraculous promise that He will build His church. Sometimes He does it in the most unlikely ways—as the unexpected story of a young Russian girl shows us so beautifully.

5
I Will Build My Church

She was ten years old, a sturdy child with tendrils of thick, brown hair escaping from a tightly woven braid. At the moment her dark eyes were focused beyond the dirty windows of her classroom. Outside, the steely sky swirled with tiny snowflakes, a rarity in the seaside city of Odessa.

Rocking back and forth at her wooden desk, wrapping one leg around the other, Irina Ratushinskaya could not keep her eyes on the teacher. Snow in Odessa! It was more precious than bread. If you waited in line long enough, you could always get a stale loaf or two. But snow was different. The stalls of the market merchants and the shelves of the miserable stores would always be bare of such magic, no matter how long you waited.

Snowballs! Forts! Scoops of snow licked from a worn woolen mitten! As she watched the flakes fall, Irina's chest tightened. Soon it would all be gone, the mysterious white lace melting away, leaving only the everyday brown of Odessa. All because she and her classmates were stuck in a boring drift of lectures.

This was atheist instruction time, and attendance was compulsory; for in Nikita Krushchev's Soviet Union, young minds represented the best hope for the future. Two years earlier, the 1961 Cuban missile crisis had nearly brought the world to nuclear confrontation, establishing the huge stakes of the superpower standoff. Krushchev saw education as the tool that would forge the eventual ideological triumph of the Soviet Union. Instructors who wanted to be part of that glorious future had to vigilantly stamp out the tiresome myths that, in spite of forty-six years of Communist indoctrination, refused to melt away.

Already Irina and her classmates had been told about a Baptist woman who had roasted her child in an oven. It seemed implausible to Irina. After all, "Auntie" Vera, the janitor at her grandparents' flat, was a Baptist, and her children were alive and well. Then the seventh graders had performed a play depicting priests as oafs and fools.

Everyone seemed to be against God: the Young Pioneers, the teachers, the headmaster, the speakers on the radio—the whole country. It didn't seem fair. Even in schoolyard games they were not allowed to gang up on one person. Also, it seemed odd that they all pitched such a furious battle against someone they said didn't exist anyway.

Today Irina was wondering, as she often had, why the teacher even bothered with the truckloads of words she was dumping from the front of the room. "God doesn't exist," the instructor said again. "Only silly, ignorant old women believe in Him."

Can't they tell they are giving themselves away? thought Irina. *Adults tell you there are no gremlins or ghosts. They tell you once or twice, and that's it. But with God, they tell you over and over again. So He must exist—and He must be very powerful for them to fear Him so greatly.*

With that logic firmly in mind, she returned to what was foremost in her mind at the moment: the snow.

Okay, God, if You did not exist, we wouldn't have to listen to this lecture. So it's Your fault we're sitting here missing the snow. If You're so powerful, make it keep snowing![1]

That was Irina Ratushinskaya's first prayer. And white flakes fell like manna for three days from Odessa's gray skies, the city's largest snowfall in sixty years. School was canceled, and Irina and her friends galloped down the wide avenues, throwing snowballs and relishing the fresh crystals that fell so softly on their faces. As she felt the gentle, melting kisses from heaven, Irina thought about this God her teachers denied, the One who could make snow fall from official Communist airspace.

She began to talk to Him secretly, late at night, asking endless questions. Not politely, but with passion and fervor. Was He kind?

If He is not kind, I don't want to have anything to do with Him, even if He is all-powerful. But if He was kind, but not all-powerful, then she didn't want to depend on Him either. What good was a God who was not powerful?

And though she conversed with Him, Irina felt it improper to ask God for anything. What had she ever done for Him that she should expect any favors? After all, here she was living in an atheistic country and doing nothing about it, so how could she start demanding that God do this or that? In fact, if she had a complaint, it was that she didn't know what He wanted from her.

This is through no fault of mine, when all is said and done; I had no choice about where to be born . . .

Yet the moment she thought this, an answer seemed to echo from within: *Don't worry, you will find out what you need to know when the time comes.*

Irina's reasoning served her well for the next few years, and when she was fourteen, a pivotal, though seemingly insignificant, event occurred—an epiphany reminiscent of Augustine's famous agony over his youthful prank of stealing pears from a neighbor's tree.

At the end of a long, dreary history lesson, when the teacher left the students alone for a few minutes, one of Irina's classmates heaved a chestnut across the room. The large nut crashed into an inkwell, which smashed on the floor, which splashed a huge splatter of black ink on a nearby wall.

Hearing the commotion, the teacher came running back into the room. "Who broke the inkwell?" she shrieked.

Silence.

The interrogation continued, with each student being questioned, one by one, by a senior teacher. When Irina's turn came, she put on her most agreeable, obedient face and began to lie with gusto, throwing in the detail that she had been searching for something in her satchel on the floor and hadn't seen anything.

After hearing Irina's testimony, the grand inquisitor moved on to the next student, Seryozha, who looked the teacher straight in the eye and said bluntly, "I'm not going to tell you."

His example pierced Irina's conscience, and much later that evening as she made her way home in the dark, she thought, *I am becoming what THEY want me to be—a cowardly, spineless creature, with no concept of honor, but ever obedient . . . One who considers a glib lie to be an act of heroism . . . Can it be that for me, the means now justifies the end? . . .*

I shall never, ever lower myself like that again before anybody, she vowed. *If I must disobey in order to preserve my self-respect, then I shall do so openly. . . I'll learn how to behave decently from books, and also I'll think a lot and talk to God more. Then my soul will remain my own: Nobody will be able to manipulate me to suit themselves.*[2]

From that point on, instinctively knowing that she would become a servant to one master or another, Irina chose her side, with a code of behavior far different than the Communist masters desired. As she explored the great Russian books lining her parents' bookshelves—for her mother was a teacher of literature—she found an enormous variety of situations and epochs, but a striking similarity among the characters' inner conditions and the situations in which life placed them.

In the writings of Dostoevsky, Pushkin, Turgenev, and Tolstoy she found a reflection of the God whom she knew was kind and all-powerful. The values of good and evil did not change, but seemed somehow to be written on the souls of men and women, regardless of their culture or training.[3]

As Irina contemplated the reflections of God and His invisible laws of human nature that she had found both in her own conscience and in the literature she loved, she wondered how she would respond to future tests. Would she compromise the straight for the crooked or trade truth for a lie? *What kind of times will I live in when I grow up?* she mused. *What kind of orders will be issued to me?*[4]

Adolescence brought its inevitable assaults of hormones and doubt. Bewildered to find herself transformed from a confident child into a gangling, spotty-faced gargoyle, Irina's childlike faith in God became more complicated. Suddenly her beloved books offered no solace, and she had no way to get a Bible.

Pushkin told her the truth lay in Russian Orthodoxy; Tolstoy's theories confused her. *Maybe I'm not a Christian at all,* she thought. *After all, I know so little about Christ. Just a few quotes here and there, picked up from various books, not enough to form a complete picture of Him. There's nobody trustworthy to ask either.*

One night as she agonized over her faith, she was gripped by a familiar urge—the fury of a poem coming on. She crept quietly from her narrow bed to the cold communal kitchen her family shared with others and scribbled out the essence of her pursuit of God:

> How the road to Him to find?
> With what the hope and pain to measure?
> People seek a God who's kind.
> God grant they find, and trust, and treasure.

Later, as an adult, she would see both the amateur nature of the poem's construction as well as the sophistication of its search. But even at that point it was not a quest without comfort, for as she traced the words with her stubby pencil, she felt a benevolent eye looking over her shoulder: *I shivered despite a delicious warmth, for I knew whose glance it was. He had not abandoned me. He was with me. And He didn't mind that I couldn't pray properly.*[5]

When Irina was twenty-three years old she obtained her first Bible. A Jewish friend emigrating to the United States gave her an eighteenth-century volume of the Scriptures printed in Old Church Slavonic. Eagerly she spent a month and a half learning the ancient, intricate alphabet printed on the delicate, thin pages. Then, finally, she was able to read the Old and New Testaments. She was excited to discover in writing a description of the God she had already come to know. She wrote in her memoirs:

> All the revelations I had either guessed or read about elsewhere fell into place, like the pieces of a jigsaw puzzle. I realized that yes, I am a Christian, and my loving God confirms that it is so, and not otherwise! Russian literature, which had earlier saved my young soul from rejection and pride, confirms the same. But I did not experience the typical zeal of a neophyte: there is one God for all, for all faiths except paganism. Is it for us, humans, to try to carve Him up amongst ourselves? He will show the way, He will instruct: for we are all His children.[6]

Meanwhile, in the world outside her mind and heart, the comparative thaw of the Krushchev years had brought about a counterreaction. By 1965 an iron yoke again choked the nation; by 1967, when Leonid Brezhnev came to power, there was a sustained, systematic persecution of those flocking to underground dissident groups. By 1983 Yuri Andropov, the former chief of the KGB who had so cruelly orchestrated the crushing of Hungary in 1956, reigned over the structures of the Soviet Union.

Human rights activists, religious dissidents, and other free-thinking citizens met in cells deep beneath that outward structure, and by this time Irina's poetry was well known to those whose resolve it steeled. It was known as well to the KGB, and the secret police targeted her work as "anti-Soviet" since it celebrated Christian faith and human rights rather than the Communist regime. She was arrested.

Irina, now twenty-eight, was sentenced to seven years of hard labor and seven years of internal exile and sent to the Barashevo labor camp in Mordovia, part of the Soviet Union's notorious gulag.

The Communist authorities had not changed, and the lessons Irina had learned as a schoolgirl served her well. Fortified by her Christian convictions, she refused to compromise with those who would have her exhibit a servile obedience by ratting on fellow prisoners, making a false confession, or praising the regime.

Despite their cruel attempt to kill her with cold and starvation, Irina survived, thin and frozen. But her soul, nourished by the peace of God and love for her fellow inmates, suffered no deprivation.

Her poetry flourished as well. She wrote verses in her head during KGB interrogations and woke in the night with her heart ablaze to commit new lines to memory. Much like one of her heroes, Aleksandr Solzhenitsyn, she recorded her writing on tiny bits of paper that would one day emerge from the gulag to tell her story.

Human rights groups and Christians in the West eventually raised an outcry over Irina's case, and in 1986, two days before Mikhail Gorbachev's Reykjavik summit with Ronald Reagan, she was released. But the KGB still monitored her every move, as well as her husband's, until they managed to make their way to the West and freedom.

Irina's first book, *Grey Is the Color of Hope*, detailed her life in the camps;

her second, *In the Beginning*, traced her early life and influences, telling how a girl in an officially atheistic country, deprived of a Bible or Christian training, found Christ and became part of the Orthodox Church. Her own story, she said, was the tale of an entire generation: young Soviets who saw through the lies of their elders, and much to their leaders' dismay, turned to God and the church.

During her prison term, Irina spent much of her time in solitary confinement. It was there that she recorded another miracle. It was an astounding sensation—something she felt not just once, but many times. After her release she compared notes with other Christian prisoners and found that they had experienced the same phenomenon. It came much as the presence of God had manifested itself to her as a child: the benevolent eye looking over her shoulder, the sense of delicious warmth in a freezing land. It was the comfort of God's presence with her, sharing her suffering, assuring her of His love.

Later Irina discovered that thousands of Christians—parts of the Body of Christ all over the world—had been praying for her, standing before God's throne in solidarity with her, petitioning Him for her. She related the effects of those prayers in her book *Pencil Letter:*

> Believe me, it was often thus:
> In solitary cells, on winter nights
> A sudden sense of joy and warmth
> And a resounding note of love.
> And then, unsleeping, I would know
> A-huddle by an icy wall:
> Someone is thinking of me now,
> Petitioning the Lord for me.
> My dear ones, thank you all
> Who did not falter, who believed in us!
> In the most fearful prison hour
> We probably would not have passed
> Through everything—from end to end,
> Our heads held high, unbowed—
> Without your valiant hearts
> To light our path.

WE BECAME FRIENDS WITH IRINA AND HER HUSBAND, Igor, in the late 1980s. They spoke at a Prison Fellowship International conference and later visited us in Washington. They met with senators and congressmen during the days of the Iron Curtain's collapse, and their insights and counsel proved helpful.

In their personal lives, however, Irina's greatest desire was to have children. But because of her tortures and deprivations in the gulag, doctors said a successful pregnancy would be difficult, if not impossible.

Months went by. We prayed. Then one night I received a phone call from Irina, breathless with excitement. She was pregnant with twins. The boys, Sergei and Oleg, were born in 1992.

Today, Irina and her family live in Moscow. Her latest book of poems, her first since 1992, has been published in the U.S. as *Wind of the Journey*. The twins, now eleven, are "healthy and optimistic little men," as Irina puts it.

"I am so thankful to God," Irina wrote me in a letter last Easter, "for being loved by my family, for the friendship with many decent people and for another Easter to celebrate. If someone told me twenty years ago that I would live to this day, I would have doubted it very much."

6
THE SIN OF PRESUMPTION

Win Over 10 Percent of Your City's Total Population to Jesus
on ONE DAY!!!

—ADVERTISEMENT IN
Religious Broadcasting

How does god build his church? Does He orchestrate snowfalls for brown-eyed girls in atheistic countries? Does He hide Himself in the pages of books repressive governments forgot to ban? Is He inevitably and irrefutably evident in the frantic denials of those who fear His rule? Does creation itself reveal "the road to Him to find"?

New life in the Spirit is conceived in the secret place of the soul, hidden from human eyes. This is the wonder and mystery of God's regeneration of men and women. And never in this life will we quite know how God calls His people to Himself.

What we do know is that the wind of the Spirit blows where He wills. We hear the sound, we see the evidences, but we cannot comprehend fully how this mysterious breath of God touches human hearts. God builds His church in the most unlikely ways and places, stirring the convictions of the heart, bringing men and women to the knowledge of sin, to repentance, to the Savior Himself—and knitting them together in His body.

In spite of all this, Irina's story can be troubling to some. After all, she did not learn about Christ in an evangelistic crusade and "make a decision"; she did not read a tract that opened her eyes of faith; she never went to

Sunday school or youth fellowship; she did not grow up in a Christian home where she learned the Bible in family devotions; she never heard the gospel preached, never had a friend give her the "Four Spiritual Laws." For many years she did not even have a Bible.

Many, particularly in evangelical ranks, believe that a person must have an experience that fits a certain pattern: The individual must know the precise moment he or she prayed "the sinner's prayer" and be able to recount that dramatic experience of "accepting Christ"—words that are almost liturgical to some.

For me, that expectation proves no problem. God intervened in my life powerfully, in a moment I will never forget. Witnessed to by a good friend and humbled by the Spirit, I surrendered my life in a flood of tears to Jesus Christ, in words that fit the pattern. For others, it's not that way.

After my much-publicized conversion, Christian brothers and sisters used to swarm around Patty whenever she accompanied me to public events. "And when were you born again, Mrs. Colson?" they would ask, eager for another gripping conversion story.

At first this drove Patty to tears, causing her at times to avoid such occasions. To this day it sometimes sets her teeth on edge.

"I don't know," she would reply. "All I know is I believe deeply."

Her pursuers would shrink away, and more than once they were heard to say, "Poor Mr. Colson. His wife isn't born again."

But Patty, like Ruth Graham and millions of others, cannot pinpoint a precise moment or sudden awakening. She grew up in a Christian home, always attended worship services, can never remember a moment when she didn't believe, and over the last thirty years has experienced an ever-deepening relationship with Christ.

For some the salvation formula has almost become a procedure whereby one makes a simple choice, as simple as walking through the right door. I once attended a service where a young evangelist displayed this attitude.

When it was time for the altar call, he strode across the platform to the congregation's left and drew an imaginary circle with a great sweep of his arms.

"In here," he explained, "is self on a chair. Go ahead. Draw it out in your own mind." Heads were nodding all around me.

Then he moved to the center of the platform and, with a grand dramatic gesture, created a second circle.

"And in this," he intoned, "is a chair, and above it is a cross. Man, you see, is reaching up to God, but He isn't there. Man is still on the throne himself." Now scattered "amens" erupted from the pews.

With deliberation he then walked to the right and drew yet another circle. By this time his words were flowing rhapsodically.

"And in here," he said, his voice breaking momentarily, "is the entrance to the kingdom of God."

Then with great emotion he called people to come forward to walk through the third circle to enter into the very presence of God Himself.

And come forward they did, as if in cadence with his words, "Come, come, all ye who are heavy laden, come into My kingdom. The third circle. Experience the forgiveness of your sins and the blessings of God." Dozens were at the altar by the time he finished a lengthy invitation that left even the choir exhausted.

It was a mesmerizing performance, and I was thankful that this young man was faithful to Scripture, that he loved God and had a heart for the lost. Probably many who came forward that day were saved and the angels rejoiced. But no doubt many also left the service having been entranced by an imaginary circle and cajoled into uttering a prayer, as if receiving Christ was a matter of jumping through a particular hoop uttering a particular set of magic words.

Over the past thirty years I've been in countless crusades and have seen thousands of people raise their hands, signifying decisions for Christ. I've seen them come forward and heard them utter the correct words. I've called them to do so myself many, many times and have seen the numbers tallied. I've rejoiced. But only God knows the mysteries of the human heart and the forensic power of the Holy Spirit to quicken a dead heart to new life. And sometimes, what we see in such situations are merely human experiences wrought by pressure or emotion, not actual belief in Christ.

People who have made only superficial decisions usually don't show up for further discipleship; they don't take part in Bible studies to grow in faith. Or they behave as Christians for a while but eventually fall back to their old ways. Jesus spoke clearly of this in His parable of the sower and the four soils.

But we encourage this sort of false flowering of faith whenever we establish our method, any method, as *the* way into the kingdom, or lead people to believe that simply uttering certain words will assure their salvation. (And if we probe ourselves honestly, the motivation behind such techniques and formulas is often so we can count scalps and claim successes. Sometimes the goal is *our* glory, not God's.)

There is a great difference between a humanly induced "decision" and a true conversion, the new birth of the Spirit. Conversion is a process that begins with God's regenerating work—an instant when the Spirit gives life—and continues as we grow in faith through the process of sanctification.

So does this mean we should abandon all tracts and banish the sinner's prayer? Not at all. I have led many in the sinner's prayer and will continue to do so. In Prison Fellowship we frequently use the "Four Spiritual Laws" and recommend Evangelism Explosion and similar evangelistic programs. They are useful techniques for presenting the good news and explaining the gospel.

But they are precisely that: techniques. They are neither sacred steps to salvation nor reliable rubrics that assure God will work in some preprogrammed way.

When Sigmund Freud said that religion is merely a wish fulfillment, that we make up God in the image of our own father, he had it exactly backward. Instead, nonbelievers disinvent the God that they know, down deep, indeed exists. Some knowledge of spiritual truth, the *Imago Dei*, is in *every* human heart, planted there by our Creator. Over the years I have found that those who call themselves atheists actually have a strong sense of the absolute truth they know exists. They just don't want to acknowledge that it's true—because if they did, they would have to change the way they live. They flee on moral grounds; refusing to submit themselves, they exchange the truth for a lie.

But God works as He wills to overcome our rebellion. Like the wind that blows through the trees, He can neither be seen nor directed. He touches the heart. He breathes through snowflakes. He calls people to

Himself, conceiving the new life in the Spirit in the secret place of the soul. He does so through one mediator between God and man, Jesus Christ.

The belief that there is but one method or formula by which we enter the kingdom is what we call the sin of presumption: presuming to know the mind of God and to program and calculate by human means who is or is not secure in the faith and hence in the church.

This mind-set is not only presumptuous, it's patronizing. Once when I was scheduled to address an evangelistic outreach gathering, the host gave me a single-spaced, typed sheet with the instructions that this was the precise script I was to use in the invitation.

I assured the man that I had given invitations hundreds of times and would feel most comfortable—and effective—using my own words to encourage people to commit their lives to Christ. But the man insisted that I follow his script.

Then, during our time of prayer together before the service, the host asked God to wipe my mind clear of anything I had prepared and replace it with "his words." (I assumed he meant the Lord's words, but I wasn't sure.)

I had worked on my talk for days, praying that God would give me the appropriate message. This man's prayer for God to expunge all that struck me as presumptuous at best. I bit my lip and prayed silently that God would not allow me to be sidetracked by this kind of manipulation.

In the end, I did not read the man's script, but followed the leading of the Holy Spirit with words that I believed were natural and appropriate for the occasion. Many people responded to the invitation to follow Christ.

When we regard any particular methodology as exclusively normative, we eventually question the faith of those who do not conform to it. This presumption, so contrary to biblical teaching, is a major cause of the disunity that plagues and cripples the witness of the church.[1] And it is all the more dangerous because it often begins with the noblest of motives: the desire that others will experience what we have. Unfortunately it can soon become harshly judgmental and can even result in writing off entire denominations or traditions.

For example, I can't tell you how many letters I've received over the years protesting my use of Mother Teresa as an example of holy living. Before her death, many suggested that I visit her in India so I could give her the plan of salvation. Picturing such a scene in my mind gave a new dimension to the word *ludicrous*. How could anyone deny this woman's faithful witness? Certainly no one who has been to India and seen the incredible impact she had upon millions of Hindus. Because of Mother Teresa, they revere the word *Christian*, even though proselytizing is against the law in that country. Who knows how many souls came into the kingdom through her witness and the worldwide fame she earned but never sought?[2]

One of our favorite examples of Mother Teresa's courageous witness occurred at the National Prayer Breakfast in Washington in 1994. None who were there will ever forget the sight of the frail, tiny nun, who had to stand on a box in order to be seen—just barely—over the podium. On one side of her were President and Mrs. Clinton, and on the other were Vice President and Mrs. Gore.

As Mother Teresa began to speak, her voice was as strong as her demeanor was frail. "I feel the greatest destroyer of peace today is abortion, because Jesus said, 'If you receive a little child, you receive me.' So every abortion is the denial of receiving Jesus, the neglect of receiving Jesus," she said. Mr. Clinton and Mr. Gore both turned crimson.

The crowd was at first dumbstruck. Then applause began, continuing and building until some people, forgetting the decorum of the event, actually stood on their chairs. No one else in the world had the moral authority to speak that way, in that setting, to that pro-choice administration. And there was no rebuttal. As Mr. Clinton said later, "No one can argue with a life so well lived."

Many who have written me about the impossibility of Mother Teresa being a Christian have not sounded particularly Christian themselves. Some letters were ugly and hateful; most were filled with outrage. Many quoted a Christian leader to whom in the course of an interview Mother Teresa supposedly expressed some universalist statements. "Thus," they wrote, "she cannot be saved."

When I finally attempted to track down the facts, I learned that the leader referred to denies that the episode ever happened. But rumors never let facts stand in their way, so this one lived on, and the letters kept coming to my office up until the time of Mother Teresa's death.

Some were downright vitriolic: "How dare you hold up someone who does not speak our language"—that is, our evangelical jargon—"someone who does not proclaim the gospel." Proclaim the gospel? She not only proclaimed the gospel often in public messages, she proclaimed it with her life. In responding to these diatribes, I often added my favorite quote from Francis of Assisi: "Preach the gospel all the time; if necessary use words."

One correspondent reacted to my use of this statement by sending me a sixteen-page treatise on why Francis himself could not have been a Christian. I confess that in exasperation I suggested that the man might make better use of his time building the kingdom himself rather than questioning the salvation of someone who was the greatest evangelist of his day and died almost eight hundred years ago.

The sin of presumption is consuming. It leads people to spend enormous amounts of precious time judging those whose views or church traditions might differ from their own. This quickly leads to arrogance and lovelessness and inevitably divides the Body, grieving the heart of God.

In the end it is a deadly form of spiritual pride, and it blinds those who practice it. It would exclude the thief on the cross next to Christ's for not praying the sinner's prayer in his dying breath; it would include any Pharisee with "perfect" doctrine and a heart of stone.

This does not mean that believers should not be discerning or challenge others when necessary. There are clear biblical warrants for doing this.[3]

Certainly there are those who claim to be Christian but clearly are not. Many New Agers, for example, call themselves Christians because they claim to believe in Jesus, though for them He is but one of the many manifestations of a pantheistic god. Others who claim to be Christians live in stubborn, unrepentant sin and need to be called to account. (More about that accountability later.)

Indeed there is widespread apostasy within Christendom, within whole denominations in fact, which any Christian should challenge. And there are those who live in egregious error, embracing a false faith and ignoring the truth.

For example, though most of us would salute Mormons for their disciplined lifestyles and strong family values, Mormonism is not simply a particular stream of Christianity.

The Mormon church, with eleven million members and an estimated worth of twenty-five billion dollars, would have people think so. During the 2002 Winter Olympics in Salt Lake City, Mormon leaders urged journalists to stop using the term "Mormon." Instead, shorthand references to the church, whose official name is "The Church of Jesus Christ of Latter Day Saints," should simply be "Church of Jesus Christ." Meanwhile, films shown to the foreign press emphasized the Mormons' relationship with Christianity by pointing out the role of the Bible in Mormon faith and practice.

But Mormonism is an entirely different religion from biblical Christian faith. For instance, Mormonism believes in many gods, not just one. Christians believe that God is eternal and is a spirit. Mormons believe that the god of this universe, like other gods in other universes, was once as we are. God "progressed" in knowledge and became divine but retained his body. For Mormons, Jesus is God's son in a very different sense than the Bible teaches.

Though many Mormons will say our beliefs are similar enough to be the same, that is not the case, and followers of Christ need to be ready to lovingly point out the differences when opportunities arise.

A few years ago I spoke at the spiritual seminar of a leading business group. I gave my presentation first, followed by a well-known Mormon author and self-help guru. He began his lecture by putting a transparency on the screen. On it was a dark curving line drawn vertically down the middle.

The author then asked people to close their eyes. As they did, he put up another transparency on which the curving line was fleshed out in the hunched figure of an old woman. He then asked one side of the room to look up and remember what they saw. Then he put a second transparency on the screen: it was the same curved line, but as the people in the other half of the room looked up, they saw it forming the side of a young woman's face.

So people on one side of the room saw an old woman, while those on the other side saw a young woman. The point, said the author, was that it was the same line—just two different perspectives. The crowd chuckled.

This is a classic Mormon technique: Both beliefs, Mormon and Christian, though they see things differently, lead to the same truth.

So I asked the man an impertinent question. "But which is the picture, an old woman or a young woman? It can't be both at the same time."

In spite of his well-renowned business mind, he couldn't answer. That's because it's a logical impossibility. *Truth cannot be both.* Just as that drawing had to be either an old woman or a young one, Mormonism (or any other belief for that matter) either affirms historic Christianity or it doesn't. Since it doesn't, it can't call itself Christianity.

Now, all this may sound confusing, perhaps even contradictory. On the one hand, we seem to be arguing, as Calvin did, that we can't know for certain whom God has called as His people. So maybe we are supposed to accept everyone? On the other hand, there is a biblical mandate to be discerning, to flee apostasy and carefully confront those in our midst who are not professing or living the truth.

The answer is neither universalism nor judgmentalism. And admittedly it means walking the razor's edge.

The means by which men and women are saved and come into the church cannot be reduced to human formulas that put God into our own little box. As Carl Henry has said, "Not even evangelicals can straitjacket the Holy Spirit." But Jesus did teach His disciples that they would be known by the fruit of their lives.[4] So the evidence of one's faith is a good measure of whether he or she is indeed part of the church of faith, and it is our duty to be discerning about that.

Another point to remember is the distinction between the church universal and the church particular. The universal body, as we've noted, is solely the work of God. Who are we to question, let alone know, whom He calls? He has the people of His own choosing in every nation, of every color and political persuasion, and from every tradition that confesses Christ and Christ alone as their Savior.

But on the particular level there is a human element. Individuals commit to one another to form a local, visible, confessing congregation in order to fulfill the purpose of the church. It is within that community that we worship and study and participate in the ordinances and sacraments. There we can, as we will discuss later, insist upon doctrinal agreement, and sometimes agreement on practices we follow. Within that body, which we help to create, we have a clear biblical warrant to hold each other accountable for faithfulness in confession and living.

Ultimately, of course, the sin of presumption hardens hearts and destroys the unity of the Body. It sets Christian against Christian, denomination against denomination, until we forget whose church this really is.

And nothing is more destructive of our communion, regardless of its cause, than disunity.

7

THE FRACTURED WITNESS

The Church is not a human society of people united by their natural affinities, but the Body of Christ, in which all members, however different, (and He rejoices in their differences and by no means wishes to iron them out) must share the common life, complementing and helping one another precisely by their differences.

—C. S. LEWIS
Letters of C. S. Lewis
7 DECEMBER 1950

In THE BEGINNING everyone loved each other. Their new church in America was a haven from the Communist repression in their old country. One by one, the immigrants made their way to the U.S., settled in a Midwest city, and found each other. They loved their freedom to worship together openly as a body of believers. They were united by their common ethnic background, common experiences, but most of all by their faith. Their fellowship became the center of their new lives.

As the years went by, the little group of foreign families prospered. They got good jobs as steelworkers at the local Ford plant. They opened restaurants. They became U.S. citizens, got married, and had children. And they decided to build a church for their growing congregation.

So they held bake sales. They collected donations door to door. They got a loan. By 1978, with twenty families and $15,000, they had enough to buy three acres of land outside the city. The only thing on the property was a broken-down garage, but the first service held there was beautiful. Sixty people gathered, singing hymns, praying, and reading aloud from the New Testament. Then they spread bright blankets on the floor and shared a hot meal. They felt like the early Christians in the book of Acts.

Within a few years the congregation had grown from the garage to a ten-thousand square-foot church and hall. It was a beautiful place for the body of believers to worship, as well as their social center. "We were the happiest church ever," says one of the longtime members about those early days.

Then the serpent entered their Eden.

A new pastor arrived. He told the congregation that further expansion would demand much more money than they could raise by bake sales alone. So he divided the congregation in half and set up an ambitious fund-raising program: The two halves would compete to see which side could help the church more. At first the church members were bewildered by this plan, but they soon got with the program. They decided on bingo . . . and the rest is history.

An average take from the Sunday and Monday bingo nights was about $7,600, and the games raised a million dollars in four years. The crowds swelled. The years went by. Then whispers began: The young church treasurer was depositing paper bags full of cash into his own account rather than the church's. Oops. An audit showed $53,000 was missing.

The treasurer's father signed a promissory note, vowing to pay back the money. New officers were elected to prevent future scandals. A professional accounting firm was hired.

But clouds of suspicion gathered again, since the professional accountant was married to the newly elected treasurer. And the new audits didn't make sense. Sizable expenses were noted as "miscellaneous."

Someone called in the state attorney general's office, but the attorney general, sensing a huge headache in the offing, backed away. The police passed as well.

So some of the contenders did the American thing and hired a lawyer. "By 1998, the church's cold war was rapidly heating," reported the local newspaper. "Police arrived at [the church] . . . to find a crowd of 50 parishioners, broken beer bottles, and a vicious fight in progress."[1]

The police officers couldn't get control of the situation. They called for backup. Several church members were arrested, one for carrying a concealed weapon.

Meanwhile, some of the church officers were busily developing a new building project and had a half-million-dollar option on eight acres of nearby land.

The founders, who wanted to stay right where they were, were furious with their former friends. They filed suit.

Meanwhile, another accounting firm did an audit and found some odd expenditures, including quite a lot of money spent on bright red leather jackets for members to wear on bingo nights.

More lawsuits were filed, several members were excommunicated and taken away by police when they tried to enter church property, and at this writing the entire proceeding is an intricate web of charges, counter-charges, suits, court orders, police arrests, newspaper articles reporting that some members have spit on each other and that the church is in the midst of a "divorce"—and miscellaneous other infighting that only the devil himself could sort out.

Of course, he's the one who started it in the first place.

THE CASE OF THE BINGO CHURCH may seem exaggerated, like a comic opera. But it really happened. And though many evangelicals would not *dream* of fighting about bingo (though they slug it out on just about every-thing else), the bingo church war highlights one of the key threats to the church as a whole, and for local churches everywhere.

No one who has spent time as part of a local church should have any illu-sions about the church being a paragon of unity and blissful accord. You need only open a newspaper to read about discord in someone's congregation. The media seem to take particular delight in reporting our failures. And in terms of demonstrating disunity, we've provided them plenty of fodder.

Take my own denomination, the Southern Baptists. When conserva-tives mounted a needed effort to restore orthodox balance to the denomi-nation, it unfortunately deteriorated into angry rhetoric and name-calling. So the Southern Baptists made headlines. Not for their outstanding mission work or the wonderful pastoral care provided to millions, but for the knock-down-drag-out battle for denominational power.

Strangely, the combatants seemed to savor the publicity. I was with one friend, a conservative, when he picked up a headline and proudly pointed to a hatchet job on a liberal—believe me, I recognize the technique—and boasted, "That will show them."

Attitudes on the other side were no different. I attended a luncheon with a group of moderate leaders, one of whom had recently given an angry sermon against the conservatives in which he threatened to withdraw his church from the denomination. His threat had been well publicized, and these men were passing around the articles, seemingly pleased at having gotten so much press. (He later carried out his threat in a nasty way, as did other churches in that state.)

Doctrinal issues have been disputed in the church since the beginning, and such debates can be healthy. When we do this unlovingly, however, we unleash our own base instincts. We become more strident to mask our own insecurity, and we use doctrinal disputes as an excuse to grab power.

Over one eighteen-month period, more than 2,100 Southern Baptist pastors were forced out of churches.[2] For doctrinal reasons in the church debate? No. According to one survey, 58 percent cited personality differences (that's spelled *split in the church);* 46 percent, failure to live up to expectations *(not enough growth);* and 42 percent, leadership style too autocratic *(power-hungry pastor).* All that church strife in a year and a half in just one denomination. (In fact, if you go on the Internet and search for the word "split" among Southern Baptists, it'll take you about .2 seconds to come up with more than 2,100 entries.)

But the Southern Baptists aren't alone. Look closely at any denomination and you'll see civil wars, slick politicking, divisions, and simmering strife among leaders and their factions. According to one survey, more than thirty thousand Protestant churches in the United States alone are in a serious conflict at any given time.[3] Author Frank Martin makes the point that "We're having so much trouble getting along in church that we've created a need for a new specialization for pastors. Most seminaries and Bible colleges now prepare future preachers for conflict through studies on conflict resolution and mediation."[4]

But the struggles aren't confined to the generals at denominational headquarters; the privates and sergeants fight in the trenches as well. Pick any community at random and odds are at least one local church is in the midst of a bloodletting. One evangelical bastion I'm familiar with has been ravaged. The pastor was charged with administrative lapses, although many believe the problem arose because he was too conservative. Open, mean-spirited sessions ensued, thoroughly covered by the press. Many left when the pastor was removed, but the denominational governing body wrote letters to other churches in the denomination ordering them not to take in the errant members. Meanwhile, the local congregation is withering.

Interdenominational strife is not as prevalent as it once was, but it still occurs—and often in a way that mars the witness of the Body. A few years ago an international group of evangelical leaders met to prepare for a large conference in a country that happened to be predominantly Catholic. Since the conference was on a universal subject—evangelism—I urged that Catholic evangelicals be invited.

"Never," one of the participants shouted, slamming his fist on the table. "We fought that battle four hundred years ago, and we're not going to surrender now." Apparently he wanted to continue the Reformation warfare. A cease-fire would spoil his fun.

He prevailed, and as a result the political leaders in the country snubbed the conference; the local Catholic bishop, himself an evangelical in the renewal movement, on the closing day of the conference led a separate evangelistic rally. All of this, of course, was widely reported by the press.

In view of all this, it is not difficult to understand the two most frequent reasons people give for avoiding church: "All Christians are hypocrites," and "Christians are always fighting with each other."

To the first I invariably reply, "Sure, probably so. Come on and join us. You'll feel right at home." But I haven't come up with a very good answer to the second.

Holding the church to its historic faith, both in its practices and institutions, is a necessary corrective. I grieve over the weakening of orthodoxy in mainline—and some evangelical—churches; stands must be taken. But shouldn't this be done in love and with understanding, showing grace instead of rancor?

Rancor not only destroys witness, it also exposes weakness of conviction. The less secure people are in their beliefs, the more strident they become. Conversely, the more confident people are of the truth, the more grace they exhibit to those who don't agree. "Tolerance is the natural endowment of true convictions," wrote Paul Tournier.[5]

Remember, Jesus said, referring to His disciples: "By this all men will know that you are My disciples, if you have love for one another."[6]

Few believers actually enjoy disunity. No, our fractured witness is most often the by-product of pride, and of acting and speaking before we think. Unfortunately, we are all subject to such human weaknesses.

The church is divinely ordained, but it is made up of fallen people. We are not yet perfect. We are all dying daily, like the apostle Paul, repenting of sin and growing in grace. As diverse individuals who make up the Body, we have many different personalities, interests, passions, functions, and odd habits that may well drive one another to distraction. But we cannot let Satan fan those irritations into full-blown disunity. We must remember God's great patience with us and, in gratitude for His great love, *love one another*. We must fix ourselves on the words of Scripture: "Make every effort to keep the unity of the Spirit through the bond of peace. There is one body and one Spirit—just as you were called to one hope when you were called—one Lord, one faith, one baptism; one God and Father of all, who is over all and through all and in all."[7]

But wait a minute. How can there really be "one body and spirit . . . one Lord, one faith, one baptism" at the same time that believers have sincere, earnest differences with one another?

It's a crucial question. And we can't really be about the business of *being* the Body of Christ until we've dealt with it.

8

ONE LORD, ONE FAITH, ONE BAPTISM

It's about time for Christians who recite the creed and mean it to come together for fellowship and witness regardless of denominational identity.

—J. I. PACKER

God is one, and all who are God's are one.
The church is a communal articulation of that truth.

—RICHARD JOHN NEUHAUS

UNITY IS THE ESSENCE OF THE CHURCH. To be one with one another as Jesus is one with the Father is a matter of biblical obedience. C. S. Lewis argued that this life is but a preparation for heaven, that there is a continuum from this life to the next. Since unity will be the condition of the church in heaven we should be preparing for it now, experiencing it as fully as possible.

But unity is also the prerequisite for evangelism. Jesus prayed for His disciples—His church—"that all of them may be one, Father, just as you are in me and I am in you. May they also be in us so that the world may believe that you have sent me."[1]

During a trip to India, Ellen saw an unforgettable example of the evangelistic power of unity when she visited a church in a remote village. There, stone by stone, the members of the congregation were building a church structure.

Women, graceful in their bright saris, were mixing the mortar. They would scrape together a clump of it, pile it into a shallow tin bowl, and deftly lift the burden to their heads. Then, perfectly balanced, they'd carry the load to the foundation, where the men would slather the mortar into place.

It was hard work under the blazing Indian sun. Yet these people sang, they laughed, they worked together with great contentment.

As the nonbelievers in that village watched the Christians building their church, they noticed their joy and cooperation. And they got curious.

"How is it that you work together and care for one another in this way?" the Hindus asked their Christian neighbors. And as they heard about the love of Jesus Christ, they received Him, were baptized, and were added to the church community in that village.

If those Hindu villagers had only *heard* about Christ, perhaps the message would have fallen on deaf ears. But because they had *seen* Him in the oneness of Christians, they came to faith.

The message is clear. Non-Christians aren't looking so much at our tracts and rallies and telecasts and books as they are looking at *us* and how we behave. When they fail to see the unity of Jesus' followers—the church—they fail to see the validation that Christ is indeed the Son of the living God. (Our Indian brothers and sisters' example can't help but make us wonder: How many neighbors in the United States have come to Christ due to the joyful *unity* exhibited in our church building programs?)

Which brings us to the third critical reason for unity: It validates our faith and enables us to influence the skeptical world around us. Aggressive secularists don't care whether we are Eastern Orthodox or Baptist or charismatic; they can't distinguish between pre- and post-millennialism, nor would they care if they could. They want only to discredit the church because its views are contrary to their own world-view. So when we are divided, quarreling among ourselves, we play right into their hands, diminishing our own already weakened influence.

While we may never achieve perfect doctrinal agreement on all points, shouldn't we at least make common cause in defense of our common orthodox faith in Christ and belief in absolute truth?[2]

Through the centuries many have echoed this fervent plea. Even in the midst of the contentious Reformation era, John Calvin wrote that when it came to standing against the Great Deep—atheism—he regarded Rome as his ally. Calvin participated in meetings with Catholic leaders, seeking to resolve differences.[3] And a century ago Abraham Kuyper, perhaps the greatest Reformed Protestant intellect of modern times, argued powerfully for an alliance between Rome and those in the Reformation tradition: "A so-called orthodox Protestant [should] perceive immediately that what we have in common with Rome concerns precisely those fundamentals of our Christian creed now most fiercely assaulted by the modern spirit."[4]

Even Dwight L. Moody, the greatest evangelist of the nineteenth century, reached across the confessional divide. When challenged over the fact that he had given funds to the construction of the Catholic Church in his hometown of Northfield, Massachusetts, Moody responded, "If they are Roman Catholics it is better they should be good Roman Catholics than bad. It is surely better to have a Catholic Church than none."[5] Equally significantly, the Catholic community provided the foundation for Moody's church when he later built it in Northfield.

The conservative scholar J. Gresham Machen called for evangelicals to recognize their common heritage with Rome. And in more contemporary times, the great Russian writer Aleksandr Solzhenitsyn reminded us that: "In recent years the major Christian churches have taken steps towards reconciliation, but these measures are far too slow; the world is perishing a hundred times more quickly. No one expects the churches to merge or to revise all their doctrines, but only to present a common front against atheism."[6]

The mandate for unity is clear, but putting it into practice is another matter. How do we deal with differences that have existed for two thousand years? Should we ignore doctrinal convictions? Do we fellowship with anyone who claims to be Christian? Is unity achieved at the price of orthodoxy?

WHAT IS UNITY?

These are not simple questions, and to answer them we need to examine exactly what we mean by unity in the church universal and in the church particular.

First of all, in the church universal it is not the kind of ecumenism that the World Council of Churches has advocated in recent years. Solzhenitsyn, in fact, was quick to point this out immediately following his statement above. He said that the WCC has done more to spawn Third World revolutionary movements than to defend the true church. Because of this, ecumenism has unfortunately come to mean "reducing all elements of faith to the lowest common denominator." The only unity this achieves is the belief in nothing, save perhaps the father-motherhood of God and the brother-sisterhood of humankind.

True unity is not sought by pretending that there are no differences, as modern ecumenists have done, but by recognizing and respecting those differences, while focusing on the great orthodox truths all Christians share.

It was in this spirit that a group of conservative Catholic and Protestant evangelicals met in New York in 1991, a meeting that led to the formation of Evangelicals and Catholics Together (ECT). The meeting was called by Richard John Neuhaus so that leaders on both sides of the divide could listen to two sociologists from England who had studied the open hostility between established Roman Catholics in Brazil and Chile and the fast-spreading evangelical churches there. They were concerned that the region might turn into another Northern Ireland, infamous for its religious strife, to the great detriment of Christian witness.

On the second day of the meetings I came under the clear conviction of the Holy Spirit. I sensed His unmistakable prodding to reach across the table and seek real fellowship with the Catholic believers there. These were the brothers and sisters with whom we stood on so many key issues of moral concern in our nation . . . couldn't we come together to defend Christian faith in a hostile world?

We began meeting regularly. In 1994 Father Neuhaus and I released our first document about unity. It was unofficial, but signed by a host of Catholic and evangelical leaders, including J. I. Packer, Bill Bright, and Pat Robertson.

What a backlash we got! We received some very hateful letters, and friends cautioned me to abandon the ECT effort in order to avoid controversy. There were even evidences that it was adversely affecting contributions to the ministry of Prison Fellowship.

But we pressed on. Father Neuhaus and I decided in 1995 to begin discussions on the most fundamental question: What does it mean to be saved? This is the key issue, after all, that led to the Reformation: Luther's rallying cry was *sola fide,* faith alone, as opposed to what the Reformers saw as Rome's doctrine of works.

Over a two-year period we met frequently, poring over the Scriptures. The resulting document, *The Gift of Salvation*, affirmed that "Justification is not earned by any good works or merits of our own; it is entirely God's gift conferred through the Father's sheer graciousness!"[7] The signers said, "We understand that what we here affirm is in agreement with what the Reformation traditions have meant by justification by faith alone *(sola fide).*"

This statement was the result of an unofficial dialogue. But Cardinal Cassidy, then in charge of interchurch relations for the Vatican, attended our concluding meeting and approved the document, later recommending it to a synod of bishops meeting in Rome in order to prepare the church for the third millennium. It is fair to say that nothing quite like this has happened since the Reformation, and it holds great promise for future efforts as ECT continues a search for common ground, for commonality that is rooted in service of the truth.

C. S. Lewis called this common ground "mere Christianity," likening it to "the great level viaduct which stands solidly over the dips and valleys of heresy and apostasy through the years."[8] Through that viaduct the mainstream of Christian belief flows from people to people, country to country, century to century. Articulated in the classic confessions and creeds, it embraces such fundamentals as the Virgin Birth, the deity of Christ, the atonement, the resurrection, the authority of Scripture, and the second coming.

While mere Christianity is a good formula for the church universal, something more is required for the church particular where believers come together for discipleship and worship. Here doctrinal agreement is essential if believers are to be of one mind and one spirit in submission to one another under the authority of their agreed-upon form of government or governing structure. Any division in the church particular destroys the ability to worship—we are commanded not to take the Lord's Supper in disunity—or to live the gospel's truth so others will believe it.

The distinction is critical: uniformity within the church particular, but unity with diversity in the Body or church universal.

This is also where our understanding of the orthodox fundamentals and doctrine provides the basis for working out the most difficult issues. For example, do we accept everyone who says he or she is a Christian? No.

Those who cannot affirm the fundamentals, such as the bodily resurrection of Christ, cannot be part of the confessing body. When we encounter this kind of disbelief, the church must correct, discipline, or disfellowship. Or, as some traditions call it, "excommunicate."

UNITY WITH DIVERSITY

Thus, within the orthodox tenets, room remains for our honest, doctrinal disagreement in the church universal. We may well hope that Christian bodies will resolve issues like the sacraments, baptism, and ecclesiology, but on these there has been disagreement for nearly two thousand years. If Calvinists and Arminians haven't been able to settle the question of free will and predestination in nearly five hundred years, there's no human reason to expect that they will anytime soon. But, of course, on all such issues of disagreement, God can and will resolve them to His own glory, either now or on that great day of His return.

Meanwhile, we have a healthy freedom to pursue these differences openly and lovingly. In fact, this kind of tolerance spares us from what might otherwise result at the hands of fallen and arrogant humans. Remember the Crusades? The Inquisition? The Catholic and Protestant martyrs of the Reformation?

Respect for differing views also provides some defense against the natural desire to incessantly probe the mystery of the gospel. (There are those who would consider it the ultimate intellectual achievement to unravel the hidden counsel of God.) But the pursuit of doctrine for the sake of doctrine can be idolatrous. The gospel will not be demystified.[9] God will not be mocked by the pretensions of those who believe that they might fully and certainly know His mind. Was that, after all, not the sin of the Garden?

Diversity within the Body, while it may chafe and bind and even pain, provides a healthy corrective. The holiness movement challenged what some saw as the cerebral, doctrinal rigidity of certain Reformers. Regardless of who was right, no one could deny that the movement breathed life into the church and brought millions to a new awareness of righteous living. Likewise, today's charismatic movement, despite some excesses, has refreshed moribund churches with the vitality of the Holy Spirit.

The fact is, we can learn from one another. Personally, while I've formed strong doctrinal convictions, I've been enriched deeply by my fellowship with those who hold different but equally strong doctrinal convictions—particularly my Catholic, Anglican, Orthodox, and Lutheran brothers and sisters. Doing so has also helped me not to trivialize the ordinances or sacraments and other acts of worship.

The sign of the cross is a good example. After praying with an Orthodox sister, Irina Ratushinskaya whose story we have related, I said my "Amen" and then watched her make the sign of the cross with such depth of feeling that I had a powerful urge to make the sign myself. I resisted—for fear it might be a betrayal of my Baptist tradition. How foolish I felt when I later discovered that believers since the very beginning and through the centuries have made the sign of the cross, signifying that they have been crucified with Christ.

Respecting and appreciating different traditions not only teaches us more about our faith, but also encourages a measure of theological humility. Abraham Kuyper wrote that he was "not ashamed to confess that on many points my views have been clarified through my study of the Romish theologians."[10]

This attitude also helps us avoid the kind of rigid conformity that human nature so desires, the "just-like-us" mentality that says everyone must look, act, talk, and think just alike. One of the most powerful evidences of Christ's reality is when skeptics look at the church and see a group of people, from different races and backgrounds, drawn together in *supernatural* unity. Not the unity the world offers, which is based on common interests or social, cultural, or economic backgrounds, but the unlikely unity that comes from Christ Himself binding together people from every tribe and nation into His one Body!

As C. S. Lewis put it, "the Church is not a human society of people united by their natural affinities but the Body of Christ, in which all members, however different, (and He rejoices in their differences and by no means wishes to iron them out) must share the common life, complementing and helping one another precisely by their differences."[11]

This truth became clear to a young man named Kefa Sempangi after he came to the United States from Uganda to study at Westminster Seminary, where he was not only educated in orthodox theology, but also in conservative Western evangelical culture. When Sempangi returned to Uganda after several years, he was horrified to see Christians dancing in the streets, hands upraised, chanting in unknown tongues. At Westminster, the young pastor had learned that worship was solemn and reverent. He distrusted charismatic expression.

As he sat in his room one night watching his exuberant countrymen dancing in the streets, it suddenly struck him: *These people could never identify with what I learned at Westminster. There's nothing unorthodox here. This is simply their natural means of expression, and they can use it to worship God just as I do.* Sempangi repented of his arrogance in judging his fellow believers.[12]

Cultures may differ and individual expressions may vary, but the intent of the heart is the same. Ecuadorians may present in drama or dance the same biblical truth that conservative Scottish preachers exposit from the pulpit. Icons in the Eastern tradition, which many of us have regarded as idolatrous, were first produced as a way to communicate the Bible to the 90 percent of the population who were illiterate.

The way in which we express ourselves through music can take many different forms. I have beloved friends who appreciate a "higher" mode of worship. Whenever they attend my church, I know they feel uncomfortable with our hand-clapping informality. That's fine—I do sometimes myself. But both forms are genuine expressions of worship. Some believers are drawn to liturgical services, others to those that emphasize teaching, still others to music. Pluralism about the form of worship is healthy; it broadens the outreach of the church.

Neuhaus puts it with his customary eloquence when he says that one should engage in "the most vigorous advocacy of what one believes to be right," but at the same time make "a mutual pledge of allegiance to reverence one with another within the mystery of our being a people led by God toward that time in which we shall 'know even as we are known.'"[13]

Calvin, who saw that the devil's chief device was disunity and division, and who preached that there should be friendly fellowship for all ministers of Christ, made a similar point in a letter to a trusted colleague: "Among Christians there ought to be so great a dislike of schism, as that they may always avoid it so far as lies in their power. That there ought to prevail among them such a reverence for the ministry of the word and the sacraments that wherever they perceive these things to be, there they must consider the church to exist . . . nor need it be of any hindrance that some points of doctrine are not quite so pure, seeing that there is scarcely any church which has not retained some remnants of former ignorance."[14]

The great German pastor, Helmut Thielicke, had a good suggestion: Rather than fighting each other, he argued, "God demands of both sister churches [Protestant and Catholic] that they relentlessly question *themselves* and grow more mature in the process."[15]

THE REAL BASIS OF UNITY

From the very beginning of the church there were doctrinal differences. In fact, such difficulties occasioned many of the epistles now in the New Testament. Yet those believers, who had to endure not just mockery or scorn but the threat of death, were united over one baptismal confession: "Jesus is Lord"—a profession that comes only under the power of the Holy Spirit.

Over the early centuries, more differences arose among the brethren, such as the Montanists, the Novitianists, and the Origenists. Yet the church achieved such a remarkable witness and visible demonstration of love for one another that they overcame persecution and won much of the then-known world to Christ.

What was their secret?

First, the church feared the Lord, about which more will be said later. And second, believers shared a core set of beliefs, which they held to be far more important than any points upon which they might differ. These have been called the *rule of faith:*

- God the creator exists in three persons, Father, Son, and Holy Spirit.
- Born of the virgin, He suffered, died, rose again, and was exalted at the right hand of the Father from whence He will come again.
- The Holy Spirit brings the benefits of Christ's saving work to people who believe in Him.

- Christians are expected to unite with a local church, submit to the authority of bishops and elders, and live a holy life conducive to the spread of the gospel.
- God will judge the world and receive His own at the end of history.[16]

Because of the assault of modernism in this century, we might add something the first-century church took for granted: belief in the authority of God's inerrant Word.

THE ROAD TO UNITY IN THE CHURCH UNIVERSAL

"By this will all men know you . . . that you love one another." One Lord, one faith, one baptism. Unity with diversity. How can we achieve what the early church did? Mere Christianity. The kind that elicits the Tertullian response, "See how these Christians love one another."

First of all, we can repent of the sin of presumption and of our ill-informed prejudices. Just think about what we are really saying when we imply that someone can't be a Christian because he or she hasn't prayed the sinner's prayer verbatim, or gone through the "Four Spiritual Laws," or responded to an altar call, or any of the other prescribed formulas that are so familiar to so many. Certainly we can discern whether the great mystery of regeneration has taken place: We see the eventual fruit of the Spirit's power. But unfortunately, many make hasty judgments according to human criteria, not divine evidence.

Probably two of the most stubbornly held beliefs today are (among evangelicals) that one can't be a Christian if he or she is Catholic, and (among Catholics) that one cannot be saved apart from the work of the Catholic Church, despite Vatican Council II's clear words to the contrary.[17]

Still, there have been encouraging signs of change in the last decade or so.[18] For example, at the worldwide charismatic gathering in London in 1991, the chaplain to Pope John Paul II, Raneiro Cantalamessa, publicly asked forgiveness from the assembled thousands for his "sin against the unity of the body of Christ." The crowd sat in stunned silence as the cleric repented for once believing that Protestants could not be part of the church.[19]

God even used the first edition of this book to stimulate evangelicals to talk about unity—and I should add, to write letters of the kind mentioned earlier ("How could you refer to Mother Teresa as Christian?" and the like). Soon after the initial publication of *The Body* came the first ECT document, with the attendant controversy we've already noted. But the debate proved to be healthy. I've received scores of positive letters and reports of ECTs being formed in different locales, including, of all places, the Republic of Ireland. Many of us on both sides of the issue have learned how to better relate to one another in the Body.

This process can be important in healing cultural as well as ecclesiastical differences. One hundred and twenty years ago in Evanston, Illinois, racial discrimination forced black members to leave the First Baptist Church. They founded Second Baptist, and for a century the two churches were separated. Then in 1991, First Baptist, with three hundred members, presented a resolution to Second Baptist, which now had three thousand members, asking forgiveness. Soon thereafter the two churches planned several joint services, and the two churches are now working together.[20]

Second, we can actively reach out and build bridges to those of different traditions. John Wesley, a giant in church history, said to those with whom he was embroiled in a serious theological dispute: "If thy heart be as my heart, give me thy hand."

Reaching out to each other can break down formidable barriers, as the experience of one of my longtime friends illustrates.

When John Aker was pastoring the Evangelical Free Church in Montvale, New Jersey, he developed a close bond in Christ with a priest from a nearby parish, Ken Herbster. Together they came up with a bold scheme: John would preach at the midmorning Mass in Father Ken's church, and the priest would preach for the Sunday evening service at John's church.

To "cut their losses," they later quipped, they chose Super Bowl Sunday when attendance might be somewhat diminished. But neither man was prepared for what happened.

Following John's message at the midmorning Mass, the Catholic congregation spontaneously stood and applauded. That evening, without prompting, the same thing happened when Father Ken preached at the Evangelical Free Church.

Later that year the two pastors led a joint Easter sunrise service on a hill just outside of town.[21]

Now, there have been many ecumenical pulpit exchanges in recent years. Protestants may preach about self-esteem in a Catholic church, and a priest may deliver a message about helping the poor in a Protestant service. What made John Aker's experience so remarkable was that both he and Father Ken preached powerful gospel messages of salvation through Jesus Christ.

Some Christians have spanned denominational divides to build communities. In places around the world there are Word of God communities and those associated with the Sword of the Spirit, groups that grew out of the charismatic renewal. One I have visited is in Ann Arbor, Michigan: a Word of God community of two hundred people, 75 percent Roman Catholic, 25 percent Protestant. Each family attends its own church in the community, but the entire community meets Sunday evenings for prayer meeting, Bible study, and worship. They make no attempt to minimize their differences, but apart from worship they have developed a complete community life. I'm familiar with a similar community in Gaithersburg, Maryland, because one of its leading members is Father Francis Martin, a great Catholic scholar and an active part of ECT.

When historians examine and record this era in church history, they will doubtless note the singular contribution of the charismatic movement toward unity in the Body. In Northern Ireland, for example, renewal movements have sprung from the rock-hard soil of old-line Presbyterianism and traditional Roman Catholicism. We've been in prisons there and seen Catholic and Protestant ex-terrorists, arms wrapped around one another, worship and rejoice as one.

There are signs of progress everywhere.

A great friend of mine, a conservative, Reformed scholar, for many years expressed concern over my association with Roman Catholics. So I was elated to read an article in which he wrote: "Fresh winds are blowing everywhere among Catholics and Protestants . . . because everybody who belongs to Jesus belongs to everybody who belongs to Jesus, I've decided to turn my polemical guns on the enemy—not so much on my family."[22]

Many are discovering, as my friend has, that when it comes to unity, biblical orthodoxy is more relevant than denominational identity. In many ways, for example, conservative Catholics have more in common with conservative Baptists than they have with liberal Catholics.

"It is a true sign of the church when true Christians love one another," said the late Francis Schaeffer. "The church is to be a loving church in a dying culture."[23] This was written in one of Schaeffer's most compelling writings, *The Mark of the Christian*, a passionate plea for Christians to obey our commandments to love one another.

This kind of loving unity has enormous implications for the common witness of the Body. It would be refreshing if, instead of squabbling with one another, churches were to join hands in meeting community or social needs. For this very reason Prison Fellowship makes a conscious effort to involve volunteers from every denomination. I remember all too well how inmates reacted to individual church proselytizing when I was a prisoner. So we go to prison not in the name of one denomination, but in the name of Jesus Christ.

And we make a concerted effort to work with other prison ministries as well. For, ironically enough, cooperation sometimes does not come easily in evangelical communities in North America. Evangelicalism, by its very nature, is entrepreneurial and individualistic. In our history, God has raised up various strong, independent leaders to begin godly ministry movements. That is good. The great strength of evangelism is its entreprenurialism.

But the great weakness of evangelicalism is also its entreprenurialism. We all go charging off, doing our own thing, and there's a lot of competition for the same donor dollars. It can be difficult for various bullheaded ministries to work together.

That's why I have been so excited about Operation Starting Line, a collaborative effort among more than twenty ministries to present the gospel to every prisoner in every prison in America over a five-year period—and to disciple those who respond. In addition to the intensive, in-prison evangelism events that draw prisoners to Jesus, OSL also presents a twenty-segment, two-year discipleship follow-up program with many additional elements, including the potential of earning graduate school theological credit. As we write, the organizations working together on OSL include:

AMEN, American Bible Society, Billy Graham Center of Wheaton College, Billy Graham Evangelistic Association, Calvary Memorial Church, Campus Crusade for Christ, Christian Hope Indian Eskimo Fellowship

(CHIEF), Council of Leadership Foundations, Crossroads Bible Institute, The DeMoss Group, Great Dads, Intercessors for America, Koinonia House, Lott Carey Baptist Foreign Mission Convention, Mission America, Moody Bible Institute, National Association of Evangelicals, Morning Star Ministry, National Black Evangelical Association, The Navigators, North American Mission Board of the Southern Baptist Convention, Pittsburgh Leadership Foundation, Prison Fellowship, Promise Keepers, Ramah International, St. Stephens Church of God in Christ, Strang Publications, Walk Thru the Bible, and Youth Direct Ministries.[24]

The miracle of unity at work here was clear to me from the beginning. OSL began in July of 1999, when about twenty-five leaders of various evangelical organizations met in Florida at Campus Crusade's headquarters. As Keith Smith gave his testimony of being in prison and his vision of taking the gospel to all the prisons in America, I could feel an almost palpable sense of unity of conviction in the room. Our human, fleshly instincts—the reserve that one Christian leader has in the presence of another, all the competitive feelings, all the turf-protection—evaporated.

By the time we had spent a few hours around the table together, all the players were not only on board, they were volunteering; they wanted to do something. I honestly cannot remember any other meeting like it in my years of Christian ministry. It was marvelous. We all left the meeting being of one heart and one mind.

Now, that doesn't mean that every detail has flowed perfectly ever since. But it does mean that when the Spirit of God calls us to ministry, He supersedes even our competitive and divisive instincts! And the result is a glorious witness for Christ—to inmates, yes, and also to the watching world.

We experienced another more recent example of unity, expressed in the most practical way possible—the pocketbook.

Good News Jail and Prison Ministry, founded in 1961, supplies chaplains to jails and to some prisons in the U.S. and several countries overseas. Two years ago, the ministry president, Harry Greene, met with then-president of Prison Fellowship, Tom Pratt, for a day of prayer and, as Greene put it, repentance for the fact that we hadn't worked more closely together.

Some months later, Harry and former Good News President Bill Simmer drove to Washington to meet with Prison Fellowship President

Mark Earley and me. "We want to work more closely together," Harry said. Then he told us that his board was aware of the Prison Fellowship deficit and that in prayer they had unanimously felt led to help the ministry of Prison Fellowship. From their surplus they decided to give us a very substantial six-figure gift. (The Good News annual budget is one-fifth the size of Prison Fellowship's.) We were absolutely overwhelmed by their love, unity, and generosity.

Now, if we were viewing ourselves as "rival" ministries vying for the same donor funds, that would never happen! But we are partners for the sake of the gospel, as the apostle Paul put it, and we share the same goal of touching prisoners' lives with the love of Christ. And there could be no better witness of that love than the unity Good News Jail and Prison Ministry demonstrated!

Wherever people cooperate rather than compete for the cause of the gospel, the witness is powerful. Mike Timmis, a Roman Catholic, is a ruddy-faced, ebullient lawyer and businessman in Detroit. In the early 1980s, Mike and his wife, Nancy, attended an executive dinner party (evangelistic outreach targeted toward business leaders) at which they responded to an invitation to make a total commitment to follow Christ. Mike and Nancy have been eagerly involved ever since. They have built hospitals in Africa, managed relief efforts in Latin America, and supported a host of evangelistic campaigns, particularly within the Catholic Church. Mike, who succeeded me as chairman of Prison Fellowship International, has traveled the globe encouraging prison ministry in ninety-five countries. But one of the Timmises' most important areas of witness has been in their own city.

A few years ago the archbishop of Detroit asked Mike to help fund a nondenominational, Christ-centered school in the inner city. A gifted entrepreneur, Mike met with Lutheran, Presbyterian, Episcopalian, Baptist, and Catholic lay leaders. They formed a steering committee, rolled up their sleeves, and in faith began serious planning. They found a site in a needy area of the city and began fund-raising in earnest.

With private funds from various denominations, three new Cornerstone elementary schools were opened in August 1991. The mission statement describes them as "Christ-centered" ecumenical schools that stress excellence and sound moral teaching. Students have consistently shown vastly improved achievements, and in the process the church is making a profound statement to the Detroit community, both through its demonstration of concern for the inner city, as well as through its members' love for one another.

A group of young people at Shively Christian Church in Louisville, Kentucky, gives us another great example of how churches must transcend traditional rivalries. Led at the time by Youth Pastor Dave Stone, the teenagers were fiercely competitive with their neighbor, Shively Baptist, in all things, especially softball. They were also serious about their Christianity, faithfully attending the summer Bible camp led by the youth pastor.

One week the Bible lesson was about Jesus washing His disciples' feet, from John 13. To make the servanthood lesson stick, Pastor Stone divided the kids into groups and told them to go out and find a practical way to be servants.

"I want you to be Jesus in the city for the next two hours," he said. "If Jesus were here, what would He do? Figure out how He would help people."

Two hours later the kids reconvened in Pastor Stone's living room to report what they had done.

One group had done two hours of yard work for an elderly man. Another group bought ice cream treats and delivered them to several widows in the church. A third group visited a church member in the hospital and gave him a card. Another group went to a nursing home and sang Christmas carols—yes, Christmas carols in the middle of August. One elderly resident remarked that it was the warmest Christmas she could remember.

But when the fifth group stood up and reported what they had done, everyone groaned. This group had made its way to none other than their archrival, Shively Baptist, where they had asked the pastor if he knew someone who needed help. The pastor sent them to the home of an elderly woman who needed yard work done. There, for two hours, they mowed grass, raked the yard, and trimmed hedges.

When they were getting ready to leave, the woman called the group together and thanked them for their hard work. "I don't know how I could get along without you," she told them. "You kids at Shively Baptist are always coming to my rescue."

"Shively *Baptist!*" interrupted Pastor Stone. "I sure hope you set her straight and told her you were from Shively *Christian* Church."

"Why, no, we didn't," the kids said. "We really didn't think it mattered."

And, of course, it didn't.

Finally, Christians must make common cause in the battle against secularism. Clearly that was the case in the twentieth century's most dramatic story, the disintegration of the Communist system in Eastern Europe.

There, in country after country, Christians of every denomination and tradition marched shoulder to shoulder in the streets—even when it came to the point of facing down tanks.

Soon after the collapse of Communism, I met with Father Vaclav Maly, one of the heroes of Czechoslovakia's "velvet revolution." He told me that even now, after the fall of Communism, he still meets weekly with Protestant brothers. I must have looked surprised, for he quickly added, "They [the Communists] tried for forty-five years to divide the Body. We must bring it together."

In the West, every area of life is being undermined by the dominant secular world-view. Myriad moral issues confront our society—the dignity of life, medical ethics, religious liberty, justice—and God's people belong out there in the trenches together. This was the appeal of Solzhenitsyn and Schaeffer and Kuyper. Nothing less will enable the church to stand against the surging forces from the "Great Deep," as Calvin called it.

What does this mean? It means attorney Seamus Hassam, a leading Roman Catholic layman and skilled defender of religious freedom with the Beckett Fund, defending the religious liberties of the Amish; it means Baptists defending Catholic cardinals, as I did in an op-ed piece in the *New York Times* when the late Cardinal O'Connor was attacked by the media for daring to criticize Catholic proabortion legislators.

When Catholic priests and Protestant laypeople stand together, peacefully praying, in front of abortion clinics, it is a powerful witness. Timothy George, eloquent theologian and dean of Beeson Divinity School, calls this "ecumenism of the trenches." Many have been arrested, but I doubt that they've sat around in their jail cells debating the Council of Trent.

Harmony and oneness in spirit can be achieved only when Christians put aside their personal agendas and submit themselves to the authority of the Holy Spirit. For the Holy Spirit, who empowers the church, can never lead believers into disunity.

I experienced a dramatic demonstration of this in the early days of Prison Fellowship's ministry. Michael Alison, who was then a senior member of the British Parliament, invited me to England to explore the possible formation of Prison Fellowship there.

Michael and his wife, Sylvia Mary, had convened more than three hundred Christians from all over the British Isles in London's historic Church House. The group included Protestants and Catholics from Northern Ireland, where open warfare was being waged in the streets; chaplains of various denominational stripes who were understandably protective of their flocks; and a number of people already working in prison ministry, who were less than excited at the idea of some upstart group sponsored, of all things, by Americans.

The meetings began on Friday night with a series of speeches, including mine, setting forth the vision of Prison Fellowship. Spirits seemed high.

The next day as we assembled in the majestic Grand Hall, it all changed. One by one the critics raised all of the objections I had anticipated, and then some. The Anglican chaplain general and his Roman Catholic counterpart might not have agreed with one another very often, but they did that day. "There is no need for any new group to be organized," they said. Some equally passionate advocates spoke up at that point. And so it went, with the debate seesawing, back and forth, throughout the day.

Still feeling the effects of jet lag, I was relieved when Michael Alison announced late in the day that after one more speech there would be a vote by a show of hands. Seated just to Michael's right, I watched the faces of the group as the final speaker concluded with a stirring appeal. Some seemed to tighten, and the chaplain general looked particularly grim. Others nodded and exchanged glances. And then all eyes riveted on Michael.

"All those in favor," Michael said, and hands went up everywhere. The result was obvious from the dissenters' moans. Then about a dozen hands were raised in opposition.

I breathed a sigh of relief. I could return home satisfied. Prison Fellowship England would be under way—and I knew that eventually the chaplains would come around. People started getting out of their seats.

Suddenly Michael banged the gavel and announced, "In view of the fact that the decision is not unanimous, we will delay any action until we can meet again."

I couldn't believe it. *What's wrong with him?* I thought. *He's just thrown the whole thing away.*

"If this be of the Holy Spirit," Michael explained, "He will say the same thing to all of us. And if it is not God's doing, we want no part of it."

I left discouraged, feeling the trip had been wasted.

Six months later the group assembled again. This time the vote was unanimous, and Prison Fellowship England has been one of the strongest ministries of the almost hundred now operating around the world.

For me, the lesson couldn't have been plainer, just as it is in the book of Acts. There we read that the believers assembled in the Upper Room in obedience to the Lord's command, waited in continuous prayer, and were of one mind. Then the Spirit came and gave life to the church, which thereafter transformed the world.

Unity is the attitude from which the church's actions flow. It is the prerequisite for effective witness both in the world arena and in any little community where the people of God show oneness.

Disunity in the church would be understandable if Christianity were only a personal relationship—"Jesus and me." In that case, of course, everyone's experience would be different. And disunity would be understandable if Christianity were nothing more than a set of creeds and confessions. But Christianity is more than these. It is centered in the One who professes to be ultimate reality, the personal God who gives us life and meaning and who calls us to be His Body at work in the world.

The early church, led by apostles who had lived with Christ Himself, understood their Teacher's call to unity. It undergirded all that they did. The book of Acts tells us the early church members were devoted to prayer, held their possessions in common, were "of one mind," and broke bread together. Linked by a common "fear of the Lord," they also knew God's power and presence among them. And they knew they were responsible to proclaim the truth. One truth.[25]

In the next two chapters we'll look more closely at these characteristics of the church, with the intent of seeing one thing clearly: When the people of God, united in His name, proclaim the Word of God, they can turn their world upside down. That happened in first-century Jerusalem. It also happened in a little church in Connecticut in the eighteenth century.

9

THE FLAMING WORD

So long then as the word of truth is on our side, never be in any wise distressed at the calumny of a lie; let no imperial threats scare you; do not be grieved at the laughter and mockery of your intimates nor at the condemnation of those who pretend to care for you, and who put forward, as their most attractive bait to deceive, a pretense of giving good advice. Against them all let sound reason do battle, invoking the championship and succor of our Lord Jesus Christ, the teacher of true religion, for whom to suffer is sweet and to die is gain.

—BASIL OF CAESAREA

THE FARMING VILLAGE of Enfield, Connecticut, had been largely untouched by the extraordinary events taking place throughout New England. A surge of revival was sweeping the populace. Cold, dry churches were suddenly being transformed, and whole communities had been changed. It was happening all over the colonies.

Just a day's ride to the south, in Middletown, thousands had recently flocked on foot, on horseback, even by ferry down the Connecticut River to hear the fiery English evangelist, George Whitefield. For miles around folks were still talking about that amazing day. After Whitefield's eloquent, moving "evangelical message of man's irremediable sinfulness and Christ's effective salvation," people wept in contrition over their sins. In response to his, "My brethren, I beseech you," they fell prostrate on the ground, crying out to God.[1]

In the midst of this, Enfield remained, some thought, the most wicked community in all of the colonies. Its smug, self-satisfied townsfolk wanted no part of the exuberant demonstrations occurring around them. Christians in neighboring areas had been praying that Enfield not remain isolated "while the divine showers were falling around them." Then on July 8, 1741, their prayers were answered.

A meeting had been called for late that summer afternoon in the Enfield meetinghouse, a white clapboard building at the town's center. The planned speaker had to cancel, but local officials had prevailed upon Jonathan Edwards, a well-known pastor from Northampton, Massachusetts, to come and preach. Since the thirty-seven-year-old Edwards was then recovering from a debilitating illness, he was somewhat frail. Some wondered if the long ride on horseback would unduly drain his strength.

The bare wooden pews of the Enfield meetinghouse were full that afternoon. But there was an air of levity as the service began, almost as if the people were challenging Edwards: *We aren't about to be carried away with all this foolish emotionalism we've heard about.*

Jonathan Edwards walked to the pulpit. He took out his sermon manuscript and began to read in calm, measured tones, "My text this evening is found in Deuteronomy, chapter 32, verse 35: 'Their foot shall slide in due time.'" Then, as he began profiling the wrath of the mighty Lord of heaven and earth, the listeners lost their smug looks. And the long sermon that followed shook not only the town of Enfield, but all of New England.

"There is nothing that keeps wicked men at any one moment out of hell, but the mere pleasure of God," Edwards proclaimed. "God holds the righteous and the wicked for His purpose. Perched perilously on the slippery slope, the wicked stand under condemnation. . . .

"The God that holds you over the pit of hell, much as one holds a spider, or some loathsome insect, over the fire . . . His wrath towards you burns like fire . . . He is of purer eyes than to bear to have you in His sight. . . . You have offended him infinitely more than ever a stubborn rebel did his prince. . . ."

As Edwards continued, the men, women, and children crowding the narrow pews before him began to shake with moans, tears, and shrieks. Several times he had to pause and ask the people to quiet down so he might continue. He did so relentlessly.

"Moreover, God is exceedingly angry with some yet living. His wrath is burning, the pit is prepared, the fire is hot. Yet, many of these do not realize their fate. They flatter themselves; they are unaware that God's wrath is like waters being dammed up before exploding. . . .

"Yet it is nothing but His hand that holds you from falling into the fire every moment. It is to be ascribed to nothing else, that you did not go to hell the last night; that you were suffered to awake again in this world, after you closed your eye to sleep."

Men and women were out of their pews now. Some fell to the floor.

"O sinner!" he proclaimed. "Consider the fearful danger you are in: It is a great furnace of wrath, a wide and bottomless pit. . . . You hang by a slender thread, with the flames of divine wrath flashing about it . . . you have no interest in any Mediator, and nothing to lay hold of to save yourself, nothing to keep off the flames of wrath, nothing of your own, nothing that you have ever done, nothing that you can do, to induce God to spare you one moment."

Men and women were on their knees, weeping. Their cries continued even after Edwards finished. Another pastor, Eleazer Wheelock, stepped into the pulpit and offered a prayer which quieted the congregation. Then he and Edwards mixed with the people.

As the people filed out of the meetinghouse, however—as an eyewitness later wrote in his diary—their countenances were cheerful. And thereafter Enfield was swept up in the wave of righteousness surging across the American colonies. It was the Great Awakening, out of which a new nation was born.[2]

Jonathan Edwards's sermon, "Sinners in the Hands of an Angry God," is most frequently thought of as a classic example of "hellfire and brimstone" preaching. Most imagine Edwards as a passionate orator, playing upon the emotions of frontier farmers, adept at producing the kind of remarkable outpouring which occurred that day in Enfield. Picturing him in the mode of our contemporary revivalists, they see him gesturing wildly, shouting words of wrath and shame at the quaking congregation. But that is far from the truth.

Standing solemnly at the pulpit, hunched over the tiny writing on the pages of his thick manuscript, Edwards *read* his sermon. As was his custom, he delivered the incendiary words in a monotone, looking up now and then to stare without expression at the back wall of the meetinghouse.

Edwards was a quiet scholar who graduated from Yale at age seventeen and who just before his death at age fifty-four was inaugurated as the second president of Princeton. Considered to be one of the greatest intellects of the Western hemisphere, he is also widely regarded as the greatest theologian America has produced.

But the reaction to his preaching in Enfield that day was not a demonstration of theological brilliance, dramatic oratory, or emotional preaching. It was the power of God's Word, convicting of sin and then offering the infinite grace of Christ's outstretched, nail-scarred hands.

The power of the Word. It is the foundation on which the church rests and the essence of its unity. It lies at the heart of the church's mission. "Go and make disciples of all nations," Jesus commanded in the Great Commission, "baptizing them in the name of the Father and of the Son and of the Holy Spirit, and *teaching them* to obey everything I have commanded you."[3]

This is why Luke, in describing the early church, lists teaching as the first task of the apostles as they gathered the new believers together. The Reformers emphasized this characteristic, and clear biblical preaching became central for the Reformed churches. But all traditions have recognized its priority. Pope John Paul II described the proclamation of Christ as the church's "supreme duty. The church's service to the kingdom is seen especially in her preaching which is a call to conversion."[4]

The ministry of the Word takes two forms: preaching, which is largely the task of the pastor and is one of the pastoral offices assigned in Scripture, and teaching, which is to be continuously carried on at every level within the church.[5]

PREACHING THE WORD

Classics have been written on the subject of preaching, and we cannot do the topic justice here. But no work on the church would be complete without some discussion of the office of the one who carries this duty. Church pulpit committees or boards must periodically search for pastors; bishops assign and reassign them to local congregations. In doing this they usually apply human yardsticks: education, eloquence, charisma, pastoral heart, administrative ability (and the often unspoken requirements: Is he a money-raiser and a church-builder?). But alongside one essential criterion, all these others pale into insignificance: Is the individual in question learned in the Word, wholly committed to preach and teach the truth, and is he anointed by the Holy Spirit for this call?[6] For the pastor is not only the one who petitions God on the congregation's behalf, but he is God's voice to the congregation—that is, charged with preaching *the* truth.

So while pastors are human and need to be held to account, which is the task of the church officers, the congregation must realize that the pastor does not just work for the church.[7] This consideration is a frequent source of confusion and even division. And because the pastor and the congregation's governing body need to be clear in their understanding, some churches have actually spelled it out in covenant agreements.[8]

Conversely, the pastor must understand his primary duty. While every pastor wants to please church authorities, keeping the church happy may not be a positive sign. Theodore Epp, founder of Back to the Bible radio ministry, realized something was wrong when he stopped receiving critical mail. Convicted that he was not challenging the flock enough, he changed his preaching. "I'm afraid that when I'm pleasing everybody, I'm not pleasing the Lord," he later said, "and *pleasing the Lord is what counts.*"[9]

We don't mean to suggest that a pastor is only successful when he is upsetting people! But he must be certain that he is first and foremost faithful to the One he serves. He is fulfilling a divine commission when he preaches. Just as an ambassador is entrusted not with his own message, but with his superior's message, so the minister is entrusted with the Word of God. Before it is delivered, therefore, every message should be laid at the foot of His throne with one question: "Is this faithful to You, my Lord?" Or as one German pastor would always pray in the pulpit, "Cause my mind to fear whether my heart means what I say."[10]

The call to preach cannot be undertaken lightly. It is the most awesome trust.

When I was a Marine lieutenant, I was conscious that I had fifty lives in my hands. I didn't dare show it, but I was frightened. Similarly, a 747 pilot knows that he or she is responsible for three hundred or more lives. But can there be anything more terrifying than to know that you are actually speaking for God—the holy, majestic "I AM"—and that at stake is the eternal destiny of those to whom you are preaching? And can there be any greater responsibility than to shepherd the church of God which Jesus purchased with His own blood?[11] Even with the anointing of the Holy Spirit, the charge is terrifying, considering our own frailty.

This sense of holy awe must have been in Paul's mind when he wrote that he preached with fear and trembling.[12] Moses and Isaiah—along with most of the major figures called by God to lead His people—at some point shrank in fear, realizing their unworthiness: "I can't speak well enough . . . I am too young . . ." "I have unclean lips . . ." Augustine, the great rhetorician, said he never gave a message he was satisfied with. He knew what was at stake.

Martin Luther felt the same holy fear. Here was a man who put his life on the line, standing alone against the combined might of church and empire. Yet when he preached, he said, his knees knocked. Luther understood that it is less dangerous to risk your life than to betray God's trust.

The great preacher Charles Haddon Spurgeon wrote, "We tremble lest we should mistake or misinterpret the word." Thousands would flock to hear this man's sermons, which were then reprinted and circulated around the globe. His intellect was extraordinary: He was reported to have read twelve thousand books in his fifty-eight years of life; he could go to his bookshelves and from memory find material on any subject. Here was a man who had every reason to be supremely confident; today he'd be heralded as an evangelical superstar. Yet Spurgeon used to counsel young men to avoid the ministry unless they felt irresistibly compelled, certain of God's call. "To preach the whole truth is an awful charge," he said.[13]

Another great intellect and preacher, Helmut Thielicke, wrote: "The men of God were never bold, brash pushers, for they were not like the false prophets motivated by their will or their urge to power," but were aware of the "thick darkness" that covers the earth and which they are called to penetrate. In referring to our natural inability to perform this holy task apart from supernatural empowerment, Thielicke said: "He who is frightened in this sense is experiencing a creative terror; he is close to the core of the matter."[14]

Even when we read the reassuring words of Matthew 10:19-20, we often miss a crucial distinction. "Do not worry about what to say or how to say it," Jesus told His disciples. "At that time you will be given what to say, for it will not be you speaking, but the Spirit of your Father speaking through you."

However, this empowerment is not, as I for one have so often prayed, that God should give us the words to speak; that is a "presumptuous assumption that the right thoughts will occur . . . at the right moment." Rather, the promise is that His Spirit will speak through us, using often, as Thielicke says, our own feeble words. Think of it: "God's own Spirit will enter into you and He Himself will confront men through your own poor words."[15]

So if we understand Jesus' words, we see that the preacher's state of mind is critical. We should not pump ourselves up with boldness and "the courage to preach"; some already have too much boldness and not enough substance to go with it. Instead, we should be "frightened by the over-whelming power of the promise but nevertheless [relying] on the power of that promise, open our mouths to speak."[16]

Today's self-important spiritual superstars who strut across the stage, so proud and confident, are far from the attitude described by Paul, Luther, Edwards, Spurgeon, or Thielicke. Indeed, the preacher would do well to stand shaking and trembling, knees knocking in holy awe. For at that moment the only source of his power is God's promise, and his only objective is to speak the whole truth, the transforming message of God's judgment and God's grace.

I know this feeling. Before speaking to a group, I always pray that God will speak through me, that He will anoint and use me for His purposes, not my own. It is human nature to want to please audiences and enjoy their favor. But the person who purports to lead others in biblical truth faces a challenge that goes far beyond himself and his own human agenda. For the charge is to preach the *whole* truth.

"Away with this milk and water preaching of the love of Christ that has no holiness or moral discrimination," proclaimed Charles Finney, one of the great preachers of the nineteenth century. "Away with preaching a love of God that is not angry with sinners every day. Away with preaching a Christ not crucified for sin."[17]

Martin Luther believed so strongly that conviction of sin must precede conversion that he would not minister comfort to "any person except those who have become contrite and are sorrowing because of their sin—those who have despaired of self-help."[18]

This is why the therapeutic gospel we discussed earlier is so dangerous. It works from the outside in to restore self-esteem by enabling us to adjust to our circumstances. Carried far enough, it can lead us to feel good about being bad. The gospel, on the other hand, is designed to transform our lives and circumstances; it works from the inside out. Therapy is concerned with changing behavior; the gospel, with changing character. Therapy gives us what we think we need; the gospel gives us what we really need.

Please don't misunderstand. Psychology and psychiatry can play a vital role. Christian counseling is a tremendous tool when it is used to open people to the Holy Spirit's healing power. But behavioral science cannot dictate the message preached from the pulpit. All of us share responsibility to see that this does not happen. Pastors should not be misled: There is no synthesis here; we are dealing with antithetical propositions. Elders and deacons must guard the ramparts to keep this false gospel out of the church. Nor should laypeople pressure their pastors to assimilate the "feel-good" marketplace.

The charge from God is to preach the whole, unadulterated truth. And when that is done with integrity—as the people of Enfield, Connecticut, learned that summer day in 1741—God does His mightiest work.

TEACHING THE TRUTH

Years ago, at the apex of her fifteen minutes of fame, a celebrated adulteress spoke to the media about her religious roots. She believed in the Bible, she told interviewers, then added the disclaimer, "but you can't always take [it] literally and be happy."[19]

We are scandalized when someone says this so brazenly. But don't many of us really operate on the same principle? We may not be breaking up other people's marriages, but many of us don't want to take the Scriptures seriously when they interfere with our comfort level. And often we do not take the Word seriously because we are not hearing it taught with authority.

The task of teaching involves all church leadership, not just the pastor.

Nor is it limited to the inquirers' class or Sunday school. Teaching is a continuous activity that permeates every level of the church, from Bible studies, youth fellowship groups, and special video presentations to Christian life courses and book discussion groups. And, as will be discussed later, a host of resources are available to aid in this: discipleship classes in print and video, doctrinal study plans, even seminary extension courses.

The church must do everything it can to equip believers with an understanding of Scripture, of doctrine, and of the application of Christian truth to all of life. And it must be teaching that affects how we live.

Make no mistake. Failure to teach is a betrayal of the Great Commission. And it is dangerous. As the prophet Hosea warned, "My people [God's covenant people] are destroyed for lack of knowledge."[20]

You may be wondering, *Why such emphasis on these basics? After all, unity and preaching of the Word are characteristics of every church, aren't they?*

Well, no, they aren't. As church squabbles and splits make all too clear, unity is not always present. And we all know of churches where the Word is not preached. Which leads to several other questions: How do we know when a particular church has fallen away from its biblical roots? How do we steer a new convert away from an apostate church and toward a faithful one? What tests can we apply to discern the fidelity of our own church? These are critical, practical questions, and they have been asked since the very beginning of the Christian faith.

Scripture itself sets the criteria, and the early church creeds built upon that foundation. The Nicene Creed, for example, speaks of "one holy catholic and apostolic church." The church is to be one—living in unity. It is to be holy—its members living righteous lives. It is catholic—that is, universal in its compass, not confined to one denomination or culture. It is apostolic—rooted in and proclaiming the apostles' teaching.

And whenever an early creed was promulgated, it came with long lists of canons: explanations in great detail of how the creed was to be implemented. So believers could not only know what it was appropriate to believe, but how to put those beliefs into practice.

Today there could be no more important question than whether our particular churches are faithful to their biblical character and identity.

After all, it's our local congregation—yes, that motley assortment of ordinary, extraordinary, flawed, eccentric, redeemed, and precious believers with whom we gather each week—that demonstrates to the watching world around us just what the unseen kingdom of God is like.

It is an awesome charge.

10
COMMUNIO SANCTORUM

The world drinks to forget;
The Christian drinks to remember.

—STEVE BROWN

WHAT DOES IT MEAN when you pray the Lord's Prayer on a Sunday morning? *"Thy kingdom come. Thy will be done, on earth as it is in heaven . . ."*?

You are asking that the kingdom of God come—and one day, in its fullness, it will. You are asking that God's perfect will, obeyed immediately in heaven, will also be done through you and the confessing community around you. So whether you are in a great cathedral or a rented hall, you are asking that your congregation will reflect, here and now, the kingdom in its eternal power and glory.

As we discussed in chapter 5, the church is a new community that God has chosen to signal or point to the coming kingdom. The church is not the kingdom of God. Historically, whenever the two have been confused, the church has brought grief upon itself and the world. The kingdom will not be brought in by our efforts; it comes when God brings it in.

But, as theologian Carl Henry so lucidly argued, the church bears present witness to what that future kingdom will look like; or, as Louis Berkhof has put it, the Body will bear the image of Christ Himself.[1] We are, therefore, a testimonial community, a holy nation, a royal priesthood, called out of the darkness into His marvelous light. We are the community that shows the world what heaven will be like! (The apostle Paul gives a wonderful snapshot of what the world should see in our community as a precursor of what is to come. "For the kingdom of God is not eating and drinking, but righteousness and peace and joy in the Holy Spirit."[2])

What are the characteristics of this new community that reflect the kingdom to come? The first is *unity*, which goes to the heart of the church's character. Then, as we examined in chapter 9, the church draws its perspective on all things from the truth of the *Word of God*. Here, let's consider several other key characteristics of this new community that mark it as supernaturally distinct from the culture around it:

- It is, of course, not individualistic or solitary. God calls people and links them together in a *fellowship*. Members bear one another's burdens and help one another through *accountability* and *discipline*.
- The *administration of the sacraments* is the visible means by which the new community celebrates the mysterious, hidden realities of God's transforming grace.
- *Prayer* and *worship* mark the new community as its people live in communication with, and adoration of, a holy God.

When the new community is faithful to its biblical identity, there is another identifying characteristic. When the church is being the Body, *the culture around it is inevitably changed.*

FELLOWSHIP

As the book of Acts depicts so beautifully, the Christians of the first churches were of one heart, sharing their material possessions and caring for their brothers and sisters in need. Surrounded by a hostile culture and convinced that Christ was returning soon, they enjoyed the intimacy of shared lives, common cause, and deep friendships that crossed the social and economic barriers of their day. Ordinary believers whose lives had been transformed by the power of Jesus, they truly were what they called themselves: the *communio sanctorum*—the communion of saints.

As the church expanded out of Jerusalem, this concept of one fellowship—one with another and with God—bound them in unity and became the very essence of the church's character and power.

Surveys show that the number-one thing people look for in a church today is fellowship. But what most modern Westerners seek is a far cry from what the Bible describes and what the early church practiced. No term in the Christian lexicon is more abused than *fellowship.*

To some it means the warm, affirming, "hot-tub" religion that soothes frayed nerves and provides relief from the stresses of everyday life. Often, with the best of intentions, Christians have turned this social notion of fellowship into an end in itself. For these folks, the object of the Christian life is fulfilled when brothers and sisters are secluded together, away on retreat. For many others, fellowship simply means coming together for church events. Instead of happy hour at the country club or the bar down the street, they have theirs with coffee and cookies in the fellowship hall (a name which, by the way, fosters the wrong impression). At the other extreme is the well-intentioned but misguided discipleship movement, where one shepherd imposes his spiritual straitjacket on his followers with unyielding discipline. This is the way cults are made.

But the word for "fellowship" in the New Testament Greek, *koinonia,* means neither punch and cookies nor cookie-cutter Christians. It conveys something much richer. Literally it means "a communion," a participation of people together in God's grace. It describes a new community in which individuals willingly covenant to share in common, to be in submission to each other, to support one another and "bear one another's burdens," as Paul wrote to the Galatians, and to build each other up in relationship with the Lord.

In Scripture, this *koinonia* embraces both the vertical and the horizontal. "What we have seen and heard we proclaim to you also, that you also may have fellowship with us and indeed our fellowship is with the Father, and with his Son Jesus Christ," wrote the apostle John to the early church.[3] It was a concept the early believers understood because it paralleled the Old Testament concept of God's people sharing together in the covenant community in which He Himself chose to dwell. Biblical fellowship involves serious commitment and obligations. An example from the early church illustrates the point.

In the second century a pagan actor was converted to Christ. Since most drama of that day encouraged immorality, and since young boys were often seduced into homosexuality in order to play the parts of women, this new believer soon realized he would have to leave the theater.

All he knew was acting, however, so he decided to support himself by teaching drama to non-Christians. Before he began, he went to his church elders and explained his predicament and his plan.

The elders immediately objected. "If it is wrong to be in the theater, then it is wrong to teach others to be in the theater," they said. The logic seemed clear, but since it was a unique situation and the young man had no other means of support, the elders decided to seek the wisdom of Cyprian, the respected bishop of the church in Carthage.

After some deliberation, Cyprian told the elders, "You are correct. What is wrong to do is morally wrong to teach." The church's duty was to hold the young convert accountable to this. "But," Cyprian added, "if the young man cannot find other employment, it is also the church's duty to care for him. And if your church is financially unable to do this, he can move over to us in Carthage and we will provide whatever he needs for food and clothing."[4]

No wonder much of the known world came to Christ in the early centuries. They could see how believers loved one another in true fellowship.

This description of true fellowship always reminds me of the way I was so lovingly and unconditionally supported by Doug Coe, Senator Harold Hughes, Congressman Al Quie, and Graham Purcell when I first became a Christian. Within the community of Christ, the fellowship of believers, we are to support each other. In the case of the young actor, his fellow believers even gave him financial support. But for equally loving reasons, they did something else: They held him accountable for disciplined behavior in his Christian commitment.

ACCOUNTABILITY AND DISCIPLINE

Fellowship is more than unconditional love that wraps its arms around someone who is hurting. It is also tough love that holds one fast to the truth and the pursuit of righteousness. For most Christians, the support side of the equation comes more easily than accountability and the subsequent discipline involved, which is one reason the behavior of Christians is often little different from the behavior of non-Christians. Maybe it's because we simply haven't taught accountability. Or maybe it's because, in today's fiercely individualistic culture, people resent being told what to do, and since we don't want to "scare them off," we succumb to cultural pressures.

Even pastors are sometimes reluctant to demand accountability. As in the case of a young couple, unmarried and living together, who asked a well-known evangelical pastor to marry them. Years earlier the young woman had belonged to the church and sung in the choir, so without further inquiry and without counseling, the pastor agreed to perform the ceremony.

Another equally prominent evangelical had on his payroll a recent convert who was living with his girlfriend. The pastor's counsel? "Think about getting married soon."

Too often we confuse love with permissiveness. It is not love to fail to dissuade another believer from sin any more than it is love to fail to take a drink away from an alcoholic or matches away from a toddler. True fellowship out of love for one another demands *accountability*.

John Wesley was so concerned with building a righteous fellowship that he devised a series of questions for his followers to ask each other every week. Some found this rigorous system of inquiry too demanding and left. Today, the very idea of such a procedure would horrify many churchgoers. Yet some wisely follow just such a practice. Several pastors I know have seven questions that they and a group of fellow pastors challenge each other with periodically:

1. Have you been with a woman anywhere this past week that might be seen as compromising?
2. Have any of your financial dealings lacked integrity?
3. Have you exposed yourself to any sexually explicit material?
4. Have you spent adequate time in Bible study and prayer?
5. Have you given priority time to your family?
6. Have you fulfilled the mandates of your calling?
7. Have you just lied to me?

The pastors and leaders who remain strong are the ones who open their lives to such questions. Those who allow the pinnacle of the pastorate to isolate them soon fall off.

I've tried to surround myself with a band of brothers who will help me look at the difficult places in my life. One of the Prison Fellowship board members reviews everything from my expense records to my daily priorities. And I make no major decision unless the circle to which I am accountable agrees unanimously. And, of course, I am subject to the authority of my home church, meet often with my pastor, and seek his counsel.

Accountability is a hollow concept unless it is enforced. There must be teeth in a church's demand for orthodoxy and righteous behavior; that is why the Reformers called *discipline* a mark of the church.[5] Yet examples of discipline are all too few in our times. Although evangelicals pride themselves on defending orthodoxy, how often have you seen questions of theological integrity actually result in discipline?

One I am aware of involved one of the evangelical movement's most ebullient and popular speakers, sociology professor Tony Campolo. Tony delights in using his glib and ready wit to shock audiences. Students love him. Others sometimes think him outrageous. And at times he does go too far.

A number of years ago Tony published a book entitled *Reasonable Faith*. It had some good apologetic material in the opening chapters, but it also contained some muddled theology. Soon after the book's publication, Tony was unceremoniously dumped from the program of a large youth gathering because sponsors of the event believed his views to be inaccurate. Tony and his friends were furious, believing he had been unfairly judged.

As we've said, the evangelical movement in America has many strengths, but cohesiveness is not one of them. Much of it is a vast, sprawling, unconnected network of rugged individualists and entrepreneurs. No magisterium, no council of bishops to settle disputes.

In this case, however, at the request of both sides, I contacted a group of leaders and asked them to serve on an ad hoc committee to judge the matter. By general agreement, J. I. Packer, a wise and scholarly man, was asked to chair the group, making him the closest thing evangelicals had to a bishop.

Despite murmurings about inquisitions and jokes about burning heretics, the committee met in a lengthy, judicious deliberation. Campolo presented his case; so did his critics.

In the end, the committee decided that Campolo had erred: His book was verbally incautious. Tony promised to mend his ways, including corrections in future printings of the book, and the sponsors of the event asked his forgiveness for their rough handling of the situation. It was the kind of accountability, discipline, and healing that should occur more often.

In a rather different situation, various arms of the evangelical community stopped supporting a best-selling author when she said that she did not hold to an orthodox belief in the Trinity. Gwen Shamblin's 1997 book, *The Weigh Down Diet,* sold more than a million copies. Its biblical principles and practical approach to changing eating habits seemed to help many people. Thirty thousand Weigh Down Workshops met in evangelical churches across the country, and Weigh Down seminars flourished.

Then, in August 2000, Shamblin posted a message on her organization's Web site indicating that she did not hold to the classic Christian doctrine of the coequal and coeternal Trinity. Soon after, several influential evangelical churches dropped her program, Shamblin was removed from the Women of Faith Web site, and key employees left her multimillion-dollar Nashville corporation. Thomas Nelson canceled publication of Shamblin's newest book, due to come out that fall.

Some observers wondered what all the fuss was about; they didn't see a huge connection between weight loss and doctrine. But by virtue of the Christian teachings that were interwoven with her program, Shamblin had accumulated a large flock of followers. And in its own way, the evangelical movement moved to censure a teacher who was leading those sheep astray.

Over the years, while the Catholic Church has not been as vigilant as it should be in protecting its parishioners from corrupt priests (though as we write, steps are being taken to redress those wrongs), it has regularly called heretics to account. Those within its ranks who teach positions anathema to historic Christian orthodoxy have been disciplined, even as the church has been subjected to media scorn.

In years past, the public reprimand of Professor Curran at Catholic University, who taught that divorce and abortion were morally justified, was a noble moment for the church. In late 1989, the bishop of San Diego refused the sacraments to a pro-choice political candidate who openly defied church teaching. The bishop was assaulted by the press and political leaders, and the candidate was elected. To this, the cleric responded calmly: "No popular vote or public opinion can change in any way the divine law that directs and guides human kind."[6] (Refusing the sacraments is not a new practice, instituted only because of the Catholic Church's position on abortion. In the sixteenth century Pope Urban VIII declared that anyone in the New World who kept Indian slaves would be excommunicated.)

When the late Cardinal O'Connor of New York suggested such church discipline for Catholic pro-choice public officials, an implied rebuke of Governor Mario Cuomo, the press went into a frenzy, particularly the *New York Times* (the same paper, incidentally, that had praised Archbishop Joseph Francis Rummel of New Orleans for denying the sacraments to a segregationist legislator in 1962).

In late 2001, Cardinal Juan Luis Cipriani instructed priests in Lima, Peru, that politicians who oppose the church's view on abortion would eventually be denied communion. In a paper called "The Moral and Legal Dimension of Abortion," the cardinal told priests that public figures who support abortion rights "are committing a grave sin, because they are supporting a crime." Pastors could "deny him or her Holy Communion in public, after warning him or her in private."[7]

Catholic Archbishop of Sydney, George Pell, has attracted much media contempt for his firm position on homosexuality. He has refused Holy Communion to Catholic homosexuals who want the church to change its teachings on homosexual behavior. He is evenhanded in his approach to unrepentant, ongoing sinful lifestyles, however, saying that communion should also be denied to "those robbing banks and whose moral life is disordered."

"Christian teaching on sexuality is only part of the Ten Commandments, of the virtues and vices," the archbishop said. Yet a biblical approach to sexuality is "essential for human well-being and especially for the proper flourishing of marriages and families, for the continuity of the human race. . . . [R]egular sexual activity, whether it is heterosexual or homosexual, is incompatible with the continued act of priestly work." Urging fellow Catholics to follow "the hard teachings of Christ," Pell has also shown compassion for those who are suffering, sponsoring hospices for people with HIV and AIDS.

Predictably, it was gay activists, including a number who are members of the media in Sydney, who most vociferously protested his appointment and installation in 2001.[8]

And the Southern Baptists, though firm defenders of individual church autonomy, have moved to oust churches that flout biblical orthodoxy. In 1999 the executive committee of the Georgia Baptist Convention cut ties with a Decatur church that allowed gays and lesbians to be deacons, Sunday school teachers, and preachers. "We came to believe that the biblical reference to homosexual behaviors do not address the Christian commitments and loving relationships of our gay and lesbian members," responded the church.

Referring to similar cases in 2001, Southern Baptist Convention President James Merritt said, "I believe in local church autonomy. I don't want any leader, agency, institution or Convention giving orders to me or my congregation. But hear me, and hear me well. The ocean of church autonomy stops at the shore of biblical authority. Local autonomy without biblical authority becomes spiritual anarchy."[9]

Such language means little to those who accuse the Baptists—or the Catholics, or Christians in general—of narrowness and repression, but the charge is absurd. The church is simply abiding by its own standards; it has never held itself to be democratic. The church is hierarchical and authoritarian and ultimately answerable only to God.

But let's just look at it pragmatically for a moment. Why should anyone join a church (which, after all, is a voluntary decision) and then expect to be able to refuse to abide by its authority (its rules, if you will). For failing to attend a few meetings, one can be thrown out of the Rotary Club. For failing to live up to a particular dress code, one can be dismissed from most private clubs. For failing to perform the required community service, one can be struck off the rolls of the Junior League. Yet when the church imposes discipline—denying the benefits of membership to those who flout its standards—it is charged with everything short of (and sometimes including) fascism. But shouldn't the church have at least the same right to set its standards as the Rotary Club? People who don't like it can and should go elsewhere.

When we fail to discipline, the church does not become more "relevant" to the world around us. It simply loses its moral authority.

Discipline should be applied not only to enforce orthodoxy, but to maintain right behavior in the church. Sermons on holy living are empty exercises unless the church is willing to back them up with action—even if doing so is uncomfortable.

Some years ago, the wife of one of the deacons in a large Southern church shocked her husband by suddenly announcing that she wanted a divorce. The following Sunday the woman came to church as usual, but this time she was accompanied by a male companion, her boss. They sat on one side of the church while the deacon and the couple's three children sat on the other side. The church soon became aware of what had happened, as the woman made no effort to disguise her intimate relationship with her boss.

The elders met with the woman and insisted that she repent of the relationship and return to her husband.

She adamantly refused. "It's over," she said. "I'm never going back to him."

The elders then told her that she could not continue coming to church with her lover because that would be flaunting her adultery. The woman responded that the church was more important to her now than ever; she believed if she could just bring her boyfriend, who happened to be Jewish, to church, he might be won to Christ. (No one in the church had ever heard of adultery being used as an evangelistic tool.)

Three elders spent many hours counseling with her. She would not repent, she would not break off the relationship, but she insisted on attending church.

Finally, one morning they called her aside, in a private room, before the worship service. All of the elders were present, and they offered her a choice. Either she would repent and work at her marriage or withdraw her membership from the church. If she refused to withdraw, she would be expelled.

In anger the woman wrote a letter of resignation to the church board.

In a similar case in Oklahoma, a disfellowshiped church member sued and, with the help of the ACLU, dragged the church through years of litigation. Although the church ultimately prevailed, it had to spend more than a million dollars in legal fees, and the elders were labeled in the press as the "goon squad" and "ayatollahs."[10]

Confrontations and cases like these are wrenching. But, "discipline guards the purity of the church, preserves the church by removing evil, and provides severe but loving correction for one who is in danger of falling into perdition."[11] Without effective discipline, there can be no accountability.

THE SACRAMENTS

The administration of the sacraments uniquely marks the community of faith as its members celebrate physical reminders of God's invisible grace. Unfortunately, believers have long used the term itself to divide their ranks between sacramental churches and nonsacramental churches. Some revere the term; others abhor it.

Not for a moment are we suggesting that the differences between Christian traditions should be minimized. In some traditions, the sacraments are considered efficacious, in others expressive. In the Lord's Supper, for example, the elements are symbolic to one tradition, the actual body to another, and invoke the actual presence to a third. These are important issues, honestly and fervently held, and they go back a long way—originating not, as most assume, with the Reformation, but with the early church fathers who held three distinct views of the sacraments. But the passion with which different traditions defend their views can sometimes blind us to the deepest reality of our Lord's commands and why He ordered them: that is, the underlying reality of the acts themselves.

A sacrament, in some traditions called an ordinance, literally means an oath or a pledge. It is an act by which we affirm our faith or swear allegiance to the lordship of Christ.

In one sense, then, believers offer *themselves* sacramentally, as Paul describes in Romans. Their obedient life is a witness, an affirmation or pledge, of their belief.[12]

Similarly, the church itself constitutes a living sign of loyalty to Christ. Just look at the biblical imagery: a holy body . . . the presence of the Lord through His people . . . the bride, pure and spotless, waiting at the altar to meet the Bridegroom for the consummation of God's grand unfolding plan for mankind. The church stands as a visible sign of faithfulness, an outward manifestation of the work of God's grace.

But these signs—whether our lives or our baptism or our worship or our participation in communion—are meaningful only insofar as they declare and manifest the reality of God's action through Christ. They are an expression of our faith in what God has done in us, what Augustine called the visible form of invisible grace.

This is why the sacraments can never be demystified, even in traditions that consider the elements to be entirely symbolic. While the Reformers were correct in insisting that the sacraments be understood in light of Scripture, God's regenerative work still contains a mystery. We can celebrate it, we can affirm His inner work with our outward acts, but we can never totally comprehend it.

So while traditions may differ on the meaning of the various acts and on which acts are specifically ordered as sacraments, all would agree that the sacraments are centered on Christ who took on flesh and died and was raised.[13] And almost all traditions agree that the administration of the sacraments is the way the community of faith expresses its very essence, and thus is an essential task and mark of the church particular. They further agree that the two we will discuss here are distinctly and unequivocally commanded by our Lord: baptism and the Lord's Supper.

BAPTISM

Infant versus adult. Immersion versus sprinkling. The work of grace in the act or represented by the act. What the act signifies. When it comes to the sacrament of baptism, I have strong convictions about the biblical pattern for adult baptism and immersion, which is why I am a Baptist. But I of course recognize that Christians hold widely divergent views and have since the days of the early church. There is one thing, however, that all believers must agree upon, and that is the need to repent and be baptized! Yet it's astonishing how many Christians profess faith and then disregard the biblical mandate.

One Christian friend told me of a new "brother," an influential Muslim he had been discipling. I was overjoyed until my friend explained that this man was continuing to read the Koran and to worship in a mosque. When I protested, he defended his new "convert."

"But he loves Jesus," my friend said. "We pray together in the spirit of Christ. He is a follower of Jesus."

"What about baptism?" I asked.

My friend shook his head. "No, he couldn't do that—it's a cultural thing—but he loves Jesus."

I never was able to convince my friend regarding that crucial dividing line. Baptism is the external witness of the invisible reality. It is the Lord's own command in the Great Commission, and it is the first oath and sign of admission into the church. Peter's first words to the new believers were, "Repent and be baptized"—and thereby was the church particular formed.

Most Westerners take baptism for granted, but for many in the world the act requires immense courage. In countries like Nepal it once meant imprisonment. In India and other nations it can bring persecution or sometimes even death.

But sometimes, even in this country, baptism demands courage. Like the nine inmates of a prison in Kentucky who, following a Prison Fellowship seminar, expressed a desire for baptism. The instructor did what all are taught to do in the ministry: to involve clergy of the denomination of the individual's choosing.

The problem was finding a place for the baptism. The prison had no baptistry in the chapel, so the only possible place to carry out the sacrament was a fenced-off exercise area inside the prison compound used by all the inmates. But there were two problems with this: one was that the other inmates could observe the service through the chain-link fence; the second was that these nine who wanted to be baptized were all from the sexual offenders' unit and were already subject to scorn and abuse from the rest of the prison populace.

But the new believers were determined. So an old galvanized horse trough was wheeled into the yard and placed beneath the guard tower. Then the men marched out, one by one, to the accompanying jeers and catcalls from the main prison yard. They went into the water and came out, as our instructor later wrote, "broken, weeping," but overflowing with God's grace.

A sacrament? Indeed it was. A bold one. And, as the instructor added, "Straight out of the New Testament."[14]

Equally clear is the command, "Do this in memory of me." The very thought that Jesus has asked us to do anything in memory of Him should fill us with awe and reverence. And think what He commands: "This is My body . . . this is My blood of the covenant, which is poured out for many for the forgiveness of sins."[15]

Again, various traditions attach different meanings to the elements. But however we view them, it is important to remember the underlying reality. And whether symbolic or actual, when we receive the elements or when we go to the communion rail, when we take the cup and the bread, we are making a physical gesture, a physical bonding. Communion is the holiest moment, when we signify our oneness with Christ. Failing to celebrate that communion, or doing so infrequently, can drain the vitality from a church body.

And failing to treat the sacrament with holy reverence is a grave error. Think of Nadab and Abihu, Aaron's two oldest sons. Nadab would have succeeded Aaron as high priest, but both he and his brother were consumed by the fire of the Lord after they "took their censers, put fire in them and added incense; and they offered unauthorized fire before the Lord."[16] Similarly, Uzzah unthinkingly touched the ark of the covenant—and died.[17] These offenses may seem trivial, the punishment harsh, but God has never lightly suffered the desecration of the holy.

For this reason, Scripture sets forth three conditions for Communion:

First, only believers can partake. Jesus' invitation to "remember Me" was to His disciples. Paul's instructions for the sacrament were to the church. And the act is the supreme signal of the inner work of grace in an individual's life.

For a nonbeliever to take Communion is to taunt God. This is why many churches—as they should—warn partakers of the meaning and significance of the sacrament and tell non-Christians to abstain.

Second, believers partaking must be at peace with one another. This is evident from Paul's anger that the church was divided and therefore should not be meeting for the Lord's Supper.[18] Before participating in Holy Communion, every believer should examine his or her heart and take whatever steps are necessary to be reconciled with fellow believers.

Third, believers dare not come to the table except with a repentant heart. "Whoever eats this bread or drinks this cup of the Lord in an unworthy manner," as Paul puts it, "drinks judgment to himself."[19] That should be a sobering warning, especially when the apostle adds that because of this offense many have fallen ill or died. Any pastor who takes the Word of God seriously should never administer Communion without adequately warning those who partake. Any who are unrepentant should flee the table rather than trivialize the sacred.

God does not view this sacred act lightly. Pat Novak, pastor in a nonsacramental denomination, discovered this when he was serving as a hospital chaplain intern just outside of Boston several years ago.

Pat was making his rounds one summer morning when he was called to visit a patient admitted with an undiagnosed ailment. John, a man in his sixties, had not responded to any treatment; medical tests showed nothing; psychological tests were inconclusive. Yet he was wasting away; he had not even been able to swallow for two weeks. The nurses tried everything. Finally they called the chaplain's office.

When Pat walked into the room, John was sitting limply in his bed, strung with IV tubes, staring listlessly at the wall. He was a tall, grandfatherly man, balding a little, but his sallow skin hung loosely on his face, neck, and arms where the weight had dropped from his frame. His eyes were hollow.

Pat was terrified; he had no idea what to do. But John seemed to brighten a bit as soon as he saw Pat's chaplain badge and invited him to sit down.

As they talked, Pat sensed that God was urging him to do something specific: He *knew* he was to ask John if he wanted to take Communion. Chaplain interns were not encouraged to ask this type of thing in this public hospital, but Pat did.

At that John broke down. "I can't!" he cried. "I've sinned and can't be forgiven."

Pat paused a moment, knowing he was about to break policy again. Then he told John about 1 Corinthians 11 and Paul's admonition that whoever takes Communion in an unworthy manner eats and drinks judgment to himself. And he asked John if he wanted to confess his sin. John nodded gratefully.

To this day Pat can't remember the particular sin John confessed, nor would he say if he did, but he recalls that it did not strike him as particularly egregious. Yet it had been draining the life from this man. John wept as he confessed, and Pat laid hands on him, hugged him, and told John his sins were forgiven.

Then Pat got the second urging from the Holy Spirit: *Ask him if he wants to take Communion.* He did.

Pat gave John a Bible and told him he would be back later. Already John was sitting up straighter, with a flicker of light in his eyes.

Pat visited a few more patients and then ate some lunch in the hospital cafeteria. When he left, he wrapped an extra piece of bread in a napkin and borrowed a coffee cup from the cafeteria. He ran out to a shop a few blocks away and bought a container of grape juice.

Then he returned to John's room with the elements and celebrated Communion with him, again reciting 1 Corinthians 11. John took the bread and chewed it slowly. It was the first time in weeks he had been able to take solid food in his mouth. He took the cup and swallowed. He had been set free.

Within three days John walked out of that hospital. The nurses were so amazed they called the newspaper, which later featured the story of John and Pat, appropriately, in its "Life" section.

Despite the differences between various traditions, would not all Christians agree that the Lord's Supper should be a moment of deepest reverence and communion when we memorialize and know God's grace in this intimate physical expression? Is not the substance of the act what is crucial?

The late Father Lawrence Jenco, who was held hostage many years ago by Islamic terrorists for nineteen months, used to tell movingly what Communion meant to him. While blindfolded and chained to a radiator in a room with three other hostages, Jenco assembled bits of bread and water. He then offered the body and blood to his companions, one of whom was Benjamin Weir, a Presbyterian minister. It was, as Jenco described later, their moment of deepest joy, sustaining them through an unimaginable ordeal.

Those who have been confined for long periods are often emotionally scarred for life, but Jenco was filled with love and forgiveness. For during that time he knew, in its most intimate sense, communion with Christ.

Later Father Jenco and Reverend Weir and the others could, I imagine, passionately discuss whether the elements were consecrated or symbolic. But none of them would dispute that together they experienced God's grace in that horrid place.

That which brings us together—the magnificent saving grace of our risen Savior—is infinitely greater and grander than any differences we might sincerely hold over the nature of our affirmations of that grace.

PRAYER AND WORSHIP

Since those called of God into the new order are a community created by and bearing witness to Jesus Christ, we are to be in constant prayer and adoration of Him.

More has been written on prayer than on any other aspect of the Christian life. Some are classics, like the work of E. M. Bounds. Others promote cheap grace: Pray so God will give you whatever you want. Others are fictionally empowering but theologically dubious.

Prayer has been one clearly distinguishing characteristic of the church from the very beginning. When the disciples gathered in the Upper Room as Christ had commanded, they stayed there for ten days continually devoting themselves to prayer.[20] After that, the Spirit came and the church was empowered for ministry.

When the believers first gathered after Pentecost, they did so to pray, feeling a sense of awe at the wonders and signs the risen Lord was performing through the apostles. Peter and John, after their first arrest, returned to the church for prayer that they might preach God's Word "with great boldness." When Peter was later imprisoned, prayer was offered fervently by the church. In prison, Paul and Silas worshiped, praying and singing hymns of praise.[21]

The apostles appointed seven others to serve the needy so that they could devote themselves to prayer and to the ministry of the Word. The church prayed and fasted before laying hands on Paul and Barnabas to send them on their first missionary journey, and Luke tells us they were thus sent by the Holy Spirit. Similarly, when Paul and Barnabas appointed elders, they prayed and fasted.[22]

Prayer is the act by which the community of faith surrenders itself, puts aside all other concerns, and comes before God Himself. It brings us, inevitably, as Archbishop William Temple once wrote, to "the nourishment of mind with his truth; the purifying of imagination by his beauty; the opening of the heart to his love; the surrender of will to his purpose—and all of this gathered up in adoration, the most selfless emotion of which our nature is capable and therefore the chief remedy for all that self-centeredness which is our original sin and the source of all actual sin."[23]

The nineteenth-century lawyer-turned-evangelist, Charles Finney, argued that the church could do nothing without what he called, "the enduement of the Spirit, the power to savingly impress," which was God's response to total God-centered prayer. Without this the church could not be the church.[24]

"God-centered" is the key phrase. The impediment to the empowerment of the church, Finney argued, was when prayer was not wholehearted, when the petitioner did not trust God to answer, or when prayer was self-directed. As the psalmist warned: "If I had cherished sin in my heart, the Lord would not have listened."[25]

We as a church pray not because it is the key to something—healing the sick, church growth, or even revival—but because God is God and worthy of our total obedience and reverence.[26]

True worship, in the same way, is radically countercultural, being directed not toward self, but toward God. Richard Neuhaus puts it in sobering terms: "The celebration we call worship has less to do with the satisfaction or the pursuit of happiness than with the abandonment of the pursuit of happiness."[27] We worship God because, in the words of the Hartford Declaration—the 1975 document designed to explode modern theologies that were emptying God of transcendence—"God is to be worshiped."

True prayer and worship also run counter to the prevailing ethos in the church, which equates God's blessings with growth and material success. Some pastors would not consider doing anything that might jeopardize their rosters and purge their pews of warm bodies. But we have known of churches whose leaders have boldly prayed that God would bring only those drawn to truly worship Him. Attendance numbers fell significantly, as those whose hearts were closed stopped coming. But the passion and intensity of worship, prayer, and teaching of the Word grew enormously, and revival followed. Older Christians began to grow in spiritual maturity, and the church itself began to grow numerically as new believers became part of the church through their witness.

Often it is in difficult surroundings—in places of deprivation or persecution—that the deepest sense of awe, reverence, and worship of our Holy God is found. That's certainly been true for a close friend and Prison Fellowship board member, Dois Rosser, who travels all over the world.

Dois has a work called International Cooperating Ministries, which connects with indigenous believers around the world to build churches and plant congregations. One day he was in India, and a friend there asked him to visit a remote village. They drove for hours, jolting and bouncing on rutted roads, and both men were soon covered with sweat and dust.

Finally they came to a small village and from there made their way along a winding dirt road up a large hill. They parked at the end of the road, and the man led Dois up a narrow path on a barren hillside. Three large gray boulders marked the entrance to the path. Painted on each one was a whitewashed sign of the cross.

In the distance Dois could see smoke rising from a buffalo-dung fire, and through the haze could make out a few ghostly figures tending the blaze. Then, people slowly began making their way toward the two men.

As they came closer, Dois realized he was looking at a leper colony.

It was like a scene from the New Testament, Dois thought, as he saw men and women with ragged strips of cloth wrapped around the stumps where their fingers had been. Many wore cloths over their disfigured faces. They shuffled forward to greet him, their toeless feet stirring up small clouds of dust.

Some of the family members were healthy, but, Dois learned, were forced to live apart here with their stricken loved ones. The government had provided them with a well, and evidently they survived by begging in the nearby town, where people would fling them a few rupees from fear as much as compassion.

"They want you to see their church," his Indian friend said. They walked further into the little camp, and as they drew close to the building, Dois was thunderstruck. It was still in the early stages of construction, but it was already four levels of heavy stone. The people were working together: Those who were able had hacked big granite slabs out of the mountain, and the others had carried them down to erect that structure—gaunt men and women edging down the mountain path on their crippled feet, cradling heavy granite boulders balanced on their fingerless hands. Then they would lay down their burden on the wall, and a skilled worker would lay it in and mortar the joints.

The people sang songs and hymns for Dois. He recognized the tune of one: "This is the day that the Lord has made; We will rejoice and be glad in it," sung in Telegu. Later, as Dois prepared to leave, the leader of the leper colony asked if they could pray together. As they gathered in a circle, Dois closed his eyes . . . but then, he heard a rustling sound.

He looked. There, lying on the ground, their saris and shawls spread out around them like ragged flags, were all the members of that leper community, prostrate before God in deep and reverent prayers, thanking Him for His goodness and grace and mercy.

"The faith of those lepers in India was absolutely humbling," Dois said later. He was "bowled over by the sight of men and women building a church with nothing at their fingertips. Not even fingers."

But that sight of weak people physically moving a mountain of stone should be no surprise. It's the same pattern by which God has chosen to work since the very beginnings of His church. He uses the weak and powerless things of the world to evidence His mighty power. He is the one who builds His church, stone by living stone. And in India, a place of terrible poverty and suffering, a land where Christians are outcast, there, worshiping the living God in Spirit and in truth, was the church, being the Body of Christ![28]

WITNESS OF THE CHURCH CHANGING CULTURE

John Calvin said that when the preaching of God's Word, the administration of the sacraments, and the exercise of church discipline—what he called the classic "marks" of the church—were present in a worshipful fellowship of believers, there would be an inevitable, organic result. When the church is being the church, reflecting the great kingdom to come, *it inevitably changes the culture around it.*

That is a radical truth, for it means that the key to changing entire societies starts on the local level, in our communities, as they are affected by our home churches. One of the best examples of that that I've ever seen—one that should give us all great hope and encouragement—comes from prison.

In 1987, I took a group of corrections officials to South America to see Prison Fellowship International's astounding work in prisons in Peru and Ecuador. In Brazil in the early 1970s, a Christian businessman named Mario Ottoboni had developed a revolutionary prison program based on the unconditional love and transforming grace of God. Since local corrections officials had experienced little but absolute failure in their ability to rehabilitate offenders, they opened the door to Ottoboni and gave him responsibility for one wing of Sao Paolo's Humaita prison.

Ottoboni's program in Humaita demonstrated incredible, long-term success. Inmates were discipled in vigorous evangelism and Bible study programs, they learned how to live in Christian community with one another, and they learned how to live as responsible citizens and family men upon their release. Recidivism rates dropped dramatically.[29] The same thing happened when Prison Fellowship took over a wing of the notorious García Moreno prison in Ecuador.

When the U.S. officials toured these prisons with me, they were astounded. As we left García Marino, Caroll Vance, then Secretary of Corrections for the state of Texas, was scribbling elaborate notes.

"What are you doing?" I asked him.

He told me he was sketching out ideas for a proposal to give to his governor so Texas could start a prison program like this.

I smiled and told him that was great. I decided not to discourage him, but I was sure it would never happen. For five years we had been trying to interest U.S. officials in these ideas and nothing had happened. Nobody wanted to take on the church/state issues involved. Even our friend, the governor of Alabama—who actually relished fighting with the ACLU—had backed away.

But Carroll Vance returned to Texas and followed through, and the next thing I knew, his governor, George W. Bush, was opening the doors to a similar program for Prison Fellowship. The state had 150,000 inmates and was spending two billion dollars a year in corrections, the state's biggest budget item. Yet half of Texas's ex-prisoners were getting re-arrested within three years of their release. The state needed a program that could change inmates from the inside out.

So Texas contracted with PF to run a faith-based prerelease program in a section of the Jester II prison unit outside Houston. PF provided programming, staff, and volunteer mentors; the state provided nonreligious aspects of the program such as security, housing, and administration. Over the months and years that followed, with every conceivable observer watching to see if InnerChange Freedom Initiative (IFI) would rise or fall—especially the American Civil Liberties Union—the program has been a clear success.

When our prison unit in Texas opened, George W. Bush came to the ceremonies. I took him through and he spoke to the inmates. Then we went into the prison yard for a press conference. Karen Hughes, his assistant who later went with him to the White House, came over as we were starting the press conference. She said that there had not yet been much response from the inmates. Could we do something to get them a little more excited?

I asked our director, Tommie Dorsett, to see if he could bring the inmates to the yard and get something going.

Next thing I knew, all the men from our program were marching in slow step out into the prison yard, their deep voices blending in the melody of "Amazing Grace." George W. Bush quickly got in line with the inmates, singing enthusiastically, and the resulting picture that made the front page of newspapers across Texas was of Governor Bush with his arms around two inmates, one a convicted murderer, singing "Amazing Grace."

Now, in Texas at the time, that was not a particularly good political move for the governor. But that convicted murderer, who had come to know Christ in prison, went on to be released from prison and is now working in a church, leading Bible studies, and drawing others to the Lord. And, of course, George W. Bush went on to the White House, where he continues to be a fervent advocate for faith-based programs in *every* arena of social need.

After the demonstrated success in Texas, the states of Iowa, Kansas, and Minnesota contracted with Prison Fellowship to start IFI programs. When the program opened in Iowa, I went to the dedication ceremony. I wasn't sure what to expect, since the program there had only been in operation for two months, and the inmates, who had been transferred into our institution from prisons all over Iowa, had not had much of a chance to bond or be discipled.

But I was surprised. Again.

As we entered, inmates began grabbing my hands, hugging me, welcoming me to their "church." And when I spoke to the men in the common area of the prison, something unforgettable happened.

The acoustics were terrible, and my words bounced off the concrete walls. But when I finished my ricocheting sermon, the inmates suddenly jumped to their feet and held their well-worn Bibles high in the air.

"This is my Bible!" they shouted, like a festal chant. Their deep voices thundered off the concrete walls. I could feel the echo in my heart.

"It is a lamp unto my feet, a light unto my path; these words I will hide in my heart so I may not sin against God!"

Tears sprang to my eyes. It was like seeing trained troops, focused, committed, and ready for battle. These believers were ready for the assault on the very gates of hell that only *they* could undertake as the church, the community of believers inside those prison walls.

I talked with our IFI staff afterward. How had it happened? I asked. How did those guys come together in such unity and purpose, after such a short time together in our program?

Their explanation was that a core group of Christian inmates had banded together immediately. They met for prayer and Bible study. They supported one another. They did not smoke or curse or read inappropriate material or cause trouble. They were honest in their prison work programs. Their behavior marked them as different.

But they didn't keep to themselves. They went out of their way to develop relationships with other inmates. They influenced each new person who came into that prison unit. And before long, a set of community values was formed, a cultural consensus of morals and behavior.

We had brought a group of inmates from several different prisons and locked them together in one compound, with Christ at the center. And what developed was not the typically depraved prison culture, but a community that, while not perfect, was marked by love, joy, peace, self-control . . . and other fruit of the Holy Spirit.

And that is the point. When we are biblically faithful as a community of believers, whether our local church is behind prison walls, in the inner city, in a treelined suburb, or in the middle of a country cornfield, the neighborhood around us will be changed by the power of the living God.

That doesn't mean that our local church will be ideal. Just as there are no perfect Christians this side of heaven, so there are no perfect churches. Even the early church in Jerusalem had its problems: Ananias and Sapphira's perjury, the dissension between Paul and Barnabas that broke up the very first missionary team, young Eutychus falling asleep during Paul's sermon and dropping out of a third-story window. Just like us, those early Christians didn't have it all together.

But they *did* have a great distinctive that we often lack in our modern experience.

11

THE GREAT DISTINCTIVE

He who admits no fear of God is really a post-Christian man;
for at the heard of Judaism and Christianity lies a holy dread.

—RUSSELL KIRK

Too OFTEN today's church takes its cues from, and defines its role by, the ways of the world. It accommodates a consumer-oriented culture that wants, above all else, to feel good. And it focuses on action at the expense of character, on doing rather than being.

There is nothing wrong with seeking to meet people's needs or creating programs to do so. The church setting should be an environment where non-Christians feel welcome. The church should grow. But when programs and growth become the central focus, the church is in danger of profaning her first love . . . in danger of trivializing the holy.

To *profane* means to take the holy and make it common. To treat the sacred with irreverence. To take the Lord's name in vain, which comes from the Latin *vanus,* or "empty." How many times do believers do just that?

Oh, perhaps we don't swear. That's too obvious. Instead, we profane the name subtly.

We forsake our assemblies. Or when we do gather, we offer empty words of devotion. We sing hymns mechanically. Our thoughts wander during corporate prayer. We shoot loose God-talk toward others: "I'll pray for you." But do we really pray for that person? Christian jargon can sound spiritual, but sometimes it hides an empty heart.

"You shall not take the name of the Lord your God in vain," the Lord thundered from Mount Sinai. Have we forgotten?

We do so at our peril. For the church is not His whim; it is His love for eternity. It is not a little business venture He founded two thousand years ago and now, in retirement, watches indulgently. Most of all, it is not our enterprise.

No, the church is the Lord's, bought with His blood on the rough wood of the cross. It is the holy city that will shine with light for all eternity. The bride of the coming King. The assembly of believers redeemed by His grace, yet whose every deed will be scrutinized by His judgment. The Body that is His holy presence now, pointing the way to the coming kingdom.

If that is so, then today, as individuals and as the corporate body of Christ, we need to know what our predecessors in less sophisticated times knew.

We need to know the fear of the Lord: the overwhelming, compelling awe and reverence of a holy God. The Proverbs tell us that the fear of the Lord is the beginning of wisdom. Why? It compels us beyond our small selves and lifts us to a right perspective of God's sovereign rule over all creation. It evokes the absolute power and perfection of the God who dwarfs mere men and women, that causes them to bow and worship and glory in His amazing grace.

Fear of the Lord was the secret of the early church. The very first Christians were Jews steeped in the Law, which demanded that they be holy because a holy God dwelt in their midst. They knew what the actual presence of the almighty God among them meant.

Early on, when Ananias and Sapphira fell to the floor and died because they lied to God, trivializing the holy, Luke describes the result: "And great fear came upon the whole church, and upon all who heard of these things. . . . And at the hands of the apostles many signs and wonders were taking place among the people; and they were all with one accord. . . . But none of the rest dared associate with them; however, the people held them in high esteem. And all the more believers in the Lord, multitudes of men and women, were constantly added to their number."[1]

Fear of the Lord would not rank particularly high on the list of modern church-growth strategies. But in the early church, it birthed multitudes of believers.

So the church throughout all Judea and Galilee and Samaria enjoyed peace, being built up; and, going on in the fear of the Lord and in the comfort of the Holy Spirit, it continued to increase.[2]

Awe is the heartbeat of the pages of Acts. The sense of worship and reverence, the conviction that Christ had risen and would return, and the vibrant, absolute joy of the first believers' faith. It was a faith based on a series of heart-stopping paradoxes: God become man; life out of death; intimate, glorious worship of the Lord they loved with holy fear. So filled were they with this awe that they could face a hostile world with holy abandon. Nothing else mattered, not even their lives.

For the church in the West to come alive, it needs to resolve its identity crisis, to stand on biblical truth, to renew its vision . . . and, more than anything else, to recover the fear of the Lord. Only that will give us the holy abandon that will cause us to be the church no matter what the culture around us says or does.

We have seen this holy fear in a way we'll never forget in the lives of two men. One was Bob McAlister, former chief of staff for the governor of South Carolina. The other was a young man named Rusty Woomer.

Rusty was not a celebrated pastor or a learned theologian. He was an unknown convict who had sinned and failed miserably. But his story struck us deeply with its jolting certainty of His amazing grace.

In fact, if members of the Body today could grab hold of what Rusty Woomer eventually knew, we might well see, in our time, a movement that would truly change the world.

12

CORAM DEO

THE CHAIR IS OAK, with wide armrests, a slightly scooped, polished seat, and a high back with four horizontal slats. It is almost a hundred years old. By 1990, 243 people had sat in it, their arms and legs restrained by leather straps, their heads shaved and smeared with gel to better conduct the two thousand volts of electricity that killed them.

Rusty Woomer was the 244th person to sit in South Carolina's electric chair.

Bob McAlister's chair in the South Carolina State House sat behind his massive mahogany desk. By 1990, Bob had sat in it for four years as Governor Carroll Campbell's director of communications and deputy chief of staff. He could lean back, prop his feet on the desk, and survey the rose damask draperies extending nearly the height of the sixteen-foot ceilings, the plush wing chairs, the photographs of himself with the governor.

But when Bob sat in his chair in 1990, jabbing a chewed blue pen in the air as he gave statements to the press on this issue or that, he wasn't totally focused on the media, the issue, or even the governor down the hall.

Rarely an hour went by that he didn't think of Rusty Woomer, the man who had become his best friend. Yet before their lives had converged five years earlier, Rusty Woomer and Bob McAlister could not have been more different.

Born in 1954, Ronald Raymond Woomer grew up in a hillbilly town in West Virginia. His parents divorced when he was a toddler, then met by chance on the street and decided to remarry. Later they divorced again.

The oldest of five children, Rusty loved the mountains and woods around his family's shack. The small, blond boy chased squirrels, ate ripe tomatoes warmed by the summer sun in his mother's garden, and watched hawks wheel in soaring circles in the sky.

But if Rusty felt free in the woods, home was prison. When his dad was drunk, he would beat his wife and children. When Rusty ran away from home, his dad would find him and bring him back, bruised and afraid.

Still, there were some good things in Rusty's life. Fishing with his mother was one of his greatest pleasures. He knew she loved him. And there was the little country church a few miles from their house. In the winter Rusty would sit in a worn pew and look out the window at long icicles hanging like fragile daggers from the eaves. Inside, an ancient potbellied stove warmed the small structure. The preacher's voice was so soft, so kind, so different from his father's screaming rages.

James Robert McAlister was born in 1949, the only child of parents who inhabited a comfortable, modest home in a comfortable South Carolina suburb. Bob's father worked in the textile industry and coached Little League on weekends; his mother baked cookies for PTA bake sales. Bob's teachers at school and Sunday school gave the quick, blue-eyed boy constant affirmation.

Early on special summer days, Bob, his father, and his grandfather would pack their tackle boxes and Mom's thick sandwiches and pile into the green family Ford. Then Bob's father would drive the three generations of McAlisters off for a day at Red's Fishing Lake. Bob's childhood passed in a happy haze of summer fishing, spring Little League, and church every Sunday.

As Rusty Woomer grew older, school bored and frustrated him, as did anything that confined him. The fights with his dad grew more violent.

Rusty would sometimes sleep in gas station rest rooms or under bridges to avoid going home.

Drugs provided an escape. He had little trouble getting marijuana. Before long, he was shooting liquefied amphetamines into his veins. He hung around with older boys who had already quit school, and when he was in the ninth grade, Rusty quit as well. He also left home.

By the age of sixteen, Rusty was a lank-haired, pale kid with habitually shifting eyes. He looked like the delinquent that he was. He was sent to a reform school. By age nineteen, he had graduated to a state prison for stealing fourteen cases of beer.

Rusty Woomer had lost his name and become a number.

In addition to fishing and baseball, by the time he entered high school Bob McAlister had developed a third all-American passion: broadcasting. At sixteen he was already a disc jockey at a radio station outside of Greenville. A year or two later he became a DJ at WQOK, the Big Q, 1440 on the radio dial of every teenager in his town. Bob rode around in the green Ford, which by now his father had given him. Everywhere he went, people knew his name.

Bob's voice rolled smoothly over the airwaves. His words made people smile or laugh, and sometimes his ideas even made them think. He wasn't changing history, spinning records at WQOK, but he had found something else. Radio gave him a sense of fulfillment, power, and influence.

By his senior year in college, Bob had moved to a Greenville television station, WFBC, as a newscaster and a reporter. Then, while covering a group of high school seniors taking a class trip to Washington, D.C., he met Strom Thurmond, South Carolina's legend in the Senate. Senator Thurmond offered Bob a job as speechwriter and assistant press secretary.

So in the spring of 1972, with President Richard Nixon at the height of his power and Strom Thurmond one of the major architects of the Southern strategy that had gotten Nixon elected, twenty-three-year-old Bob McAlister arrived in Washington. As he accelerated his Dodge Charger up the incline of Capitol Hill, he thought with awe, *I am now a part of Washington. This is reality.*

Bob's job kept him in the office from early in the morning until late at night. Senator Thurmond was an affable, though demanding, boss who took Bob with him to the White House, onto the floor of the Senate, and on trips back to South Carolina.

Eventually Bob returned to South Carolina, where, through the balance of the 1970s, he steadily built his career in broadcasting—and his bankbook. He married. But since he was wedded to his job more than his wife, the marriage crumbled.

His ambition sharpened. He met every goal he set for himself, and then some.

While Bob McAlister was flying high, Rusty Woomer was plunging deeper and deeper into trouble. After serving three years in prison for the beer burglary episode, he spent his newfound freedom in a constant cycle of drugs, alcohol, and stealing to get money for more drugs and alcohol. He married, but after a brief high, his marriage crashed.

Rusty was convicted of statutory rape after he picked up a fifteen-year-old girl in a bar. That gave him a year in a Kentucky prison. After his release, he returned to West Virginia, where his drug use escalated. He mainlined a homemade mix of amphetamines, twitching along without sleep for five days at a time. To come down, he chugged whiskey, vodka, and beer. In between he popped Quaaludes, Valium, and PCP.

Though dimly aware that he was breaking his mother's heart, he didn't care.

He hung around with men ten and fifteen years older than himself, realizing even in his druggy haze that he was looking for a father figure. One who filled that role was an ex-con named Eugene Skaar, who owned a grocery store where Rusty shopped. Neighbors said Skaar would come and go at odd hours of the night. Friends said he was infatuated with guns. Police said he was a sexual offender. He also had been convicted for possessing and selling altered U.S. coins.

Rusty sometimes said Skaar was his father when he introduced him to acquaintances. He bragged about how well Skaar could hold his drugs and alcohol and was flattered when the man let him in on a plan that could net them both a bundle of cash. All Rusty had to do was go with Skaar to South Carolina and help him steal a coin collection.

Armed with guns, Quaaludes, Valium, whiskey, and marijuana, the two men arrived in the rural South Carolina town of Cottageville on February

22, 1979. Skaar found the coins; Rusty shot the coin collector, John Turner.

Next Skaar picked out a house at random some miles northeast. There, Rusty shot and killed the occupants, Arnie Richardson and Earldean Wright, and wounded Richardson's daughter. They stole more guns and money before moving on.

Still drinking and popping pills, the two continued toward the coast. They stopped at Pawleys Island, where they robbed a convenience store and kidnapped the two clerks, Della Louise Sellers and Wanda Summers. Taking the women to a remote wooded area, the two men raped them; then Rusty shot them. Della Louise Sellers died; Wanda Summers lived but lost the lower half of her face to a shotgun blast.

Rusty and Skaar finished their night at a Myrtle Beach motel as the police closed in. Just after midnight, Skaar shot himself rather than surrender; police took a drugged-out Rusty into custody. The next day, shaking and still high, he confessed to the murders.

Bob himself got a bit caught in the early 1980s. News-talk radio was expensive, and budget crunching began to crunch on him. When the management changed in his company, new executives began tearing down what Bob had built over the previous five years—firing people, cutting budgets, changing formats and programming.

Bob had married again, and his wife, Carol, could see that he was slowly being pulverized by the pressure.

"Look," Carol finally said one morning. "When you come home tonight, I want you to come home without a job. I would rather have a live unemployed husband than a dead one with a job."

Bob knew she was right. He went to his office and gave notice, all the time thinking: *This is the worst day of my life.*

He had just resigned from his position as news director and assistant general manager for the most prestigious radio station in South Carolina. His entire identity was gone. He had no idea who he was apart from a title and a position—and soon he discovered that many of the people in his social and professional circles didn't care who he was apart from all that either. He was shocked when "friends" who once couldn't do enough for him now didn't even return his phone calls.

At the time Bob didn't understand his situation in theological terms; that would come later. But he knew enough to realize he was being broken.

"I came back to reality," he says. "The reality that no matter how meticulously you plan your life, no matter how diligently you pursue your goals, no matter how many hours you work, no matter how dedicated you are, the bottom line is you just don't have total control over your life."[1]

When you do everything right and it turns out wrong, then what happens next? Bob wondered. In desperation, he began to reach out to God.

Bob had no dramatic conversion, apart from the miracle of a proud man yielding himself to Jesus Christ. He began to read his Bible, began to pray, began to consciously seek to please God. Submitting his will to God's meant some big changes—the kingdom of heaven was a kingdom with very different values from the world of media and politics. His parents had "trained him up in the way he should go" during his happy childhood; now Bob was returning to those spiritual roots.

In January 1984, he and a friend started a public relations firm. It was a tough business. Yet Bob found that his old self-sufficiency had been replaced by a new dependence on God. He worked as hard as ever, striving for excellence, but his perspective had changed. Now he knew there was a lot more to life than public relations, political illusions, and personal advancement.

But if God took hold of Bob McAlister's heart in the marketplace, He broke it on a Columbia thoroughfare. Bull Street became Bob McAlister's Damascus Road.

It was a sweltering day in July 1984, and Bob was tooling along Bull Street's lanes at forty-five miles an hour in his gray Chrysler New Yorker when he noticed the traffic ahead diverting around some sort of obstacle.

It was a frail black man in a wheelchair, sweat running off him as he strained to roll his chair along the pavement at about half a mile an hour, right in the middle of traffic. Cars were passing him on the left and the right, drivers shouting at him to get out of the road.

What's this guy doing? Bob thought. *He's going to get killed. And he's going to make me late.*

Then Bob did something he had never done before. For the first time in his life, he stopped.

As Bob pulled over, the man wheeled toward his car. He was slight, glistening with perspiration, his clothes worn and reeking of sweat. His legs were thin, undeveloped, hanging uselessly like two bony sticks.

"Thank you for stoppin'," the man said with a grin. "I'm Odell."

"Odell, I'm Bob McAlister," Bob said, forcing himself to shake the dust-caked hand the man offered. "What are you doing in the middle of the highway? How can I help you?"

Odell explained that two friends of his, a mother and her thirty-year-old daughter, were ill. They lived in a shanty in one of the poorest parts of town; they had absolutely nothing and were too weak to get any food for themselves. So Odell was wheeling his way to a rescue mission he knew would wrap up some hot food for the women. Then he was going to take the meal back to his friends. Sort of a personal Meals on Wheels.

When Bob calculated Odell's proposed journey, he realized this man was talking about a seven-mile round trip.

"Odell, I'll take you to the mission," he said. "Let's get you in the car."

Bob helped the man into the passenger seat, pushing aside his briefcase as he lifted Odell's useless legs. Then, after wrestling the wheelchair into the trunk, Bob drove to the mission, got the food, then took it and Odell to the sick women's house.

Bob McAlister had written speeches about poverty, reported news stories about indigent families, given to charities. But he had never seen poverty up close. He had never smelled it.

All of this is within a stone's throw of the luxury of the State House and historic downtown churches, he thought. *How could I have been so near, yet so far away?*

And he had never met anyone like Odell. He had seen people give out of their excess; he had never seen anyone give like Odell. This frail old man was giving everything he had—two arms and a wheelchair—to help those whose need was greater.

Later, on his way home and for weeks to come, Bob couldn't get the question out of his mind: *When was the last time you gave everything you had to anybody?*

As he read his Bible, verses popped out at him in the apostle Paul's first letter to the Corinthians: "God has chosen the foolish things of the world to shame the wise, and the weak to shame the strong. God has chosen the base and the despised of the world. God has chosen the things that are not to shame the things that are, so that no man should boast before God."[2]

For days after meeting Odell, Bob felt paralyzed. Paralyzed with a burden for the man and his suffering, for the hungry, sick women, for the pain of poverty and need. Bob was seeing the heart of God's love for the unloved.

Soon after that, he signed on as a volunteer at Providence Home, a Christian shelter for the homeless. His advertising agency even did some free fund-raising and publicity. Then one of the social workers at the mission called Bob with a request he never would have anticipated: Could he go to visit a man on death row? The man, a Black Muslim named Wardell Patterson, needed a friend.

Bob had never set foot inside a prison, but he agreed to go.

As Bob entered death row the first time, he was terrified. It was located in the old Central Correctional Institution (CCI) near the river in downtown Columbia. Legend had it that General Sherman had quartered his horses there during the Civil War, and as Bob saw the long, dark row of stinking cells, he thought, *This is worse than a stable. You can't treat men worse than horses. Even if they are murderers, they are still human beings.*

Bob visited Wardell for months, and their friendship grew. Soon other inmates began to ask if Bob could visit them too.[3] Because he had known the corrections commissioner from his days as a reporter, Bob was able to make arrangements to get through the usual security barriers so he could regularly visit death row. Before long he was there every Friday night.

By now, Bob realized that he had found his true calling. For it was on death row, among men convicted of the most heinous crimes, that for the first time in his life he felt wholly alive. God was using him, giving him the power to love these powerless, condemned men with the love of Christ.

In his new prison sphere, he soon met Ernie Pannal, then Prison Fellowship's area director in South Carolina. And Ernie got both Bob and Carol involved in a weekly PF Bible study with some hundred inmates at nearby Kirkland Correctional Institution.

Through that Thursday evening group, Carol's Christianity caught fire. The faith of those imprisoned men seemed more real: an all-or-nothing choice rather than a social convention reserved for a proper Sunday morning pew.

"Without Odell," Bob says, "I don't know that we would have ever learned the heart of God for the suffering and the oppressed. I wonder if anything further would really have happened in our Christian lives."

One Friday night in October 1985 after Bob had visited a few of his "regulars" on the row, he was getting ready to leave the prison. It had been a long day, a long night, and Carol was waiting for him at home. Before he left, however, he stopped at one more cell.

By now Bob was accustomed to some horrible sights, but he had never seen anything like this. The inmate was sitting on the floor of his cell, looking like a pale, dirty shrimp. The concrete floor was strewn with papers, half-eaten sandwiches, toilet paper, old copies of *Playboy* and *Penthouse*. The cell stank. The man stank too, his long, dirty, blond hair and beard matted and greasy. His face was chalk-colored, like a rubber mask, like a dead person. And all over his cell, all over the man, crawled dozens of cockroaches. He didn't even move as they swarmed over his shoulders, his hair, his legs.

Bob had met this inmate and exchanged a few words with him. His name was Rusty Woomer.

Seeing the state he was in, Bob spoke to him—called his name. No response. It seemed like the man was trying to talk, but something wouldn't let him.

Bob was a Southern Baptist. He didn't often think in terms of demonic warfare or the physical presence of evil. But that night he knew he was facing it. Satan had a hold on this man.

So Bob called on the name of Jesus to cast out the evil and death in that cell. Then he said, "Rusty, just say the name, 'Jesus.' Call on Jesus."

Nothing happened for several minutes. Then the man's lips moved slowly. "Jesus," he whispered. "Jesus. Jesus!"

Bob gripped the bars of the cell so hard his hands hurt.

"Rusty," he called again. "Look around you, son. Look at what you are living in!"

To his amazement the man slowly sat up straighter, his eyes actually focusing on the floor and walls of his cell. They widened as he saw the roaches.

"Your cell is filthy and so are you," Bob said gently. "The roaches have taken over, and you're spiritually a dead man, son. Jesus can give you something better. Don't you want to pray to give your life to Him instead?"

Rusty nodded, his eyes glistening, then streaming with tears—the first tears he had wept in fifteen years—as his heart cracked open. He bowed his head like he remembered from his childhood.

"Jesus," Rusty prayed, "I've hurt a lot of people. Ain't no way that I deserve You to hear me. But I'm tired and I'm sick and I'm lonely. Please forgive me, Jesus, for everything I've done. I don't know much about You, but I'm willin' to learn, and I thank You for listenin' to me."[4]

As Bob left CCI that evening, he hurried through the night to his car, chased through the dark by a sense of terror he had never before experienced. Once again he prayed in the name of Jesus, and whatever the feeling was, it left him.

On Monday, Bob could wait no longer. Had Friday been a dream? Had he imagined Rusty Woomer's transformation? The sense of struggle not with flesh and blood, but with powers unseen? After work he drove to the prison and made his way to death row.

The guards let him in, good-naturedly joking, "We're gonna have to get you a cell of your own if you're going to spend so much time here."

Bob laughed with them, but once he was cleared to enter, he almost sprinted down the long row to Rusty's cell.

Once there he stopped short, breathing hard. He couldn't believe his eyes.

The walls were clean, bare, and glistening from the scrubbing they had received. The smell of disinfectant still hung in the air. The garbage was gone, the bed was made, and the roaches were history.

Rusty stood smiling and erect, enjoying his surprise.

"How do you like it?" he asked. "I spent all weekend cleaning out my cell 'cause I figured that's what Jesus wanted me to do."

"Rusty," said Bob, his heart swelling, "it may have taken you all weekend to clean your cell, but it took Jesus only an instant to clean your life."

And thus began a relationship that would last the rest of Rusty Woomer's life on earth—and change Bob McAlister's life forever.

Rusty now had no hesitation about accepting responsibility for his horrible crimes. He wept over the pain he had caused others. He knew that Christ's blood was sufficient to cleanse even the vilest sinner, but he could not undo the death and pain he had caused. He wrote letters to the families of his victims, asking their forgiveness—and was not surprised when he did not receive it.

Though he was only five years younger than Bob, Rusty called him "Paps." Carol was "Moms." Rusty loved to listen to Bob read the Scriptures aloud. In his concrete world, the fresh breezes of Psalm 104 sent his heart soaring.

> Bless the Lord, O my soul!
> O Lord my God, Thou art very great;
> Thou art clothed with splendor and majesty . . .
> He makes the clouds His chariot;
> He walks upon the wings of the wind;
> He makes the winds His messengers . . .
> He sends forth springs in the valleys . . .
> Beside them the birds of the heavens dwell;
> They lift up their voice among the branches. . . .
> O Lord, how many are Thy works!
> In wisdom Thou hast made them all;
> The earth is full of Thy possessions. . . .
> They all wait for Thee. . . .
> Let the glory of the Lord endure forever. . . .
> I will sing to the Lord as long as I live;
> I will sing praise to my God while I have my being.

He would lie on his narrow bed dreaming of the hawks circling in the skies of his childhood, thinking of the clouds, the wind, and the springs flowing through the West Virginia valleys. *If only I had known the Lord then,* he mused. *If only I could have lived to serve Him on the outside. If only I had not caused such hurt to innocent people.*

Seeing his remorse, Bob could only take Rusty deeper and deeper into the Scriptures, assuring him of God's forgiveness and exhorting him to make peace the best he could with anyone he had not yet forgiven. Rusty thought about the man he had hated for so many years—and he asked God to enable him to forgive his father.

In 1986 Governor Carroll Campbell approached Bob about taking a position as one of his senior aides. Bob's company, Coulter-McAlister, Inc., was doing well, but Bob was ready again for the challenge of politics. He no longer had any illusions about how much the political world could really accomplish, but he wanted to help the governor. He took the job.

Governor Campbell knew about Bob's involvement on death row when he hired him. Still, with the political and public attention on crime, Bob was fearful that this aspect of his private life might someday hurt the governor politically.

When he brought it up one day, Governor Campbell assured him, "McAlister, if I couldn't understand that you're doing what you feel God wants you to do, then I don't deserve to be sitting in this chair." Not every politician would be so gracious, Bob knew.

Then in 1988, after the election of George H. W. Bush to the presidency of the United States, the invitation of a lifetime came to Bob. The president needed a top-notch speechwriter on his White House team. Was Bob interested?

Yes, he was. But when Bob and Carol prayed and talked about it, they couldn't imagine packing up and moving to Washington. The frenetic and costly lifestyle did not appeal to them at all, and their daughter, Denise, was in the midst of her senior year of high school. Also, it would mean leaving the men on death row.

Bob thought about Andy, who had developed making birthday cards into an art form. Every year he sent Carol an elaborate birthday card, signed with Bob's name, because he was afraid Bob would forget. Or Elmo, who took rags and leftover material and made beautiful pillows, embroidering them with designs and names. The McAlisters had three of the pillows. Or Mad Dog Mullins, whose pet cockatiel rode contentedly on his shoulder—except when Bob came to death row. As soon as the guards cleared Bob onto the cellblock, the cockatiel would swoop for him and perch on his shoulder, cocking its head this way and that while Bob talked with the inmates. With his cotton pinstriped shirts, khaki pants, conservative striped ties, and the elaborately feathered bird draped next to his head,

Bob looked like a cross between a deranged Republican and a Las Vegas showgirl.

Then there was Sly, who had made Carol a wonderful heart-shaped jewelry box out of cardboard and felt paper. Or Ron, a severely retarded man who had taught himself to draw beautiful pictures. Or Fred, the mature Christian to whom Bob himself would occasionally go for advice.

He thought about Christmas the previous year, when the death-row inmates had learned in a worship service about a family in a town nearby who would have no Christmas—there were three little children and the father was out of work. The men had taken up a collection from the canned goods and clothing they received from home, the only time during the year they were allowed this luxury. Then they had packed the food and clothing into three paper bags and asked Bob and the other prison volunteers to take the supplies to this family and wish them a Merry Christmas on behalf of death row! Rusty had led the way in giving.

Rusty. Going to Washington would mean leaving Rusty. President George Bush could find plenty of others to help him, but Rusty Woomer could not.

So in the end, Bob and Carol stayed in Columbia.

By early 1989, Rusty had been on death row for ten years and his appeals had run out. In March, the U.S. Supreme Court let stand his conviction and death sentence, and his execution date was set for June 16.

Three days before his scheduled execution Rusty was moved from his cell at CCI to South Carolina's new Capital Punishment Facility, what everyone called the Death House. His few possessions were put into storage. He was photographed and fingerprinted in a final check to make sure officials were executing the right man. And he settled his funeral arrangements, asking to be buried next to his mother.

While the execution team ran through daily training drills and the electricians tested and retested the new wiring, Rusty spent his final days with Bob McAlister.

When Bob asked if he could interview Rusty on videotape, he agreed. Bob hoped the weight of a man's perspective days before he was to die would be riveting. "Maybe I can make this into something to show to kids in school," he said. "A warning."

"What would you say to kids about drugs, Rusty?" asked Bob.

"What about drugs? Well, 'just say no' isn't enough—because the human side of us isn't strong enough to do that. We need the power of God that comes through Jesus to say no to evil and to do what is right. That's the bottom line. And we don't get very long in our lives to make sure about where we're gonna spend eternity."

"Rusty," Bob asked, "what will your thoughts be when they strap you in that chair?"

"The human side of me is scared to sit down and be electrocuted," Rusty said slowly. "They tell me I won't feel nothin'. But I've stuck my finger in the socket and it hurt plenty. So even if it hurts for a millionth of a second, that's frightening. But I'm gonna be holdin' Jesus' hand. Long as He's my partner, what more can I say?

"After all, there's no way I'm gonna lose. If they execute me, I'll be in heaven. If they don't, I'll never be the same. God's made it impossible for me not to praise and love Him and tell people about what He's done."

Rusty also used the video to gently chide a friend. "You are out on the streets," he told her. "But I am the one that's free. I'm behind bars, but I can lay down at night and sleep. You can't."

How many people are like that? Bob thought. *Free on the outside, but tossing on their beds, unable to sleep, prisoners of a guilty conscience.*

Though Rusty appealed for clemency to the governor, Carroll Campbell's office issued a statement saying that the governor would "not intervene in the workings of the judicial process."

Bob McAlister was in an agonizing position. As the governor's director of communications, he was usually the one who presided over such press statements. In this particular instance, however, he had removed himself from the process. He had worked shoulder to shoulder with Carroll Campbell for years; he loved and respected the man. Now his friend and boss was refusing to exercise his power to spare the life of Bob's friend and "son" in prison.

But to Bob's relief, the South Carolina press handled his situation with grace and sensitivity. He had taken two weeks of vacation leave to be with Rusty during his final days and to spare the governor any potential embarrassment. The media seemed to respect the integrity with which Bob was handling his position—and they seemed to respect the governor for respecting Bob.

On the night before the scheduled execution, Rusty received an unexpected visitor: South Carolina's top prison official, Corrections Commissioner Parker Evatt, a United Methodist firmly opposed to capital punishment but required by his job to uphold and enforce it.

"If I'm going to kill somebody, I've got to know who I'm killing," Evatt once told reporters bluntly. "I couldn't do this if I didn't meet him first."[5]

So Parker Evatt met with Rusty. The two men shared a final communion service together, along with Bob McAlister; Zeb Osbourne, head of a local Christian prison ministry who had become one of Bob's closest friends; J. Michael Brown, the prison chaplain; and Frankie San, a Christian man who had devoted his entire life to ministry in the prison. The men prayed together, swallowing grape juice portioned out in small plastic cups.

After the others left, Bob stayed on with Rusty. About two in the morning Rusty asked Bob to read the Bible. Bob opened to John 14 and began reading, "Let not your heart be troubled . . ." When he was halfway through the chapter, he heard a snore. Then another.

Rusty! That rascal was sleeping! By that point, Bob was totally broken. His friend would be dead in twenty-three hours. But Rusty's peace and tranquillity were so certain that he was able to sleep. Bob tucked a blanket around him and whispered good night. Then, at three in the morning, he walked to his car and drove to a Denny's to have breakfast, the first real meal he'd had in days. Rusty's peace had given him peace.

The next morning, Bob and Rusty worked on what Rusty would say as his final statement:

"So many things are on my heart tonight that I cannot find the words for. But I want to say some things the best way I know how to some people. I have written letters to the families of my victims asking them for forgiveness. I understand if they can't forgive me. I have lived with my actions all of these years. I would die a hundred times over if it would put one breath of life back into them. I have prayed for the families over and over again and my last prayer before my death tonight will be for them. . . .

"I want to tell Governor Campbell that I love him too. I appreciate him and I am sorry that I put such a load on him by asking him to spare my life. No man should have to bear that kind of load.

"I want to thank all the prison officials from Mr. Evatt on down for their kindness to me and my family. You have made it easier.

"I want to tell everybody that I am fine. I have never known peace like I have known it in my final days on earth. I know some people say I got jailhouse religion and they are right. I turned to Jesus in prison when I had no place else to turn. Words cannot express what He did for me but He knows and that's all that counts. . . ."

But Rusty never had to make that particular statement. As he and Bob sat in the death cell thirteen hours before the execution, the phone rang. It was Rusty's attorney, Gaston Fairey. The Supreme Court had granted a stay of execution.

Rusty asked a few questions, then hung up the phone. Bob stared at him as Rusty stared back. Reprieve! Bob glanced at his watch, then jotted the time on Rusty's laboriously typed final statement.

"12:17 P.M., 6/16/89," Bob wrote. "Praise be to God!"

Later when he got home and fell exhausted into his bed, he took his watch off and noticed it had stopped. At 12:17 P.M. The watch never worked again.

In spite of the reprieve, both men knew that Rusty's final journey was just a matter of time. But the stay gave Rusty a new urgency to share his faith, to seek to live for Jesus only.

"I want to live," he told Bob fervently. "And even if my sentence was somehow commuted to life in prison, Jesus is here just the same as He is on the outside. I can serve Him here."

But the reprieve also gave Rusty an incredible gift, one he knew he did not deserve.

That summer of 1989 a letter made its way through the prison security checks to Rusty's cell. He eagerly picked up the plain envelope—then trembled when he saw the return address. It was from Lee Hewitt, the younger brother of Della Summers, the woman whose murder Rusty would die for.

"For years I hated you with all my heart. I could have blown your brains out for what you did to my sister. I only regretted you were in prison where I couldn't get to you.

"But I've spent time in jail myself—fifty-six different times over the years. I felt like a failure. But then I became a Christian. And the more I learned about being a Christian, the more I knew I had to forgive you. I didn't want to. But it got to where I couldn't even pray the Lord's prayer—'forgive us our trespasses as we forgive those who trespass against us.'

"It made me so mad—now I had to forgive you. Now the ball was in my court. I've prayed about it, and God has done a miracle in my heart. I forgive you. We are brothers in Christ. I love you."

Rusty looked up, blinded by tears and the radiance of God's goodness to him. Forgiven! Not only by Christ, but now by the man he had offended most here on earth. It seemed the greatest blessing he could have ever hoped for.

Rusty wrote back to Lee, tears dotting the penciled pages of his letter. Watching, Bob was humbled by the enormity of Lee's obedience to Christ and overwhelmed by the absolute joy Lee's gift of forgiveness sealed in Rusty's heart.

Months passed. When he wasn't visiting death row, Bob traveled with the governor, wrote speeches, put in long days at work. He led a Wednesday morning Bible study at the State House and a Thursday evening group at his church, and he sometimes went fishing on Saturdays. He and Carol looked at wallpaper samples and priced countertops, thinking about re-decorating their kitchen.

Meanwhile, Rusty finished out the year in his daily routine. By now all the condemned inmates had been moved to the new death row facility, so their physical conditions were much improved. Rusty's family never visited, but when other men's wives and families came, they almost always stopped to talk with him. One little girl, Patrice, was his favorite. In fact, her mother, Wanda, claimed that Rusty was the reason Patrice was even alive.[6]

Several years earlier, during a visit to the row, Wanda had tearfully confided to Rusty that she was pregnant, out of wedlock, and that the father of the child refused to acknowledge the baby was his. She had made an appointment to have an abortion.

"Don't do it," he pleaded. "Life is precious. I don't have no money, but I'll do whatever I can to support that child. If you need a name for the baby, it can have my name. I'll be its father. Just let it live."

Now Patrice was a beautiful little toddler with big, dark eyes and a special smile just for Rusty. *The man who took lives has saved a life,* Bob thought as he watched Rusty and Patrice. *That's the difference Jesus makes.*

Rusty had no money, but he was rich in one thing: time. Until his time ran out, of course. So he spent hours reading the Scriptures, visualizing the glories of God in nature and the love of God for him. "I will sing to the Lord as long as I live; I will sing praise to my God while I have my being."

Early in 1990, the Supreme Court again decided not to hear Rusty's appeal. And once again an execution date was set: Friday, April 27, 1990, 1:00 A.M.

Good Friday, April 13, 1990

Rusty lay in his cell thinking about Jesus: He had been executed. He had gone through it all—arrest, trial, sentencing, death penalty. Except He was innocent.[7]

Jesus went to His death for me already, Rusty thought. *And He'll be with me when I go to mine.*

Easter Sunday, April 15, 1990

"I am the resurrection and the life; he who believes in Me shall live even if he dies."[8] *What an amazing thought,* Rusty mused. *A promise to me.*

Later that afternoon an unexpected gift arrived: a bright basket filled with chocolates, candies, and cookies. Rusty sat for fifteen minutes, picking each piece up, looking it over, putting it gently back in the basket.

"Paps," he said to Bob, who had brought in the gift, "I ain't never had an Easter basket before in my whole life."

The basket was from Lee and Barbara Hewitt. Lee had set Rusty free with his letter of forgiveness the previous summer. Now he wanted to visit, but he and his wife had not been able to get into the prison. So they had asked Bob to take their gift basket in to Rusty.

Before the week was over, Bob got special permission to bring the Hewitts and Rusty together in a prison conference room.

Initially there was an awkward moment as they sat down across from one another at the table. Bob sat in a corner, chewing a blue pen and taking notes so he could remember later what everyone had said. Lee slid a Good News "God Loves You" Bible across the table to Rusty.

"It's hard to know what to say," Lee began, "except I wish we could have met you long ago."

Rusty slid a small devotional book across the table to Lee and listened while he told about giving his life to Christ after years in and out of prisons.

Then Rusty told about his years on death row, how he had been spiritually dead even though his body was alive, and how Jesus had changed his life.

"You know," Rusty said slowly, "when I first accepted the Lord, I thought everything would change right then and that there would be no more hurt. Then when Mama died, I blamed God, and I asked Him why I done all these things. Then my brother died and my uncle died. But Bob here just kept me from giving up. . . . When I realized Mama was in heaven, I just said, 'When I get there, I'm goin' fishin' with Mama again.'"

Then Rusty turned to Lee, his voice thick with tears, but his blue eyes shining. "Your forgiving me has done more for me than anybody's ever done. I know I done these things. That day [of the murders] is like two minutes to me—just there and gone—but even with God's and people's forgiveness, I've never gotten the hurt out of my heart. I prayed and prayed. When I got that letter from you, I can't explain how I felt. Is my faith strong enough to do what you're doin'? I'd like to think I could, but I'm not sure."

"I can do nothing without Jesus," said Lee. "I have to draw from Him. I see Him hanging on the cross, saying, 'Father, forgive them.'"

"It's amazing, ain't it?" said Rusty, thinking of his Easter morning reflections. "I believe with all my heart in the Bible. Sometimes I'd like to see an ocean partin'. But God's already given me miracles I'd never dreamed of."

"What God can do, people can't comprehend," Lee nodded. "I don't have hurt or anger. I wouldn't want to walk around like that for nothin'. I have no anger because God took it and done away with it and threw it into the sea of forgetfulness. He loves you, and He don't want to remember.

"The only time He knows about it is when we bring it up. There's no words to describe hate. It's an ugly feeling. If you don't forgive, you don't deserve Jesus as your Lord. It took almost four years—now I hope the rest of my family can change. This is the way it's gonna be, no matter if my family talks to me or not." Lee's family had publicly castigated him and cut him off for forgiving Rusty, but he had chosen to obey God rather than please his family.

Rusty nodded. "Trust in God is the only way I've kept sane in this place," he told Lee. "If they took me over there to the chair right now, I could do it. What you have done has made God's Word complete to me."[9]

And Bob thought, *Both of these men have learned that God's will is the ultimate reality.*

By now their time was up and the guards motioned that Lee and Barbara and Bob had to leave. Before they did, however, Rusty and Lee held hands and prayed together in the name of the Lord Jesus, who had saved them, forgiven them, and made them brothers in Him. They knew they would not see each other again this side of heaven.

Tuesday, April 24, 1990

At one o'clock that morning the officers came to get Rusty, giving him time to say good-bye to the other inmates on the row.

South Carolina's Capital Punishment Facility is a small, clinical structure cordoned off into a maze of rooms, each with a strategic function in the execution process. The inmate is brought from death row and kept in one of four narrow, blue-barred cells, each about six by ten feet, with nothing but a cot and a stainless steel washbasin and toilet. Each cell has a narrow, vertical window, four inches wide by four feet high. More bars separate the cell area from a central hall and a guard center.

At the center of the small building sits the electric chair itself, facing a small connected room with two rows of chairs. Here the witnesses view the condemned man's final moments.

As the sun rose on the morning of April 24, Rusty found that even in this grim house of death God had not neglected to give him a reminder of His grace. In the triple spiral of razor wire coiled over the fence that Rusty could see outside his cell was a bird's nest.

If the nest had been inches to the right or to the left, Rusty would not have been able to see it. But there it was, dead center in the view from his narrow window. And as he watched throughout the morning, he saw a mother bird swooping in and out of that razor-nest, threading her way between the deadly wires with precision, tending her eggs.

When Bob arrived, Rusty took hold of his shoulders and pointed him toward the nest. Then the two men smiled at each other. No matter how horrible the next few days would be, God would provide for them. And in that simple bunch of twigs and grass He had sent a sign.[10]

"When Noah was riding out the floodwaters, God sent him a bird with an olive branch as a sign of hope," Bob told Rusty. "When Jesus was baptized, the Holy Spirit appeared in the form of a dove. And now here's this crazy bird with her eggs, right outside your death house window! God's sign of new life!"

Through the rest of that day and the next, Bob and Rusty read the Bible, prayed, and talked about the hills of West Virginia and the fishing holes of heaven. Also, a phone line had been installed, so Rusty was free to talk with anyone he could reach.

Thursday, April 26, 1990

His last sunrise.

Rusty watched the mother bird tend her nest. She was warm gray with a black mask, and the officers guarding Rusty were frustrated; they hadn't been able to figure out what kind of bird she was. This morning one guard had brought in a bird book. Rusty could feel their urgency: got to find out what kind of bird this is before Rusty goes.

His last lunch.

At this time a year ago the Supreme Court had come through for Rusty. No calls from the court today. The governor's office announced his refusal to intervene.

His last interview.

Rusty talked about Christ with a reporter from the *Charlotte Observer.*
His last visit.

At 4:00 P.M. Rusty's family came to say good-bye, and Rusty demonstrated the forgiveness he had long ago given his father. His dad's face looked like mountain granite as they stood in a circle for a final farewell.

"I wish y'all would stop living so far apart," Rusty told his family. "And

I wish y'all would fight less and hug more." Then he commanded them, "Bow your heads. We're gonna pray.

"Our precious Lord, I'm not cryin' 'cause I feel bad, but 'cause I'm happy. I'm gonna be with You, and You've done everything for me far beyond what I ever deserve. I ask You to watch over my family and take the hurt and sadness from their hearts. I pray that all this hurt and sufferin' will be gone, and I just praise You with all of my heart."

With that, Rusty lifted his head and broke the silence by gently patting his father's bulging stomach. "You need to lose some of that, Pappy!" he joked. And then they left.

His last meal.

Rusty could order anything he wanted—his first non-prison-prepared meal in more than a decade. A pizza with everything but anchovies. Rusty couldn't eat, but he had gotten it to make sure the guards would. But they weren't hungry either.

As the evening ticked by, Rusty drank several cups of coffee.

"Normally this would keep me up," he said dryly. "Tonight I guess it don't matter."

He returned a phone call from a girl who had called earlier—Patti, the friend of a friend.

"Oh, Patti's out," her roommate told Rusty, obviously unaware of his situation. "She'll be back about one in the morning. Can you call back then?"

"No," Rusty drawled, grinning at Bob. "I'm afraid that'll be a little too late for me."

As the sun's rays angled lower and lower, the light on the bird nest fading, Rusty watched in silence. A golden sense of peace washed over Bob. Rusty felt it too.

"Ya know, Paps," he said finally. "I feel real happy. I just want to go on home now. I don't want to stay here; things are just too bad down here. I just feel real peaceful, and I know Mama's waitin' on me up there."

At 11:00 P.M. the execution team arrived, checking their equipment one final time. At 11:45 officers came to get Rusty and took him to the preparation room.

A final shower. Clean prison clothes.

Bob sat on the floor at Rusty's feet while a prison barber shaved his head and right leg in preparation for the application of the conducting gel that would help make a strong connection for the electric charge. The preparation room was filled with about a dozen officers and several corrections officials.

"Paps," Rusty said, "read me the Bible one last time."

As the electric razor buzzed, Bob turned to Revelation 21.

"And He shall wipe away every tear from their eyes; and there shall no longer be any death; there shall no longer be any mourning, or crying, or pain—" A clump of Rusty's blond hair felt onto Bob's open Bible.

Bob looked up. And when he saw Rusty's half-shaven head and his face filled with a heavenly expression—his eyes fixed not on the dark efficiency of the death house, but on the new heaven of Revelation—at that moment, Bob's emotions got away from him. It was the only time he lost his composure in front of Rusty. He handed his Bible to Chaplain Brown, who read the rest of the chapter.

At 12:40 A.M. George Martin arrived. Not in his official role as warden—that would come later. His stomach tense, George sat down beside Rusty on the cot, patting him on the shoulder.

"Are you doing all right?" he asked.

Rusty smiled at him. "Yep. Like I told you before, I have been taken care of, and I am gonna be all right. But what about you?"

George hadn't expected that a man who was to die in twenty minutes would have others on his mind. "I'm okay," he said.

Rusty's bald head, glistening as the light reflected off the conducting gel, made a surreal image as he talked with the warden. It was a hideous sight, and Bob thought about his own weaknesses during the past weeks, compared to Rusty's strength. How he would wake up in the middle of the night in a cold sweat, sobbing. And how Carol would just snuggle up close to him and hold him without saying a word. But somehow his fears and trembling vanished when he was with Rusty. The worst times were away from Rusty, not with him.

Rusty had never broken down during those last days. His sense of the imminent reality of seeing his Lord seemed to obliterate almost everything else. Bob couldn't help but think, *If only that reality were as vivid for all of us, the Body of Christ would be transformed—and the world as well.*

The only thing that really hurt Rusty was seeing the pain and anguish of his friends. "I know this has been about as tough on you as it has on me," Rusty was telling Warden Martin earnestly. "But don't let it ruin you. These guys in this prison need you here too bad for you to leave them because of this."

George Martin smiled at Rusty. "All right, son," he said and left the room.[11]

Fifteen minutes later he returned, this time with the death warrant in his hand, the paper that signified the will of the state in carrying out the sentence of death on one Ronald Raymond Woomer.

"Rusty, it is time to go," George Martin said.

"Let's go," Rusty replied.

The officers escorted him to the execution chamber, just thirty paces away, shuffling because they were so tightly bunched. Rusty was shackled with steel arm restraints. A line of officers stood stiffly as he passed out of the guard area. Bob, following, saw tears in some of their eyes.

Earlier, Bob and Rusty had agreed not to say good-bye. Though they had always ended their visits together with a brotherly hug, this time it would seem too final. So Bob put his hand on his friend's shoulder, looked into his eyes, and said, "Look to Jesus, Rusty."

Throughout their friendship, Bob had always felt Rusty needed him, and he had given everything he had. But now, he realized, there was nothing more he could give. Rusty had already moved beyond Bob's reach. Now it was all between Rusty and Jesus.

The group of officers, Rusty, Warden Martin, Chaplain Mike Brown, and Bob entered the death chamber. The official witnesses sat in two short rows facing the electric chair. In the room adjacent to the death chamber, three executioners waited beside buttons recessed into the wall; the electrical current would alternate between the three buttons, so no one would know which one had actually activated the current.

The warden took the microphone nestled in an alcove in the wall that also held three telephones: open lines to the deputy commissioner's office, the attorney general's office, the governor's office.

They strapped Rusty into the chair, buckling the thick leather restraining straps over his chest, legs, and arms.

"Do you have a final statement?" Warden Martin asked, walking toward him with the microphone.

Rusty had not prepared a formal statement this time. Since his first trip to the death house, he had read about how Jesus told His followers not to worry about what they would say, for the Holy Spirit would give them the utterance they needed.[12]

He thought for a moment, then spoke simply. "I'm sorry," he said. "I claim Jesus Christ as my Savior. My only wish is that everyone in the world could feel the love I have felt from Him."

The electrician fitted Rusty's head into a leather beanie connected to the main, thick electrode that descended from the ceiling like an ugly stalactite. Another electrode was strapped to his leg. They placed a leather strap under Rusty's nose, which pulled his head back into the cap. Then they fastened the copper headpiece over Rusty's head and dropped the leather death hood over his face.

Darkness.

Rusty could hear the warden's voice making the final phone check to the deputy commissioner to see if the governor or the Supreme Court had intervened. It sounded very far away. He could hear an officer escorting Bob out—a few footsteps, and a door closing. He could sense the executioners nervously waiting for the warden's order to hit the triggers that would activate the killing current.

The seconds ticked by. Darkness under the hood.

Then the jolt of two thousand volts.

Light.

A FEW DAYS BEFORE HE WAS ELECTROCUTED, Rusty Woomer talked about fear.

It was not the terror of imminent death. It was the fear of the Lord: the immanence of God.

I saw this in Rusty when I visited him on Easter Sunday, just eleven days before he died. And Bob McAlister, who knew Rusty best, was there to the very end. He saw his friend's eyes fill with tears when he thought about that quick step from the shadowed chair of death into the light.

In his simple way, Rusty spoke to Bob of the holy awe he was experiencing: "I think of His radiance, His power, His love. Doesn't it scare you that someone loves you enough that He can forgive you for anything that you do? It scares me sometimes. He is something that we have not got any idea what it is going to be like when we meet . . . His love is so strong that it might hurt us when we meet Him . . ."

Few of us will know the mystery that for Rusty was solved by the state of South Carolina: the exact time of our own death. Rusty was not caught unaware, unrepentant, distracted by the things of this world and distant from his Lord.

But we must be prepared, living every day as if we'll see Jesus at midnight. Or sooner. Rusty's final perspective is one the church at large must have if we are to truly be the Body, the holy people of God, in these times of both catastrophe and opportunity.

Do we really know the radiance of the Lord? His glory? His astounding love? Do we know that we are but a breath away from union with Him?

We live in a world where many have lost the holy dread of the Creator—and exchanged His truth for a lie. How, then, should we live against the world . . . yet for the world?

That's what we'll look at in the second and third sections of this book.

PART 2

THE CHURCH AGAINST THE WORLD

13
WHAT IS TRUTH?

THE LEGEND SAYS that the pool is in the Alps, somewhere between Italy and Switzerland. It is hidden by early mists in the morning, ringed by mountain peaks, inaccessible except by a narrow footpath that forges a slender passage into the high valley.

Those few who have discovered it over the centuries find also a tall figure draped in the toga of imperial Rome. He kneels beside the waters. Dipping his hands into the liquid ice bubbling up from underground springs, he rubs one hand over the other.

"I am innocent," he mumbles over and over, dipping and cleansing and wringing as he has for two thousand years. "I am innocent of the blood of this just person."

THE REALITY BEGAN early one morning in first-century Jerusalem when an aide awakened Pontius Pilate.

"They're causing trouble again," the soldier told the Roman governor.

This time it was the Jewish leadership, elders and scribes of the synagogue. The chief priest himself was there. They were gathered outside the Praetorium, holding torches aloft in the predawn darkness, and shouting for Pilate. They had a prisoner with them. They were screaming about treason and blasphemy.

Pontius Pilate groaned. He hated Jerusalem. He hated the Jews. Normally he governed Judea and Samaria from his palace in Caesarea by the sea, far from this foul city and its feverish Jews. But his superiors required him to come to Jerusalem for feast days and other occasions that might breed turmoil. The Jews had been ruled by the Romans for decades, but that didn't mean they were docile.

In Jerusalem, Pilate and his entourage made their headquarters in the Praetorium, a grand palace built by Herod the Great. Despite the splendid setting, the air felt old and Pilate felt trapped. He tossed in his elegant bed; his wife complained of headaches and dark dreams in the walled city.

Pilate usually addressed the Jews from a distance. He was a practical man, and the moldy mysteries of their ancient faith irritated him to no end. Their contempt for things Roman didn't help, nor did their stubborn refusal to honor the image of Caesar, their obsessive observances of religious rules, their endless prayers and sacrifices and incense floating in clouds above their temple courtyard, their stiff-necked allegiance to an unseen God whose name they would not even say.

The Romans had a pantheon of colorful gods, one for every situation. But this solemn theocracy, this business about a king of the universe who demanded absolute allegiance, was unfathomable and offensive.

A year or so earlier Pilate's disdain had slipped out of control. The Jews had protested his use of funds from their temple treasury to finance the construction of an aqueduct. Their accusations were an affront to Pilate. After all, as procurator he controlled the temple and its funds, and the aqueduct brought water to the city in which they lived. But in their usual illogical fervor they had accused him of sacrilege. Thousands of motley Jews—trooping in from all over the province for one of their strange festivals—had demonstrated outside the palace, shouting and shuffling dust.

Pilate had decided to teach them a lesson.

He ordered a special detachment of city troops to sweep in and slaughter those who had led the revolt. Then they ascended the steps of the temple and cut the throats of Jews who had just offered their lambs for sacrifice. Pilate had relished the grim justice of the bodies of men and beasts heaped together, their blood mingling on the holy altar.

The massacre became the talk of Judea. Pilate even heard about it from Sejanus, his old friend and mentor. "Good work," Sejanus had said. "Those Jews need to know just who is sovereign."

Until recently, Pilate had envied Sejanus as much as he admired him. The tribune had risen decisively through the Roman ranks, and Pilate had clung to the tails of his toga. Last year when the seventy-year-old Emperor Tiberius left Rome for a rest at his residence in Capri, he had placed most of the government affairs in the hands of Sejanus.

Sejanus, along with his supporters like Pilate, had been inducted into an elite group known as "friends of Caesar." The semiofficial title carried power and prestige. Pilate thrilled every time someone called him Caesar's friend and thanked the stars for Sejanus's sponsorship.

Until recently. Now, the more distance from Sejanus, the better. His ambition had driven him too far.

Sejanus had declared it his goal to "exterminate the nation [of Jews]." He had expelled every Jew from Italy.[1] Counting on allies like Pilate, he hoped to flush the race from the eastern provinces as well as Palestine. In the process he would consolidate his power among the military, which also had no great affection for the Jews. Then, in the end, he could push the elderly Tiberius aside and become emperor himself.

A bold plan. But the Roman legion of Syria had refused to honor Sejanus's leadership. Loyal forces alerted Tiberius, and the emperor returned to Rome. Sejanus and his key supporters were tried and executed. Case closed.

When the news reached Palestine, Pilate knew he would survive only if he followed the emperor's leadership to the letter. His link to the traitor was well known. But one of the first of Tiberius's orders was the worst. The directive announced a new Roman policy regarding the Jews: tolerance. Tiberius would be watching for any infractions. He wanted no more unrest in the provinces.

So, grinding his teeth, Pilate had extended an olive branch to the Jews. He had ceased minting the official Roman coins that had angered the Jews ever since Roman occupation. Gone was the elaborate image of the emperor, which they said violated one of their commandments. Pilate replaced it with a plain, ordinary coin.

But now here they were again, outside his palace, disturbing the peace, milling and shouting and beating their breasts like madmen. He would just love to set his troops loose on them and shut them up for good.

Pilate cursed and took his time. He splashed his puffy face with cool water and called for his barber. A slave draped Pilate's toga around him, arranging the folds of wool expertly and flinging the bulk of it over his shoulder and around his left arm. Pilate straightened the rings on his hands, drank down a healthy draught of Judean wine, and went to meet the Jews.

He had to go outside to the balcony to do so, since their detestable religion prohibited them from entering his "defiled" Gentile home.

The faces of the crowd below him were illumined by the glare of torches. The Jews were shouting, pushing, shoving. Even the priests were screaming, gesturing wildly at a man bound with ropes. Pilate's soldiers had encircled the prisoner. When they saw the governor, they hustled the man up the steps to the inner hall of the Praetorium.

"What accusation do you bring against this man?" Pilate shouted down to the mob.

"If he were not an evildoer," yelled one man, "we would not have delivered him to you!"

Pilate flushed. *The insolence of these people!* "You take him," he shouted. "Judge him according to your law."

Another priest shouted. "It is not lawful for us to put anyone to death."

At least they know their limits, thought Pilate. The Jews retained the power to condemn a man according to their strange laws, but they needed the sanction of Rome to execute a criminal.

"He's perverting the nation," another screamed. "He is forbidding people to pay taxes to Caesar! He says that he himself is a king!"

By now Pilate could hear the booted feet of his soldiers as they led the prisoner into the hall behind him. He turned away from the crowd and went back inside.

The prisoner was in bad shape. He had deep circles under his eyes, and he was covered with grime where the Jews had flung dust and sand on him.

His robe was stained with blood in a few places. But the man met Pilate's gaze, eye to eye. Pilate wasn't used to that. Prisoners usually hung their heads and stared at the dirt from which they had come.

He sat down and motioned for his aide to pour him another goblet of wine. "Are you the king of the Jews?" he asked the prisoner, raising an eyebrow.

"It is as you say," the man replied. "Are you speaking for yourself, or did others tell you this about me?"

"Am I a Jew?" Pilate responded, controlling his anger with difficulty. "Your own nation, your chief priests, have delivered you to me. What have you done?"

"My kingdom is not of this world," said the prisoner, returning to Pilate's initial question. "If my kingdom were of this world, my servants would fight so that I would not be delivered to the Jews." He glanced toward the armed soldiers on either side of Pilate and then at the ornate room, reflecting Rome's great pomp and power. "But my kingdom is not of this world."

The riddle caught Pilate's attention. He'd never seen anyone quite so self-confident, yet at the same time utterly lacking in self-consciousness.

"Are you a king then?" he asked.

"You say rightly that I am a king," the man responded. "For this cause I was born, and for this cause I have come into the world: that I should bear witness to the truth. Everyone who is of the truth hears my voice."

Truth, Pilate thought. *In Rome the truth doesn't have much to do with whether one is king or not. In fact, truth doesn't have much to do with anything. It's all upside down. Sejanus is dead because he killed Jews and wanted to be king. These Jews want this prisoner dead because he claims to be their king. What does any of it really matter? What is truth? It's all a matter of who holds the scepter.*

Pilate looked up. *Well, I hold it now. The eagle of imperial Rome.*

The prisoner was looking at him steadily, composed in the midst of the guards, the spears, the shouts of the crazy Jews filtering up from the court-yard outside. The man even had a look of compassion in his eyes. Pilate couldn't stand it.

"Truth," he said tiredly, shrugging as he got up from his seat and arranged the folds of his toga. "What *is* truth?" And he went back out to the balcony.

The truth of the matter was really irrelevant, he thought. But one thing he knew: These stubborn, screaming Jews should be taught a lesson—if he could do so without causing a riot.

He stepped to the railing of the balcony. "I find no fault in this man," he said softly, so the people would have to shut up to hear him. When his words registered, they burst into shouts of anger and accusation.

Pilate threw up his hand. They had shouted that this man was from Galilee. Well, Galilee was in Herod's jurisdiction. Let him deal with it.

"Send him to Herod," he told his soldiers. "Let him decide this case."

But within just a few hours, the prisoner was back in Pilate's court. Herod hadn't done anything except play with him: Now the man was wearing a crown of spiked thorns, his face covered with wounds and abrasions. A soaked purple robe covered his shoulders and stank of blood.

So it began all over again. Pilate questioned the prisoner and offered options to the Jews. But they were bent on execution.

Then a dark-skinned messenger, bodyguard and attendant to Pilate's wife, appeared. The soldiers standing guard on either side of the governor let him through. The man slipped behind the judgment seat and bent toward the governor's ear.

"A message from your wife," he whispered. "She has had another of her dreams. She told me to come to you as quickly as I could. It is about the Galilean."

Pilate looked down at his lap. His wife often had troubled night visions in Jerusalem: sleeping shadows of tumbling walls and broken stones. What could she have dreamed about this strange prisoner?

The aide bent again. "She said to tell you this: 'Have nothing to do with that innocent man, for I have suffered a great deal today in a dream because of him.'"

Innocent! The thought made Pilate's stomach turn over.

He dismissed the messenger and turned back to the people.

"I have examined this man and have found no basis for your charges against him," he shouted. "He has done nothing to deserve death. Therefore, I will punish him and then release him."

Back came the cries from voices hoarse with hatred. "Away with this man! Crucify him! Crucify him!"

"What?" Pilate shouted back, infuriated by their fury. "Shall I crucify your king?"

Then it happened. Led by a priest who knew Rome's ways, they howled like dogs that had picked up the scent of the quarry. "We have no king but Caesar!" The incredible words never before heard from the mouth of a Jew now issued from the lips of the chief priest himself.

"Whoever makes himself a king speaks against Caesar!" the priest continued. "And if you let this man go, *you are no friend of Caesar!*"

They had him. Pilate saw the jaws of the trap spring tight. Sejanus had been stripped of his title; he was *no friend of Caesar,* the tribunal had ruled. Then they had executed him.

Emperor Tiberius had made the choice quite clear: Friends of Caesar need have no other friends. If Pilate's choice was between this man and Caesar, he would take Caesar. He wasn't about to lose his life over someone who spoke riddles about kingship and truth, no matter how much he wanted to trounce the Jews.

"Water," called Pilate hoarsely. "Water!"

A slave brought a big basin. Pilate had him hold it high so the crowd could see—and then he dipped his hands in the water and wiped them with a linen towel. "I am innocent of the blood of this just person," he said loudly. "You see to it."

And they did.

14

I AM THE TRUTH

One word of truth shall outweigh the whole world.

—ALEKSANDR SOLZHENITSYN

WHAT IS TRUTH?" Pilate asked Jesus.

Scripture provides no inflection, no gesture, so we don't know how the Roman governor asked the question. But the account does tell us that after asking it, Pilate turned away and offered Jesus back to the Jews. He didn't wait for His reply. It doesn't seem that he was really looking for an answer.

One thing is certain. Pilate didn't understand, or he didn't accept, what Jesus had been telling him. If he had, he would have turned toward Him—not away.

During His ministry, Jesus made many remarkable claims. That He and His Father were one. That He could forgive sin. That through faith in Him, people could have eternal life. Christianity itself rests on the astonishing claim that Jesus rose bodily from the dead and ascended into heaven. But of all these claims, the most remarkable is His bold statement: *I am the truth.*

In the great drama of the gospel account, we often pass right over Christ's statement. Of course Jesus is the truth, we say. Just like He called Himself the "way" or the "door" or the "vine." It's a metaphor. Jesus was claiming that He was who He said He was. He was confirming that He truly was the Son of God, the Messiah. We then go on to the rest of the biblical account without considering the full import of His declaration.

But Jesus was not just speaking metaphorically when He said "I am the truth." He was telling us something that, if properly understood, *radically* affects our view of the essence and character of the Christian faith, as well as the very nature of the world in which we live.

The dictionary defines *truth* not only as "genuineness or veracity," but also as "that which conforms to reality or fact—that which is in accordance with what is, what has been, or must be."

The first part of that definition is quickly understood. Truth is veracity. Which means something is true when we can prove it, when it is evident through physical examination, demonstrated through physical phenomena, known through experience. It is true that you are alive. It is true that if you jump off the roof of your home, you will fall down rather than up. It is true that the sun will rise at a precise, determinable minute and hour tomorrow morning.

We can also attest to the veracity of personal experience. It is true that I cannot digest milk. It is true that I love my wife: Forty years of experience testifies to that truth; it represents the accurate condition of my will and emotions.

Some phenomena may be true even though they are beyond known physical laws or experience. It is true, for example, that Jesus was resurrected bodily from the grave. Though skeptics have for two millennia tried to explain away the bodily resurrection of Jesus, the historical evidence for it is overwhelming. We can conclude that it is true.

But Jesus' claim to Pilate is astonishing because He does not just assert veracity *about* Himself. He told Pilate he had come to "testify to the truth."[1] That claim fits the second part of Webster's definition, "Truth is that which conforms to reality or fact, what is, what has been, or must be."

And so Jesus does not claim to be just one truth or one reality among many, but to be *the* truth—that is, *the ultimate reality*, the root of what is and what was, the point of origin and framework for all that we can see and know and understand. It is the assertion that in the beginning was God, that He is responsible for the universe, for our very existence, and that He has created the order and structure in which life exists. Everything we know—all meaning—flows from Him.

Interestingly, the NASA satellite discovery of radiation fluctuations in the atmosphere, which could account for the formation of earth and other planets and galaxies arising from a Big Bang, profoundly affects scientific understanding of ultimate reality. And it does so in a way that confirms the ancient biblical view.

Since the Enlightenment, astronomers have asserted, as did the pagan world, that the cosmos is eternal. The most well-known contemporary advocate of that view was Carl Sagan, who said that the Cosmos (with a capital C) is all there is, ever was, or ever will be. Thus there was no need for a God to have created the world.

But NASA discoveries undermine that premise, detecting through physical evidence that there was a point from which, by some extraordinary force of energy, the universe was created. One scientist puts it this way: All matter started as a small superdense ball—the size of a basketball, he suggests—that exploded with such spectacular force that it expanded across millions of light-years. It had a beginning at a point in time—and that astonishing force persists today as the universe continues expanding across the incomprehensible reaches of space.[2]

Incomprehensible? Indeed it is, by any known law of physics. Matter cannot come out of nothing, let alone with a force of such unimaginable magnitude. Yet while this might defy known physical laws, in this one critical respect it affirms the process described in Genesis.

Ultimate reality embodied in God and Christ is the most consistent theme in Scripture. When God described Himself in His extraordinary encounter with a terrified shepherd named Moses, what did He say? *"I am who I am."* Nothing more need be said. As the creator, God is the ultimate source of authority and meaning, the very essence of what is. Thus the Jews used the phrase "I AM," *Yahweh,* as their way of identifying God throughout the Scriptures. *Yahweh* appears more than six thousand times in the Old Testament; it is the expression of the One who lives eternally from everlasting to everlasting without beginning or end, the One alone who does not change.

No wonder the unbelieving Jews wanted to stone Jesus for blasphemy!

He told them, "Most assuredly, I say to you, before Abraham was, I AM."[3] He was not claiming to be *like* God or sent *by* God. He was claiming to *be* God: *Yahweh*—the great "I AM."

Note as well the New Testament writers' use of the Greek word *logos* to describe Christ. We translate that as "word" because there is not an exact corresponding term in English. But in fact, *logos* embraces what we would call intelligence, reason, and truth—that which is embodied in the very plan of creation itself.[4] From Yahweh to Logos, the biblical accounts present God and Christ as the ultimate reality. *The* truth.

Understanding this provides an objective basis for knowledge and a foundation to understand reality, a holistic perspective that our splintered world lacks. For under the influence of Enlightenment thinkers, the modern mindset began to separate faith and reason; and over the last two centuries the divide has become virtually unbridgeable. On one side are those things that people believe can be proven—scientifically observable phenomena. On the other side are those things, like God, that modern man believes cannot be empirically validated and thus can only be accepted by faith.

A chair is in the room, goes the proposition in philosophy class. You see it. But when you leave the room, how do you know that the chair is still there? You don't know for sure. Perhaps it was only an illusion; perhaps it was only there when you were looking. At best we can establish phenomena only by empirical observations—or so we have been taught. This means that unless a phenomenon can be proved, it has no objective standing. This modern view erodes not only historic Christianity but the props of civilization itself, as discussed later.[5]

But understanding Christianity as *the* truth means more than simply deducing reality through physical examination. The truth—ultimate reality—is not limited to what we observe. Thus, the Christian believes that there is no gap between faith and reason. He or she perceives "that all truth is the truth of the one God revealed in Jesus Christ."[6]

Truth exists—it is not just subjective interpretation. And truth, as we'll show later, is knowable. Jesus is the Alpha and Omega, the beginning and the end from which all else flows—the Logos from which all creation sprang, the past and the future and what will be. And thus it is in Christ that all things are held together.[7]

All meaning and understanding are rooted in the ultimate reality of the God who is. Apart from Him, nothing was created. No wonder Malcolm Muggeridge, the great writer and inveterate iconoclast, asserted with supreme confidence that he could be more certain of the reality of Jesus Christ than of his own reality.

This concept, what Francis Schaeffer described as "true truth," is so ultimate and absolute that it is difficult to articulate, and even more difficult to grasp. But ponder it . . . do not pass quickly over this point. For throughout history, this very point has been men and women's greatest quest, the most significant search of any civilization, the most intimate and meaningful questions for any individual: *What is reality?* Is there meaning? How do we know it? How did we get here? Is there a purpose in my life, or is everything that happens simply the result of the random occurrence of chaotic events?

HOW FIRM A FOUNDATION

Through the centuries the answers to these questions have ranged from the biblical view to a host of different philosophies and religions. In the past, the common thread was that people looked outward, beyond themselves, for ultimate meaning. In our times, however, the quest has turned inward. The forces of Eastern mysticism and secular naturalism—particularly the emphasis on the "imperial self," as one observer calls it—have propelled people to seek meaning not in some god or moral system or grand ideal beyond themselves, but within. (As we'll see in the next chapter, that narrows the quest quite a bit.)

From the beginning, Western thought and civilization assumed the existence of objective truth. The prevailing intellectual consensus was rooted in the Judeo-Christian tradition and the Greco-Roman idealistic tradition which explained the universe, humanity, and the purpose of life. This consensus became the cornerstone upon which the great philosophical systems rested, giving a form, substance, and context in which science, art, music, and commerce could develop and creating an environment in which political and ethical discourse could be measured. Whether individuals believed in the God of the Bible or not, this consensus provided secure philosophical ground upon which civilization could flourish. It provided order, coherence, and a common focus outside of self.

At the most basic level, men and women could relate their own existence to the supernatural, a connection that provided a sense of personal significance. Without a personal God and a meaningful universe, we are adrift in time and space, lost in the cosmos. Life, with all its pain and suffering, is a random and meaningless experience. A cruel hoax.

Consider how science has been influenced by the order and coherence of the Judeo-Christian tradition. It is a modern myth that Christianity and science are mortal enemies. In fact, most of the early scientists were Christians. Copernicus, Kepler, Galileo, Newton, Pascal . . . all believed the world had an orderly structure that could be scientifically studied because it was created by an orderly God.

Several science historians have recently published works documenting the historical relationship between science and Christianity. While many civilizations demonstrated great technical expertise—Egypt with its pyramids, Rome with its aqueducts—only one, they say, produced the experimental method we call science. That was a Christian culture: Europe at the end of the Middle Ages. The reason, says one historian, was the biblical teaching of a rational God: "Experimental science began its discoveries . . . in the faith . . . that it was dealing with a rational universe controlled by a Creator who did not act upon whim."[8] And the scientific method has always depended on the assumption that the universe is ordered.[9]

The same point can be made with respect to learning. Western scholarship assumed that truth was an objective to be pursued. Because of this, the model of the liberal arts university was instituted in the Middle Ages as a Christian undertaking expressly for the pursuit of truth.[10] Harvard University's great coat of arms bears the word *veritas,* Latin for truth.

Similarly, Western art, music, literature, and politics flourished as they reflected the order and significance of a meaningful universe. Remove order and you are left without form, void. With no objective standard to point to what is true or real, music echoes discord; art reflects nothingness; literature stutters into chaos.

When it came to ethics and philosophy, the moral consensus based on biblical revelation provided a framework for moral behavior through most of Western civilization. Francis Schaeffer recounted a time when he shared a platform with former cabinet member and urban leader John Gardner, during which Gardner spoke on the need to restore values to our culture. After he finished, a Harvard student asked him: "On what do you build your values?" Gardner, usually articulate and erudite, paused, looked down, and said, "I do not know."[11]

I repeatedly encounter the same reaction. When I have contended before scholars and college audiences that in a secular, relativistic society there is no basis for ethics, no one has ever challenged me. In fact, in private they often agree.

Nowhere is the existence of an absolute standard more vital than in politics and government. In the West, nations built sound political structures on the belief that ultimately man's laws were to be but a reflection of God's immutable, moral laws. This undergirded English law and the founding documents of the United States.

But if there is no truth—no objective standard of what is good or just and, therefore, no standard of what is unjust—then the social contract is always threatened by the whim of the moment. And tyranny, either from the unrestrained passions of the majority or from a ruthless dictator, inevitably follows.[12]

PEOPLE OF THE TRUTH

"What is truth?" Pilate asked.

If the implications of Jesus' statements are overwhelmingly significant for the world, they are no less profound for the church. For if we understand what Jesus meant by His extraordinary assertions, *I am the truth . . . I have come to testify to the truth,* our view of Christianity will be utterly transformed.

Christianity is not some religious structure or social institution. It is not merely a set of beliefs or creeds about the nature of reality. The Christian faith rests on *the* truth: ultimate reality. It is, therefore, a world-view: an explanation of all of life, of how the world works and how we fit into that world. The Christian experience begins with a personal relationship with Jesus Christ, made possible as men and women are declared righteous by their faith. But these born-again individuals then constitute a new society that points to the coming kingdom, which is centered on the core of all meaning—the God who was, who is, and who is to come, and the God who has revealed Himself in human history.

The One who said, "I am the truth," also said that "[the Father's] word is truth."[13] Truth is propositional and revealed. God has spoken through Scripture, giving us a comprehensive revelation of reality. Thus the orthodox creeds, which flow from Scripture and which have historically been regarded as the fundamentals of the Christian faith, are rooted in absolute and ultimate truth.

In the middle of the darkest night of Pilate's life, Jesus told him, "Everyone who is of the truth hears My voice."[14] Pilate had ears, but he did not hear. And so he turned away, asking, "What is truth?" even as he stood before the Truth Himself.

But Pilate is more than a tragic figure of Shakespearian proportions, condemned to wash his bloodstained hands forever. His cynical mind-set is all around us today. You can see it in your office, classroom, or courtroom . . . in your local newspaper, national news magazine, or scholarly journal. And, oh, yes, on the most ubiquitous medium of all. Your television.

15

LOST IN THE COSMOS

Some people are uncomfortable with the idea that humans belong to the same class of animals as cats and cows and raccoons. They're like the people who become successful and then don't want to be reminded of the old neighborhood.

—PHIL DONAHUE

Decadence is the decay that results from the hollowing out of meanings. When decadence is in full swing, meanings are not simply hollow but we exult in the gutting of them. This we call autonomy, liberation, freedom, the ultimate goal of postmodernism.

—RICHARD JOHN NEUHAUS

POPULAR CULTURE has always been not only a reliable reflection of a people's tastes, dispositions, and habits, but a powerful influence in shaping who we are—what we think, believe, and do. Ten years ago when we surveyed the landscape of American popular culture, we categorized its primary influencers as Donahueites and Goodmanites. Those names identified two points of view controlling much of America's airtime and print media.

The Donahueites were named, of course, for Phil Donahue, the gifted interviewer who popularized the feel-good, whatever-is-right-for-you, sexually scandalous staple fare of the television industry. The Goodmanites were named for syndicated writer Ellen Goodman. They represented those cultural elites—writers, educators, politicians, media executives—who aggressively advance tolerance for any and all lifestyles and people except those informed by religious beliefs rooted in absolute truth. Those the Goodmanites will not tolerate.

Now, a decade later, let's assess the influence and development of these two groups.

THE DONAHUEITES

Back in 1967, talk-show host Phil Donahue began interviewing celebrities and political personalities. He eventually became a household word; his then-new television format spawned dozens of imitators seeking to attract ratings with increasingly bizarre, explicit material. By the mid-1990s, he was losing viewers to others who had taken his format to new depths. Desperate, Donahue wore a dress for a show on transvestism, interviewed male strippers, and did an unfortunate feature on the Australian "sport" of dwarf tossing.

By 1996, Donahue retired, leaving much of his earlier audience in the gutter with trash TV. He came back in the summer of 2002 but failed to create quite the stir he did the first time around. But his legacy is clear.

Today's shows continue to feature just about anything and every-thing—as long as it is erotic, depraved, melodramatic, and sensational. And no matter how twisted the subject matter, the audience always applauds the tremendous heroism of those who appear, for they are being faithful to modern culture's main mantra: Only *you* can decide what is right for you. Just please, oh, please, let the audience watch.

This led right into "reality" shows, the ultimate voyeurism. The fad started with *Survivor*, which proved so successful that the spin-offs quickly vied wildly to top each other. We were treated to *Temptation Island*, in which four scantily clad couples competed to see who could tempt who to be unfaithful to whom. Then there's *Meet My Parents*, in which a young woman's parents decide just which of the three hunky contestants their daughter will go out with. They subject the suitors to a lie-detector test, in which the big question, "Do you want to sleep with my daughter?" meets with a roar of hilarious approval from the audience as the kid says "No," and the test administrator gives a big thumbs-down, indicating a lie.

If you want a break from sex, shows like *The Chamber* and *The Chair* feature contestants answering quiz questions while an air cannon blasts 120-mile-an-hour winds at them or they are subjected to electrical shocks. Or *Fear Factor*, where contestants eat spiders, slugs, and submit to other slimy forms of humiliation for cash and prizes.

On dramas and sitcoms like HBO's *Sex and the City* and *Queer as Folk* or Fox's *Boston Public,* the focus is pubic. One recurring storyline on *Boston Public* featured a teacher having a sexual relationship with a seventeen-year-old student—which is a crime in some jurisdictions. When asked about viewer complaints, a Fox spokesman replied that the network had received more complaints about the lack of accurate Boston accents than about the show's sexual content.

Sometimes when Christians complain about the depiction of sex on television, we're derided as prune-faced, puritanical killjoys. Yet the fact is that the biblical view is far more celebratory of the beauty, true passion, and priority of the sexual relationship than the cheap junk on TV. The problem with society's obsession with sex is that, taken out of its biblical context and the gracious intentions of its Creator, the physical relationship is degraded. Men and women, particularly women, are treated as simply the sum of their body parts, the bigger the better. Teenagers and children are shown relationships devoid of meaning and commitment. Nothing is cherished, protected, or secure. Life itself is cynical and banal. That kind of television is the *real* killjoy.

OPRAHFICATION

Some argue, however, that television is essential for our national survival, that it is the one instrument which provides national cohesion. Certainly this can be so, particularly in times of national crisis. After the terrorist attacks of September 11, 2001, citizens gathered around television screens, not only to try to begin to understand what had happened, but to take comfort from the inspiring words of our leaders and the heroic deeds of our countrymen and women.

At times like that, television really is the instrument of our modern American religion, since the word *religion* derives from the Latin *religiare,* meaning "to bind together." While Scripture and its common bonds and values provided the most cohesive force in culture fifty years ago, today the chord of common understanding and communication is transmitted by television and cable networks.

In this, the dominant influence is Oprah Winfrey. Her authority is such that the *Wall Street Journal* used the phrase "Oprahfication" to describe "public confession as a form of therapy." And *Vanity Fair* described her as more powerful "than any university president, politician or religious leader except perhaps the Pope."[1]

To her credit, Oprah set herself apart from gutter TV in the 1990s. She established her own hugely successful brand identity, not only as the great public confessional, but by providing a range of services and products like the Oprah Book Club and *O Magazine*. This has made her enormously wealthy and powerful—and "with a congregation of 22 million viewers, one of the most influential spiritual leaders in America."[2]

Raised by a devout grandmother and evangelical father, Oprah was a precocious child. She gave recitations in church, and on Monday mornings she would often provide a devotional critique of the Sunday sermon. In her youth she became a spellbinding speaker in Nashville churches. She overcame personal violation and tragedy; raped at nine and abused sexually for years, as a teen she gave birth to a premature baby who died. She strove on, won beauty and talent pageants, and began a career in television broadcasting that eventually led to the opportunity to host a Chicago talk show.

Her journey to television screens in millions of American homes has paralleled her evolution from an orthodox faith to a postmodern eclecticism. New Age gurus have been frequent participants on her programs, including Dr. Phil McGraw, the psychologist who dispenses psychotherapy to audience participants and has since spun off with a show of his own.

Oprah has a remarkable capacity to connect with her audiences and to draw out their spiritual hunger. "Stand still inside yourself," she'll say, "and know the truth"—the perfect postmodern homily. As one viewer described her feelings about being part of Oprah's congregation: "I always say I am a member of the Church of Oprah, and Dr. Phil [McGraw] is my Higher Power."[3]

In the Church of Oprah it is up to us to find our own spiritual truths. "One of the biggest mistakes we make is to believe that there is only one way," she says. "There are many diverse paths leading to God." Oprah's "blurring of the popular and pastoral, the self-help and the sacred," has, as *Christianity Today* put it, made Oprah an icon, the high priestess of postmodernism.

Twelve days after the Twin Towers collapsed, an interfaith prayer service was held at Yankee Stadium. Thousands of people, mostly victims' families, flooded the stadium to mourn; millions more watched on television. Christian, Jewish, Muslim, and Hindu clergy filled the stage around the event's host—Oprah. Standing center stage, she confidently assured the crowd in low, comforting tones that though they had lost a loved one they had gained an angel whose name they knew.

What Oprah is preaching is not particularly new. It's just that the combination of her public access and immense influence, as well as the particular appeal of her own earnest search for meaning, make it uniquely twenty-first century. The Church of O encourages people to ask all the right questions about life, meaning, service to others, identity—and then to look in precisely the wrong place to find those answers. Within.

This is the logical consequence of postmodernism, popularized by television's pervasive presence and its hollowing out of meaning. In different ways, the Donahueites and the Church of O lead people on equally futile pilgrimages. There is no ultimate truth, so we must each find our own truth—either through pleasure and diversion, or by looking deep within ourselves. And we must feel good about ourselves—even when we do wrong.

But while Donahue's style is combative, Oprah is gentle, caring, and calming—precisely what Americans want most. And so the dominant movement today bears not Donahue's name, but Oprah's.

THE GOODMANITES

What, then, of the Goodmanites, those who virulently oppose Christianity's place in the public square? What's become of them?

Well, we have a new term for them as well. For today their tone has even more of an edge, captured most clearly by writers from both ends of the political spectrum, showing that intolerance toward Christians is not confined to the left.

In an article in the *New York Times*, Andrew Sullivan suggested that the war on terrorism was a "religious war—but not as Islam vs. Christianity and Judaism, [rather] a war waged by fundamentalism [both Christian and Islamic]."[4] His definition of fundamentalism? "The blind recourse to texts embraced as literal truth, the injunction to follow the commandments of God before anything else."[5]

Other *Times* columnists like Thomas Friedman and Anthony Lewis have equated Islamic fundamentalists with Christian fundamentalists. In an interview Lewis compared John Ashcroft with Osama bin Laden, saying, "Certainty is the enemy of decency and humanity." (Ashcroft, you see, commits the unpardonable sin of praying alone in his office each morning.) Conservative Christians were on occasion labeled the "Taliban wing of the Republican Party."[6]

Based on these remarks, we'll call those with such derision for Christians "Talibanizers."

I have felt their ire.

Early in 2002 I was accused in the press of "making one of the most ill-conceived and dangerous proclamations heard anywhere in the world today," words that "bring back memories of armies of Western Christians sweeping across Muslim lands during their Crusades, forced conversions of Jews during many dark periods of Christian history, and bloody wars between Protestant sects following the 16th century reformation."[7]

After I read that about myself, I hurried to look at the speech in question to see just what "ill-conceived and dangerous" proclamations I had uttered. Ah, here they are: "I see this time as an opportunity of evangelism of Muslims, proclaiming the Gospel, the wonderful Good News, to people—who when they hear it are deeply affected. They may not show it, but are deeply affected. . . . We do [so] by using our minds and making a defense of Christian truth. 'Always be prepared to give a reason for the hope which is within you, but do it with gentleness and reverence,' Peter said."[8]

In the post 9-11, politically correct assumption that all religions worship the same God, it seems that any probing of Islam, or any suggestion that one might evangelize Muslims—even with "gentleness and reverence"—was labeled intolerance, bigotry, or worse. Franklin Graham and others who did so were accused of "hate speech."[9]

Such "Talibanizing" could be dismissed as simply more of the anti-Christian bias we've long heard from the media. But in fact, it reflects an utterly dogmatic rejection of truth itself and an open, virulent hostility to any truth claim. Hence the dreaded label of "fundamentalist" is bestowed on anyone who believes in any literal truth.

RELATIVE RELATIVISM

The Oprahites and Talibanizers clearly reflect a profound cultural and philosophical revolution in societal values. Secularism has steadily eroded the Judeo-Christian consensus at the root of the Western value system.

British journalist and historian Paul Johnson pinpoints the scientific verification of Einstein's theory of relativity in 1919 as *the* decisive event in secularism's development, because relativity in the field of science was confused by Western elites with relativism in the field of ideas. This skepticism about truth grew until it came of age in the 1960s, when many college and university campuses were invaded by modern existentialism: the belief that God was dead and human beings could overcome the resulting void by their own heroic individualism. Gone was any adherence to common moral standards or belief in absolute truth. The individual now created his or her own world.

During the same period, deconstructionism—the notion that a written text has no objective meaning and thus is defined solely by one's own interpretation—invaded literature and the law, erasing any notion of a transcendent reality or objective truth. By the 1980s this mind-set was so entrenched in American life that Dr. Alan Bloom opened his bestseller *The Closing of the American Mind* with the bold statement that "almost every student entering the university believes or says that he believes truth is relative."[10]

By the late 1980s, absolute truth was openly proclaimed as the enemy of civilization. Harvard historian Arthur Schlesinger decried the perils of *absolutism:* "It is this belief in absolutes that is the great enemy today of the life of the mind." And then he added this heroic call, "The mystic prophets of the absolute cannot save us. Sustained by our history and traditions, we must save ourselves at whatever risk of heresy or blasphemy."[11]

It is difficult to find campuses in America today where Schlesinger's views do not reign.[12] "There is no knowledge, no standard, no choice that is objective," says Barbara Herrstein-Smith, a leading feminist academic.[13]

And academics are, if nothing else, determined in their beliefs. Walt Kaiser, a distinguished Christian scholar, tells of his experiences when he was a graduate student at Brandeis University. After a lecture by a professor who contended there was no absolute truth, Kaiser asked the question, "Are you saying there is no case in which a truth can be said to be absolute?" Kaiser asked.

"That's correct," the professor replied.

"Are you absolutely sure?" Kaiser asked.

"Absolutely!" the irritated professor snapped.

In the modern era, the late eighteenth century to the late twentieth century, truth was considered knowable, but by reason, not by faith as had been previously accepted. What is called postmodernism holds that truth is unknowable by either faith *or* reason, thus reducing all ideas to social constructions shaped by class, gender, and ethnicity. The individual finds meaning only in whatever category, usually a grievance group, he or she can best identify with. And in postmodernism, all beliefs and lifestyles and subgroups are equally valid.

Postmodernism traveled quickly from the campuses to the court-rooms, where decision after decision revealed hostility to truth, and then hostility to its adherents and defenders. The Ninth Circuit's Judge Steven Reinhardt, for example, in his celebrated 1996 decision permitting assisted suicide (later reversed by the United States Supreme Court), demonstrated an obvious irritation with people "with strong moral or religious convictions. . . . They are not free to force their views, their religious convictions or their philosophies on all other members of the democratic society."[14]

The issue before the court, mind you, was the constitutionality of a *democratically* enacted referendum in Washington State. Were people with strong moral and religious convictions not free to participate in the process? To vote? To participate in arguments in a court challenge? If that's the case, then the Talibanizers are not just in the media; they wear black robes and interpret, if not make, our laws.

Similar antagonism was evident in the case of *Romer v. Evans,* when the U.S. Supreme Court struck down another democratically enacted referendum in Colorado barring special civil rights benefits based on sexual orientation. Justice Kennedy, writing for the majority, said, "Laws of the kind before us raise the inevitable inference that the disadvantage imposed is born of animosity toward the class of persons affected."[15]

With these words, a truth claim held by Christians, Jews, and Muslims (as well as much of civilized society) for millennia was summarily dismissed and characterized as nothing more than prejudice. This is classic postmodernism—the triumph of group grievances over the common good, even when that common good was determined by popular vote and reflected long-held moral traditions.

Judges who cling to these reviled absolutist notions are subject to open censure. A few years ago Justice Antonin Scalia, in a private speech to a prayer breakfast, expressed belief in the resurrection. This is not particularly surprising since he is a devout Catholic. But the Talibanizers of Washington were scandalized. Scalia was excoriated in the press, ridiculed and attacked brutally for his "bias." One columnist went so far as to propose that Scalia disqualify himself from sitting on any church/state cases. (Perhaps only atheists are qualified to hear such cases?)

The postmodern world-view and its hostility to truth claims has gripped not only the structures of power, but has been thoroughly popularized. The primary virtue in today's relativistic world is unbridled tolerance: the jovial broad-mindedness that purports that any and all values, if sincerely held, are equally valid. Therefore one cannot assert his claim to be superior or even normative. To do so is to invite a charge of bigotry. Of course this suppresses free and open discussion, which has always been the historic meaning of tolerance.

Even in this quick overview of postmodernism's effects in American life today, one can see how its tentacles grasp everything from television to politics to court decisions to education. The world-views of the Church of O and the Talibanizers have consequences.

World-view is not an arcane term only for eggheads. Everyone has a world-view. It's the set of suppositions that each person holds about how the world works and how we fit into it. It's what we believe to be true and untrue. It forms the basis of our values and determines how we behave.[16]

It's vital for the Body of Christ in the world today to understand the dominant secular world-views of those around us if we are ever going to love, serve, challenge, and communicate with them. The job of the church, living as it does in alien country, must always be to be a beacon of the truth, not only in evangelism, but in bringing Christian revelation to bear on every aspect of life. When we don't do so, we have little influence on the shape and direction of our culture.

So what are the characteristics of the postmodernist world-view that the Talibanizers, Donahueites, and the congregation of O have reflected and perpetuated?

THE PREVAILING WORLD-VIEW IS SECULAR

As an adjective, the word *secular* means merely "of this world," or "of the present age." As a world-view, however, it becomes secular*ism,* an ideology that places emphasis on the here and now.

The anthem of modern American secularism is the old beer commercial: "You only go around this way once, so grab for all the gusto you can." That's actually the same creed the ancient Epicureans delighted in: "Eat, drink, and be merry, for tomorrow we die." Or, as the popular T-shirt slogan proclaims, "Carpe diem"—*Seize the day!*—the ultimate existential expression.

If you do not have any sense of the future, now is all that matters. Such an attitude demands instant gratification: Money, sex, power, food, vacations, cars, wardrobes, drugs, and pleasure, pleasure, pleasure are the ends of life. Then there's the midlife crisis, with plastic surgery, an affair, or a younger spouse to turn back the clock. Attempts to have it all—now—become increasingly desperate.

Haven't we seen this mind-set in America's corporate scandals? It seems that many an executive rationalized something like this: *All that matters is this quarter's per share earnings which will lift the stock price 20 percent, which means I can cash in my options and salt away 10 million dollars and buy the second house in golfing paradise; and if I have to hide some liabilities to get those earnings up—well, so be it.* The focus that subsumed all else— like any moral considerations—was on *this* quarter's earnings and what that gets me *now.*

The tragedy is that secularism strips life of purpose. It's all linear. When a certain number of years have elapsed, it's over. Period. So divert or medicate yourself however you can, and you won't have to confront the hard reality of the inevitable passage of time.

Comedian Billy Crystal's character in the old movie *City Slickers* captured the essence of the linear life. He's a bored baby boomer in the middle of a midlife crisis. One day he visits his young son's school to tell about his work. Suddenly overcome by life's brevity, he spews the following monologue to the bewildered youngsters.

> Value this time in your life, kids, because this is the time in your life when you still have your choices. It goes by so fast.
>
> When you're a teenager, you think you can do anything and you do. Your twenties are a blur.
>
> Thirties you raise your family, you make a little money, and you think to yourself, "What happened to my twenties?"
>
> Forties, you grow a little pot belly, you grow another chin. The music starts to get too loud, one of your old girlfriends from high school becomes a grandmother.
>
> Fifties, you have a minor surgery—you'll call it a procedure, but it's a surgery.
>
> Sixties, you'll have a major surgery, the music is still loud, but it doesn't matter because you can't hear it anyway.
>
> Seventies, you and the wife retire to Fort Lauderdale. You start eating dinner at 2:00 in the afternoon, you have lunch around 10:00, breakfast the night before, spend most of your time wandering around malls looking for the ultimate soft yogurt and muttering, "How come the kids don't call? How come the kids don't call?"
>
> The eighties, you'll have a major stroke, and you end up babbling with some Jamaican nurse who your wife can't stand, but who you call Mama.
>
> Any questions? [17]

If that's all life is, then we may as well live for the moment. Any questions?

THE PREVAILING WORLD-VIEW IS ANTIHISTORICAL

Since postmodernism exalts the moment—right now—it dispenses with any belief in the objective reality of the past. Otherwise the past might have some influence on the present.

This disdain for the past has expressed itself in deconstructionism. Without objective truth, there is no reason for an objective interpretation of history, law, or politics. Past events or writings, which reflect only the viewpoint of the class that was in power at the time, have no binding effect on us today. What authors intended in literature or history books, for example, is irrelevant. What matters is our interpretation of what they wrote. So we freely revise the past to conform to current politically correct values. This is why today's history books often portray Christopher Columbus not as a courageous explorer seeking to discover new parts of God's great world, but as a white European male oppressor who destroyed the pristine utopia enjoyed by natives on these shores.

I encountered elementary deconstructionism firsthand when I sat down a few years ago with our then ten-year-old granddaughter, Caroline, an eager fifth grader, to look through her history lesson.

Flipping through the section on the Bill of Rights in her brand-new history textbook, we saw a caption that read, "The Bill of Rights promised individual freedom to many people but not to women, blacks, and Native Americans."

Caroline burst out, "Grandpa, that not fair! Why did they leave out women, blacks, and Native Americans?"

"The book is wrong," I replied. "That simply isn't so."

Caroline looked me in the eye and gravely told me that I must be wrong. She knew the Bill of Rights discriminated because, after all, "the book says so."

There was only one way to convince Caroline that her shiny new book was giving an incorrect interpretation. We sat down together and read the Bill of Rights aloud. Article 1 talks about the right of the people to practice their religion freely. "Is there anything in those words that excludes women, blacks, or Native Americans?" I asked.

"No," Caroline admitted.

We went to Article 2, which describes the right of the people to keep and bear arms. "Anything there that excludes women, blacks, or Native Americans?" Caroline shook her head.

Article 4 speaks of the right of "the people" to be secure in their persons and their property. No one excluded there either.

After we'd read the last one, Caroline looked up at me, amazement written on her face. "Grandpa, you're right!" she said. "The book is wrong."

Now, it is true that women, blacks, and Native Americans couldn't vote at the time the Bill of Rights was adopted. No nation in the world at that time in history provided universal suffrage. It wasn't a matter of our founders denying such rights to blacks, women, and Native Americans, as the textbook implied; the truth is that the founders went far beyond anything that had ever been tried anywhere in the world. And in succeeding generations, blacks, Native Americans, and women were enfranchised—largely, we might add, at the instigation of those motivated by Christian conscience.

A more careful explanation—one the textbook writers, for whatever reason, chose not to make—would have avoided the strong anti-American impression created by the book.[18]

Deconstructionism has also wormed its way into classic fiction. Consider the adventure story of Robin Hood, the noble rogue of Sherwood Forest who robbed the rich to give to the poor. One of Hollywood's more recent versions, featuring Kevin Costner, updated and politicized the old story. The heroine is no longer Maid Marian, maiden in distress, but a tough Ms. Marian. Friar Tuck is a drunk whose Christianity is depicted as the same superstitious ignorance that fueled the horrific Crusades from which Robin has just returned. And the new hero, a character not appearing in the original story, is Azeem, a Muslim Moor who repeatedly demonstrates the superiority of Muslim culture over the flawed Christianity of Crusade-era England.

What's a Muslim doing in Sherwood Forest? Deconstructionism at work. Since white males are no longer politically correct heroes, history—even the history of legend—has to be rewritten.

For another flavor of postmodern revision, consider the film version of the classic work *The Scarlet Letter* that came out a few years ago. The author of the book, Nathaniel Hawthorne, was a Christian who believed in original sin and the redemptive power of confession and absolution, and he wrote a story about redemption before a forgiving God and the nobility of service to others. This, however, was not going to fly in postmodern Hollywood, so, as Richard Grenier of the *Washington Times* put it, filmmaker Roland Joffe simply converted heroine Hester Prynne into a liberating, feminist heroine. "Massachusetts Puritans, in Mr. Joffe's view, were really sensual, sexy people, lusting for nudist bathing, hot tubs, and extracurricular love. But someone has imposed an oppressive theocratic system on these sexy Massachusetts people. Probably greedy capitalists . . .

"How does the film end? Well, forgiveness by God is obviously not a happy ending in Roland Joffe's prayerbook. So, just as Hester [is] about to be hanged for [her] sins by these horrible Boston Puritans, good Indians attack and massacre the Puritans, leaving untouched the nice, sexy Massachusetts proletarians—although how the Indians can tell them apart beats me."[19]

Now granted, movies have never been known for their historical accuracy. John Wayne and Doris Day seldom got it right either. So all this might seem rather harmless. After all, isn't this just artistic license—putting a new twist on an old tale and updating its historical context?

We think not.

Nor is the issue here *just* concern over political bias or politically correct revisionism or even the trashing of Christianity. It is that skewed movies that rewrite history—and their underlying philosophy—erode our sense of *real* history. And if history has no meaning, then a society has no tradition to draw upon, no lessons learned from or debts owed to the past.

The very heart of our republican tradition is respect for the covenants of the past, for civic values and virtues passed from generation to generation, for the restraints the wisdom of the past imposes on today's behavior. Take away a society's common history, and you remove that which binds it together. Take away a sense of history, and you eviscerate the Christian faith, which is a religion of historical fact.

THE PREVAILING WORLD-VIEW IS NATURALISTIC

For a generation, Christians have railed against the enemy called *secular humanism.* So called because it was secular—of the moment—and humanistic, which meant that man, not God, was the center of the universe. But as the contemporary world-view has evolved, humanism no longer seems an appropriate term.

If the universe is preexisting and eternal, and if life arose by cosmic chance out of the primordial soup, then of course nature is supreme. If there is nothing beyond what we can see, hear, taste, smell, or touch, then there is no supernatural and the material world is ultimate—and there is no reason to think of humans as the height of creation. We are simply one species among many. It is perfectly logical, therefore, that activists fight for the rights of endangered baby seals while not blinking an eye at the abortion of unborn humans. Or, as the president of People for the Ethical Treatment of Animals once put it: "A rat is a pig is a dog is a boy."[20]

In a strange perversion of Darwin, some even hold that the higher species owe a special debt to the lower species. So animal rights terrorists poison products intended for humans to protest the alleged inhumane treatment of rats. And ecological terrorists booby-trap loggers in the Northwest to protect the spotted owl.

All this is madness, of course, but perfectly logical for the devout naturalist. Since all life forms allegedly arose out of the same primordial slime, then it is no surprise that Stephanie Mills, coauthor of *Whatever Happened to Ecology?* would describe humans as "debased human protoplasm."[21]

THE PREVAILING WORLD-VIEW IS UTOPIAN

In calling humans "debased," however, Mills has inadvertently exposed one of the inner contradictions of this modern view of the world. On one hand, naturalism holds that we have no intrinsic worth—we're just "protoplasm." The contradiction is that postmodernism, in its disdain of Judeo-Christian teaching about original sin, holds that all human beings are intrinsically good. So the poster people of postmodernism hold that basically good men and women—who are, come to think of it, no more than debased protoplasm—will, with education and protoplasmic progress, become better slime over time.[22]

The roots of this myth go back to Aristotle, who believed that education would eventually erase sin and evil. This belief gained wide acceptance during the Enlightenment, when the philosophical focus shifted dramatically from God to man. The philosopher Georg Friedrich Hegel, for one, embraced and expanded the Aristotelian view.

The eighteenth-century writer and philosopher Jean Jacques Rousseau argued that children were born good and were corrupted by social structures and the oppression of civilization. "Vices belong less to man than man badly governed," he wrote.[23] So wise politics and social engineering could, he reasoned, achieve universal remedies for man's ills.

Building on Rousseau, Karl Marx argued that freeing the proletariat would lead to a classless society. As a result, government would "wither away." But Marxism created no utopia. Rather, it led to a totalitarian state that slaughtered tens of millions of its own citizens and enslaved one-third of the world. And when it ran its course, the government didn't "wither away." It was trampled, torn from flags and toppled from monuments by the masses parading joyously through the streets.

The twentieth century produced the most staggering advances in knowledge, education, and technology in history. It also gave us Hitler and the Holocaust, the horrors of mass slaughter in two world wars, and countless other conflicts. It gave us brutal rulers like Stalin and Pol Pot (who read Rousseau while condemning millions to the gulag and the killing fields), genocide of millions in Africa, serial killers, greed, rape, horror, bloodshed, and evil of unimaginable proportions. Yet the myth of man's goodness endures.

In the 1960s, even as communist utopias were gripping the East, we in the West were experimenting with our own utopianism, with devastating results. When President Lyndon Johnson declared war on poverty, the message went out that the poor were unable to extricate themselves from their plight. In a landmark speech at Howard University in 1965, he told black students that they were the victims of society's oppression and racism and that their government would rescue them.

LBJ, his compatriots in Congress, and the socially conscious elite who championed the war on poverty were well-intentioned. They really believed that institutional programs could solve poverty. They really believed that the poor were victims. Unfortunately, they were also very convincing. Up until then the work ethic had been strong among the inner-city minorities. Now all that changed. *If my condition is not my doing,* they now reasoned, *then why work to try to get out of it? And if society is at fault, then why not steal from it?*

The result was a crime rate that soared from the 1960s into the 1990s, a fivefold increase of the prison population, millions on the public dole, a permanently subsidized underclass, and crumbling infrastructures of inner-city schools, families, and housing.

The utopian myth of human goodness also creates our greatest modern dilemma: If we are basically good people, how do we explain the wrongs we do? We can't. So we simply deny that the wrongs are wrong—or else we blame them on sickness or on someone else. Thus, we all become victims. So years ago when former mayor of Washington, D.C., Marion Barry, was filmed by the FBI with his hand in the cocaine jar, he claimed he was the victim of a racist plot. Or when militant gay activists suffer from AIDS, they rarely acknowledge that their disease might be a consequence of their own behavior. Instead, they angrily blame the government for not yet finding a cure.

This culture of victimization has resulted in mind-boggling court cases. A woman who developed lung cancer after smoking a pack and a half of cigarettes a day for forty years—despite all the well-publicized warnings by the government and the tobacco companies—sued the cigarette manufacturer.[24] And won. Across the country in the 1990s, in state after state, juries held tobacco companies liable for billions of dollars, even though those smokers made their own choices to smoke.

Now, in addition to Big Tobacco, we have Big Fat, the latest twist on the victimization of addiction. A fifty-six-year-old New York man sued four leading fast-food chains for contributing to his obesity, heart attacks, and other health problems. Lawyers claimed that fast food creates an addiction, or "craving," among those who eat it and that the restaurants had been deceptive about the health ramifications of digesting their food. (The four chains in the suit have published nutritional information about their meals since 1990, according to law, and they all offer salads and other low-fat options on their menus.)

When the chairman of Sotheby's—who amassed a fortune worth nearly $800 million by planning and building shopping malls—was accused of running a price-fixing scheme, his defense team argued that he has no head for numbers, has dyslexia, and suffers a sleeping disorder that caused him to snooze through meetings. He's therefore innocent, they claimed.[25]

Thankfully, sometimes these far-fetched excuses still don't work. When a student who was arrested in 1999 for allegedly e-mailing a violent threat to a Columbine high school student, his attorney claimed that the young man was "hypnotized by too much Web surfing" and therefore was not responsible for his actions. He was found guilty anyway.[26]

But the trend is clear. If we are victims, caught in the Web, or by racism or a sleeping disorder or whatever, then somebody else must be to blame. And whoever it is should have the pants sued off them. (Which is why Americans have the highest per capita representation of lawyers in the world and spend billions of dollars a year on insurance to protect against litigation.)

But sometimes blaming and suing aren't enough. So in this relativistic, utopian world when we can't blame something or sue someone, when our conscience finally convicts—when we are truly cornered by the reality of our sin—how do we respond? Filmmaker Woody Allen gives us a chilling answer in his movie *Crimes and Misdemeanors*. (It was released years ago, but it's worth renting; it's a modern classic.)

The story is of Judah Rosenthal, a prosperous ophthalmologist and pillar of the community who happens to be cheating on his wife. He is enjoying his successful double life until one day when he opens a letter meant for his wife. It is from his mistress, and it threatens to unravel everything.

Judah goes first to a rabbi friend who urges him to repent and make a clean break with his past. Then he consults his brother who has ties to the mob and offers a cleaner way out: murder.

Although flooded with memories of his religious upbringing, Judah tells his brother to go ahead and kill his mistress.

Most of the film deals with Judah's subsequent anguish. At first he is ravaged by guilt. Haunted by nightmares, he can talk with no one but his brother. He is close to a nervous breakdown.

Then something marvelous happens. No one discovers his crime! A burglar is blamed for the woman's death.

Judah's guilt fades. His life is rich and full, his business thrives, he lies to his rabbi friend. He feels wonderful, better than ever. The film ends with Judah back on top, at peace with himself and his world.

And the lesson is plain: Judah committed two murders; he killed not only his mistress, but his own conscience as well.

In a culture where the tiresome vestiges of guilt still hang on, that's the answer. If there is no one else to blame and you still feel bad, then just kill your conscience. You'll feel so much better in the morning.

THE PREVAILING WORLD-VIEW IS PRAGMATIC AND UTILITARIAN

If there is no objective truth, how are we to decide which of two possible actions is preferable? The answer is provided by choosing from two somewhat related philosophies: pragmatism (do what works best) or utilitarianism (do the greatest good for the greatest number).

Pragmatism is the philosophical system made in America. In the late nineteenth century William James, Charles Pierce, Oliver Wendell Holmes, and John Dewey, the father of modern education, met at Harvard and formed what was called the metaphysics club—although their philosophy began with skepticism about metaphysics and theology. In essence, they argued that one cannot know truth, so good can only be measured by what works, and what works is therefore good. As James said, "Truth is the cash value of an idea."[27] Or, Oliver Wendell Holmes Jr. observed, "the best test of truth is the power of the thought to get itself accepted in the competition of the market."[28]

Today, without a moral compass to gauge direction, "Does it work?" has replaced "Is it right?" as the question to ask in business decisions and lifestyle choices. If it works for you, then go right ahead. Thus, the only question about abortion is whether the pregnancy is "wanted" (read: convenient). If not, flush it away. Is your marriage working? If not, get out of it. Can you make a questionable deal to increase your corporate profits . . . just so long as it doesn't get in the newspapers? If so, go right ahead. The consequence, as we saw in 2002, was entire companies wrecked and bankrupted, ordinary shareholders ripped off, Wall Street in retreat, and those pragmatically minded CEOs and business leaders under indictment for their actions.

The 1960s adage, "If it feels good, do it," became a new mantra in the new millennium: "If it works, do it."

Our neighbors, friends, and colleagues who are not followers of Christ won't necessarily articulate their world-views in the tidy categories we've just listed. But make no mistake: Philosophical relativism, which is embraced by two-thirds of the American people, leads to the dominant secular, antihistorical, naturalistic, utopian, and pragmatic world-view. The Christian concept of truth—that ultimate reality is found in Jesus Christ— is held today by a small minority.

Modern man, as Francis Schaeffer once quipped, has both feet firmly planted in midair. To take his metaphor further, we might say that today's culture is, as Walker Percy's marvelous essay puts it, "lost in the cosmos."[29] It's like a spacecraft that has broken its ties with the home ship, and is whirling randomly, lost in the furthest reaches of a cold and darkening void.

But it's not just a "culture" that's lost in space. On board that spinning vessel are millions of individual travelers. Countless human beings who are cynical, defiant, desperate, afraid, and everything in-between . . . souls who have lost their way and long, down deep, for a fixed star to steer by—a still point in the turning world.

16

THE PILLAR OF TRUTH

*There is not a square inch in the whole domain of our human existence over
which Christ, who is sovereign over all, does not cry, "Mine!"*

—ABRAHAM KUYPER

By now you may be wondering what all this discussion of deconstructionism, relativism, Oprahism, Donahueism, postmodernism, and
Talibanizing has to do with Christians.

Sadly, for many the answer is "not much."

Every week millions of believers settle into church pews to hear soothing words from our pastors. We sing our favorite hymns or praise songs, do
our church duties, and study our Bibles. It's somewhat comforting to view
a decaying world from the safety of our sanctuaries, while we strive to
strengthen our own personal relationships with God.

Not that striving for personal holiness is wrong; it is central to the
Christian life. But the Christian faith is absolutely incomplete if it stops at
the individual level.

When believers recite the ancient baptismal confession, "Jesus is Lord,"
we refer to His rule over our own lives, of course, but we are also acknowledging His sovereignty over all He has created. That means we have the
awesome responsibility of affirming that rule—of proclaiming His truth—
in a world that is full of the same cynicism Pontius Pilate expressed. We
cannot sit back in the comforts of our sanctuaries, where people talk and

think like we do, and refuse to take up this challenge. We cannot forgo the corporate consequences of Jesus' lordship. For we alone can provide the answer and point a weary and skeptical culture to the ultimate and only reality, Jesus Christ Himself.

His Body—His church—is charged with the obligation to defend His truth. As the apostle Paul described in his letter to Timothy, the church is to be "the pillar and support of the truth."[1] We are to be the body that raises up the truth and makes it visible to the world.

That means we must know the truth, and we must understand the mind-set of those we meet each day in the marketplace. We are engaged, after all, in a great struggle. The historic Christian world-view is being confronted on the world stage by Islam, whose fundamental tenets are, as we have written, at sharp odds with the Christian world-view. At the same time, we face a constant cultural conflict with the forces of the postmodern mind-set we described in the last chapter.

Postmodernism has created a huge gulf between contemporary American culture and those who adhere to traditional and Judeo-Christian views of life. Gertrude Himmelfarb described this in her excellent book, *One Nation, Two Cultures*. To coexist as a distinct, separate culture is an unfamiliar role for the Western church, but we have to get used to the fact that we are no longer part of the American mainstream. This demands that we radically rethink our role and our strategy for reaching our own society. We must be like missionaries to our own culture, even to the point of learning a new language, as missionaries do. For the two cultures, thanks to postmodernism, speak the same words but with totally different meanings.

For example, take a verse that is familiar to any serious Christian: "the truth will set you free."[2] *We* know this means *the* truth—that is, Jesus, who says I am *the* truth, or ultimate reality—will set us free from sin and death. But when a pastor preaches on this verse, what does the postmodern ear hear? The truth—that is, *my preference*—will set me at liberty to do whatever I please.

So we have to translate for postmodern listeners, which means presenting what truth is—objective reality. It also means letting them in on the great news that we can actually know truth.

Is the church today prepared to do this?

Not very well. The Barna poll that found that 72 percent of the American people believe there is no such thing as absolute truth also revealed a shocking response from believers: 67 percent of those claiming to be Bible-believing, conservative Christians also said there is no such thing as absolute truth. A large majority of those who follow the One who says, "I am the truth," profess not to believe in truth.[3]

So how do we engage in this struggle? If we are to be the pillar and support of the truth, it seems obvious that the first thing the people of God need to do is to understand that there is truth and it is knowable.

IS TRUTH TRUE?

Some years ago, I received a letter from the Commanding General of the Second Marine Division in Camp Lejenue, North Carolina, the division in which I had served as a young lieutenant commanding a platoon in the mid-1950s. The general had seen a video of a speech I'd given on ethics at the Air Force Academy. If I would give the same talk at Camp Lejeune, General Jones promised he'd turn out all of the officers and noncommissioned officers on the base. It was an offer I couldn't refuse.

The general kept his word, and it was a moment of great nostalgia for me, watching two thousand marines, in combat fatigues with spit-shined boots, march in to take their seats in the base theater. Seated in the front row was General Jones.

When I finished my talk, the presiding officer invited questions. The marines sat ramrod stiff in their seats. No one blinked. Then General Jones, 6'6" and the epitome of a marine general, stood, turned to face the officers, cupped his hand around his mouth, and announced in a voice of unquestioned authority, "There *will* be questions!"

Then the questions came one after another, better ones than I had gotten on any college campus. Near the end, a marine major stood erect at the microphone in the aisle. "Mr. Colson, you've made a good argument that absolute moral standards are necessary to prevent social decay," he said, "but that's a pragmatic argument. I want to know, sir, is it true? Is there such a thing as moral truth—and if there is, how do we know it?"

I stared at the officer. I had spoken on this subject all across America and no one had ever asked this—the key question. The issue is not whether moral standards are useful in propping up society but whether they are true. Is there truth? Is it knowable?

"Yes," I said, "there are moral absolutes, and we know them because God has revealed them in Scripture." I then briefly shared my experiences that we can know God through His Word.

But beyond that, "We also see that there is an objective order in our regular experience." With that I took my pen out of my pocket and dropped it repeatedly on the podium. It landed beside the microphone, the sound reverberating through the auditorium.

"When I let go of this pen, it falls," I said. "Every time. We call that the law of gravity. There are known physical laws. We can see them in operation, predictable consequences to physical acts. Why shouldn't we understand that there are predictable consequences to moral acts? If there are physical laws, can we not conclude there are moral laws?

"I think it's demonstrable that there's an order to the moral universe just as there's an order in the physical universe. We can determine these things from empirical observation.

"And if there are physical laws and moral laws," I concluded, "can we not assume that there is a Lawgiver?"

It was fascinating to watch the light of understanding dawn on the faces of the officers in that auditorium.

This is but one of five ways that we can know Truth.

For Christians, we start with what is the most straightforward proposition: God is, He is not silent, and He has spoken. First, *we have special revelation:* Scripture inspired by God, authoritative, and without error in its original autographs. More about that in a moment.

Second, *we have general revelation.* In Romans 1:19–20, Paul writes, "What may be known about God is plain to them, because God has made it plain to them. For since the creation of the world God's invisible qualities—his eternal power and divine nature—have been clearly seen, being understood from what has been made, so that men are without excuse."

Long before I came to Christ, I can remember looking at the sky and the mountains and the ocean and *knowing,* as much as I've ever known anything, that there was a God who created the wonders that I could see.

As I wrote in *Born Again*, I prayed to that God without understanding Christ, the atonement, the resurrection, because what was made was evident to me. Ask scoffers and cynics to go out on a clear night and look at the stars and planets and galaxies hundreds of millions of light-years away, and explain the power and majesty of what they see apart from a Creator. It's impossible. People know that there is a God, though many spend their lives running away from Him because they don't want to pay the moral price of living according to His laws.

There is a third level of knowing truth related to the second: *Truth is in us*. As J. Budziszewski writes, "These are the laws we *can't* not know."[4] Paul evoked this in Romans 2:15: "The requirements of the law are written on their hearts, their consciences also bearing witness, and their thoughts now accusing, now even defending them."

Though it is further strengthened or weakened by early environmental influences, human beings are born with a conscience. We know certain things are right and certain things are wrong because our conscience convicts and informs us.

I recently spoke at my granddaughter's baccalaureate service at a large public high school on the outskirts of Atlanta. I knew that almost all the six hundred students graduating would go on to universities where they would learn that there is no truth, no absolute right and wrong, simply preferences. So I gave them the illustration that theologian R.C. Sproul frequently uses. You're standing on a street corner, and there's a frail old lady with a heavy shopping bag in front of you. Trucks, buses, and cars are zipping by. You have three choices. You can ignore her. You can help her across. Or you can push her into the ongoing traffic. What is the right thing to do?

When I asked that question of the graduating seniors, I watched their expressions. Of course they know which of these choices is right, just as anyone does. That truth is in us. It is, as C. S. Lewis elegantly argued, the Tao, the ongoing moral law of right and wrong, which people have known from the beginning of time. They know it because it is in them, instilled by their Creator.

I learned from my Caroline later that many of her fellow students were talking about that simple example afterward. They had not heard it before. And they got it.

Fourth, we can know truth because even if it isn't determined by the five senses—that is, even if it can't be seen, felt, heard, touched, or smelled—*truth is intelligible.* It is understandable to the intellect.

Drawing on the teaching of Plato, Augustine made this distinction. If you see a complex mathematical formula on the blackboard in front of you, at first it may not make sense. You labor through it, and it's still hard to comprehend. Then you finally get it, all at once: the aha! phenomenon. The light dawns and the concept becomes clear and intelligible.

Or consider another example. Love cannot be understood by any of the senses. Yet we know when it exists. It is as real as any physically demonstrable phenomenon.

Yet in our society, largely because of the influence of Immanuel Kant, that which can be reduced to a phenomenon and empirically validated is considered objectively true. But that which can only be known by faith cannot be established as objective truth. That's a modern myth. The fact is, it requires faith to know *anything,* even what you empirically observe. (How do you know you're not dreaming right now?)

And fifth, we can test things empirically to see what conforms to reality because *what conforms to reality is truth.* Just as I dropped the pen for the marines, so too we can make observations and conclude from repeated applications that something is true.

If I want to drive from Washington to Providence, Rhode Island, I will get a map. If I follow the map and end up in Alabama, I'll know the map isn't true. If I try it a second time and end up in Pittsburgh, Pennsylvania, I'll know the map isn't true. But if every time I follow the map, I end up in Providence, I can say that that map is true. It's an empirical test: Road maps—and world-views—that take you to the wrong place cannot be true.

It is important to understand these arguments if we want to engage people around us in critical conversations. And sometimes the terms can get foggy. For example, University of Illinois dean and English professor Stanley Fish quibbles over the semantics. He says he believes there is truth. It's just that you cannot know it or establish it. We should not be put off by such sleight of hand: To say there is truth but "no independent standard of objectivity" is a slippery way of saying there is no truth.[5]

Since truth is an independent standard of objectivity, postmodernists have to resort to arguments like this to soothe what would otherwise be a desperate despair. If there is no objective road map that takes you through life, you're left in chaos, caught in cul-de-sacs and dead-end streets.

What a bankrupt world-view! Its captives can be liberated only by the rich perspective of truth: the reality of what we see with our own eyes and experience in our own beings, by the existence of moral law over centuries, and by the revelation of God in nature and in Scripture.

THE TRUTH ABOUT GOD

The Christian must always start with and return to the question of Scripture. History is on our side, which is another way to validate truth. In theology, as in other areas of life, fads come and go, but truth is validated as it survives the assaults that come its way. Tested through the centuries, the central tenets of Christian orthodoxy have been passed on and entrusted to us. And here we must stand—without equivocation—even when the world hangs labels on us that represent everything considered ugly and backward.

A *New York Times* article, for example, labeled me a "theocrat" (if the author had bothered to read almost anything I've written, he would have discovered that I'm an outspoken critic of theonomy), implied that I was anxious and confused about my faith, given to apocalyptic visions, possibly a sadist, opposed to fiction, psychology, journalism, and assertive women. In short, a dreaded *fundamentalist*—a word that conjures up images of uneducated bigots, backward Bible-thumping preachers, and the Taliban. Yet fundamentalism is really akin to Lewis's "mere Christianity," or the rules of faith in the early church. It means adherence to the fundamental facts—in this case, the fundamental facts of Christianity. It is a term that was once a badge of honor, and we should reclaim it from its inaccurate caricatures.

At the end of the nineteenth century, evolution and the new higher biblical criticism began to challenge biblical authority. This assault affected even great theological institutions such as Princeton Seminary, which, though once orthodox, began questioning fundamental doctrines such as the Virgin Birth and inerrancy of Scripture. Meanwhile, a lively social gospel was also surfacing. Strong in good intentions, it was weak in biblical doctrine and orthodoxy. So a group of theologians, pastors, and laypeople published a series of volumes titled *The Fundamentals*. Published between 1910 and 1915, these booklets defined what had been the nonnegotiables of the faith since the Apostles' Creed:

1. the infallibility of Scripture
2. the deity of Christ
3. the Virgin Birth and miracles of Christ
4. Christ's substitutionary death
5. Christ's physical resurrection and eventual return[6]

These were then, as they are today, the backbone of orthodox Christianity. If a fundamentalist is a person who affirms these truths, then there are fundamentalists in every denomination—Catholic, Presbyterian, Baptist, Brethren, Methodist, Episcopal . . . Everyone who believes in the orthodox truths about Jesus Christ—in short, every Christian—is a fundamentalist.

Whenever other believers ask if I'm a fundamentalist—and when they do, they usually lower their voices and look around to see if anyone is listening—I reply, "Certainly." When I then trace for them what it really means, my questioners often have said, "Well, that's what I believe! What a relief!"

We must get over our timidity. Secularists misinterpret it as insecurity and a weakness of faith. Some years ago, the late atheist spokesperson, Madalyn Murray O'Hair, was asked why so many people were afraid of her. "I'll tell you why some Christians are," she replied. "They are not sure what they say they believe is true. If they were, I wouldn't be a threat to them at all."[7] Precisely.

Nor should we be defensive about what we believe or the authority by which we believe it. The argument is made that those of us who are orthodox are simply out of touch; doctrine should be determined by what the majority believe, and that's the only way the church can be relevant.

Could there be anything more relevant than the spiritual salvation of each human being who, apart from Christ, is absolutely lost? The historic gospel is the most immediate, encompassing, and necessary news anyone could ever proclaim.

Besides, truth is not determined by majority vote. It is, by definition, objectively true whether anyone believes it or not. The world was still round even when most of its inhabitants believed it was flat. God is still God even when millions deny Him. His word is still His Word, notwithstanding all those who try to explain it away.

The church is not a democracy and never can be. We can change rules and practices and sing new hymns and use different styles of worship. We can change forms, but not our foundation. For the church is authoritarian. It is ruled over by Christ the Head and governed by a constitution that cannot be ignored or amended.

THE TRUTH ABOUT HUMAN BEINGS

Scripture and our orthodox confession teach us the truth, not only about God, but also about men and women. The Bible says that every person has sinned and fallen short of God's glory. Jesus said, "The things which proceed out of the man are what defile the man . . . these evil things proceed from within."[8]

This, of course, is where we directly challenge and offend the predominant world-view that sees men and women as innately good victims of corrupt social influences. Scripture teaches that people are not victims but independent moral agents who make moral choices and must accept responsibility for those choices.

For people to see their need for a Savior, they must first see this truth about themselves. And if the truth about God challenges the secular mind, the truth about man is terrifying.

In 1960, Israeli undercover agents orchestrated the daring kidnapping of one of the worst of the Holocaust masterminds, Adolf Eichmann. After capturing him in his South American hideout, they transported him to Israel to stand trial.

There, prosecutors called a string of former concentration camp prisoners as witnesses. One was a small, haggard man named Yehiel Dinur, who had miraculously escaped death in Auschwitz.

On his day to testify, Dinur entered the courtroom and stared at the man in the bulletproof-glass booth—the man who had murdered Dinur's friends, personally executed a number of Jews, and presided over the slaughter of millions more. As the eyes of the two men met—victim and murderous tyrant—the courtroom fell silent, filled with the tension of the confrontation. But no one was prepared for what happened next.

Yehiel Dinur began to shout and sob, collapsing to the floor.

Was he overcome by hatred . . . by the horrifying memories . . . by the evil incarnate in Eichmann's face?

No. As he later explained in a riveting *60 Minutes* interview, his response was such because Eichmann was not the demonic personification of evil Dinur had expected. Rather, he was an ordinary man, just like anyone else. And in that one instant, Dinur came to the stunning realization that sin and evil are the human condition. "I was afraid about myself," Dinur said. "I saw that I am capable to do this . . . exactly like he."

Dinur's remarkable statements caused Mike Wallace to turn to the camera and ask the audience the most painful of all questions: "How was it possible . . . for a man to act as Eichmann acted? Was he a monster? A madman? Or was he perhaps something even more terrifying . . . was he normal?"

Yehiel Dinur's shocking conclusion? "Eichmann is in all of us."[9]

I saw this myself in 1981 when I visited death row at the maximum security prison in Menard, Illinois, and one of the prisoners asked to speak with me. He was a middle-aged man with neatly brushed, silver-streaked hair, a warm smile, and intelligent eyes. Except for his shackles and chains, he could have been a genial high school principal or a friendly pharmacist. He could have been anyone.

In reality, he was John Wayne Gacy Jr., the man who had sexually abused and murdered thirty-three young men. As we sat in a small interview room and talked, Gacy spoke quite rationally. And as I thought of his crimes, I kept telling myself that he had to be sick.

He was sick all right. Not mentally ill, but sick with sin that had erupted into horrific evil. Only as I reminded myself that he was sick with the same sin that dwells in us all was I able to spend one hour facing him across a table—and then to pray with him.

The terrifying truth is that we are not morally neutral. A renowned psychologist and orthodox Jew often makes the point that left to their own devices, with the assurance they would never be caught or held accountable, individuals will more often choose what is wrong than what is right. We are drawn toward evil; without powerful intervention, we will choose it.

Eichmann is in all of us. And that sin can be cleansed only by Christ's shed blood.

That fundamental message sounds harsh and archaic in today's society, even in many of today's "enlightened" churches. And it certainly doesn't conform to some of the strategies of the church growth movement. As discussed earlier, most pastors are under pressure to grow their churches; that's how we measure success. In many instances the pastors' jobs are on the line if they don't. So they look to the great untapped market—Americans who are daily conditioned not to think about the great questions and for whom pleasure is the chief aim of life.

Businesses penetrate new markets by giving people what they want. The temptation is great for the church to do the same: to offer pleasure, but in a spiritualized form. "If you think the world can give you a high, wait until you see what God can do."

Give people what it takes to get them into the tent; then let them have the whole message. This is good strategy, goes the argument. And many innovative churches have developed excellent techniques for drawing in the unconverted. But while we shouldn't frighten people away, we must take care to tell the truth. At some point people need to see the truth about themselves and God, and that is not a comfortable experience, for it by definition leads to the reality of sin.

SPEAK THE TRUTH BOLDLY

"The true Christian . . . is not only to teach truth but to practice truth in the midst of such relativism," said Francis Schaeffer, and this will "bring forth confrontation—loving confrontation, but confrontation."[10]

Yet confrontation is something most Christians seem to want to avoid. Not only because we want people to come to our churches, but because of our fear of offending and being rejected.

Christians want to be nice people. Nice Christians are genial and well-mannered, wrote novelist Walker Percy, but one would barely know they are Christians at all.[11] Nice means not ever offending anyone with a gospel that is, by definition, offensive.[12]

But when we speak the message boldly, with love, God often surprises us, as I discovered several years ago when I met with a prominent business leader in a southeastern city.

Mr. Abercrombie, as we shall call him, was not only a pillar of the community and an active church member, he also hosted a weekly Bible study luncheon at his office. Since I was in the city to speak at the governor's prayer breakfast, Mr. Abercrombie invited me to attend the study luncheon.

Nineteen men in all, dressed in dark suits, conservative ties, and white shirts, filed in at the appointed hour. They filled the large conference room, which was paneled on one side in beautiful rosewood and on the other with plate-glass windows offering a breathtaking view of the city that these men ran and owned. Although this was the city's power establishment, each man showed deference to our host, who had recently been featured in a national magazine as one of the up-and-comers of the corporate world.

Mr. Abercrombie had asked me to speak at the luncheon and then allow time for questions. Somewhere in my talk I referred to our sinful nature. Actually, "total depravity" was the phrase I used. I noticed at the time that a few individuals shifted uncomfortably in their leather chairs, and, sure enough, it must have hit the mark. Because after I finished, the first question was on sin.

"You don't really believe we are sinners, do you? I mean, you're too sophisticated to be one of those hellfire-and-brimstone preachers," one older gentleman said, eyeing my dark blue pinstripe suit just like his. "Intelligent people don't go for that backwoods stuff," he added.

"Yes sir," I replied. "I believe we are desperately sinful. What's inside of each of us is really pretty ugly. In fact we deserve hell and would get it, but for the sacrifice of Christ for our sins."

Mr. Abercrombie himself looked distressed by now. "Well, I don't know about that," he said. "I'm a good person and have been all my life. I go to church, and I get exhausted spending all my time doing good works."

The room seemed particularly quiet, and twenty pairs of eyes were trained on me.

"If you believe that, Mr. Abercrombie—and I hate to say this, for you certainly won't invite me back—you are, for all of your good works, further away from the kingdom than the people I work with in prison who are aware of their own sins."

Someone at the other end of the table coughed. Another rattled his coffee cup. And a flush quickly worked its way up from beneath Mr. Abercrombie's starched white collar.

"In fact, gentlemen," I added, drawing on a favorite R. C. Sproul shocker, "if you think about it, we are all really more like Adolf Hitler than like Jesus Christ."

Now there was silence . . . until someone somehow changed the subject.

When lunch ended and I was preparing to leave, Mr. Abercrombie took my arm. "Didn't you say you wanted to make a phone call when we were finished?"

I started to say it wasn't necessary, then realized he wanted to get me alone.

"Yes, thank you," I said.

He led me down the corridor to an empty office. As soon as we were inside, he said bluntly, "I don't have what you have."

"I know," I replied, "but you can. God is touching your heart right now."

"No, no," he took a step back. "Maybe sometime."

I pressed a bit more, however, and moments later we were both on our knees. Mr. Abercrombie asked forgiveness of his sins and turned his life over to Christ.

Martin Luther was right. "The ultimate proof of the sinner is that he doesn't know his own sin. Our job is to make him see it."[13]

Of course the sledgehammer that worked with Mr. Abercrombie might not be quite right for everyone. That's okay. Approach the issue lovingly and gently and tactfully, if you wish, but one way or another, *do it*. Conviction must precede conversion. You cannot present the gospel truth until you have also presented the fact of sin.

Without this message we are simply offering our own brand of therapy. And therapy can only modify behavior. It is the gospel that transforms character.

The object is not to make people able to live with themselves; it is to make them able to live with God. Forever.

Yet the huge gulf between the Christian and the secular view of human beings is sometimes underestimated because there are so many people with a Christian veneer. Many of our neighbors and coworkers don't seem so different from us—on the surface. But their world-view is utterly in conflict with Christian values, and their relativism dominates a culture that was, until the last several decades or so, at least nominally Christian.

The scandal is that we in the church have allowed this to happen. We have failed to stand for truth, failed to articulate, defend, and advance an intelligent and coherent Christian world-view.

Which brings us to the third and perhaps, because it is little discussed, the most daunting challenge of all—to develop and live out a biblically informed view of life.

SEEING GOD'S TRUTH IN ALL OF LIFE:
THE BIBLICAL WORLD-VIEW

It is impossible to read the Scriptures from Genesis to Revelation and not see the clear pattern of God's sovereignty, as well as His charge that the people of God be His body, doing His work as stewards of His entire creation. This is a matter of obedience.

According to the Genesis account, God created the world and was pleased with His creation. Then He ordered Adam to "cultivate and keep" the garden. "To cultivate" means increasing creation's bounty, while the Hebrew verb *shau mar*, translated "keep," means literally "to guard." Adam was to guard the garden against anything that might jeopardize its reflection of God's goodness.

The Fall did not negate this mandate. It just made it harder to obey. The curse of sin extended into every arena of life. But so did Christ's redemption.

Eventually, because of Christ's completed work on the cross, all creation will be restored to its former glory. Until His return, however, Christians must persevere in their role of "cultivating and keeping" the garden of a fallen world.

Even before Christ came, the men and women of the Old Testament understood this. The Psalms are filled with King David's exultation over

God's rule and His mandate to us. And David's son Solomon understood his father's words; his proverbs touch on everything from child-raising to neighborly relations to work to economic justice to international relations.

Later, the central message of the prophets was to call God's people to account for their failure to apply His truth to every aspect of their lives. They decried Israel's cavalier attitude toward the family, the tendency of the wealthy to treat the poor with injustice, and the self-serving ways of government officials.[14] They also led the people in carrying out their educational responsibilities to the generation to come.[15] And the prophets looked forward to a day when the application of God's truth to all of life would shape the nations of the world.[16]

Throughout His public ministry, Jesus evoked the kingdom mind-set that consciously takes "every thought captive to the obedience of Christ."[17] Likening the kingdom of heaven to leaven, Jesus described God's rule as having a transforming effect on everything it touches.[18] And in the parable of the talents He taught that God expects a "return on investment" from His faithful stewards,[19] who are to bring glory to Him as they cultivate and keep that which He has entrusted to them.[20]

Not surprisingly, the apostles took pains to teach the church not to be conformed to this world but to be transformed by the renewing of the mind, to guard against being taken captive by the empty deceptions and philosophies of the world or cleverly devised tales, and to seek truth according to Christ.[21]

What is clear from this, from creation onward, is that God's rule extends to everything from the most intimate details of our personal lives to the most public outworkings of our corporate lives. From our bank accounts to our business dealings to our educational curricula to our social justice issues to our environmental concerns to our political choices in the voting booth—*everything* must reflect the fact that God's righteous rule extends to all of life.

As writer Harry Blamires put it in *The Christian Mind,* "As a thinking being, the modern Christian has succumbed to secularization. He accepts religion—its morality, its worship, its spiritual culture; but he rejects the religious view of life, the thing which sets all earthly issues within the context of the eternal."[22]

When Christians set all issues in the context of the eternal, when we shape our view of all of life in light of the Truth, what does that view look like? Point by point, it is the antithesis of the dominant world-view described in the previous chapter:

- The world's view is shaped by relativism; the Christian's view flows from the objective, revealed truth of Scripture. It rests on absolutes.
- The world's view is secular, rooted in the "now." The Christian's view is eternal. What we do now counts forever.
- The world's view is antihistorical. The Christian's view respects the historical account of God's work from the beginning of time.
- The world's view is solely naturalistic. The Christian's view is based on the *super*natural.
- The world's view is pragmatic, judging actions by what does the greatest good for the greatest number. The Christian's view is idealistic—we see to do what is right and just by firm, objective standards.

One man who saw clearly this clash of world-views and the scope of God's call was Abraham Kuyper, a scholarly Dutch pastor. Following his sermon one day at a country church, a peasant woman from the congregation approached him.

"Dr. Kuyper," she said, "that was a brilliant sermon, but you need to be born again!"

While the learned doctor was stunned at her words, he later discovered what she meant and gave his life to Christ. For twenty-five years he edited a Christian journal, wrote, preached, ultimately led a Christian political movement, and became prime minister of Holland in 1900. He also became one of the great modern proponents of a well-realized Christian world-view.

"If everything that is exists for the sake of God, then the whole creation must give glory to God," Kuyper argued. And after intense study of Scripture, he realized that the holy writings disclose "not only justification by faith but the very foundation of life and the ordinances that regulate human existence."[23]

In describing the burden that God placed on his life, Kuyper, who might have been speaking for the church today, said, "[Our call] is this: that in spite of all worldly opposition, God's holy ordinances shall be established again in the home, in the school and in the state for the good of the people; to carve as it were into the conscience of the nation the ordinances of the Lord, to which Bible and creation bear witness, until the nation pays homage again to God."[24]

We do this not by attempting to usher in God's kingdom now—the mistake triumphalist, overzealous believers have made since the time of Augustine. Nor do we seek to capture control of political structures— although Christians should certainly seek office if God calls them to do so. Rather, we should be contending for truth in every area of life. Not for power or because we are taken with some trendy cause, but humbly to bring glory to God and affirm His good reign.

For this reason, Christians should be ardent ecologists. Not because we think trees are our brothers, but because we are mandated to be good stewards of God's garden, to ensure that the beauty and grandeur God has reflected in nature is not despoiled.

We should care for animals. Not because whales are our sisters, but because animals are part of God's kingdom over which we are to exercise dominion. Francis of Assisi should be our role model, not Ted Turner or Ingrid Newkirk.

We should care for human life. If we are concerned about baby seals, we should be far more concerned for unborn humans. Not because of some prudish Victorian morality or a desire to interfere in people's private lives, but because every human being is created in the image of God. For the same reason we oppose euthanasia, assisted suicide, or human cloning. And when lives are at stake, we take a stand against the world.[25]

Thus, the Christian world-view is what makes the church a passionate defender of human liberty and civil rights. The very term our founding fathers used, "endowed by their creator with certain *unalienable* rights," reflects a Christian view of human liberty that is nonnegotiable. Governments can neither confer nor take away human rights; these rights are given by God. It is this conviction that put Christians in the forefront of the campaign for the abolition of slavery, the civil rights movement, and the crusade for human rights in oppressed nations around the world.

Thus, Christians zealously seek reforms in the prisons and in criminal justice laws. Not because it's part of some party platform or vague humanistic idealism, but because our view of institutions must always be measured by God's clear standard of justice.

Thus, Christians celebrate the arts—painting, music, dance, drama—and all creative expressions that bring glory to God, the Great Artist. It's sad that the National Endowment for the Arts controversies have siphoned off so much attention in this area. Obscenities parading as art are pathetic abominations designed to shock and profane; they express a world-view that depends on moral chaos rather than the celebration of God's created order.

In the same way, Christians must champion ethics. Not because it is good business—the dominant pragmatic view—but because moral standards come from God. Objective truths are neither arbitrary nor irrational; they are just and enduring, reflecting God's just and unchanging nature.

Thus, Christians are not enemies of academic freedom, but true defenders of education. Because the purpose of learning is the pursuit of truth, open inquiry is critical.

DEFENDING THE TRUTH AND EXPOSING TODAY'S LIES

It is also the task of the Christian to defend truth in every area of life. The apostle Peter tells us that we are always to be prepared to give a reason for the hope that is within us, but with gentleness and reverence.[26] This means we must be prepared at all times to defend a biblical world-view against the competing world-views arrayed against Christianity.

The great theologian Cornelius Van Til argued that the apologetic task of the Christian is to assert the truth of our basic presupposition: God is, He has created us, He has spoken, His word is clear. At the same time, we are to show that any other formulation, any other presupposition, leads to conclusions that are simply not rational.

This is why people like Princeton ethicist Peter Singer are such convenient adversaries. Since he believes, for example, that all species, animal and human, are equal, he openly advocates bestiality. It's the logical consequence of his belief system: Go ahead, if you feel like it, have relations with the family dog. Or a consenting pig or horse.[27]

Singer favors everyone living on $30,000 a year and giving away anything left over to others in need, a good utilitarian philosophy. The problem is he doesn't do it himself. And though euthanasia is the utilitarian choice for those at the end of life so resources can be diverted to healthier specimens, Singer keeps his own Alzheimer's-stricken mother in a nursing home.

The truth of a world-view is determined by whether one can rationally live with it. If a proposition about life and the world around us is true, then it will conform to the moral order and will lead to healthy or right consequences. If the proposition is false, odds are that one can't really live with it. It is, as scholar Neal Plantinga writes, "cutting against the grain of the universe," or "spitting into the wind." If people say there are no physical laws, they will discover their supposition is false just as soon as they slip at the top of the stairs. Someone like Peter Singer who claims there are no moral laws is probably not going to carry his propositions to their logical conclusions and abandon his mother and have sex with his dog.

So the apologetic opportunity is for Christians to help the secularist to see that his belief system is simply unsustainable in real life. Michael Novak tells the story of a friend who was debating an ardent feminist on National Public Radio. The issue was whether there were moral absolutes; the feminist stubbornly maintained there were none. At that point, the female interviewer cut into the debate, asking Novak's friend if he could come up with one absolute they would all agree on. In a moment of inspiration he answered, "Rape." End of discussion.

Sometimes the secularist's predicament is not so obvious. I watched a TV report of Christopher Reeve testifying before a congressional committee in favor of "therapeutic cloning," the process by which an embryo is created to be used in medical experiments. Therapeutic cloning has been touted by the biotech industry as the key to finding cures for Parkinson's, spinal injuries, diabetes, Alzheimer's, and a host of other dreaded illnesses. No one calls it for what it is: a human being created to be killed for research.

Of course Christopher Reeve is a sympathetic figure, strapped in a wheelchair, his familiar face as handsome as ever. He speaks with difficult pauses, his oxygen supplied by a breathing tube. It required several people and elaborate equipment to maintain Reeve in the hearing room.

During his appearance, Reeve made the following statement as part of his argument why the government was responsible to allow this research: "Our government is supposed to do the greatest good for the greatest number of people."[28]

Congressmen nodded, the press scribbled furiously, flashbulbs popped. Not a member of the committee raised an objection—including the ugly, obvious one. Or was it obvious? Perhaps they were all so immersed in a postmodern mind-set that they didn't see it.

For if government really embraced the philosophy Reeve advocated, he wouldn't be sitting in the committee room able to advocate it. After all, it cost vast sums to save Reeve's life and to rehabilitate him to even be able to speak. It costs millions each year to support him in his condition. If our philosophy were to use finite medical resources to do the greatest good for the greatest number, Reeve would have been allowed to die. That's the harsh calculus of the greatest good for the greatest number.

Force the secularist to embrace the logical conclusion of his own view of life and reality and you will discover he cannot live with his own beliefs. I experienced this at a small luncheon for a dozen Christian men. I thought it was to be an informal time of fellowship until I discovered that one of the men had brought a guest, a well-known intellectual and writer who was a thoroughgoing skeptic. And he was seated beside me.

We made it through the first course without incident. But when we began discussing the differences between Islam and Christianity, he turned to me in irritation. "That's what offends me about you Christians," he said. "You think you have the only way to heaven."

"Of course," I replied. "But it's not just Christians. Jews and Muslims believe they have the only way also." I tried to explain that any truth claim is by its very nature an exclusive claim.

He wasn't buying it. As I pressed him further, I realized he didn't believe in any kind of truth claim. I dropped my trusty pen on the table and we talked about the law of gravity. He argued that we couldn't know if the pen was actually dropping, that quantum physics might explain it otherwise.

"Just tell me what you see," I pressed him.

Finally, he grudgingly nodded. "Well, okay," he said. "There may be certain things we can say are true. But religions are all the same, seeking the same God."

This is one of the most widely held beliefs in our culture, but it is a specious argument, and I knew he was trapped. Judging by the reddening of his neck, he did too.

"But two exclusive claims cannot both be true," I said. "The law of non-contradiction says something cannot be one thing at the same time it is something of an entirely different character." The man scanned the eyes around the table and then shook his head dismissively, saying, "Okay, it's extra-natural."

His logic was not sustainable, and therefore his world-view could not be true. The task of the Christian is to press those who embrace the world-view so prevalent in America to examine their own beliefs. If they are willing to do so honestly, postmodernism's lies are baldly exposed.

WAR OF THE WORLD-VIEWS

We are engaged in the war of the worlds. The problem is that we neither understand the other side nor hold our position well. At the very time when we are being attacked by powerful and wholly alien forces, the church is weakest.

And it's a multifront war. As we've said, we are contending against two world-views. One is the postmodern view that we've been discussing in this chapter. This view is stealthy, subtle, and sometimes well-camouflaged. Supported by intellectuals in every walk of life, this relativistic world-view can afford to be subtle because, by its very nature, it appeals to the weakest and most vulnerable aspects of human nature. In this radically individualistic age, people flee authority and are naturally drawn to postmodernism's gleeful autonomy.

The other growing and aggressive threat is the world-view of militant Islam. Islam is a theocratic system that teaches that all areas of life are within its reign. Being submitted to Allah means being fully integrated into a society with rules, values, and standards.

In the 1992 edition of this book, we wrote about the incursion of Islam. We did not know how prophetic those words would be. Islam is breeding at an unprecedented rate in our nation's prisons. It appeals to inmates because it provides order and concern for the whole person and a strong community (as Christians should but often don't). It has a similar appeal in countries where men and women live with the constant chaos of coups and revolutions, and for the same reason thrives in America's inner cities.

Because of Islam's monolithic structure, its officials can—and do—carefully plan evangelization campaigns from country to country. Christians, on the other hand, rush off in a hundred different directions, arguing over which methods to use, and end up giving a truncated message.

Not since the barbarian hordes overran Europe has the influence of Christianity been weaker. We hear all about church growth in various parts of America, or Christianity exploding in African countries, but look at the cold, hard facts. Look at what we really are up against.

There are approximately 2 billion members of various Christian churches: 983 million Roman Catholics, 17 million Eastern Catholics, 250 million Eastern Orthodox, approximately 300 million mainline Protestants, and perhaps 300 million conservatives, Baptists, Pentecostals, and assorted evangelical sects (the latter growing rapidly). And the heart of the church—those with serious, alive faith? No one knows the number for sure, but they are spread throughout myriad denominations and traditions, scattered in various corners of the globe, widely separated by theology and tradition, and in some cases not even speaking to one another.

Compare that with more than 1.2 billion, well-organized, relatively well-disciplined Muslims (not to mention 800 million Hindus, 362 million Buddhists, and one billion "atheists or nonreligious" individuals).[29] Though in much of the world Christianity is the fastest-growing faith, Christians are actually a minority, and the odds against us are overwhelming. Which is why it is so crucial for us to put aside our less significant differences and join forces to defend the truth.[30]

But the church must not only stand together; it must stand free. Remember, ideology constantly changes; it is from man. Truth is immutable; it is from God. So if the church is to be the pillar and support of the truth, ideology and truth can never be mixed.

And wherever and whenever it has stood for the truth, independent from tyrants who would enslave it, the church has demonstrated a power nothing on earth can contain.

Historians are still sifting the tumultuous history of the most astonishing development of the twentieth century: the fall of Communism. Yet even the best of Western intelligence did not see the changes coming in the former Soviet empire, nor discern the real inner workings of these quiet revolutions.

Perhaps that's because at the heart of this globe-shaking shift was the church: that body of persecuted Christians who stood apart from the culture around them, fearing God rather than men. They were just ordinary men and women, but they stayed true. They kept their independence. They trusted God. And in the end, they made history.

17

BETWEEN TWO CROSSES

In some ways the story began in the town of Nowa Huta, Poland, soon after World War II.[1]

Planned in the late 1940s and constructed in the 1950s as a living monument to Communist utopianism, Nowa Huta, or "New Town," was originally designed as a center for the workers who would make up the backbone of the new Poland. Adjacent to the medieval city of Krakow, ancient seat of Polish kings and golden centerpiece of Polish art, culture, and spirit since the thirteenth century, Nowa Huta was an industrial center. Its only artifacts were mammoth steel works and ugly chimneys spewing smoke and sulfuric fumes into the skies of southern Poland.

Early in the town's construction, an open square attracted the workers' attention. It testified to the vacuum the Communists had left in the rigid grids of their urban planning.

We need a church, the workers said. A place to worship.

What was the problem with these Poles? the authorities wondered. After all, their new housing was the best planners could design (discounting the fact that in a typical flat the kitchen was so narrow that a woman could barely enter it sideways after her sixth month of pregnancy). And now they even had hot and cold water. Why in the world did they need more? Especially a church!

The Communists bought time, however, by nodding agreeably. Fine, they said. No problem.

So several young Christians and a Polish priest nailed together two rugged beams and pounded the rough timber cross straight and solid into Polish soil to mark the site where their chapel would be built.

Soon, however, the authorities returned with a different verdict. We are sorry, they told the workers. This space is needed for something else. You cannot build a church here.

But the people wanted their church. Night after night they gathered around the cross. Priests offered mass, and the people sang and celebrated communion with one another and their Lord.

The authorities retaliated with water cannons, but this vigorous baptism didn't faze the faithful. Then the Communists tore down the cross, as if sundering its heavy beams would somehow cleave the people. But the citizens of Nowa Huta were determined, and in the morning the cross was once again stretching toward heaven for all to see.

This went on for years—the authorities tearing down the cross and the people restoring it. And in the midst of the struggle the people came to a realization that would steel their faith in a way that Communism could never steal their souls.

"The church is not a building," they said to one another. "The church is us, celebrating the presence of our Lord among us! Praise be to God!"

MEANWHILE, students in Romania were discovering the reality of the choice Communism posed for them.

In a small classroom in Cluj the temperature was cold and the lighting low as a philology teacher finished his lecture. Joseph Tson shifted uncomfortably in his wooden chair. Earlier he had asked a question that seemed to enrage his teacher—something about the historicity of biblical literature. Now Joseph felt the professor's attention return to him.

"We no longer need the old fables," the teacher said abruptly. "And you watch. Within a generation, the church will die out."

At first his vehemence startled Joseph. But, he reasoned, people don't usually become angry unless they feel threatened. Then he thought about the words of Jesus Christ in the Gospel of Matthew: "Upon this rock I will build my church; and the gates of hell shall not prevail against it."[2]

What Joseph had seen of Communism seemed a fair translation of "the gates of hell." And paraphrasing the verse in his mind, Joseph realized that to those like the professor and the present regime, the church did indeed pose a threat: "I will build my church in Eastern Europe, and Communism will not prevail against it."

When the class ended, Joseph stuffed his books into his battered briefcase and thought, *What I believe will determine how I act. So I have to decide who I will believe: this Communist professor—or Christ.*[3]

THE SAME CHOICE faced Hanani Mikhalovich, a major in the army of the Soviet Union, stationed at a remote compound near Vladivostok. Like his father before him, Major Mikhalovich was a good soldier and faithful Communist party member. His wife, in fact, was the local party secretary. Aligned with the state, their future looked bright.

But one day Major Mikhalovich heard a shortwave radio broadcast that changed his life. He heard the gospel, and the Holy Spirit touched his heart.

The Wednesday after his conversion, Major Mikhalovich went to the weekly, compulsory party meeting. Always he had sat at the front of the bare hall, focusing on the huge portrait of Lenin, straining to take in everything that came from the podium. But this night he took a straight wooden chair in the last row.

The following Wednesday he didn't show up at all.

The next morning the commanding officer and the political officer demanded an explanation.

"I have become a Christian," Mikhalovich said simply.

The commanding officer looked at him for a moment in shock, but the political officer jumped from his chair, his face red with fury. "Shut up!" he screamed. "You are never to say those words again! Get out!"

That evening orders were issued for a special parade to be held the next day; all personnel were to wear ceremonial dress.

The next morning the parade grounds were full. Even citizens from Vladivostok were there, Mikhalovich noted with surprise, filling long bleachers along the gray gravel square of the marching area.

Precise lines of troops passed the reviewing stand, followed by an array of tanks and heavy artillery. Then the loudspeaker system crackled. Mikhalovich's name was called.

His throat suddenly dry, the major made his way to a raised platform in the center of the parade grounds on which the commanding officer and the political officer were standing. The band had stopped; the crowd was silent.

The political officer began shouting hoarsely into the microphone, reading an official charge accusing Mikhalovich of desertion from the Communist party because of indulgence in a religious belief. Then the commanding officer stripped the narrow crimson stripes off Mikhalovich's sleeve, ripped his navy blue tunic from top to bottom, and tore his cap from his head and tossed it to the ground.

Two armed soldiers stepped forward to escort Mikhalovich, not with their usual deference but with the distaste reserved for traitors. They marched him around the parade ground, his tunic gaping open to reveal his undershirt. From the troops he sensed a chill wave of derision; in the bleachers he could see civilians laughing and poking one another. In the front row his wife sat tight-lipped, furious. His older son kept his eyes down. The young one, oblivious, waved happily.

That afternoon Mikhalovich was handed a stiff-bristled push broom.

"This is the last time I will ever address you," the commanding officer said. "Your job is to clean."

THE COMMUNISTS were also subduing their opposition in the German Democratic Republic.

In June 1953, tanks ground through the streets of East Berlin, armed with the party's indignation. In this workers' state, fifty thousand laborers had dared to protest when the government announced a 10 percent increase in production quotas without a corresponding raise in pay.

Now, as masons and carpenters crowded the streets, throwing rocks at tanks and tearing up boundary markers between East and West Berlin, the Soviets sealed the border. Mine, factory, and rail yard workers all over the German Democratic Republic joined the protest in support of their comrades in Berlin. But tanks and guns carried the day.

The Soviet commandant declared martial law, and police herded the people into their homes. Premier Otto Grotewohl urged "loyal citizens" to join the search for workers leading the insurrection, and the party purged thousands of "doubters" from its ranks.

TWO YEARS LATER, a group of grim, gray men gathered around a fragile Queen Anne table to sign the Warsaw Pact: the military unification of the Soviet Union, Poland, Czechoslovakia, Hungary, Romania, Bulgaria, Albania, and East Germany. With this counterbalance to NATO, the world was officially divided. The Cold War had begun.

IN THE FALL OF 1956, the Hungarians revolted. Demonstrators in Budapest cheered wildly at the sight of a decapitated statue of Joseph Stalin, even as they demanded the heads of their current rulers and an end to Hungary's hard-line Communist regime.

Secret police opened fire on the crowds. Hundreds fell. But by this time the protesters had won the regular army's heart, and many troops joined the rebels, distributing arms to students and workers.

During the weeks of the rebellion, two reform-minded Communists who had been jailed and tortured under Stalin, Imre Nagy and Janos Kadar, were made prime minister and first secretary by the people. These new leaders declared Hungarian neutrality and disbanded the secret police.

At this, the Soviets throttled Budapest with two hundred thousand heavily armed troops, a thousand tanks, and an armada of planes. While the Hungarians hurled sticks, stones, and Molotov cocktails at the invaders, the advancing weapons leveled buildings and hundreds of Hungarian patriots.

At 9:00 on the morning of November 23, Soviet troops marched into Budapest's elegant parliament buildings to arrest Prime Minister Imre Nagy and most of his government. At 9:30 the Soviets opened fire on the American embassy, where Hungary's spiritual leader, Joseph Cardinal Mindszenty, had taken refuge just days earlier after being released from seven years in a Communist prison.

By the end of the day, the streets of Budapest were littered with rubble, bodies, and broken dreams. Some estimate that ten thousand Hungarians were killed, thirty thousand wounded.

But Janos Kadar emerged unscathed. In the midst of the uprising he changed sides, denounced the freedom fighters, and was made puppet prime minister by the Soviets as they put Hungary back together again—their way.

IN BERLIN, the authorities responded to the people's quest for freedom not with bullets, but with concrete blocks.

By now, two thousand people were escaping from East Germany to the West every day. So on the morning of August 13, 1961, soldiers left their barracks in East Berlin before dawn, driving trucks loaded with tons of concrete blocks and coils of barbed wire. By the time most Berliners awoke, an ugly barrier snaked its way through the heart of their city.

While soldiers with machine guns spiraled barbed wire over the Berlin Wall, battle-ready Soviet divisions surrounded the city, poised to enforce the point: No more East Germans would cross to the West.

AROUND THE SAME TIME in Poland, Karol Woytyla, bishop of Krakow, looked out over the sea of people and grinned, his rosy face shining with pleasure as he prepared to celebrate the triumph of the Christians of Nowa Huta.

Communists or Nazis, he sighed inwardly, in the end Poland's oppressors had all been the same, with their hard, narrow minds that shut out love and shut up people. He himself had been conscripted by the Nazis during World War II, forced to break up rocks in a stone quarry in Zakrzowek. In his labor camp work he had seen the toughest stones broken by sustained pressure and precise blows. But he had also seen stones, built together in a wall, resist even the mightiest of opposing forces.

It was like what the apostle Peter had written about the church: "You are living stones, being built up as a spiritual house for a holy priesthood, to offer up spiritual sacrifices acceptable to God through Jesus Christ."

Karol Woytyla believed the words of Scripture. And he believed his country would withstand the Communists—and in the end prevail. Just as this beloved church of Nowa Huta had prevailed.

The struggle had gone on for years: the workers of Nowa Huta demanding their church, erecting their cross, and the authorities tearing it down, only to have the cycle repeated. Perhaps the Communists had just worn down and given up. Whatever it was, Woytyla himself had finally led the church building campaign and set the cornerstone. And today fifty thousand people packed the square to consecrate and celebrate the result of their years of faithfulness.

"This city of Nowa Huta was built as a city without God," Bishop Woytyla shouted to the people. "But the will of God and the workers here has prevailed. Let us all take the lesson to heart. This is not just a building. These are living stones."[4]

SUCH MOMENTS OF TRIUMPH were sweet during the Communist occupation. Like the spring of 1968, when the Czech people enjoyed a season of hope during Czechoslovakia's "Prague Spring."

Students flocked to the Balustrade, Prague's avant-garde theater, to see the works of the artistic director, playwright Vaclav Havel, which mirrored socialism's absurd impositions on his country.

Czech leader Alexander Dubcek, determined to break the Soviet grip on his land, had stirred his countrymen with the vision of "socialism with a human face"—a loosening of policy that did not please Leonid Brezhnev, the heavy-browed face in the Kremlin.

The crushing Soviet response came quickly, as troops from obedient Warsaw Pact members—Poland, Hungary, Bulgaria, and East Germany—moved in to help subdue the Czechs.

Soon the resisters were gone and so was Alexander Dubcek, removed from power and replaced by a more reliable socialist with a less human countenance.

Five months later Jan Palach, a Czech student, stood in Wenceslas Square before the statue of Czechoslovakia's great saint and drenched himself in petrol, protesting the Soviet invasion of his nation. A match, a flame, and he was gone.

A FEW YEARS LATER, a young woman with as fiery a passion stood before a KGB court in Lithuania.

As a schoolgirl Nijole Sadunaite had been taken on tours of old cathedrals. When she insisted upon genuflecting at the altar, she was ordered to stop. She did not. Likewise, her parents refused to stop attending mass, even though her father was threatened with the loss of his job. And when the Communists threatened to throw Nijole and her brother out of school for refusing to join the party's youth league, their mother told the authorities that her children would never be "hypocrites and compromisers." And they weren't.

Nijole underwent a profound experience of the Holy Spirit at eighteen and then joined an underground order of nuns. In the early 1970s she published and distributed the *Chronicles of the Catholic Church*, which detailed the Soviet persecution. In 1974 she was caught and tried, but she turned the courtroom into a forum against her accusers.

"Are you happy with your triumph?" she asked. "What have you triumphed over? Over the moral ruins of the country, over millions of unborn children whom you have killed, over people robbed of their human dignity, poisoned by fear and evil passions?" And then she made a defiant prophecy. "Every day your crimes are bringing you closer to history's junk heap."

The flustered, angry members of the tribunal sentenced her to the gulag.[5]

IN ROMANIA, the threat to Christians was as constant, but perhaps more subtle. Doru Popa was a young chemical engineer when he met some Christians from the West connected with Campus Crusade for Christ. By law all Romanians were required to report any contact with Westerners within twenty-four hours. Popa neglected to do so, and his relationship with these believers resulted in extended theological training and his decision to become a pastor.

Popa became very influential among the Baptists in Arad, a city of three hundred thousand near Romania's Hungarian border. One day the secret police approached him and asked if he would like to travel all over Western Europe and the United States at their expense. All he needed to do was cooperate with them.

The idea of the Securitate as his personal travel agents didn't appeal to Popa, a fiery, passionate preacher who loved Christ a lot more than he loved the dictator, Nicolae Ceausescu. He declined the invitation—and soon found himself transferred from the guestlist to the hit list.

Agents broke into his apartment, bugged his phone, stole his work permit, and regularly arrested him for questioning. His car sometimes did strange things while he was at the wheel, and one day the steering mechanism failed to respond. Popa ran off the road and into a tree. Two of his passengers were injured, and Popa found himself at the center of a government-rigged lawsuit designed to put him in prison.

VACLAV HAVEL'S BOOKS and plays had been banned in Czechoslovakia since the crackdown during the 1968 Prague Spring uprising. Havel continued to publish outside of the country, but he was still writing in his homeland as well. With a group of writers and intellectuals he drafted the declaration of the 242-member Charter 77 movement.

The document, released on New Year's Day, 1977, called for "freedom of religious belief," "the right to freedom of expression," and an end to "tapping telephones, bugging homes, opening mail, carrying out house-searches, setting up networks of neighborhood informers."[6]

The Czech authorities didn't care for this New Year's resolution, and by January 2, Vaclav Havel was in prison.

IN OCTOBER of the following year, an election took place that would profoundly affect the battle between the cross and Communism. At the Vatican, the College of Cardinals announced the name of the 262nd successor to the throne of St. Peter.

Karol Woytyla, archbishop of Krakow, planter of crosses, was now Pope John Paul II. He was the youngest pope in 132 years, the first non-Italian in 456 years, the first pope from Poland, and the first pope with direct experience of life under totalitarian atheism.[7]

The following year when Pope John Paul II joyously returned to his beloved homeland, Warsaw's Victory Square—named for the Communists' triumph over the Axis powers in World War II—was packed with hundreds of thousands of Poles, crowded shoulder to shoulder to welcome home their own. Standing before an altar erected for the occasion, an immense cross in place behind him, the sturdy pontiff with the rosy complexion and the smile crinkles around his eyes raised his arms into the air.

"Holy Spirit, descend upon this ground," he shouted in a loud, exultant voice. "Holy Spirit, descend upon this ground! Holy Spirit, descend upon this ground!"

The people looked at one another with a sense of wonder. "Where are the Communists?" they asked. "Here we are. So many of us! Together with our pope!"

And in an instant came the realization that this truly was "victory square." Not the stale victory of one rival atheism supplanting another, but a spiritual victory. Gathered together that summer day the people saw with the eyes of their hearts; in the cross raised high they saw hope for the future.[8]

That hope would stand them in good stead in the dark days to follow. For life in Poland was bleak. The land had been bled of its fruitfulness, the heart and blood pressed from its workers. Conditions in the mines and factories were atrocious. Unions were outlawed. Food was scarce and lines were long.

Then at the end of the 1970s came *Solidarnosc,* or Solidarity. Many in Poland say it began more as an ideal than as a workers' union—a concept of oneness rooted in the spiritual values the Polish people clung to in those times of physical and spiritual repression. But what the world first saw of Solidarity appeared dramatically in the summer of 1980 when workers in Gdansk's Lenin Shipyard, in northern Poland, went on strike.

It began after Anna Walentynowicz, a thirty-year shipyard employee, was abruptly dismissed on August 7. The management did not care for Anna's activity in the Free Trade Union, a movement she had cofounded with Lech Walesa, a former shipyard electrician.

At six in the morning on August 14, sections of the Lenin Shipyard went out on strike. By the next day the strike had spread to fifteen other plants. That afternoon the authorities cut telecommunication links between Gdansk and the rest of Poland. Yet word of the strike seeped throughout the country, even as rumors flew of Soviet troops poised to enter Polish soil.

On August 17 workers erected a timber cross in front of Gate 2 of the Lenin Shipyard. Workers' families brought food, and priests entered the locked-in yard to celebrate mass.

As the tense days and nights of August ticked by, strikers and government representatives continued to negotiate, and on August 31 came the miraculous: The Gdansk Agreement was signed. The strike was over, and the workers had won twenty-one new rights. Lech Walesa, the young electrician, had become an international name, and Poles had a new sense of hope in their national movement.

But Solidarity's summertime hopes dimmed in the dark days of December 1980.

The Soviet leadership, concerned about the party's authority in Poland, had put Defense Minister General Wojciech Jaruzelski in charge. And in the early hours of December 14, Jaruzelski's government declared martial law. Tanks, troops, water cannons, and guns hedged in Poland's citizens, while police rounded up the leaders of the trade union and hustled them off to jail. By morning, the country had become one vast prison.

But something else was happening in the gray light of dawn: Priests across the nation were announcing that anyone who wanted to be of help in this terrible situation should make themselves known. Thus, only hours after the crackdown, the people were once again resisting—all over Krakow, all over Poland.

The first act of these "committees of social help" was to serve as information networks, finding out where people were imprisoned and informing their families. Then they gathered care packages—soap, toothpaste, warm clothing—and assisted prisoners' families who were left with no means of income. And as the people connected with one another to help, they broke the barrier of fear and isolation that martial law imposed.[9]

In seeing Solidarity as merely a trade union, the authorities had miscalculated. Solidarity was not simply an organization; it was a movement, a linkage of hands and hearts across Poland. And the Communists could not stop it, no matter how many troops they shuttled through the streets of Warsaw and Krakow.

But the linkage of hands and hearts didn't stop at Polish borders. Even as Soviet tanks massed outside of Poland, ready to quell any uprising, Pope John Paul II defied their oppressive authority. He announced to the press that if the Soviets invaded his homeland, he would return to stand with his people.

The tanks did not invade.

Hours after martial law began, a Warsaw priest named Father Jan Sikorski was knocking on the doors of the city's prisons to celebrate mass for the incarcerated. He encountered resistance, but Father Sikorski had a blunt, amiable, if unorthodox way of dealing with prison guards. After staring down more than one prison officer and dousing more than one guard with holy water, he was given permission to celebrate mass in the prisons. They didn't want to tangle with Father Sikorski, so he soon got his way.

Another Warsaw priest, Father Jerzy Popieluszko, dealt with the troops with his own brand of ecclesiastical love. On Christmas Eve he slipped away from his church, St. Stanislaw Kostka, and went into downtown

Warsaw. There he gave the thin Christmas Eve wafers—a traditional gift the Poles give friends and family to celebrate the coming of Christ—to the soldiers enforcing the hated martial law. "Be not overcome with evil, but overcome evil with good," was his creed.

MEANWHILE, in the Soviet Union, the former Major Mikhalovich thought often of the suffering Christ on the cross. For decades, since he had been publicly demoted because of his conversion, he had cleaned the soldiers' barracks in Vladivostok.

At first the men had harassed him, urinating on floors he had just swept, kicking over his water bucket while he mopped. His wife had left him, taking the children with her. He had only his faith to cling to.

But as the years went by and the soldiers were transferred, those who had known Mikhalovich as an officer dwindled. The commanding officer was killed in a train accident; the political officer was appointed to a key post in Moscow.

Hanani Mikhalovich was allowed to retire the year he turned seventy. He had no money, so he could not leave Vladivostok. But after all, his home was there—Dhom Baptista, a house church filled with sixty fervent Christians sharing three Bibles. Among these men and women, Hanani was a white-haired saint, his once-square shoulders now bowed, his hands gnarled from years of scrubbing floors, his black peasant's pants a bit tattered but impeccably clean, as if he were expecting inspection at any time.

IN POLAND, Father Jerzy Popieluszko was walking his own pilgrimage of suffering. Father Jerzy's lifelong hero, Maximilian Kolbe, had given his life for another inmate at Auschwitz during World War II. Now Father Jerzy felt a call to lay down his own life for his brothers.

Soon after the birth of Solidarity, Father Jerzy preached among the striking workers in Warsaw's huge steel works. He showed them how alcohol contributed to their oppression: If their drinking caused absenteeism or mistakes at work, it could be used to blackmail them. After that, alcoholism dropped dramatically. "Somehow we felt they owned us," said one foundryman, "and we became their slaves. Father Jerzy changed that."[10]

Not long after martial law was imposed and his foray into the night with Christmas peace for the soldiers, Father Jerzy instituted a monthly "Mass for the Homeland," dedicated to all victims of the repressive regime. Eventually thousands, then tens of thousands, attended these services at St. Stanislaw Kostka, with Father Jerzy ministering from a balcony and the people fanned out in the courtyard and streets below.

The pale, gaunt priest spoke without flair or passion. Yet his words themselves were filled with power.

"A man who bears witness to the truth can be free even though he might be in prison. . . . The essential thing in the process of liberating man and the nation is to overcome fear. . . . We fear suffering, we fear losing material good, we fear losing freedom or our work. And then we act contrary to our consciences, thus muzzling the truth. We can overcome fear only if we accept suffering in the name of a greater value. If the truth becomes for us a value worthy of suffering and risk, then we shall overcome fear—the direct reason for our enslavement.

"A Christian must be a sign of contradiction in the world. . . . A Christian is one who all his life chooses between good and evil, lies and truth, love and hatred, God and Satan. . . . Today more than ever there is a need for our light to shine, so that through us, through our deeds, through our choices, people can see the Father who is in Heaven."[11]

Father Jerzy's influence did not escape the notice of the authorities. He was far too popular, far too independent, far too threatening to the regime's control. He must be silenced.

The secret police followed Father Jerzy everywhere. He received unsigned, threatening letters. On the first anniversary of martial law, a pipe bomb sailed through the front window of his small flat, exploding in his sitting room.

Then, on October 19, 1984, while driving back to Warsaw from Bydgoszcz where he had celebrated a special mass and delivered a homily called "Overcome Evil with Good," Father Jerzy disappeared.

Thousands prayed for him in churches all over Poland. The steelworkers stopped their work in order to pray and threatened a national strike if their priest was not returned to them. The universities smoldered with unrest.

On the last Sunday of October, as fifty thousand people filled St. Stanislaw Kostka in an emotional Mass for the Homeland and listened in tears to a tape of Father Jerzy's final sermon, Father Antoni Lewek, one of the thirty priests at the altar, received word: "Just a moment ago it was announced on television that Father Jerzy's body has been found in the Vistula River."

"I shall never forget what happened," Father Lewek said later. "In a second people went down on their knees, crying and shouting; what we had feared most, the worst, had happened. . . .

"And then something very moving happened. This crying crowd managed to show that they could forgive. Three times they repeated after the priest: 'And forgive us our trespasses as we forgive them that trespass against us.' It was a Christian answer to the unchristian deed of the murderers."[12]

The body pulled from the Vistula, bound tightly and weighted with stones, was almost unidentifiable. Only when his brother saw the birthmark on the corpse's chest could he be sure it was Father Jerzy. His body was covered with deep wounds and horrifying bruises. Hair had been ripped from his scalp; his eyes, nose, mouth, and skull were gouged and smashed. His teeth had been broken to bits, his tongue reduced to pulp, as were his inner organs. His final agonies were unimaginable.

Yet on November 2, the day of Father Jerzy's funeral, people marched the streets past the secret police headquarters bearing banners reading, "We forgive."

Regardless of their expertise in murdering the body, the executioners could not kill the soul. Father Jerzy had taught his people well.

FIVE MONTHS LATER there was another funeral, this one in the Soviet Union.

Konstantin Chernenko, leader of the USSR, lay in a mound of roses, medals, and scarlet bunting, flanked by Soviet flags. Somber funeral music played on television and radio stations across the vast nation as the Communist leaders gravely deliberated over the choice of a new general secretary, sobered by the fact that they were burying their third leader in three years.

In the end, they chose Mikhail Sergeyevich Gorbachev, former KGB deputy and Politburo member who, even as he led Chernenko's funeral procession, vowed to free the Soviet Union from its own rigor mortis.

IN ROMANIA there were no new vows. Just Nicolae Ceausescu's relentless grip on his nation, where Christians continued to endure persecution.

Joseph Tson, the student who had heard his teacher's prophecy that the church would die out in a generation, had purposed to use his life to equip and strengthen the church for its battle.

Trained first as a philologist, Joseph taught Romanian literature for a decade. In 1969 he was able to travel abroad and subsequently studied theology at Oxford. Returning home in 1972, he taught for two years at the Baptist Seminary in Bucharest, but was fired when he wrote about the persecution of believers in Romania. He then became pastor of the Second Baptist Church of Oradea, the largest Baptist congregation in Eastern Europe.

Over the years, Joseph was arrested many times and beaten for his faith. By September 1981, the authorities presented him with a choice: prison in Romania or exile. Tson chose the latter.

He also chose to go to America, where he founded the Romanian Missionary Society and began to translate Christian books to smuggle back into Romania.

Back in his homeland, Christians who weren't exiled were hounded mercilessly.

Peter Dugulescu, a Baptist pastor in Timisoara, was warned by the Romanian secret police, "If you don't obey us, don't be surprised if a truck or a bus crosses your path."[13]

On September 30, 1986, Peter, his wife, and their thirteen-year-old daughter were driving down a one-way street when a large bus, empty except for its driver, ran a stop sign and appeared in the intersection before them, perpendicular to their car. Peter tried to stop, but it was too late.

After seeing that his wife and daughter appeared to be all right, Peter sat there stunned in his wrecked car, his right arm hanging useless by his side, but feeling the Holy Spirit nudging his mind back to a sermon he had preached three weeks earlier. That morning he had exhorted his congregation that the Christian must give thanks to God for everything that happens, even problems, troubles, and accidents.

"I tried to concentrate," Peter said later. "I tried to use my last strength to say, 'Oh, Lord, I don't understand what has happened. But I want to thank You—because You reign over all these things.'"

The police arrived, but neglected to question the bus driver, measure Peter's skid marks, or do any of their usual accident investigations. They just took Peter and his family to the hospital, where they were treated for shock, bruises, and broken bones. Two days later, they took Peter's driver's license away from him.

Peter knew the Communists had murdered other outspoken church leaders—like Jerzy Popieluszko in Poland—so he asked a friend to visit the bus driver. "Look deep into his eyes, without blinking, and ask him, 'Was it just an ordinary accident, or were you ordered to kill Pastor Dugulescu?'"

Peter's friend visited the driver, and when he asked the question, the man looked away. "I can't talk to you about that," he said. "Go away!"

Later, Peter visited the driver himself. "I forgive you," he said. "Take this Bible, in Jesus' name."

TWO YEARS LATER, in 1988, Nicolae Ceausescu stood on the balcony of the Central Committee headquarters in Bucharest, smiling the best smile his unpleasant face could muster, waving as the parades passed below him.

"Ceausescu, Peace!" read one bright banner. Schoolchildren carried another reading simply "Romania!" The crowd, swelled by thousands of Securitate agents and compliant citizens dressed in colorful native costumes, marched and sang of Romania's glory.

Meanwhile, Christian leaders across the nation were acknowledging the anniversary as well. "Look at the newspapers," one told his congregation, noting the authorities' emphasis on this forty-year mark and comparing the believers' situation with that of the ancient Israelites. "The newspapers are preaching to you that your time in the desert is almost over. Get ready!"

IN JANUARY 1989 a small group of Czechoslovakian students peacefully made their way to St. Wenceslas's statue in Prague to commemorate another anniversary: the twenty-year anniversary of Jan Palach's suicidal protest of the Soviet invasion of their country. Before they could reach their destination, however, a group of policemen moved toward them with water cannons and tear gas.

As the officials advanced, a short, fair-haired man watched in disgust from the other side of the square. A plainclothes agent grabbed the man and shoved him into a police van—only to find that this was Vaclav Havel, known throughout the West as Czechoslovakia's greatest human rights champion. No matter. A judge sentenced Havel to nine months in prison for inciting the demonstration.

When he was released on parole five months later, pale and thin, Havel met with Alexander Dubcek, deposed hero of the 1968 Prague Spring uprising. It was the first time the two visionaries had met. But it would not be the last.

MEANWHILE, POLAND'S PROBLEMS, including a $38.9 billion debt and continuous consumer shortages, had driven the government to desperation. As a result, the authorities did the unthinkable: They opened avenues for discussion with their longtime opponents.

Solidarity representatives who had spent time in jail during martial law now found themselves being wooed by party members offering to reinstate the union and give it a share of parliamentary power—if Solidarity would, in turn, assure the government's continued control of the parliament.

THE SOVIET UNION was attempting an equally surprising exercise in democracy, with general elections held in March 1989—the first nation-wide, competitive election since the autumn of 1917.

When the votes were tallied, Communist party officials, including those who ran without opposition, found themselves ousted. A substantial number of independent and reform-minded candidates swept into office, including a bold, opinionated iconoclast named Boris Yeltsin.

IN JUNE, Poland's elections made it clear that Solidarity had won every-where. Many leading Communists, running unopposed, had failed to get enough votes to win. The power struggle continued through the summer, however, since the party still controlled a portion of the government. But by August 19, President Jaruzelski had appointed Tadeusz Mazowiecki as prime minister of Poland.

Mazowiecki, a journalist, a devout Roman Catholic, and an adviser to Solidarity leader Lech Walesa, had the heady distinction of being the first non-Communist to head a government in Eastern Europe since Stalin had imposed his Soviet-style Communism there after World War II.

IN HUNGARY, during that same summer, processional music filled Budapest's largest square as Imre Nagy, who had led the nation's 1956 uprising against the Communists, was buried. Again.

Thirty-one years after he had been hanged and flung in a common grave with hundreds of other rebels, the former prime minister was honored by a state funeral—the type of tribute usually reserved for top party officials. Four companions who had led the revolt with Nagy were reburied with him, and the government network broadcast the proceedings.

Though the nation's top leaders marched solemnly behind the coffin in the funeral procession, Nagy's former ally, Janos Kadar, the turncoat leader who had been Hungary's Soviet-backed leader for thirty-two years, was not present. Deposed in 1988, Kadar was said to be physically and mentally ill.

Then, in September, came another procession, when Hungarian troops tore down their barbed-wire fences and watchtowers on the border with Austria. Since early 1988 the Hungarians had been able to travel more freely, but this physical opening of the border crossing meant that it was now possible to walk from Hungary into Austria—and on into West Germany.

And at midnight on September 13, 1989, the Hungarians went further, formally suspending their agreement with East Germany and officially opening their western border. According to the East German penal code, "flight from the republic" meant long prison terms. But within three days, fifteen thousand East Germans had headed for freedom.[14]

Meanwhile, the unimaginable happened: A thirty-five-year-old Lutheran pastor, Gabor Roszik, challenged a sitting member of parliament. For his impertinence, Roszik was defrocked by his Communist-sympathizing bishop. Undeterred, Roszik preached all the harder and campaigned to a stunning upset, making him the first non-Communist to win a seat since the Soviet occupation of the Eastern bloc.

AS MORE AND MORE special trains were added to the freedom railroad from east to west, the hundreds of thousands who chose to remain in East Germany took to the churches and the streets.

In Leipzig, Dresden, Halle, Weimar, and Wittenberg, churches were filled. Monday evening prayer services at St. Nikolai's in Leipzig overflowed, and after the services, the people spilled out to the Karl Marx Platz to march for freedom.[15]

Fifteen hundred people crowded into Leipzig's Evangelical Reformed Church on Monday evenings, though the building seated only 550. Meanwhile, people were spilling out of the doors of the larger churches in the city centers. The huge Church of the Cross in Dresden was packed, as was Gethsemane Church in East Berlin.

During that time, says Juergen Weidel, pastor of Peace Church in Leipzig, "People saw that the church was a living and viable organism, not the decaying institution Marxism said it was."[16] The church had indeed survived the Communists.

Yet, maintains Johannes Richter, pastor of St. Thomas Church in Leipzig, "We didn't encourage disobedience. The responsibility would have been too great. What we did was encourage obedience to God. We said, 'Do you want to be free and obey the Ten Commandments? Or do you want to be a slave and have a car and a good job?'"[17]

Clearly the people of East Germany had had enough of slavery, and Communism's triumphal forty-year anniversary celebration on October 7 was not quite the event the party had planned. In East Berlin, Lutheran bishops boycotted the affair, and riot police broke up a peaceful candlelight vigil of some fifteen hundred protesters. In Dresden, Leipzig, and other cities, police used water cannons and swung riot sticks to beat back the crowds.

On October 9, after the usual Monday night prayer meeting at Leipzig's Nikolai church, 150,000 people took to the streets.

"We are the people!" they shouted.

State security forces and riot police stood by with live ammunition. Tanks sat ready in the garage of the state university, and armed troops surrounded every church in the city.

But this time, at least, blood was not shed. Church leaders pleaded with government leaders for nonviolence, and the order to fire was never issued.

On October 19, Bishop Leich arrived at the party offices for his scheduled meeting with Communist leader Erich Honecker. After the mass demonstrations of October 9 and the averting of disaster, Honecker had sent for the bishop to discuss the church's role in the protests erupting all over East Germany. Instead of meeting with Honecker, however, Bishop Leich found himself the first official visitor of a new prime minister.

Secretly, the day before, the man who had been the leader of the East German Communist establishment for eighteen years had fallen from power, but not before replacing himself with his protégé, Egon Krenz. No matter, thought Bishop Leich. All would soon be changed. He could feel it coming.

Krenz hastened to present himself as a younger, more sophisticated leader, aware of the people's discontent. Within a day or two, however, angry citizens were bold enough to shout down the East German party chief.

"You are finished!" they cried. "Give us free elections!"

A FEW WEEKS LATER, on the first Sunday of November, all of the Romanian Baptist churches spent the day in prayer and fasting for their nation.[18] As they had for years, they prayed for religious freedom in their country. They had heard rumors about upheaval in Eastern Europe, but they dared not dream such changes could come to Romania.

For his part, Pastor Doru Popa had had enough of the petty Communist oppression. He was due to preach at a funeral service in a small town north of Arad, and now the ever-troublesome secret police had called him to Timisoara, the university town south of Arad, for questioning regarding his case. Popa went to the prosecutor in Arad to explain his situation.

"Sir, you can arrest me if you want," he said, "but today I have to go to a funeral service. I am a pastor, and that is where I am needed. I will stay here only if you arrest me. But know this: You will stand before God one day."

The official blanched, then responded in typical bureaucratic fashion.

"Reverend Popa, I have nothing to do with this," he said. "Your case was given to me, and you will be in prison. That is the plan. It's not up to me. It's beyond my powers. The case will go before the court in December."

Popa went on to preach at the funeral. And by December, events the officials had not foreseen had overtaken Romania. Doru Popa did not go to prison.[19]

ON NOVEMBER 9, work crews in Germany embarked on a deconstruction project the people had awaited for twenty-eight years. Several days earlier the entire Communist cabinet of the German Democratic Republic had resigned, and this time the army crews did not come at night while the people slept. They came openly, their progress marked by cheers and tears of joy, and watched with amazement and celebration around the world.

The Berlin Wall was coming down!

As the wall broke open, citizens of East Berlin poured through. Crowds of West Germans waited to greet them with uncharacteristic fervor, hugging strangers and throwing bouquets of flowers. Friends who had not seen each other for twenty-eight years were reunited. East Germans gleefully picked up their 100-mark "welcome money," hungrily eyeing the sights in the sumptuous West German shop windows.

Whatever lay ahead, it was a celebration they would never forget. Nor would the rest of a watching world.

"We Germans are now the happiest people on earth," declared the mayor of West Berlin.

THE PEOPLE OF CZECHOSLOVAKIA were also on the road to freedom. During the third week of November, all of Czechoslovakia seemed to be in the streets, shouting for change and demanding the resignation of Milos Jakes, Czechoslovakia's hard-line Communist leader.

Those not crowding Wenceslas Square watched in fascination as the rallies unfolded on television. There was Vaclav Havel, with hundreds of thousands cheering him madly. A worker named Honza Lexa, interviewed by a reporter, was saying openly that she thought the government had been lying. "What is the government afraid of?" she asked.

Suddenly their screens went black. The voice of an announcer soon came on, explaining that some unidentified television workers had disagreed with Lexa's statement. Thirty-five minutes later the broadcast was reinstated and the people heard the strong voice of Father Vaclav Maly from Wenceslas Square.

"There can be no confidence in the leadership of a state that refuses to tell people the truth," shouted Maly, a Catholic priest whose propensity for truth telling had annoyed the government for years. Long barred from performing priestly duties, Maly was reading from an open letter from Cardinal Frantisek Tomasek, who had prayed for the day when the people would no longer accept lies.

Maly had prayed for this day as well. Not for his own advancement, but for the proclamation of gospel truth against the government's lies. After his clerical license had been revoked in 1979, he had cleaned toilets in the Prague subways and worked as a coal stoker in a hotel.

When a religious foundation in the West heard about him and began sending a small stipend, he was able to quit stoking coal and study theology instead—sitting at a small kitchen table in the tiny apartment he shared with his widowed father. Maly knew the police listened in on his conversations through a microphone hidden in a ceiling light fixture; he hoped they paid special attention when he prayed aloud to God for his nation.

Ironically the priest found that his tormentors' harassment helped, rather than hindered, his devotion to Christ.

"They stripped our faith of all the superfluous things," he said. "They took away church property. Only someone willing to make a personal sacrifice could make a confession of faith. Young people entered the church because they understood this sacrifice."[20]

And in a demonstration along the Letna Plain, the huge riverfront park bordering the northern edge of downtown Prague, Father Maly had an unexpected opportunity to practice the faith he had learned from years of sacrifice.

As Maly was speaking before a crowd of half a million demonstrators, a young police officer pushed his way forward, climbed the steps to the podium, and explained to the shocked crowd that he had been among the police officers who had beaten a group of student protesters several weeks earlier. "I am sorry," he stammered. "Please forgive me."

Maly put his arm around the weeping officer, then spoke firmly to the crowd about the Christian duty to forgive. "Let us pray," he shouted.

And in a voice five hundred thousand strong, they affirmed the faith the Communists had not been able to steal: "Our Father, who art in heaven . . . Thy will be done on earth, as it is in heaven . . . forgive us our trespasses, as we forgive those who trespass against us."

BY NOW THE PEOPLE in Wenceslas Square had cheered themselves hoarse. Yet still singing, dancing, screaming, 350,000 protesters welcomed back a man they had not seen in public since 1968: Alexander Dubcek, leader of the Prague Spring uprising. For the past two decades he had worked in an obscure state forestry office.

As he stood on the balcony, Dubcek's eyes filled with tears. "An old wise man said, 'If there once was light, why should there be darkness again?'" he shouted. "Let us act in such a way to bring the light back again!"[21]

Soon after his speech, the people received the news that Czechoslovakia's Communist party leadership had resigned, including Milos Jakes.

Their long-ago springtime dreams were finally coming to harvest.

IN ROMANIA, Nicolae Ceausescu was open to no such dreams. On November 20 he harangued his way through a five-hour speech in Bucharest. His party delegates chanted slogans, jumped up, applauded, and sat down in unison, uniformly—too uniformly—affirming their support for Ceausescu's disdain for democratic changes elsewhere in Eastern Europe.

Meanwhile, from his exile in the West, Dr. Joseph Tson had stepped up his assault on Romanian airwaves via Radio Free Europe.

"Change is coming to Romania," asserted Dr. Tson. "Christians, be ready!"

Believers in western Romania heard his challenge with a mixture of joy and wonder.

THERE WAS WONDER at the Vatican, too, as media from around the world recorded the culmination of an unprecedented event: the first encounter between a Soviet leader and a pope. Clasping hands at the close of a tumultuous decade, John Paul II and Mikhail Gorbachev stood at a crossroads.

During the historic meeting the pope pressed for religious freedoms for Soviet Catholics. In response, the Soviet leader acknowledged that all believers "have a right to satisfy their spiritual needs" and that his country had made the mistake of treating religion in "a simplistic manner."[22]

The ironies of the meeting were not lost on the *New York Times,* which observed, "At an earlier time, Stalin had scornfully asked how many divisions the pope had. Now, a successor intent on undoing Stalin's legacy has crossed St. Peter's Square in open recognition that he must reckon with the Vatican as a moral and political force."[23]

Three days later the Soviet Union and the four Warsaw Pact allies that had taken part in the invasion of Czechoslovakia in 1968 issued a joint statement condemning the Soviet-led military suppression of the popular Prague Spring uprising.

BACK IN PRAGUE, a prisoner from that uprising was on his way to becoming president.

For years Vaclav Havel's most common form of transportation had been paddy wagons and police cars. Now, during the first week of December 1989, people had glimpsed him riding in government limousines. What was going on?

Then came the announcement the people had hoped for: Havel was willing to become president of Czechoslovakia.

"I have repeatedly said my occupation is writer," the dissident told an American reporter. "I have no desire to be a professional politician. But I have always placed the public interest above my own. And if, God help us, the situation develops in such a way that the only service I could render my country would be to do this, then of course I would do it."[24]

AT THE SAME TIME, though heartened by the democratic changes coming elsewhere in Eastern Europe, the people in Romania could not believe that such changes might possibly come to their own land. Nicolae Ceausescu was too powerful, his Securitate too insidiously pervasive.

Nevertheless, believers in Timisoara spent hours in prayer. Lying prostrate on the cold floors of their small flats, they were warmed by a spiritual passion that caused them to thunder a bold and unlikely prayer: "Lord, help our nation. Turn Your face to our land. Bring revival to Romania—and bring it through Timisoara!"[25]

God answered that prayer. And help for Romania did indeed begin in Timisoara. Government agents came to the home of a pastor named Laszlo Tokes. Protesters from his church blockaded the door. Their numbers swelled, and soon thousands of citizens filled Timisoara's central square. Christians from all over the city rallied and prayed that this might be the beginning of the end of the godless tyranny of Ceausescu's regime.

Some believers held back from the protest demonstrations at first. Was this their answer to prayer? Surely they would give their lives for Christ and the cause of the gospel—but was this that time? Or was it merely a political situation? They were ready, but they wanted to be wise.

As they prayed for wisdom, they also brought tea and soup and blankets to warm the people in the square. And as they did so, they believed God was leading them to join these demonstrations against a dictator who had despised His name. For the sake of the university students with whom they worked, the ones who would ask in the future, "Were you there?" they had to be able to answer, "Yes, we were there. We were in solidarity with those who stood for the cause of freedom and justice."

Gelu Paul, his wife, Rodica, and Peter and Gina Bulica were part of the small group that fasted and prayed over their decision to join the people. They also prayed, as they had for years, for the downfall of Nicolae Ceausescu.

Meanwhile, in Bucharest, Ceausescu convened a meeting of the Political Executive Committee of the Romanian Communist party, furious that the military had yet to open fire on the Timisoara demonstrators.

"Why didn't they shoot?" he asked Defense Minister Vasile Milea. "They should have shot to put them on the ground, to warn them—shot them in the legs."

Addressing the group, Ceausescu continued, "Everybody who doesn't submit to the soldiers—I've given the order to shoot. They'll get a warning, and if they don't submit, they'll have to be shot. It was a mistake to turn the other cheek. . . . In an hour, order should be reestablished in Timisoara."[26]

Supposing the situation resolved, Ceausescu left for a three-day trip to Iran, leaving his army and faithful Securitate agents to carry out his violent measures. What he didn't realize was that his army was not entirely with him.

Marius Miron was on the streets of Timisoara on the evening of

December 17 after Ceausescu had given his order to shoot. Miron saw cars driving the wrong way down one-way streets, and near Laszlo Tokes's church he saw tear gas canisters and water cannons. On the city square a huge bonfire raged in front of a bookshop: People had broken the windows and were dragging out books by and about the Ceausescus, throwing them into the flames. Near the opera house he saw soldiers firing their guns into the air; he heard the sounds of breaking glass and people shouting slogans.

He was at the corner of Liberty Square and Karl Marx Street when he saw a group of ten people shot down by soldiers. Miron, a trained medical assistant, ran and bent over the man closest to him; the man's femoral artery had been severed by a bullet, and he was bleeding to death.

When Miron stood up to take off his belt to make a tourniquet, he saw a soldier take deliberate aim at him and fire. He felt no pain. His leg just suddenly blew up. He hit the ground, his limb shattered, and began to drag himself backward by his elbows until someone picked him up and took him to the hospital.[27]

The shooting continued.

Gradually hundreds, then thousands, of people flooded the streets, making their way toward Timisoara's main square, carrying signs and banners. One held a stick aloft with a shoe on top—a reference to Ceausescu's original vocation.

"Down with the shoemaker!" he cried.

"Liberty!" shouted others. "Freedom!"

Adina Jinaru, watching the procession go by her home, felt as if the whole of Timisoara had been in prison—"and now they were all to be released at once."

Rumors spread everywhere in the bullet-torn city: Nicolae Ceausescu had given the order to level Timisoara and annihilate everyone in it. Elena Ceausescu had urged the use of chemical weapons. The army's special code, "Blue Rain," was about to be activated and would signal the city's utter destruction.

During the night Adina and her family huddled in their basement with a few provisions while the air-raid siren wailed across the city. Somehow Adina got an open phone line and called her friend Nellie Iovin in Arad.

"I don't know what will happen to us," she cried into the phone, "but if we are wiped out, call my brother in Germany and tell him what happened!"[28]

Nellie Iovin lived in a small, detached house in Arad on Scolii Street, just off the main highway through town. Like Nellie, most of Arad's citizens knew about the drama being played out in neighboring Timisoara. Then their own uprising began as a hundred thousand people gathered in Arad's main square in front of the city hall, where they were soon ringed by tanks and soldiers.

As Nellie and other Christians approached the square, they had to pass these tanks and a line of soldiers. Would they shoot? Fearful but determined, Nellie and the others knelt in front of the guns and began to pray; some stuck flowers into the gun barrels. The soldiers let them pass.[29]

Here, as in Timisoara, the crowds were shouting, "Down with Ceausescu! Down with Communism!"

And here, as in Timisoara, the Christians in the crowd added other slogans. For forty-five years the citizens of Romania had been told there was no God. Now a hundred thousand people were shouting as one, "God exists! God is with us!"

Across the street from city hall, Baptist pastor Mihai Gongola was given a microphone, wired with electricity from the tram lines. His main theme was the people's slogan: "God is with us!"

Pastor Doru Popa preached to the crowd as well. "Finally we are free," he shouted. "But some of us here were free already: We had been made free by God."

Then Popa gestured toward the Communist headquarters, a building where he had been searched and interrogated many times.

"We will write on this building three words," he said. *"Via, veritas, vita:* the way, the truth, the life. We need a way: For forty years we had no leadership. We need the truth: For forty years all we heard were lies. And we need life: For forty years we have had only an existence."

Popa closed his sermon with a traditional Romanian carol that people had not sung in public for forty years: "What wonderful news is coming from Bethlehem, that we have now a Savior."

Holding candles aloft in the night, a hundred thousand people took up the melody. A song of good news in a land that had known only bad for so long.

On December 21, with Romania on the verge of total upheaval, Ceausescu staged a rally in Bucharest. Such rallies had been the staple of his regime for years: pro-Ceausescu banners displaying carefully retouched, attractive portraits of the unattractive dictator and his wife; the Ceausescus on a balcony high above the people, who obediently brayed their shouts of approval and adulation.

But this time something went awry.

When Ceausescu appeared on the balcony, he intoned with unintended irony, "I would like to extend to you . . . warm revolutionary greetings."[30]

At first the usual cheers and applause came back to him: "Ceausescu! Ceausescu! Romania!"

Suddenly there was a movement in the crowd, as if people in the back of the throng were pushing those in front of them. Undistinguished shouts. A sense of confusion.

Then a faint cry began: "Timisoara!" "Timisoara!" and several young people unfurled a banner they had hidden under their coats: "Down with Ceausescu!" Some in the crowd began to run away.

Perplexed by the disorder, Ceausescu began waving his arms, muttering into the microphone, "Hello? Hello?" assuming something was wrong with the sound system. Elena Ceausescu strode forward, shouting for silence, and then her husband resumed his speech.

But it was too late.

Even as a few supporters still cheered the dictator, a group of people began singing "Romanians, Awake," the same song the crowd had sung outside the church of Laszlo Tokes. And then came the cry: "Yesterday Timisoara, today Bucharest!"[31]

As Nicolae Ceausescu tried once more to speak to the crowds, his once-docile people booed and threw shoes at him. Furious, the ugly little man turned back into the Central Committee building and ordered the army to fire.

By this time, however, many members of the army had defected to the people. Also, Vasile Milea, minister of defense, refused to give the firing order to his troops; soon after, his death was announced as a traitor's suicide. Milea had shot himself rather than carry out Ceausescu's lethal order.[32]

When a crowd stormed the Central Committee building, Ceausescu, his wife, and a few aides fled by helicopter from the roof.

Just as the news of Ceausescu's flight reached Timisoara, Pastor Peter Dugulescu was poised to speak to the two hundred thousand people assembled in the city square. For hours speakers had been addressing the crowds from the balcony of the opera house—the same balcony from which Ceausescu had spoken to the people during his annual visits to Timisoara.

On this night, just hours before Christmas, people in the crowd had requested that a pastor come to preach to them. A committee of sorts was reviewing each speaker's material. When Dugulescu told them his plans, they nodded. "Just end with the words, 'Down with the tyrant,'" they said. "I can do that," Dugulescu replied.

"I'm Pastor Peter Dugulescu from the First Baptist Church, Timisoara," he began as he took the microphone, "and I have come to speak to you in the name of God, as you wanted. For almost forty-five years—my age, unfortunately—we have been told there is no God. The Communists wanted to take God away from our hearts, from our minds, from our families, from our schools. I want to speak to you in the name of this God."

From the balcony Dugulescu could see thousands of upturned faces, hear the shouts of voices hoarse with tears.

"God exists!" they shouted. "There is a God. There is a God. God is with us!"

Dugulescu continued. "The Communists tried to kill me a few times— but I am still alive, because God protected me. And I have asked the government to bring Pastor Tokes back to Timisoara; we must have real religious freedom in Romania!"

Cheers interrupted him periodically as he continued for a few minutes, then asked the people to pray with him. "This is a historic moment. Let us turn our hearts to God. Please follow me in the Lord's Prayer."

He hadn't asked the people to kneel, but as he looked out he saw a sight he would never forget.

On this square where people had been forced to sing the praises of

Ceausescu for years, before this balcony that had been an altar to the Communist regime, now, as far as he could see, a tidal wave of people knelt on the pavement. And sentence by sentence, with one voice, they thundered out the ancient prayer: "Our Father, who art in heaven, hallowed be Thy name."

Believers in the crowd looked at those beside them and sensed a unity that set their hearts afire. They could see hope on the faces of young people who had known nothing but socialism for their entire lives. They saw joy on the faces of old people who had long yearned for Romania to return to God, long prayed for God to turn His face back to their beleaguered nation. In their eyes was the wonder of the truth, the life, the way: *God is sovereign. It is His kingdom, His power, and His glory.*

AS CHRISTMAS DAWN CREPT across the land of Romania, the church bells rang for the first time in forty years. Good news blared from television sets across the country: "God has turned His face back to Romania!" Christians who had not sung carols in public during their lifetimes sang out the good news of Christ's coming: "Immanuel, God with us!"

Since Nicolae Ceausescu had denied that fact during his entire political career, to many Romanians it seemed fitting that his execution came on Christmas Day.

Ceausescu and his wife had been captured almost immediately after their flight from Bucharest and kept in army custody for several days. Then on December 25, having been tried by a military tribunal for crimes against the people, they were convicted of genocide. Hundreds volunteered to serve on their firing squad.

Video images of the dictator and his wife sprawled in pools of blood were transmitted across Romania—and around the world.

What a man sows, so shall he reap, thought Pastor Mihai Gongola as he saw the fallen tyrant. Then he went through his forty-four-unit apartment block distributing New Testaments and wishing his neighbors a merry Christmas, relishing his extraordinary new freedom to do so openly.

THE BELLS RINGING IN ROMANIA rang across the rest of Eastern Europe as the people gathered in the streets, hugging each other and weeping for joy, singing Christmas carols with the fervor of newfound freedom.

And even as the citizens of the East shook off their bonds, the pundits of the West lost no time in analyzing the story.

Time magazine held nothing back in its enthusiasm for the end of the Cold War, declaring Mikhail Gorbachev "Man of the Decade." Ignoring the complexities and the heart of Eastern Europe's revolutions of 1989, the journal effused, "A catalyst for reform from Moscow to Bucharest, Gorbachev has transformed the world."[33]

Surely Gorbachev's policies created an atmosphere wherein change seemed more accessible than at any time in the Eastern bloc's history. But had the glasnost cowboy riding the buckling brontosaurus of his ailing nation really pulled off such a miracle?

No. Even as they affirmed the wonder of the Cold War ending, not with a bang or a whimper, but with shouts of joy in the streets, the media missed the heart of the biggest story of the century.[34] Surely bad politics and dismal economics played their part in fueling the unrest. But man does not live by bread alone, and in Eastern Europe the people were not marching for bread alone. They were marching for a freedom that transcends the physical—the freedom of the human spirit.

While the "Man of the Decade" issue filled Western newsstands, President Vaclav Havel adjusted his glasses, took a deep breath, and began his New Year's Day address to the people of Czechoslovakia. His theme was the same one that had gotten him arrested thirteen years earlier.

The worst thing about the legacy of Communism, he told the people, "is that we are living in a decayed moral environment. We have become morally ill, because we have become accustomed to saying one thing and thinking another. We have learned not to believe in anything, not to have consideration for one another, and to only look after ourselves. . . .

"When I talk about a decayed moral environment . . . I mean all of us . . . all of us are responsible, each to a different degree, for keeping the totalitarian machine running. None of us is merely a victim of it, because all of us helped to create it together."

Shocking words for people accustomed to forty years of Communism, but words they had staged a revolution to hear. Then Havel took it further:

"Our first [pre-Communist] president wrote, 'Jesus and not Caesar.' . . . This idea has once again been reawakened in us."[35]

CHRIST OR CAESAR? This was the choice made all across Eastern Europe. And what began in Nowa Huta with the raising of the cross in the public square came to its denouement three decades later in, of all places, the heart of the Communist behemoth.

It was May Day, 1990. The place, Moscow's Red Square.

"Is it straight, Father?" one Orthodox priest asked another, shifting the heavy, eight-foot crucifix on his shoulder.

"Yes," said the other. "It is straight."

Together the two priests, along with a group of parishioners holding ropes that steadied the beams of the huge cross, walked the parade route. Before them had passed the official might of the Union of Soviet Socialist Republics: the usual May Day procession of tanks, missiles, troops, and salutes to the Communist party elite.

Behind the tanks surged a giant crowd of protesters, shouting up at Mikhail Gorbachev. "Bread! . . . Freedom! . . . Truth!"

As the throng passed directly in front of the Soviet leader standing in his place of honor, the priests hoisted their heavy burden toward the sky. The cross emerged from the crowd. As it did, the figure of Jesus Christ obscured the giant poster faces of Karl Marx, Friedrich Engels, and Vladimir Lenin that provided the backdrop for Gorbachev's reviewing stand.

"Mikhail Sergeyevich!" one of the priests shouted, his deep voice cleaving the clamor of the protesters and piercing straight toward the angry Soviet leader. "Mikhail Sergeyevich! Christ is risen!"

A FEW MONTHS AFTER that final May Day celebration, the Soviet Union was officially dissolved.

Christ is risen indeed. And regardless of the prevailing political powers, be they the reigns of the Caesars or the Communists or the cultures of moral decay, He will build His church. And the gates of hell will not prevail against it.

18

THE CHURCH IN CAPTIVITY

Literalistic Christians will learn that a God or a faith system that has to be defended daily is finally no God or faith system at all. They will learn that any god who can be killed ought to be killed. Ultimately they will discover that all their claims to represent the historical, traditional, or biblical truth of Christianity cannot stop the advance of knowledge that will render every historic claim for a literal religious system questionable at best, null and void at worst.

—JOHN SHELBY SPONG,
retired Episcopal bishop

A DECADE AGO, as the world watched in astonishment, long-entrenched Communist regimes collapsed. Oppressors fled. The persecuted church emerged triumphant. A miraculous deliverance.

But oppression of the church did not end, of course. It continues today in China, North Korea, Vietnam, parts of India, and in a number of Islamic nations. One place in particular cries out for our attention. Here is how our brothers and sisters in Sudan describe their plight:

> If we say Jesus is God, we do not eat. We starve within sight of the U.N. planes filled with food you sent us, denied to us by our government. . . .
>
> It is mutilations, our ears, lips, hands, feet gone. It is another generation without education. It is mass rapes—our daughters, many men. It is slavery, the real thing.
>
> It is running barefoot . . . before the utterly incessant tracking of the spraying, hissing, whining bullets spitting at our heels from helicopter gunships.
>
> It is our pregnant women in jails so hot that the babies in their

wombs are essentially poached and born, of course, dead. They have held us down and pierced our lips so hot and through the bloody perforations forced the locking arm of padlocks, which when shut prevent the tortured ones from speaking or eating.

One day, government forces came to my brother's home. . . . They tied his hands behind his back and tied the other end of the rope to their vehicle. They dragged him three miles. His skin was worn off his bones. They poured gas on my brother and set his body on fire.[1]

Macram Max Gassis, bishop of the Diocese of El Obeid in south central Sudan, has testified before the U.S. Congress, the U.N., and the European Parliament, documenting the slave raids that steal children from Christian parents, the bombing of Christian schools, churches, and hospitals, the forced famines, the crucifixions, the Islamic indoctrination of young boys of Christian families, the creation of concentration camps for Christians who refuse to convert to Islam.[2] For this, Sudan's dictators have placed him under indictment. But still the gentle priest brings food, medicine, Bibles, and the attention of the West to Sudan.

And against all hope, against all logic, in spite of these tortures, the church in the Sudan continues to grow. The English translation of a song sung by Sudanese believers goes something like this:

> God has not forgotten us.
> Evil is departing and holiness is advancing.
> These are the things that shake the earth!

In the darkest places, the light shines the brightest, and it can't be extinguished in the hellhole of Sudan. In the midst of the horror and carnage, believers celebrate and worship with joy. As Gassis puts it, *"The church is the reality of hope."*

Baroness Caroline Cox, a member of the English House of Lords, has seen that hope firsthand. A great advocate for the persecuted church around the world, she has been to Sudan many times. She once told me about an experience there that shows the truth of Bishop Gassis's beautiful phrase.

Baroness Cox traveled into the bush area in southern Sudan, bringing supplies and a Catholic priest to a church which for lack of clergy had not celebrated mass in years. The church was being systematically repressed by the Muslims. Many of their number had disappeared, while others lived in a primitive camp with barely enough food and water to survive.

As the sun rose on another oppressive day in Sudan, that little band of believers gathered under the leaves of a big mango tree, the only protection for miles around. At great personal risk, the priest had brought bread and wine. He passed the elements. In that sweltering African savannah, even as the blood of many was being shed in the neighboring province, these Christians, on their knees, celebrated the Body and blood of our Lord Jesus, the One whose shed blood saves us. It was the most moving worship service Baroness Cox had ever experienced.

Halfway around the globe, in America, congregations also gather to worship. But sometimes the scenes are strikingly different.

In January 2002, the congregation filed into the twelve-hundred-member Plymouth Congregational Church in Denver. When the worshipers had settled in, the minister, Rev. Scott Landis, made his announcement.

He was, he told his congregation, gay, and therefore terminating his twenty-five-year marriage. His three children had been "remarkable," he said, in understanding and supporting his decision. So were his congregants: After Landis concluded his remarks, they stood and applauded.

Would the church members have applauded, one commentator asked, if, say, the reverend announced he was dumping his wife for the twenty-year-old daughter of one of the congregants?[3]

Doubtful. Why, then, the thunderous applause? The answer is that to be gay and come out is seen as heroic: One takes a stand against such repressive customs as marital fidelity and heterosexual sex and is liberated, able to fulfill his biological destiny. Infidelity is transformed into a form of existential heroism or self-actualization.

Reverend Landis told the *Denver Post* that his decision was the result of a long struggle between his homosexual feelings and his Christian beliefs. When he told his church of the choice, he said later, "they showed me compassion, love and support beyond my wildest dreams."[4]

But, of course, this is a liberal church, some may say. This wouldn't happen in our evangelical congregations. But remember when Mel White, who had impeccable evangelical "credentials," came out a few years back, divorced his wife, and founded a church for homosexuals?

As for the divorce question, we evangelicals aren't all that different from the culture at large: Barna research has found that born-again Christians are just as likely to get divorced as non-born-again adults.[5]

Consider the scene in a big evangelical church a few years ago. Six years earlier the pastor had come to the congregation with sad news. He was separating from his wife of over forty years. He had promised that if the separation turned to divorce, he would, in accordance with the covenant of the church, resign his post as pastor.

But now he had changed his mind. He and his wife were divorcing, but instead of resigning as promised, he vowed to stay on as senior pastor, being faithful, as he put it, to God's call. According to news accounts the congregation stood and gave him a sustained ovation.

Applause? The pastor in question is someone I know and respect. I am very sorry about his personal tragedy. But I found the action of the congregation incomprehensible. As pleased as they were to have him stay, as much as they wanted to show him their love, there could be no justification for applauding the violation of church covenants.

One of the church deacons told the press, "We hate it when things like this happen, but our church is moving right along."[6] An assistant pastor even suggested that God would make the senior pastor more valuable because his personal pain through this divorce would enhance his ability to minister to others.

Where is the church in bondage? Where it worships in a land filled with Islamic troops who kill, maim, torture and sell Christians into slavery? Or in beautiful sanctuaries in America, where the church has accommodated and embraced the worst of American secular culture? While the church has refused to buckle under the heavy hand of its Muslim oppressors in Sudan, in the U.S. it has become, with each passing year, more difficult to distinguish from the culture around it.

The question should haunt us: Which church is it that is in captivity?

There are at least five reasons that many churches in the affluent West are in captivity.

- First, many churches imitate the culture around them rather than using Scripture as their guide.
- Second, many Christians lack a biblical world-view, focusing instead on personal issues.
- Third, many mainline and evangelical churches have become politically coopted.
- Fourth, many churches put more emphasis on recruitment than repentance.
- Fifth, many churches have converted worship into entertainment and praise into performance.

Let's look at each of these and consider how churches can break free of their often-unconscious cultural captivity.

CHRIST OR CULTURE?

The greatest threat to the church comes not from persecution, but from the spirit of the age, the *Zeitgeist*, the values and beliefs in vogue in the culture at any moment. The spirit of the age does not break down church doors like Communist agents or militant Muslims. It drifts in the side window, largely unnoticed. It's like the air we breathe: We don't even think about it unless it is unusually foul. And even then we can get accustomed to it, breath by breath, until we don't even recognize the stench.

This is particularly noticeable when you step back and consider both mainline and evangelical standards of sexual purity. For many who claim to follow Christ, the norms come from the culture around them rather than the uncompromising declarations of biblical truth.

At a "WOW 2000" conference attended by activists from United Church of Christ, Presbyterian, United Methodist, Episcopalian, and Roman Catholic churches, participants were passionate about the inclusion of every sexual preference in every level of church involvement: "good news for all transgendered, transsexual, drag kings and drag queens, intersex people, [and] bearded women."[7]

The conference featured a number of unorthodox interpretations of Scripture. For example, one Presbyterian minister who teaches at the

Episcopal Divinity School in Cambridge, Massachusetts, spoke on Pentecost. "There was [sic] 40 days between Christ's resurrection and when the disciples 'came out' into public," she said. "The Holy Spirit 'came out' that day. Pentecost is a miracle of 'coming out.'"[8]

The sexual agendas spilled into political ones. A Roman Catholic lesbian author stated, "Inclusivity is the heart of our faith. . . . Either all are welcome or none are [sic] welcome." She went on to welcome God: "The Divine is welcome . . . the Divine, the holy, God, Goddess, whatever term you use to describe this reality is welcome. Though our movement is religious in name, the demands of justice-making can quickly become just one more political struggle."[9]

An Episcopal theologian picked up that theme, rejecting the "savaging effects of global capitalism on human and other creatures." She concluded, "To be queer is to refuse to accept any injustice."[10]

But wait, you may say, these are fringe heretics. Yes, but they are only extreme manifestations of a broadly based movement that is influencing core members as well. One can only wonder what John Calvin and Martin Luther would think about the deliberations that have virtually shattered the denominations that purportedly carry on their theological convictions. The Presbyterian Church USA General Assembly has been torn apart with debates over the recommendations of a task force on human sexuality. The Church, it was said, had to adjust to cultural norms, which meant optional celibacy for those who were unmarried. Sex is okay if it is "full of joyful caring," so joyful, caring adultery is acceptable, as is the ordination of practicing homosexuals. The task force argued that it was time to dump "the pervasive fear of sex and passion . . . and embrace the erotic as a moral good."[11] Each time the Assembly meets, these issues are at the forefront of their discussions.

Once movements like this begin, they gain momentum. Similar debates are now under way in many Protestant denominations and among some breakaway Catholic groups. Sadly, as *Christianity Today* observed about one denomination's infighting on this issue, "The battle over sexuality has occurred against the backdrop of further membership decline, including a drop of 22,000 last year. For some, the divisive sexuality debates have distracted church leaders from focusing on the familiar work of evangelistic outreach and mission projects."[12]

Signs of this same erosion in biblical morality are evident in evangelical ranks. Three out of ten adults who say they are born-again also say that cohabitation, gay sex, and watching sexually explicit movies is morally acceptable. All the poll data cited earlier points to the fact that on sexual issues, evangelical Christians are indistinguishable in their behavior from mainline Christians or, for that matter, non-church members.

Anecdotal evidence supports this. Even in Christian ministries, we see a lowering of the standards of biblical morality. One major Christian organization monitored Internet access by its employees and discovered a shockingly high percentage visiting X-rated Web sites. Mark Earley, president of Prison Fellowship and former attorney general of Virginia, told me about his church experience during his political career. He belonged to three different churches over a period of years; in each one, the pastors had to leave the pulpit for moral failures. And of course the evidence of widespread moral failures among Catholic priests gives further credence to the assertion that sexual standards are not uniformly strong in conservative wings of the church.

The media has highlighted the same thing among prominent laypeople. In just the last few years, four of the most visible pro-family, conservative Christian leaders on Capitol Hill left their wives and families, reportedly embroiled in affairs, and were divorced and remarried. This kind of behavior gives rise to the charge of hypocrisy, and is devastating to the witness of the Body.

Other moral failures among evangelicals hurt our witness as well, such as those in our ranks who succumbed to temptation during the rash of corporate fraud cases in 2002. Bernie Ebbers, for example, head of WorldCom, was active in an evangelical church. After he was forced out of the company and the investigations began, Ebbers assured his fellow church members, in Nixonian style, "You aren't going to church with a crook." Then he added, "I hope my witness for Jesus Christ will not be jeopardized," to which statement the church responded with a standing ovation.[13]

Cultural accommodation doesn't just take the form of sexual compromise and moral failure. It also comes when churches, in an effort to appear relevant, take their cues from the world rather than from the truths of Scripture.

We are not talking here about the church being aware of and sensitive to prevailing cultural attitudes. To be sensitive is both wise strategy and a loving witness. But so often, in our zeal not to offend nonbelievers, and in our fear of being different, the church gradually, almost imperceptibly, slips into accommodating the culture.

Take the issue of language itself—how we communicate. Many churches have jumped on the political correctness bandwagon and ridden it all the way to non-biblical ends.

Some mainline denominations have eagerly embraced secular fashions, reworking hymn books and changing liturgy. Lest they offend anyone by talking about the Fatherhood of God, some have rewritten prayers to address "our Creator" rather than "our Father"; "our Redeemer" rather than "Jesus"; and "the Sustainer" rather than "the Holy Spirit." A church in which one of my evangelical friends worships now offers a unisex service at one of its three morning services, during which prayers are offered to "Our Father and Mother in heaven."

Several hymns from a recent United Methodist Hymnal supplement move to a "to whom it may concern" mode of address. "Womb of Life" refers to God as "Mother, Brother, Holy Partner, Father, Spirit, Only Son," and asks him/her to "aid the birthing of the new world yet to be." This is about as confusing as another hymn, "Bring Many Names," which refers to "strong Mother God," "young, growing God," and "old, aching God."

CALLING ON THE NAME OF NUT

These influences come from the Re-Imagining movement within the United Methodist Church. It began with congregants who were dissatisfied with the predominance of male images of God. Their pastor responded by exploring the Greek figure of Wisdom, "Sophia." Soon a Sophia Bible study grew into a Sophia movement, which opened a Pandora's box of goddess worship, pantheism, earth veneration, and New Age fusions.

At a United Methodist–affiliated seminary a few years ago, a chapel "service of the Word" liturgy went like this:

> People: O Prehistoric Goddess, reveal to us Your names so we can call You when we need You.
>
> Caller: Who are You, O Holy One? How have Your daughters named You?
>
> Voice: I am Ishtar and Inanna . . . I am Isis of Egypt, manifest wisdom, eye of Re the sun god, Universal Goddess. . .
>
> Caller: Who are You, O Holy One? How have Your daughters named You?
>
> Voice: I am Nut of the sky, of Egypt, Goddess of Affection.
>
> People: Nut, we call upon your name and long for your affection.[14]

Most evangelicals are not yet calling on the name of Nut. (Of course, most mainliners aren't either.) But subtly, insidiously, gradually, in the way that these things go, evangelicals are being lured in the same direction, usually in the name of drawing more people into our pews (usually beginning in ways that seem quite harmless).

Years ago I was invited to give an address on the sanctity of life at a symposium held at an evangelical Christian college. My remarks were transcribed for later publication, then edited by one of the professors. When I reviewed the draft, I discovered that all references to "man" and "mankind" had been changed to "human" and "humankind," which made for some very awkward constructions.

I returned the draft, changed back to its original wording. I knew the professor wouldn't like it, but I was unprepared for his reply, in which he accused me of advocating "Christian Archie Bunkerism."

Another time, I was not so vigilant. An evangelical publisher excerpted a chapter from one of my books, and I failed to read the proof sheets. When I saw the copy in print, I discovered that the publisher had substituted inclusive language throughout. After my protest, subsequent printings were returned to the original language.

I dismissed these as isolated incidents—until the thought police struck with a vengeance. A few days before I was scheduled to address a large evangelical gathering, I received a letter from one of the event organizers, a professor at a leading evangelical seminary, sternly warning me against the use of sexist words such as *mankind*. They were, the professor said somewhat imperiously, the equivalent of racist slang and violated "ethical biblical guidelines." (I'm still searching for these guidelines.) I was also told that if the translation of the Bible I used contained such offensive references, I was to substitute "correct" wording when reading those verses aloud during my presentation.

This was more than I could stomach. I changed what I had planned to speak about and, in language straight out of the "insensitive" Scripture, argued for the inerrant Word of God and the need to guard orthodoxy. One of the event organizers later told me, "You just don't understand how strong some people's feelings are." (Not surprisingly, the organization has not invited me to speak again.)

But the issue here isn't *feelings;* the issue is objective truth.

Of course we should craft our words, whether speaking or writing, in a way that shows respect and courtesy for both sexes, for people of color, for any community of listeners. And over the years I have sincerely tried to become more "inclusive" with my language.

Also, I recognize that women have historically not been recognized or treated as equals in the workplace, in the culture, or in the church. That inequity has changed some—and it needs to change more.

But the politically correct movement is interested in much more than fairness or sensitivity or equality. Lurking just beneath its surface is an angry, militant agenda that is not really concerned with the words themselves. Rather, the words are part of a litmus test that separates those who agree with an extremist agenda from those who don't. Sort of a not-so-secret handshake or a campaign button that classifies the wearer. These are code words of what one writer calls "a feminist orthodoxy"—and this inclusive language represents subscription to the entire agenda.[15]

The issue, then, is not whether the word *mankind* is incorrect; it is not. It still remains the generic term for "the human race: the totality of human beings" according to Webster. The issue is whether we agree with militant feminist orthodoxy. When people are forced to use the feminist dialect, they are being forced to signal agreement with the agenda. If they don't use it, they're accused of being bigots.

So when Christians uncritically take up the language of the movement, they are, perhaps without even realizing it, embracing an ideology that inevitably raises serious attacks on biblical authority. For what the militants seek is not equality, but the elimination of all gender distinctives. This, despite the empirical fact that there are biological differences, and despite the clear distinctions in Scripture: Men and women are created by God as equal partners, but with different gifts and roles relating directly to the biblical character of the family and the patriarchal character of God Himself.

Thus, while it may parade under the banner of sensitivity and relevance and other benign terms, the militant feminist agenda at root is an assault on the revealed, propositional truth of God and His plan for men and women. And the tragedy is that it has duped a lot of people, preying on the understandable frustration of some Christian women and imposing unwarranted guilt on some Christian men.

So believers must not be intimidated. We must make sure our language is loving and respectful, recognizing the God-given dignity of every person. But we need not, in a headlong rush to seem relevant, salute the god/goddess of political correctness and his/her/its underlying opposition to the biblical world-view.

We accommodate the culture as well when, in an effort to swell our ranks, we give moral and spiritual equivalence to all religions. The cultural pressures on Christian churches to do this became particularly intense in the aftermath of 9-11. As noted earlier, those of us who have dared to point out the unloving and even dangerous characteristics of Islam, or who have suggested that we evangelize Muslims, have been stomped on by the press.

I can understand politicians and the press championing this position, for the stakes are high in dealing with the Muslim world. What is bewildering, however, is that so many Christians share this sentiment, genuflecting to the rampant belief that all religions are alike.

Walt Kaiser, president of Gordon Conwell Seminary, wrote a letter to all seminary alumni and friends a few weeks after 9-11. In it he wrote about the terrorists' commitment and offered a challenge for Christians: a "challenge and call to love and serve Christ . . . the living God who stands majestically over all men, movements and time." A few months later, Kaiser received an angry response from an alumnus returning his letter and discontinuing his support for the annual fund. Kaiser's statement, the alumnus wrote, could be "misunderstood as a challenge to Islam—or any [other] religious faith—and will not contribute to solving the larger issue: an exhaustive and profound understanding of all causes of terrorist activity."[16]

This is just one letter, of course. But does it suggest that some believers have decided it's better to offend the living God than our secular neighbors or Muslim friends?

Our willingness to embrace cultural fads, along with our surrender to today's definitions of tolerance, also make us vulnerable to both New Age and occult influences. Once we start believing that all roads lead to the same place, we easily slip into the practice of making up our own religion, finding God in ourselves and everywhere else, and fashioning our religious practices to our own tastes.

Christian apologist Peter Kreeft says that most students who enter Boston College, where he teaches, are pantheists. "'God is in everything,' they say. So they see no need to be saved, only 'to recognize our intrinsic value and accept ourselves as we are.'"[17]

Of course secular students see no need to be saved. All they need do is look at one of Christendom's most prominent leaders, and they see a mirror of their own pantheistic views.

Just before his investiture as leader of the world's Anglican and Episcopal communions, Archbishop of Canterbury Rowan Williams was also installed as an honorary druid. According to the *London Times,* he donned "a long white cloak while druids chanted a prayer to the ancient god and goddess of the land." The archbishop, adopting a new Bardic name, was accepted into the "White Druids order."[18] The archbishop's defenders insisted that druids are not actually pagans; it's only a ceremony, sort of an honorary thing.

Perhaps so. But his action creates a troubling symbol at a time when so many in the church at large are eagerly embracing pagan and worldly influences.

PERSONAL PERSPECTIVE OR CHRISTIAN WORLD-VIEW?

One reason the Christian movement has lost much of its influence is that we have failed to really understand our cultural responsibility. If we think of Christianity *only* as personal salvation, then we fail to see that Christian truth applies to all of life. If we think of Christianity as therapy or a nice spiritual fix to get us through the week, then we're really irrelevant.

As we discussed in chapter 16, biblical belief covers every arena of human endeavor, not just the narrow view of self-comfort. Christian truth looks outward, not just inward. This is the key to reviving our witness in today's culture.

Many Christians are discouraged by a sense that we are losing the culture war. They speak glumly about withdrawing altogether, pulling back to enjoy like-minded fellowship in Christian enclaves. That would be the worst thing we could do. In large part, our lack of real cultural influence in the past has to do with our own truncated view of Christianity. Only when we see our faith as an all-encompassing life system that vigorously brings hope and redemption to every arena will we have an effect on reversing the prevailing cultural tides and resist the accommodation that can so easily ensnare us.

THE CHURCH AS PAWN OR PROPHET?

Believers are to be the best of citizens, said Augustine, because they do out of a love for God what others do only because the law requires it. Christians are commanded to pray for those in authority and obey those who are appointed as magistrates over them. And that means Christians must vote, work for candidates, express their views on political issues, contend for biblical and moral truth in the public square, and, of course, respect and obey the law.

Sadly, we often fail to get this simple formulation right. The experience of the mainline denominations from the 1960s on is a case in point. Genuinely, and correctly, outraged by racial discrimination in our country, the major denominations joined the civil rights movement with a fervor. (Evangelicals should have stood more solidly with them than we did; Christian conscience compels moral passion for human rights.) But church leaders quickly moved from sit-ins and street marches into a thoroughly politicized agenda. Church bureaucracies slid quickly down the slippery slope, churning out press releases on every imaginable political issue, including ones on which they were conspicuously uninformed.

The Vietnam War intensified the politicizing of mainline churches, so much so that most of them went beyond moral judgments about Vietnam. Abandoning "just war" doctrine, they declared all war to be immoral. Through the 1970s and 1980s, many sold out completely to the agenda of the radical left. So much so that by fall 2001, at the annual meeting of the U.S. Committee of the World Council of Churches, speakers condemned the U.S. war against terrorism as morally unacceptable. Their convictions were intensified, they said, because the WCC had designated this as the "decade to overcome violence."[19] (It's unfortunate that nobody seems to have informed the September 11 terrorists that the WCC had issued such a decree.)

Liberation theologian Elsa Tamex of Costa Rica equated U.S. actions with those of the September 11 terrorists: "The attack of September 11 was revenge, the same as Bush's response to that attack. . . . The terrorists will never admit that they had an objective to kill innocent victims. At the same time, Bush will never affirm that his objective is to kill the Afghan people. . . . No one proposes attacking innocent victims, but all do it without wanting to."[20]

In the spring of 2002, an Argentinian Methodist Bishop denounced capitalism as inextricably linked to racism and exploitation. "Racism is in a strong relation to capitalism," Bishop Aldo Etchegoyen said at a Methodist commission on religion and race. "The wrong use of power is producing a new racism around the world to perform [the work of] the capitalistic system."

"The speech was like a blast from the past, so loaded was it with the rhetoric of liberation theology, which captivated left-wing theologians in the 1970s and 1980s," reported the Institute on Religion and Democracy. Etchegoyen went on to comment that global capitalism, led by the U.S., is the logical outgrowth of the genocide European colonizers waged against native peoples of America and the slaves they brought from Africa.

"After September 11, the war against terrorism has targeted poor countries," said the bishop, "especially those within the Islamic tradition."[21]

Sometimes the obsession with political involvement becomes surreal. During Easter 2001, at the very time that Christians in the Sudan were being enslaved, raped, beheaded, and crucified, the NCC had other priorities. During Holy Week, Christian coalitions from both left and right were remembering Christ's passion by calling attention to the suffering believers in the Sudan. Where was the NCC concentrating its energies? It was issuing statements supporting the McCain-Feingold finance reform bill—and curiously silent on the matter of persecution in Sudan.[22]

What began in the 1960s as a concern for justice and human suffering, issues that all Christians should care about passionately, led in time to the complete marginalization of the mainline Christian movement. Why? Because the church bureaucracies and many of the churches themselves lost their balance, focusing all of their energies on politics. They were taken in by the modern utopian myth that people are basically good and if we can simply correct the structures of society, they can live in peace, justice, and happiness. Hence our salvation is in politics.

Above all, the militant mainliners forgot that the primary task of the church is to win and disciple men and women to Christ and then to equip those changed lives to be instruments of justice and righteousness in every walk of life.

The evangelical movement came perilously close to suffering a similar fate.

In the 1980s, the religious right organized the Moral Majority. For a while it seemed that it had become as much an adjunct of the Reagan White House and the Republican party as the mainline churches had become an adjunct of the Democrats. Conservative Christians enjoyed access to State dinners, the Oval Office, and quickly lost their prophetic edge.

I recall a conversation with one evangelical leader who was outraged, as I was, when George H. W. Bush invited a homosexual activist group to the White House for a bill signing; it was the first time an American president had officially recognized gay militants. At the same time, of course, President Bush was entertaining evangelicals. One leader told me he would not say anything publicly, however, because "I'm going to have dinner with the president next month." He was well aware that those in power dump those who rock the boat. In fact, shortly afterward the White House liaison to the evangelical community who did protest the bill signing invitation was fired.

The evangelical political movement of the 1980s and 1990s accomplished some good things. Family and life issues to which Scripture clearly speaks have been brought to the forefront in court decisions and political debate. (Just as the 1960s mainline movement achieved some good ends, like civil rights advances.)

But when we become more concerned with power and access than with the gospel and our prophetic responsibilities, we've carried political action to a nonbiblical excess. Christians must never become just another interest group, the handmaiden of one political party or another. Politics is like the proverbial tar baby: Embrace it too tightly and you're stuck to it. Christians have to navigate a narrow path of prophetic involvement without becoming political pawns.[23]

The demise of the Moral Majority and the weakening of other Christian movements is in some ways a healthy development, as long as it doesn't cause Christians to turn away from the political process. On the whole, I think most evangelicals are more sophisticated today. Perhaps we are closer to finding the right balance between the propagation of the gospel and defending Christian truth in every area of life . . . as long as we resist the seductive snare of spiritual compromise because of political access.

RECRUITMENT OR REPENTANCE?

Descartes' famous formulation *cogito ergo sum*—"I think, therefore I am"— might be restated for the modern church: "We grow, therefore we are." In this age that prizes size as an indicator of success, churches, as we have written, often measure their success by numbers. Pastors are under intense pressure to increase their flocks and build bigger facilities.

Of course we must fling open our doors and seek to draw in the lost. It is good for a church to be sensitive to seekers, who would not be seeking at all if the Holy Spirit was not wooing them to Christ. But a *seeker-driven* church takes its lead not only from what will intrigue nonbelievers and get them in the doors, but what will please them and keep them coming. If interested nonbelievers are not confronted with solid doctrine, the hard yet liberating truths of Jesus, and the demands of Scripture, the church has betrayed them.

How well are churches making disciples? The polls again paint a depressing portrait. Biblical illiteracy is rampant. According to George Barna, 45 percent of all born-again Christians believe if people are good enough they can earn a place in heaven. This is a denial of the central issue of the Reformation, of which the born-again movement today is heir.

It gets worse. Barna's research shows that one-third of born-again Christians do not believe that Jesus was sinless or that He was *bodily resurrected from the dead.* That means that one-third of those who call themselves evangelicals deny the central belief of Christianity.

Similarly, George Gallup reported in 1999 that 20 percent of self-described born-again evangelicals believe in reincarnation, 26 percent in astrology, and 16 percent have visited a fortuneteller.[24] Wade Clark Roof, in his book *The Spiritual Marketplace,* says that one-quarter of born-again baby boomers claim to communicate with the dead.[25]

These are staggering statistics. But we shouldn't be surprised. These kinds of heresies flourish when churches focus on recruitment rather than real Christianity. It's easy to be so focused on getting people into our churches that we end up doing whatever we can to keep them there. Like blending trendy Eastern thought with Christian teaching—and ending up with churchgoers who believe in reincarnation.

Such sacrileges begin with a small step, something almost unconscious. Like the pastor who never quite gets around to teaching about sin and repentance, or the one who simply smoothes the edges off some of the hard sayings of the gospel. Or those who shade the message, subtly equating the "abundant" life with upper middle-class affluence. Or the church leaders who are unwilling to challenge sinful behavior.

The pressures are great to avoid the tough demands of Scripture. I know one associate pastor of a large, seeker-friendly evangelical church, who, when filling in for the senior pastor one Sunday, preached a tough message on sin. When the senior pastor returned, he chastised the young man and cautioned him never to preach that message again. Soon thereafter the associate pastor was asked to leave.

Softening and shaping the gospel into a user-friendly version also leads to immature believers who, while seemingly orthodox in their beliefs, are unable to discern spiritual truth.

During a visit some years ago to a Christian bookstore in a midsized American city, I noticed packets of blank church bulletin forms for sale, obviously for smaller churches that didn't print their own. They had nicely decorated covers for Easter, Christmas, and, of all things, Kwanzaa.

When I questioned the store manager, he informed me that Kwanzaa was included out of respect to African-American Christians, and he saw no reason not to sell the bulletins. His sensitivity may be admirable, but the truth is, Kwanzaa has nothing to do with Christianity. Nor is it, as many think, a spiritual holiday brought to the U.S. from Africa.

Kwanzaa is the invention of a professor at Cal Tech, Maulana Karenga, who in 1966 came up with the idea of affirming African customs as an alternative to the Christmas celebration of the birth of Christ. Karenga has been amazingly successful in promoting his "holiday"; school districts across America set aside days for Kwanzaa celebrations. But certainly Christian churches should know better. And so should the Christian bookstore manager. His lack of discernment allowed him to sell materials promoting a cultural alternative to the celebration of Christ's birth.

Sometimes lack of discernment among Christians is far more egregious. In February 2002, for example, Della Reese, costar of *Touched by an Angel,* was featured in a TBN interview. That seems appropriate: After all, Reese plays an angel, and *Touched by an Angel* is produced by an evangelical, Martha Williamson, who frequently brings a strong gospel message to the screen.

But the fact not noted on the TBN show is that Reese is a New Thought minister who believes, according to the Christian Research Institute (CRI), that every person is part of God (pantheism) and who rejects Christ's unique divinity and atoning sacrifice on the cross. According to the CRI report, Reese explained her spiritual beliefs while the host nodded approvingly and offered no objection or biblical perspective. The audience applauded and cheered, either unwilling or unable to see the difference between Christian truth and New Age pantheism.[26]

PERFORMANCE OR PRAISE?

When churches adulterate biblical teaching and take their cues from the culture around us, another tragic result is that worship services become self-focused performances rather than God-focused worship. The tendency in seeker-driven churches is to add high-tech accouterment, lighting, special audiovisual effects, and dramatic music, all brilliantly choreographed. There is nothing intrinsically wrong with such tools if they enhance worship. But too often the platform becomes a stage, the cross a backdrop. Worshipers are ushered into their seats to watch the stage and be entertained, thrilled, and inspired. But they aren't participants. It's all a grand show, more like Hollywood than the holy of holies.

According to Al Mohler, the president of Southern Seminary, the biblical model of worship is found in Isaiah 6, where Isaiah enters the temple and sees the Lord seated on the throne, the Seraphim crying out, "Holy, holy, holy is the LORD Almighty." Isaiah was overwhelmed and filled with awe in the presence of the Holy One, the one and only all righteous God. He cried out, "I am ruined! For I am a man of unclean lips, and I live among a people of unclean lips, and my eyes have seen the King, the LORD Almighty." These words reflected Isaiah's deep repentance and recognition of his own inadequacy in the face of God's holiness.[27]

As we assemble to worship, believers are to come into the presence of the living God, filled with awe, wonder, and repentance, as Isaiah did. The purpose of our gathering, Mohler argues, is not to be entertained or fulfilled or comforted; it is to offer ourselves in total adoration and reverence for the one true God.

We dare not trivialize our worship. As mentioned earlier, Nadab and Abihu,[28] Aaron's sons, were struck dead for doing so, as was Uzzah who touched the ark of the covenant, contrary to God's commands.

Worship inevitably demands a repentant spirit. Remember the vivid story Jesus told "to some who were confident of their own righteousness and looked down on everybody else"? The Pharisee in Jesus' parable was supremely smug and self-righteous, praying, "God, I thank you that I am not like other men—robbers, evildoers, adulterers—or even this tax collector. I fast twice a week and give a tenth of all I get."[29]

But, said Jesus, "the tax collector stood at a distance. He would not even look up to heaven, but beat his breast and said, 'God have mercy on me, a sinner.'

"I tell you," Jesus concluded, "this man, rather than the other, went home justified before God. For everyone who exalts himself will be humbled, and he who humbles himself will be exalted."[30] The tax collector understood repentance.

What might Jesus say at our church services that are more about performance and exalting ourselves than humble, holy fear? What might He say of the worship team that manufactures pious passion for the jumbo TV screens, or the would-be rock stars and classical sopranos alike who focus on their own performance, rather than losing themselves in the worship of the holy God?

Please note that we are not criticizing any particular form of worship. For all of us, at the front or in the pews, this is a matter of the motivation of our hearts. Are we exalting self or God?

Worship, Mohler says, involves coming into the presence of God, repenting, hearing the gospel, and confronting the cross. Sobering demands for the therapeutic church, which often looks and behaves much more like a concert performance exalting the players than a place of worship exalting the King.

IT IS DIFFICULT TO STAND FOR RIGHT AND WRONG, to defend truth in love, to wholly worship a holy God in today's secular culture. Daily, in a hundred different ways, by little things we scarcely notice, we are subtly enticed to accommodate the values of those who scorn the living God.

Of course our fellowship must be loving and attract those who hunger and thirst. But we must never forget that the early church did not explode because it was a comfortable haven for those weary of life's pressures or because it accommodated the culture's values. The early church turned the world upside down because the believers confessed that Jesus, not Caesar, was Lord. They didn't embrace the culture; they scandalized it.

And lest we forget, the early Christians were seen not as enlightened and progressive folks. One charge hurled against the church was cannibalism: Opponents said that Christians gathered to eat and drink the flesh and blood of their Savior. Their contemporaries were shocked, but the believers made such a dramatic and bold witness that no one could ignore them.

The church will again be the church—against the world, yet for the world—not when it's applauded for being politically correct or sexually liberated or therapeutically comfortable, but when it is slandered for "cannibalism" . . . for consuming a truth so bold and vibrant that it makes the world's most glittering attractions pale and insipid by comparison.

19

THE TERROR OF THE HOLY

MARTIN LUTHER did not set out to reform the world—or even the church for that matter. In the beginning he was simply a near-mad, maddening monk searching for sanity. Throwing inkwells in his cloister cell, he wept and ground his teeth in frustration and fear because he sensed too little of God's presence, too much of the devil's.[1]

The medieval world lent itself to such terrors. People lived short, brutal lives. Which was worse, they wondered: the plagues and pestilence of this life, or the hell and purgatory of the next? To attempt to ward off the evil spirits, they mingled the gnomes and witches of old German paganism with elements of Christianity.

Churches dotted every town, and religious processions routinely passed through the narrow, muddy streets. Crippled men dying of pneumonia stationed themselves near churches, hoping to be cured by the ringing of the vesper bell. Beggars shouted for coins and consigned passersby to the fires of hell for their lack of charity. The dying saw fiends that tempted them to abandon faith.

Playing upon these tensions between terror and hope, the church re-inforced images of hell, despair, and ghastly purgatory so that people might be driven to the sacraments. Artists carved the Great Judgment into their woodcuts. Christ the Judge sat on a rainbow, with a lily emerging from His right ear—symbol of the saved, taken by angels into paradise. From His left ear shot a sword—symbol of the damned, dragged from their tombs by devils and cast into the flames of hell. Young Martin Luther would stare at these pictures, fascinated in fear: Christ the Judge was coming for him.[2]

His father wanted Martin to be a lawyer so he could provide for his parents in their old age. But while he was attending the University of Erfurt, a July thunderstorm altered his path forever.

Returning to school after a visit with his parents, sturdy young Martin was startled by a bolt of lightning. The flash, the heat, the crash of power flung him to the ground, scattering his books like ashes. And that instant he saw in the power of the storm all that his soul feared in the dark hours of the night: God could incinerate him in a moment.

In his terror he cried out for the surest safety he knew. "Saint Anne, help me!" he screamed. "I will become a monk."

Singed, scared, and sobered, Luther was off to the monastery. And there, after a quiet first year of study, spiritual discipline, and austerity, his struggles began in earnest.

The crisis came the day he celebrated his first mass. It was a family celebration as well; his father had ridden into town in a company of twenty horsemen. The cloister bells chimed, the music of the glorious psalm ascended to the heights of the cathedral: "O sing unto the Lord a new song." The young monk, robed for ecclesiastical duty, took his place before the altar.

But as he approached the bread and wine of the holy rite, Luther's senses began to spin. In this ceremony the sacrifice of Calvary would be reenacted, and he, a spurious worm, was to handle the holy host. When he came to the words, "We offer unto Thee, the living, the true, the eternal God," he was suddenly filled with terror.

Who am I that I should lift my eyes or raise my hands to the divine Majesty? he thought. *The angels surround Him. At His nod the earth trembles. And shall I, a miserable little pygmy, say 'I want this, I ask for that'? For I am dust and ashes and full of sin, and I am speaking to the living, eternal, and true God.*

His knees shook. After all, the God of the Old Testament had smitten those He deemed unworthy. Sinai had rumbled with His fury; no man could look on His face and live. And now he, Martin Luther, dared stand before the altar. Pale and shaking, he remained standing. Barely.

During the winter of 1510–11, Luther journeyed to Rome. There, the basilica of St. Peter's was just being built. From his swaying scaffold, Michelangelo was painting the Sistine Chapel's grand ceiling. An elderly Leonardo da Vinci was still designing and inventing. And Vasco de Balboa was preparing for the voyage that would lead him to discover the Pacific Ocean.

Yet it was not the Renaissance splendor of Rome nor her past pagan glories that interested Luther; it was her Christian history. The city of the martyrs. The holy city of the church. He visited the catacombs, venerated the bones of the saints, prayed and fasted and performed the daily devotions of his order. But he was shocked by the Italian clergy. They rattled through prayers and masses as quickly as possible. They mocked the bread and wine of the holy sacrament. And they mocked the young monk for caring.

Luther returned to Erfurt downcast over what he had seen, but he was soon busy enough to put it behind him. That same year, 1511, he was transferred to the village of Wittenberg, invited by Frederick the Wise, prince and elector of Saxony, who had high hopes for his university there.

Luther lived in the Augustinian cloister at one end of the town; less than a mile away, at the other end, stood the Castle Church. At the cloister, once again, he wrestled with his old fears: How did a man know he was saved from the yawning pit of hell? How did he meet the demands of an utterly holy God?

Others struggled with such fears as well, but they found a miserable degree of solace by purchasing pieces of grace called indulgences. The church sold its people these dubious favors, based on a kind of spiritual banking system. Their premise was that the goodness of the saints of old, as well as Christ and the blessed Virgin, created an inexhaustible store of goodness— sort of an immense bank account from which the spiritually needy of this world could draw. If your personal account was low, depleted by sin's withdrawals, then you could draw from the account of the saints. All you had to do was view a holy relic belonging to one of them, pay the prescribed price, and you could count on a specific deposit in your own account.

In one of Rome's great storehouses, a single crypt held the bones of forty popes and seventy-six thousand martyrs. Among thousands of other items, Rome also had a piece of Moses' burning bush, the chains of St. Paul, and one of the coins paid to Judas for betraying Christ. Just viewing the coin ensured fourteen hundred years off one's sentence in purgatory.

In Wittenberg, Frederick the Wise had amassed his own storehouse of relics, with more than five thousand items listed in a 1509 catalog. Among these were a tooth of St. Jerome, four pieces of St. Augustine and six of St. Bernard, four hairs from the Virgin Mary, a piece of Christ's swaddling clothes, one piece of the Wise Men's gold, one strand of Jesus' beard, one of the nails driven into His hands, one piece of bread from the Last Supper, and, not to be outdone by Rome, one twig from Moses' burning bush.

By viewing these relics on the designated day—the Eve of All Saints, October 31—and making the proper contribution, people could receive indulgences to reduce time in purgatory by up to 1,902,202 years—either for themselves or for others.

For his part, Martin Luther fastened his dim hopes on penance, seeking absolution from confessors who wearily heard his painstaking reviews of his soul and conduct. One session lasted six hours as Luther, fearful of missing some sin that would cast him into perdition, worked his way through the Ten Commandments and the seven deadly sins several times over.

In order for sins to be forgiven, Luther reasoned, they must be confessed. And to be confessed, they must be remembered. If not remembered, not confessed, then they were not forgiven. Frantic that he had not recognized or remembered every transgression, he would lie awake at night, hearing fiends in the dark coming to bear him to hell. The moaning of the wind stirred terror in his soul. His vitality drained away.

"Your problem is not so much sins as sin," his mentor Staupitz counseled. "It is not single wrongdoings that damn men, but their nature itself. The whole nature of man must be changed."

Luther could no longer look at a crucifix without seeing Christ seated on the rainbow, judgment emanating from Him as men were tossed into hell. To him it seemed that God capriciously titillated men with the hope of heaven, then hardened and damned them, as if He delighted in tormenting the wretches for eternity. *I wish I had never been created,* he thought. *Love God? I hate Him!*[3]

The unspeakable had been spoken. Luther haunted Staupitz, wondering if he was the only man alive plagued by such doubts and fears. "No," responded the vicar dryly. "But I think they are your meat and drink."[4]

Perceiving that the troubled monk needed to focus on Scripture rather than his own struggles, Staupitz gave Luther the chair of the Bible at the university. As an Augustinian monk, Luther was required to do frequent Bible readings; now, in his focused study, the Scriptures themselves pointed him to two central truths about their Author.

The first spike to pierce Luther's heart was his study of Psalm 22: "My God, my God, why hast Thou forsaken me?"

Christ had cried these very words from the cross, knowing despair, desolation, and the withdrawal of God's presence. Bleeding, sweaty, abandoned, He had cried out in desperation.

But Christ was without sin; no ashy worm He. Why, then, had God turned away His face? Luther questioned.

The answer hit him like a lightning bolt.

By becoming man, Christ had taken upon Himself the sins of the world. He didn't deserve the alienation. The Judge on the rainbow had chosen to be the helpless man dangling from a bloody cross. Christ was forsaken and damned. For him.

Luther saw that his desire to repent was right, but it was sin itself that must be killed.

"When lightning strikes a tree or a man," he mused, "it does two things at once—it rends the tree and swiftly slays the man. But it also turns the face of the dead man and the broken branches of the tree itself toward heaven." As Christ had died, so must he; as Christ was raised, so would he be. Because of Christ's righteousness.

If Psalm 22 crystallized a new understanding of Christ the Savior, Paul's epistle to the Romans cured Luther's confusion about Christ the Judge.

"I greatly longed to understand Paul's Epistle to the Romans," he later wrote, "and nothing stood in the way but that one expression, 'the justice of God,' because I took it to mean that justice whereby God is just and deals justly in punishing the unjust.

"My situation was that, although an impeccable monk, I stood before God as a sinner troubled in conscience, and I had no confidence that my merit would assuage Him. Therefore I did not love a just and angry God, but rather hated and murmured against Him. Yet I clung to the dear Paul and had a great yearning to know what he meant.

"Night and day I pondered until I saw the connection between the justice of God and the statement that 'the just shall live by his faith.' Then I grasped that the justice of God is that righteousness by which through grace and sheer mercy God justifies us through faith. . . . I felt myself to be reborn and to have gone through open doors into paradise. The whole of Scripture took on a new meaning, and whereas before the 'justice of God' had filled me with hate, now it became to me inexpressibly sweet in greater love. This passage of Paul became to me a gate to heaven."[5]

Justification by faith! Luther's heart thumped with the liberty of it. No longer a slave to fear, but freed by faith in Christ!

"If you have a true faith that Christ is your Savior," he wrote, "then at once you have a gracious God, for faith leads you in and opens up God's heart and will, that you should see pure grace and overwhelming love."[6]

As Luther reveled in his new freedom, he could not help but see that so many around him were still fettered by fear. And he saw that the church fueled those fears. If men and women were in bondage, it was the church that was selling the bonds. The indulgences.

He grieved. People were paying for nothing, their pockets plundered to line the coffers of the church. The indulgences of Rome were funding St. Peter's new basilica. And Pope Leo X seemed to relish hunting, gambling, and devotion much more than assuaging the fears of his flock.

A Dominican monk named Johann Tetzel was the most notorious of the pope's indulgence peddlers. Tetzel was not allowed in Wittenberg because the church could not sell indulgences without the consent of the civil authorities, and Frederick the Wise was not interested in having his own collection superseded. But Luther's parishioners could easily cross the border when the Dominican was nearby and return with all kinds of spiritual benefits—for a price.

Whenever Tetzel entered a town, he was met by dignitaries who ushered him down the main street with great fanfare. A cross bearing the papal arms preceded him, then was planted in the marketplace, where people quickly gathered to seek peace for their souls.

"Listen to the voices of your dear dead relatives and friends beseeching you and saying, 'Pity us, pity us. We are in dire torment from which you can redeem us for a pittance,'" Tetzel would shout. "Open your ears. Hear the father saying to his son, the mother to her daughter, 'We bore you, nourished you, and you are so cruel and hard that now you are not willing for so little to set us free. Will you let us lie here in flames? Will you delay our promised glory?' Remember that you are able to release them, for as soon as the coin in the coffer rings, the soul from purgatory springs."[7]

Tetzel was not much of a poet, but he was a great salesman. The people flocked to him, and he fleeced them mercilessly.

Luther, meanwhile, mourned for the sheep and knew he could not remain silent.

ON OCTOBER 31, 1517—Eve of All Saints, the day that Frederick the Wise would again display his holy collection of bones, teeth, hair, and twigs—Martin Luther fired his warning shot. It was in the form of a placard posted on the thick door of the Castle Church in Wittenberg: Ninety-Five Theses, or propositions, for debate. Written in the heat of anger, they were designed to expose the business of selling grace.

One, for example, crisply pointed to the underwriting of St. Peter's basilica with German funds from anxious souls: "First of all, we should rear living temples, not local churches, and only last of all St. Peter's, which . . . we Germans cannot attend. . . . Why doesn't the pope build the basilica of St. Peter out of his own money? He is richer than Croesus. He would do better to sell St. Peter's and give the money to the poor folk who are being fleeced by the hawkers of indulgences. If the pope knew the exactions of these vendors, he would rather that St. Peter's should lie in ashes than that it should be built out of the blood and hide of his sheep."

Luther's posting was nothing unusual. Such signs were a routine means of provoking debate. And he had penned his affirmations in Latin, the language of the clergy and the collegiate. This was not necessarily a matter to put before the people, and Luther took care at this point not to bring them into the debate. In his introduction to his points, he said he spoke "out of love and zeal for truth and the desire to bring it to light."[8]

But Luther did send a copy of the theses to Albrecht of Mainz, his archbishop, humbly writing, "Forgive me that I, the scum of the earth, should dare to approach Your Sublimity. The Lord Jesus is my witness that I am well aware of my insignificance and my unworthiness."[9]

Such pleasantries dispensed with, he warmed to his subject as he wrote the archbishop about indulgences. "God on high, is this the way the souls entrusted to your care are prepared for death? It is high time you looked into this matter. I can be silent no longer."

Luther could not have known that his challenge would rock his church. He had not even intended his theses for wide distribution. But scholars translated them into German and reproduced them. Soon people everywhere were taking sides in the growing battle between the reluctant reformer and the assembled powers of the church.

Pope Leo X was not particularly concerned, reportedly telling an aide, "Luther is a drunken German. He will feel differently when he is sober."[10]

Perhaps Luther was drunk—in the Spirit. At any rate, the years between 1517 and 1521 found him defending his growing convictions before church councils, in the face of a papal bull or official pronouncement, threats of excommunication, and more warnings of assassination than he cared to note.

Luther's prince, the earnest and pious Frederick the Wise, was devoted not only to the church, but also to Luther. So was his old mentor, Staupitz, who wrote to Luther, "The world hates the truth. By such hate Christ was crucified, and what there is in store for you today if not the cross I do not know. You have few friends. . . . Leave Wittenberg and come to me that we may live and die together. The prince [Frederick] is in accord. Deserted let us follow the deserted Christ."[11]

In 1520, after appealing in vain to the pope, Luther put his case before the civil authority of his day, Emperor Charles V: "I prostrate myself before your Imperial Majesty. I have published books which have alienated many, but I have done so because driven by others, for I would prefer nothing more than to remain in obscurity. For three years I have sought peace in vain. I have now but one recourse. I appeal to Caesar."[12]

Luther would later assert that no one had so championed the civil state as he. He believed that the civil magistrate was ordained of God to punish evildoers, and that the state had the power to protect citizens from ecclesiastical corruption. The church's claims to theocracy must be repulsed.[13] Hence his appeal to the emperor.

Luther's books were burned in Rome and other cities. Theological students, however, threw the papal bull condemning Luther into the river Elbe, calling it a "bulloon" and seeing if it would float. All the while, Luther continued to furiously write books and articles.

Finally, in the spring of 1521, he was requested to appear at an assembly in the town of Worms to answer questions regarding his teachings. The emperor and church officials assured him safe conduct. Luther, well aware of the possibility that the meeting could well end with his execution, was resolute. He would go to Worms, he said, "though there were as many devils as tiles" on the roofs of the city.[14]

Late in the afternoon of April 16, Luther and a few companions entered Worms by oxcart. An imperial herald escorted them. Two thousand citizens turned out to march with the monk to his lodgings. Whether hating or admiring, few were neutral about Luther or his cause.

The following day, Luther was escorted to the assembly where, gaunt and pale in his Augustinian habit, he stood before the resplendent Charles V, heir of a long line of Catholic sovereigns and scion of the House of Hapsburg, lord of Austria, Burgundy, the Low Countries, Spain, and Naples, Holy Roman Emperor.

The examination began when an official of the archbishop of Trier pointed to a pile of Luther's books resting on a wooden table. Among them were his *Address to the German Nobility,* a treatise presenting his strategy for the reform of the church; *The Babylonian Captivity of the Church,* which examined the sacraments of the medieval church; and *On the Freedom of the Christian,* Luther's discovery of justification by faith in Christ alone.

"Are these yours?" asked the examiner.

"The books are all mine," said Luther. "And I have written more."

"Do you defend them all, or do you care to reject a part?" The examiner seemed to be giving him an out.

Luther paused, his heart pounding, then spoke: "This touches God and

His Word. This affects the salvation of souls. Of this Christ said, 'He who denies Me before men, him will I deny before My Father.' To say too little or too much would be dangerous. I beg you, give me some time to think it over."

The assembly began to buzz. Think it over? Surely the man had had years to evaluate his positions! Was this the fiery reformer who had so boldly challenged Rome? Where was the firebrand they had expected?

At the moment, the firebrand was shaking and sweating, experiencing a terror not unlike the holy fear he had experienced at his first mass. How could he, a lowly monk, challenge the assembled powers of his day? More important, his stand would affect, as he put it, "the salvation of souls." Whatever he said, there was no going back. He had to be sure. Was he?

Luther's request was granted, and the assembly reconvened the next afternoon. This time a larger hall had to be used, with a packed, standing crowd filling every space. Only the emperor was seated.

The examiner repeated the question of the day before. This time Luther was ready.

"They are all mine," he asserted. "But as to the second question, they are not all of one sort." This tactic gave him the opportunity to make a speech, rather than simply affirm or deny.

He went on to describe some of his books, telling how they dealt "with faith and life so simply and evangelically that my very enemies are compelled to regard them as worthy of Christian reading." A second class, continued Luther, denounced "the desolation of the Christian world by the evil lives and teaching of the papists. Who can deny this when the universal complaints testify that by the laws of the popes the consciences of men are racked?"

At this point, the emperor broke in, shouting, "No!"

Luther continued, describing a third class of his works that "contains attacks on private individuals. I confess I have been more caustic than comports with my profession, but I am being judged, not only my life, but for the teaching of Christ, and I cannot denounce these works either. . . . If I am shown my error, I would be the first to throw my books into the fire. I have been reminded of the dissensions which my teaching engenders. I can answer only in the words of the Lord, 'I came not to bring peace but a sword.' . . . God it is who confounds the wise. I must walk in the fear of the Lord. . . . I have spoken."15

"Martin, your plea to be heard from Scripture is the one always made by heretics," responded his examiner with passion. "How can you assume that you are the only one to understand the sense of Scripture? Would you put your judgment above that of so many famous men and claim that you know more than them all?

"You have no right to call into question the most holy orthodox faith, instituted by Christ, the perfect lawgiver, proclaimed throughout the world by the apostles, sealed by the red blood of the martyrs, confirmed by the sacred councils, defined by the church in which all our fathers believed until death and gave to us as an inheritance, and which now we are forbidden by the pope and the emperor to discuss lest there be no end of debate.

"I ask you, Martin—answer candidly and without horns—do you or do you not repudiate your books and the errors which they contain?"

Luther was sweating again, trembling as he spoke with the resignation of a man who has counted the cost and is ready to pay.

"Since then your majesty and your lordships desire a simple reply, I will answer without horns and without teeth. Unless I am convinced by Scripture and plain reason—I do not accept the authority of popes and councils, for they have contradicted each other—my conscience is captive to the Word of God. I cannot and I will not recant anything, for to go against conscience is neither right nor safe. God help me. Here I stand. I cannot do otherwise. Amen."

He had spoken in German. Now the examiner asked him to repeat his statement in Latin.

A friend called out, "If you can't do it, Doctor, you have done enough."

Then Martin Luther repeated his statement in the language of the church, threw his arms up into the air, and left the crowded hall . . . hisses and boos echoing behind him.

20

JUSTICE UNLEASHED: A WORLD TRANSFORMED

The task of the people of God is, as far as possible in a sinful society,
to reclaim the cosmos for God's created purpose.

—CARL F. HENRY

WHEN MARTIN LUTHER strode out of the assembly hall at Worms, he could never have dreamed of the consequences of his courageous confession.

After pondering the monk's position, Emperor Charles V proclaimed his own: "I am descended from a long line of Christian emperors.... I have resolved to follow in their steps. A single friar who goes counter to all Christianity for a thousand years must be wrong. Therefore I am resolved to stake my lands, my friends, my body, my blood, my life, and my soul ... I will proceed against [Luther] as a notorious heretic."[1]

And proceed he did, forbidding his subjects to offer Luther food, drink, or shelter and ordering anyone who came upon the beleaguered monk to arrest him.

But the emperor was distracted by convulsions elsewhere in his empire: revolts in Spain and threats from the Turkish ruler to the east, Suleiman the Magnificent. Meanwhile, the French king, Francis I, claimed a number of territories that Charles claimed as his own, and Pope Leo X often cast his lot with the French king over Charles. Thus, busy monitoring rebels, fighting infidels, squabbling with the pope, and trying to keep his own balance on the slippery slope of sixteenth-century politics, the emperor let Martin Luther slip away.

Immediately after the Diet of Worms, Luther was "abducted" by friendly forces and hidden in the castle at Wartburg, where he lived, disguised as a knight, until early in 1522.

Cut off from the heat of battle and shut up in the chilly, silent castle, Luther's natural disposition began to manifest itself again, as it had in the cloister. As he wrote furiously, producing nearly a dozen books and translating the New Testament from Greek into German, he also suffered from constipation, insomnia, and depression—woes even lesser writers know quite well!

Modern distortions—and reductions—of Martin Luther abound. Many lay-Catholics know him only as the mad monk who broke up the Catholic Church and was somehow responsible for Protestantism. Many Protestants know him only as the dissident who nailed up the Ninety-Five Theses, whatever those were, and composed "A Mighty Fortress Is Our God."

Secular observers see Luther as simply an odd textbook figure sandwiched somewhere in the midst of the Middle Ages and the Renaissance. Or they celebrate his autonomy as the new man, standing "counter to Christianity as it had been practiced for a thousand years," the modern man emerging from the stultifying domination of the superstitions of the Middle Ages.

But Martin Luther was more than a mad monk, a composer of theses, or an enlightened liberator. And this is why we tell his story. For Luther, one of the most significant figures in Christian history, not only began the church's reformation, but in fact launched a movement that rejuvenated the character of Western civilization. Many of the structures of our modern world bear his stamp.

What compelled this man to take his stand and loom so large in modern history?

First, he was compelled by the flaming truth: Christianity is no mere creed or confession; it is ultimate reality in Jesus Christ. The Scriptures are God's authoritative revelation of truth. Convinced of this, Luther had no choice but to stand for truth, even if it meant taking on the power structures of his day.

Second, he was compelled by his radical discovery within the Scriptures. For as he sat in the flickering candlelight, poring over the Word of God, Luther discovered that the central theme of all Scripture was the justice of God.

When Isaiah admonished the Jews to "do justice" and Amos thundered, "let justice roll down like living waters," the Hebrew word they used, *tsedeq*, literally meant "righteousness." It was God's declaration that men and women and social structures must be in conformity with the righteous standards of a just and holy God.

The New Testament sets forth the same standard. Using the language of debt and payment, it shows how Jesus Christ—who alone could meet God's holy demands—bore God's judgment for *our* sins. Because of Christ's payment, God's justice has been satisfied. And for those who "believe in him who raised Jesus our Lord from the dead," as Romans 4:23 puts it, God credits Christ's perfect righteousness to our account. We are declared righteous! Thus the apostle Paul could write in Romans 5:1–2, "We have been justified through faith, we have peace with God through our Lord Jesus Christ, through whom we have gained access by faith into this grace in which we now stand."

The biblical theme is consistent from Genesis to Revelation: The justice anticipated in the Old Testament, called forth by the Law and the Prophets, is fulfilled in the New through Christ the Mediator. There is no dichotomy then between justice and faith.

So in that great moment when "the gates of heaven" swung open for him, Luther saw the whole biblical vision: God demands justice—that is, *righteousness*—in all of the created order, and He declares men and women righteous by their faith. The Christian, then, must see all the world through God's eyes: righteousness for the world, for the structures of society, and for people. This leads to the biblical world-view, which affects all of life.

Our own age needs that same holistic view. Many Christian endeavors have traditionally divided into two camps: social activists in one and soul-winners in the other. Those seeking to right injustices and meet human needs have been accused of abandoning the classic Christian call to evangelize the lost. Meanwhile the social activists deride soul-winners for being concerned only with altar calls and notches in their Bible belts.

Failing to see the true definition of justice, many Christians slice the Scriptures in two, evoking images of an angry Old Testament God bringing vengeance upon those who disobeyed His laws (exacerbated by the King James translation of justice as "judgment"), or the New Testament caricature of a God who has discarded His law in favor of showering grace on everyone.[2]

How desperately the modern church needs to recapture the full biblical vision of justice! And we need also to take hold of Luther's third great contribution to the church: the unity of biblical truth and its relevance to all of life.

In his monastery cell, Luther was reborn. The justice he had so feared as a tumbrel to God's gallows became the chariot to God's throne of grace. Galloping in that chariot with the winds of grace and freedom rushing through his head, Martin Luther cast his eyes over the landscape of his day and saw that it was all the Lord's. From the farmer tilling the soil, to the prince hearing the pleas of his people, to the merchant selling his wares, to the child singing a small song . . . all of it was to reflect the righteous justice of the Lord of heaven and earth. All of it was to reflect right relations between people and their Lord, and right relations between people and their neighbors. All of it was to proclaim the glory of God.

Luther's vision for biblical justice shaped not only his own perspectives and actions, but launched a movement that swept across Europe, its currents surging with new leaders. John Calvin . . . Ulrich Zwingli . . . Philip Melanchthon . . . John Knox . . . soon the entire continent was in the midst of a mighty—and far-reaching—Reformation.

Seized by this biblically informed view of life and the realization that Scripture made truth plainly known to men and women, these Reformers were moved by a holy passion. Filled with the fear of God—the deepest reverence of the Lord Almighty—their cry became *Coram Deo,* "in the presence of God."

And nothing could stop them.

AS LUTHER SOUGHT TO RECLAIM Christian faith from cultural corruption, his work was less a radical new beginning than it was a re-formation in the truest sense of the term—a return to the essence of what the church had been in its noble past.

But the Reformation was more than a cleansing of ecclesiastical structures. Nothing was left untouched: the arts, commerce, government, and education all came under its powerful influence. In chapter 16 we discussed the foundation that absolute truth provided for the whole of Western history, but it was during the Reformation that the consequences of that belief had their most profound influence.

Consider just a few examples of that influence as we now see it from the perspective of nearly five centuries.

POLITICS AND GOVERNMENT

State and church had been wed in an unholy alliance since the time of Constantine, each using the other for its own purposes. With the gospel held hostage, the church could bring little reforming influence on culture. But the Reformers, seeing God as sovereign and the church as the people of God, wrenched free from the emperor's clutches, enabling the church to make a profound difference in societal values and structures.

For one thing, the Reformers changed the view of man in relation to the state. Luther's belief in the priesthood of all believers—that men and women had direct access to God and need not go through any earthly mediator—provided the philosophical foundation for political change. All men and women, whether sovereign or peasant, were equal in God's sight. All were created in the image of God and imbued with intrinsic dignity. And all were fallen and in need of divine grace.

And since the rights of the individual came from God, the state's power could no longer be regarded as absolute, nor could a ruler's "divine" authority be a charter for arbitrary rule. The Reformers developed a doctrine which became known as sphere sovereignty. Each structure that God ordained had its own sphere of responsibility: family, church, and state. The job of the state was not to rule over the others, but simply to create an environment in which all structures might fulfill their God-given responsibility.

One who expounded such radical ideas with particular cogency was the Scottish minister Samuel Rutherford, a great scholar and disciple of John

Knox's ministry. Rutherford wrote the classic work, *Lex Rex* ("The Law Is King") in 1644, arguing that the truth of Christ could never be subordinate to Caesar. Only Christ's authority is absolute and arbitrary. God is the true seat of government; rulers are merely trustees and stewards of God-given authority. The sovereign must administer law—not break, abrogate, or dispense with it. Public magistrates are public servants. Even the king, highest authority in the land, is a servant.

Lex Rex laid the philosophical foundation for a constitutional republic— the form that best balances man's intrinsic dignity with his inherent sinful nature which demands restraint. These principles were soon transported across the Atlantic.

John Witherspoon, president of what would become Princeton University, and the only clergyman to sign the Declaration of Independence, advanced Rutherford's ideas in America's great constitutional debates.

Thomas Jefferson also drew on Rutherford—indirectly—when he borrowed from John Locke. Locke, one of the Enlightenment's great thinkers, had himself been influenced by *Lex Rex*, secularizing Rutherford's concepts into his view of a social contract: inalienable rights, separation of powers, consent of the governed, and the right of revolution. Though not a Christian (he cut-and-pasted his own Bible, excising with scissors all references to miracles), Jefferson nonetheless brought Christian-influenced social and political ideas to the New World debate.

Thus two crucial doctrines of the Reformation—sphere sovereignty, or limited government, and *lex rex*, the rule of law—profoundly influenced America's founding fathers. While Enlightenment thinkers influenced the founders as well, clearly the most powerful ideas came from the Reformation. These streams of thought converged to form the first truly constitutional republic in the world. (The Catholic doctrine that is similar to the Reformers' sphere sovereignty is called subsidiarity.)

Meanwhile, the forces unleashed in the Reformation were producing massive political and social reforms in England. The Reformation's biblical world-view and vision of justice drove John Wesley, William Wilberforce, Lord Shaftesbury, Elizabeth Fry, and thousands of others in their crusade for the abolition of the slave trade, the reform of values, and the prevention of exploitation of children and workers in the mines and prisons.

VOCATION

While the Reformers' views of limited government profoundly influenced the political sphere, Luther's view of God's sovereignty also altered established concepts of work and vocation. For one thing, it rent the veil between the sacred and the secular. In God's sight, Luther wrote, the work of monks or priests was "in no way whatever superior to the works of a farmer laboring in the field, or of a woman looking after her home."[3] All work was noble and worthy if it was done to the glory of God.[4]

His reasoning here was that God's creation was good, and human beings were to be stewards of it; therefore, work was holy. In the Reformation era, vocational training was considered one of the first steps of discipleship. People were to discern their skills and use them fully, to seek excellence and shun idleness. The belief that people should pursue their individual callings broke down the rigid caste system, not only in the church but in society as a whole, paving the way for new economic and social freedoms.

By the seventeenth century, those whose religious convictions made them unwelcome in the Old World fled to the New and brought with them this high view of work, later known as the Protestant work ethic. The virtues of industry, frugality, respect for property, and duty to community were firmly planted in the soil of the new colonies, producing the most vibrant and productive economy in human history. In time, that distinctively Christian ethic was secularized, and, until recent years, its virtues remained ingrained in the American character.

ECONOMICS

The church had long embraced Thomas Aquinas's teaching that most work carried on for profit was immoral. But the Reformers' insistence that all work could and should be done to the glory of God legitimized successful commerce and profit. Thus, in a very real sense, the Reformation made possible the emergence of what we know today as democratic capitalism.

This recognition of legitimate commerce could not have been more timely. The plagues of the Middle Ages had decimated much of Europe's population, but by the 1500s there was a population surge—an 80 percent growth in Germany, for example, in one century. Increased forms of mobility aided commercial expansion, and the craft guilds shifted to more capitalistic modes of production. Banking, trade, and commerce prospered. All of which set the stage for the great Industrial Revolution with all that meant to the development of Western society.[5]

But along with this high view of work and commerce, the Reformers demanded stewardship and social responsibility. "Man does not live for himself alone . . . he lives also for all men on earth," wrote Luther, while John Calvin encouraged workers to produce more than they needed so they could give to those less fortunate.

It has taken five hundred years, but the Reformation has borne fruit around the globe. Apart from a few intellectual strongholds and holdout tyrannical governments, where is socialism not in retreat today? The Marxist vision has been thoroughly discredited; the welfare state is an acknowledged failure.

In one of the wonderful turns that history often takes, the head of the church against which Luther and others rebelled has been for years one of the most articulate defenders of democratic capitalism—more articulate, ironically, than the present-day spokespersons for mainline Protestantism.[6]

EDUCATION

Protestantism has often been described as "the religion of the word," with an emphasis on oral instruction. Protestants used both press and pulpit to propagate their message, and wherever Lutheranism and Calvinism spread, new schools were founded.

The study of history was particularly important to the Reformers, who took seriously the obligation to examine original sources. This also affected their attitude toward ancient languages. The Renaissance had already focused on classical literature and languages; the Reformers broadened the intellectual horizon of the day, calling attention to the ancient world, arguing that the chronology of history was the evidence of God's sovereign working.

These convictions directly affected the spread of education. At the popular level, Luther wanted to end illiteracy so people could be instructed in the Scriptures. So he advocated mandatory education for all children. And Luther's colleagues from the University of Wittenberg, including Philip Melanchthon and student Joachim Camerarius, championed classical learning in various German universities.

William Tyndale, among the first generation of English reformers, skilled in seven languages, translated and published a vernacular Bible in Britain. In Scotland, John Knox, influenced by both German and Swiss Reformation teaching, drew up the *First Book of Discipline,* which essentially provided the basis for a national system of education in Scotland.

The Reformation restored the university to the cultural leadership it had known in the thirteenth century and stimulated popular education throughout the West.

SCIENCE

In 1530 the publication of scientific books outnumbered that of religious books. This was no passing phenomenon, but a mirror of the sixteenth century's fascination with nature. The spiritual awakening created a hunger to understand the wonders of the universe, the work of the Creator.

During this period, science claimed no conflict with religion, contrary to what is popularly thought today. Instead, the notion of an orderly universe provided a context for the development of the scientific method, and progress was made in a number of fields.

The Reformation was a golden age for the increase of knowledge. Astronomy's burgeoning views of the universe challenged conventional medieval myths. The fields of botany, zoology, and geology flourished; musicians studied the mathematics of harmony; thinkers explored anatomy, metallurgy, plants, inertia, polar magnetism, optics, and acoustics; and inventors harnessed new knowledge to make practical tools of all kinds.

ART

Though the Reformers are often pictured as iconoclasts, their world-view actually caused them to perceive art of all types as a means to give glory to God and to reflect the goodness and beauty of His creation.[7]

Among the best known of the artists influenced by the Reformation is the Dutch painter Rembrandt van Rijn. His famous *Raising of the Cross* includes a self-portrait, in which he painted himself wearing a painter's beret and a cruel look on his face, helping to erect the cross. *My sin,* proclaimed Rembrandt, *sent my Lord to the cross.*[8]

Luther, himself a hearty singer with an excellent voice, considered music the noblest of the arts. "Next to the word of God, music deserves the highest praise," he wrote.[9] His love for music reflected his holistic view of life: All art reflected theology.

Luther's focus on music was truly reforming, bringing the church back to the practice of the early centuries. (Ambrose, fourth-century bishop of Milan, for example, had written hymns and then taught them to his congregation.) And in providing music and hymns to be sung by the common people, not just the priests, Luther reinstated a tradition that went back as far as the early apostles singing in their house churches in Jerusalem.

The German Reformation in particular stressed music and singing, giving rise to the chorale, which led to the cantata and oratorio of the baroque period.

The baroque era mirrored the exuberance of a "golden age" in European history, and many of its artists, composers, and writers were products of the Reformation heritage. In architecture, it appealed to impressiveness and grandeur. In literature, it came to expression through Shakespeare. In music, it was dominated by German Protestants.[10]

Johann Sebastian Bach was the zenith of the composers emerging from the Reformation. Inscribing his scores with the letters *S.D.G.—Soli Deo Gloria,* "To the glory of God alone"—Bach wove the words and chords of music in a conscious effort to please and exalt the God from whom his gifts had come.

ECCLESIASTICAL

While the Reformation went far beyond Luther's original focus, we cannot ignore the theological reform it sent throughout the Body of Christ. For here again, history has made one of its great sweeping circles.

To see this, we must stand back from our partisan passions and view the past five hundred years with some detached perspective. When we do, the picture is remarkable.

The Reformers, for example, assailed the corrupt practices of indulgences; today they are gone for the most part (save for the modern equivalent practiced by some television hucksters who promise healing and blessing for contributions).

And consider the view of the church. Calvin insisted it was not an institution that stood between man and God as it had become in the Middle Ages, but that it was the very people of God. Today's Catholic doctrine describes the church as the people of God, saying, the lay faithful should be conscious "not only of belonging to a church but of *being the church*."[11]

Or take the central issue for the Reformers: *sola fide* ("by faith alone"). The widest and deepest chasm was opened between Protestants and Catholics over this issue.

In recent decades, however, Catholic and Protestant doctrine has dramatically converged. In the fall of 1991, Pope John Paul II and Lutheran bishops from Scandinavia joined in an ecumenical celebration—not ignoring differences, but emphasizing growing unity on matters of orthodoxy, including justification. In his message, the Swedish primate said: "Dialogue has proven the existence of a basic unity, for instance, in the question of justification by faith," to which the pope agreed that both sides were "very close" to a common understanding.[12]

In the years that followed, Lutherans and Catholics reached a historic accord on the question of justification. The agreement was released in 1999.[13] Though significant differences remained unresolved, great progress was made, and affirmations were agreed to that would have been unthinkable during the Reformation.

Also, as we explained earlier, the informal process of Evangelicals and Catholics Together arrived at a resolution of the question of justification, which was in turn taught in all the Catholic synods meeting in Rome prior to the new millennium. Cardinal Ratzinger, whose Vatican task it is to guard church doctrine and who has written on the orthodox principles of Christianity, has elaborated on the issue of justification as well. Faith in Jesus Christ, writes Ratzinger, is "truly 'personal faith'" that comes from hearing.[14]

One would be hard-pressed to find instances today in which the Catholic Church has been coopted by the state, a condition the Reformers rightly assailed. As we saw in chapter 17, the church's heroic refusal to bow to the Communist state in Eastern Europe helped to bring that corrupt and oppressive regime to its ruin.

Examining the larger sweep of history, we see that although the Reformation brought great upheaval, of course, eventually it also stimulated profound renewal and reform to the church as a whole. The final chapters are yet to be written, but even today there are signs of an emerging movement, crossing traditional lines, bringing together conservative, confessing believers in a new expression of orthodox unity.

WHAT IF . . . ?

What if Martin Luther had not been inflamed by holy passion, had not taken his courageous stand? What if he had retreated to the cloister, cowed by the mighty forces arrayed before him? What if he had turned away, feeling helpless or indifferent?

One thing is certain: Our modern world would look distinctly different.

Many of today's sharp-tongued critics of Christianity's influence in public matters seem totally oblivious to this; and in their oblivion, they are sawing off the very limb on which they rest. For it was the religious influence of the Reformation that secured the very civil liberties they enjoy and which permit them to attack religion.

Viewed in its full historical perspective, we can now see why Luther's stand was so important.

First, the church of his day was in captivity, just as the Jews had been in Babylonian captivity two thousand years earlier. The movement Luther spawned broke the church free, gave it an evangelical thrust, made it an instrument of justice and compassion in the great awakenings that followed, and restored its theological heart.

Second, the movement influenced all of culture. The Reformation provided the most sweeping political, economic, and cultural benefits for Western civilization.

What would it take to free today's church from its own captivity—from the enculturation we described earlier? Some of the very same things that characterized the Reformers.

First of all, it would require *a commitment to the truth*—the One who says He is ultimate reality—and from this a renewed passion for what God has propositionally revealed, His inerrant Word, and the orthodox confession of faith by which the truth has been preserved and passed through the centuries.

It would mean *an awakening to the fact that the church is the people of God and that the church must be the church.* Away with consumer religion, the edifice complex, slick marketing plans, and syrupy sermons. Equip the people of God with spiritual weapons so they may serve the living God in the world.

It would mean *a healthy fear of God.* No trivializing of the sacred, but a sense of living in the day-to-day, hour-to-hour, minute-to-minute presence of the holy, majestic God.

It would require *the realization that God is sovereign over all and that we must, therefore, have a biblically informed view of all of life and a commitment to be agents of God's justice in society at large and to see His whole world from the perspective of His truth.*

It would require us *to have Luther's courage: to declare our independence from the world and to take our stand.*

But our vision of another great Reformation is easily blurred. When we survey the state of the world around us, it's easy to feel that we couldn't possibly have the kind of culture-changing influence that the Christians of earlier centuries did.

Our fears would be well-founded. For such influence would clearly be impossible . . . *except* for the awesome secret that Jesus left with us.

21

THE BODY

The holiest moment of the church service is the moment when God's people—strengthened by preaching and sacrament—go out of the church door into the world to be the Church. We don't go to church; we are the Church.

—ERNEST SOUTHCOTT

I<small>T WAS AN ASTOUNDING EVENING</small>—the last supper Christ shared with His disciples. He washed their feet, broke their Passover bread, and passed them the common cup. He spoke of His death. He comforted them, confused them, and challenged them.

Today we read the biblical account of that meal and feel some of the same emotions. But we know, as His disciples soon discovered, that the Last Supper was not an end, but a beginning. The beginning of a whole new era. For within the extraordinary words Christ spoke to them is one of the most powerful secrets of His plan for us and for the world.

"I tell you the truth," said Jesus to His friends, "anyone who has faith in me will do what I have been doing." The disciples must have looked at one another in bewilderment. They had seen Christ cast out demons and raise the dead. How could they possibly do that?

But then Jesus went even further, adding, "He will do even greater things than these, because I am going to the Father."[1]

Greater things than these? How could this ragtag lot of people do *more* than Jesus? What in the world was He talking about?

Consider the context. Christ was poised at the juncture between the conclusion of His earthly ministry and His death, resurrection, and ascension into heaven. Confined in the human experience—God incarnate in a human body, with the limitations of time and space—He had for thirty-three years done the works and ministry to which God had called Him. Now He was preparing to return to the right hand of the Father.

"I will ask the Father," Jesus promised them that night, "and he will give you another Counselor to be with you forever—the Spirit of truth."[2] God would send in His Son's place the Holy Spirit, who would enable His people to do all Jesus had commanded them to do.

True to Christ's promise, the Holy Spirit arrived a few weeks later at Pentecost. The disciples were filled with new power. They began to fulfill His commission for His new church: They proclaimed the good news; they baptized new believers and gathered them into communities; and under the seal of the Holy Spirit, the church began to grow.

Hundreds, then thousands, then millions of believers became part of that body. Generations of Christians, gifted in a thousand different ways and empowered by the same Holy Spirit, invaded *every* arena of human life, *every* country, *every* field of endeavor, bringing the truth to bear on their surroundings.

In His earthly ministry, Jesus was limited to one human body; now the Body of Christ is made up of millions and millions of human bodies stamped with His image—His followers. That includes you and me, for Jesus prayed for *us* that last evening, not just for the disciples who were with Him. "My prayer is not for them alone," He told His Father. "I pray also for those who will believe in me through their message."[3]

Astounding. Jesus ascended. But His Spirit descended to empower His Body—the church—to do more than He could accomplish as one Person.

In light of this awesome truth, it is scandalous that so many believers today have such a low view of the church. They see their Christian lives as a solitary exercise—"Jesus and me"—or they treat the church as a building or a social center. They flit from congregation to congregation—or they don't associate with any church at all. That the church is held in such low esteem reflects not only the depths of our biblical ignorance, but the alarming extent to which we've bought into the obsessive individualism of modern culture.

Of course every believer is part of the universal church. But for any

Christian who has a choice in the matter, failure to commit to a particular church is failure to obey Christ.[4] For it is through a confessing, local body of believers that we carry out the work of the church in the world. It is within the church particular that we commit ourselves to intimate relationships with fellow believers and submit ourselves to accountability, duties, and responsibilities. In this community our Christian character is shaped, our spiritual gifts developed and exercised. It is the family whose ties cannot be broken. It is the training camp that disciples and equips believers to be God's people against the world and for the world.

If we don't grasp *the intrinsically corporate nature of Christianity* embodied in the church, we are missing the very heart of Jesus' plan.

But when we do understand that the church is Christ's body, what next? What does this one body with many parts look like? What does it do? What is its mission in the world? These are questions we will examine in the final section of this book.

ONE OF OUR FAVORITE PICTURES OF THE CHURCH comes from the late Richard Halverson, friend and mentor. Dick was chaplain of the U.S. Senate, but before that he was pastor of Washington D.C.'s large Fourth Presbyterian Church. He had been leading that church for years when suddenly, one night, he saw his church clearly for the very first time.

He was flying into Washington one day at dusk. At that time the approach path to Washington's Reagan National Airport happened to pass directly over Fourth Presbyterian Church. Dick pressed his face against the window to catch a glimpse of the building from the air. But everything on the ground was shrouded in the shadows falling over the city as the sun set. Dick could not find his church.

He leaned back in his seat, gazing at the Washington skyline, always an inspiring sight. As his eyes followed the Potomac River, he could see the skyscrapers of Rosslyn, just across Key Bridge from Georgetown. Then, in the distance to the left, the White House, the lights of the Labor Department, the distant glow of the Capitol dome.

As he stared out the window, he began mentally ticking off the names of members of his congregation who worked in those office buildings and government bureaus. Disciples he had equipped to live their faith. And suddenly it hit him.

"Of course!" he exclaimed to the startled passenger in the next seat. "There it is! Fourth Presbyterian Church!"

The church wasn't marked by a sanctuary or a steeple. The church was spread throughout Washington, in the homes and neighborhoods and offices below him, thousands of points of light illuminating the darkness.

And that is the way the church should look in the world today. The people of God—one body with many different parts—spread throughout every arena of life, twenty-four hours a day, seven days a week, doing even "greater things" than Christ Himself!

PART 3

THE CHURCH
IN THE WORLD

22

EQUIPPING THE SAINTS

*Every member of the Body has the potential to be—and should be fed and
led toward functioning as a fully equipped agent of Jesus Christ,
as His minister.*

—JACK HAYFORD

Ask about the local church's role in the world, and most
Christians immediately begin hauling out mission statements, action
plans, and strategy schemes. They are already lacing up their Nikes, asking,
"What should we do?"

Action plans and mission statements are great things. But first, like
Dick Halverson, we need to see the church from a higher perspective. We
need the big-picture view of the Body, alive and vibrant—the holy presence in the world. The church's role in the world is not a series of independent items on an action checklist. Instead, the church's role (what it
does) is dependent on its character (what it is) as a community of believers.

What we do, therefore, flows from who we are.

Remember the bold believers in Eastern Europe who brought down
their Communist rulers? They didn't hold congregational meetings and
discuss their goals and objectives as part of a five-year plan ("Year One:
Tear Down Berlin Wall"). Their strength derived not from their to-do list,
but from who they were—the church. Their very presence as the people of
God, loyal to a greater kingdom, invoked a power that even the most ruthless government could not repress.

The same was true of the early church. The first Christians worshiped God and lived as a holy community, conforming their character to the demands of Christ rather than Caesar. They didn't purpose to change history. They did so because of who they were.

This character-oriented perspective is foreign to our achievement-oriented society. Particularly in the U.S., we focus on what people do rather than who they are. We evaluate, classify, and prioritize with that all-important question: "So, what do you do?"

Our consumer-oriented religious culture tends to run the same way. Many Christians measure churches by their status in the community or by what they do: their outreach programs, musical repertoire, and fellowship opportunities. Seldom do you hear a person say, "I decided to join this church because of its character as a holy community." Nor do most believers choose a church for its capacity to disciple and equip them for ministry.

Yet these fundamentals of character should be our very first considerations. If the church is the Body, the holy presence of Christ in the world, its most fundamental task is to build communities of holy people who are just like Jesus. And the first priority of those communities is to disciple men and women to maturity in Him and then to equip them to live their faith in every aspect of life and in every part of the world.

MAKING DISCIPLES

The most familiar of our mandates is the Great Commission: "All authority has been given to Me in heaven and on earth," Jesus said. "Go therefore and make disciples of all the nations, baptizing them in the name of the Father and the Son and the Holy Spirit, teaching them to observe all that I commanded you."[1]

Note that this is not a charge to individuals. It is a commission to the church. Baptism, the public display of faith in Christ and the visible sign of entry into the church, can only be carried out by the church. And only the church can truly teach all that Christ has commanded, equipping believers to grow in maturity and to be the people of God.

And note also that "making disciples" involves more than evangelism.

Though the church must be passionate in its calling to introduce people to Jesus Christ, that is only a part of God's commission to us. Evangelism must be fully integrated with *discipleship* in order for the church to truly be obedient to Scripture.

Yet discipleship sometimes gets lost in the focus on evangelism. Ask evangelicals what the first priority of the church is, and most will invariably answer, "Evangelism." In their fund-raising letters, many ministries focus solely on evangelism, because supporters love to read about, and tend to give money to, the work of lost souls coming to Christ.

Sometimes an erroneous understanding of evangelism creates false guilt. I vividly remember hearing a visiting missionary use his entire message one Sunday morning to berate the congregation. "The only purpose of the church is soul-winning," he charged, pounding the pulpit and glaring at the people. "Each and every one of you are failing if you are not out there winning souls for Christ."

Of course evangelism is crucial! We'll discuss it at length in an upcoming chapter. But it is not the end of the story, as in so many testimonies we hear. In my life, Tom Phillips introduced me to Christ. I was born again. But I was an infant in the faith. Then a group of faithful brothers in Washington fed, taught, encouraged, and corrected me, even as my new membership in the church further sustained and equipped me.

Once a person receives Christ, his or her growth in holiness—sanctification—is a lifelong process. And it happens in the context of the local congregation.

BUILDING UP THE BODY

In his letter to the church at Ephesus, Paul described this process when he sketched the anatomy of a healthy church:

> And He gave some as apostles, and some as prophets, and some as evangelists, and some as pastors and teachers, for the equipping of the saints for the work of service, to the building up of the body of Christ; until we all attain to the unity of the faith, and of the knowledge of the

Son of God, to a mature man, to the measure of the stature which belongs to the fulness of Christ. As a result, we are no longer to be children, tossed here and there by waves, and carried about by every wind of doctrine, by the trickery of men, by craftiness in deceitful scheming; but speaking the truth in love, we are to grow up in all aspects into Him, who is the head, even Christ, from whom the whole body, being fitted and held together by that which every joint supplies, according to the proper working of each individual part, causes the growth of the body for the building up of itself in love.[2]

Paul is speaking here of the whole body, the church universal. But since the process described can only take place in a local community of faith, theologian and writer T. M. Moore uses this passage as a model for the progression of vigorous development for the church particular. And *discipleship* is the key to that process.

Moore breaks down the major elements in Paul's description of how God builds up the church:

- Unity of the faith. The church must have a oneness of confessional creed (common understandings, vision, goals, and aspirations), as well as a oneness of experience (shared lives).
- The knowledge of the Son of God. The church must have full assurance of salvation, grounded in right doctrine.
- A mature man. The church must manifest maturity in critical areas of discipleship: committed to growth achieved through the Word of God, prayer, worship, and fellowship; producing the fruit of the Spirit, demonstrating love, keeping God's commandments, and bearing witness to the Lord.
- No longer children. Members of the Body must be able to discern false doctrines and to distinguish truth from error. To put it in terms we've already discussed, believers must be equipped with a Christian world-view. [3]
- Speaking the truth in love. Church members articulate the truth of Christ to one another and to those outside the Body. They confront errors with love rather than condescension.

- Every joint supplies. The individual members cultivate their spiritual gifts, using them to the glory of God in ministry to one another and for the community.
- The growth of the Body. All of this increases the church both quantitatively and qualitatively.[4]

Note the role Paul assigns to the pastor in the process of building the Body.[5] Contrary to popular impressions today, the pastor is not paid to do ministry. Pastors and teachers are to equip the saints—that's us—to serve, to build the Body, to *be* the church in the world and do the work of ministry. Every layperson is to be equipped as a minister of the gospel.

French social critic Jacques Ellul put it well:

The channel through which the Holy Spirit brings truth to the world is the pastor, who teaches it to the laity, who in turn translate it and put it to work in the marketplace, infiltrating the world. The problem in the modern church, however, Ellul says, is that the channel is blocked. The pastor doesn't engage in the secular world on a day-in, day-out basis, and the laypeople, who do, tend to keep their faith in a compartment separate from the rest of their lives.[6]

So Sunday after Sunday congregations sit passively—like spectators watching the entertainment up front—missing the fact that they should be absorbing the truth and applying it to their lives, training to be effective soldiers of the cross.

I cannot help but see parallels here with my experience in marine officers' basic training. The marines, if you'll pardon an old leatherneck's pride, do it right.

During the first grueling weeks we were put through intense physical training on death-defying obstacle courses. We learned to handle and clean a rifle, and to disassemble and reassemble it blindfolded. We memorized the marine handbook of military rules and regimen (and no one argued about whether the rules were relevant or accepted by a majority of marines). Our hearts and minds were imprinted forever with the meaning of discipline. (I remember once cracking the slightest smile during inspection. The result? "Fifty push-ups, Colson!")

From there it was on to the rifle range and small-unit tactics. Then field maneuvers. And while all of this was simulated warfare, no one treated it like a game. When I was in training, the Korean War was at its bloodiest; young men just out of school were leading other young men in deadly combat. Many came home in pine boxes. So we were serious not only about surviving combat, but about winning it.

It should be the same for the soldiers of the cross. Yet rather than being well-trained, well-disciplined, functioning members of the Body, many of us act more like reserve units: weekend warriors whose real jobs occupy them during the week and who just turn out for occasional drills.

If we take our Handbook seriously, we have to conclude that the church is the basic school of discipline and training for all Christians. And shouldn't our training be at least as serious as the military? After all, we are in warfare. And the battle is not just for flesh and blood; it is for eternal souls.

Nineteenth-century British missionaries knew this. Departing from England for Africa, many packed their possessions in long, narrow wooden boxes: their own coffins. They knew that, more than likely, they would return home in those coffins. Felled by disease, exhaustion, and violence, many did.

Every part of the church should be geared for the training (discipling and equipping) of the local units that fight this battle. Evangelistic ministries should be directing new believers into the church particular. Discipleship ministries should be working hand in hand with local congregations. Specialized ministries—such as service to the disabled, to youth, to executives, to the inner city, to prisoners—should be guiding those they reach into local congregations, even as they are equipping those same local churches with the skills, resources, encouragement, and education they need to do effective ministry in these unique areas.[7]

In fact, whether these parachurch ministries are building up the Body is perhaps the best test of their biblical fidelity. Those that aren't cooperating with and equipping the work of local churches run the risk of ending up promoting their own cause over the good of the Body and thus being outside of God's plan. (This has been a real problem among evangelicals. One great strength of the movement is its vitality: independent, dynamic leaders raising up powerful organizations to do important work. But human nature being what it is, this can also be a weakness when those same leaders become protective of their turf or fall into the trap of the personality cult.)

So the church must first build strong disciples and then equip its men and women for battle in the world.

TRAINING FOR BATTLE

Since a biblical world-view involves all of life, the church must equip its members for all of life. Like the military, this begins with the basics and moves on to building the mature character of the seasoned warrior.

There are hundreds of diverse and creative ways to train Christians to be the people of God so that they, together, can do those "greater things" to which Christ referred. We cannot cover all the areas of equipping, let alone include even a fraction of the particular churches doing a great job preparing their people for ministry. But we can touch upon training areas that should be a part of every church—with a few representative examples.

At the most fundamental level, the church must equip its members to know and defend their faith and to apply it in the world. The ministry of the Word is the beginning. The Christian disciple must be grounded in the Word and historic Christian orthodoxy. Without this basic training, we are unable to give a reasonable defense for the hope within us.[8]

Most churches do a good job with Sunday school and Bible studies, but they can also make use of parachurch resources like the Navigators, which produces excellent discipleship material. Or they might take advantage of Walk Thru the Bible, which gives Christians a big-picture perspective on the Old and New Testaments. And I personally have profited greatly from Ligonier Ministries' seminars, tapes, and videos on doctrine.

Those seeking more advanced skills can take advantage of lay seminary training like that offered by the Seminary of the East, located in New York and Philadelphia. Some larger churches like Elmbrook in Waukesha, Wisconsin, provide similar courses, enabling students to receive credit through nearby Trinity College and Trinity Evangelical Divinity School. A number of Catholic dioceses do the same thing, as in Washington, D.C. where Education for Parish Service (EPS) requires two years of academic study combined with practical work in the attendee's parish. And then there's Prison Fellowship's Wilberforce Forum, which offers college credit courses in biblical world-view, with credit given by Union University of Jackson, Tennessee. We will soon have courses for the seminary level as well as for pastors and Christian leaders.[9]

Discipling can also include applying a biblical perspective to current events. Some friends in Florida initiated a tough-minded "life issues" course in their parish. They met weekly to study timely issues, from just-war theory to the New Age movement to abortion to the question, "Does truth exist?" One hundred people turned out for that last one.

Why leave it to the League of Women Voters or the local university to lead discussions on the concerns of the day? The church should be aggressively training its people to be discerning and to speak out of the convictions of an equipped Christian mind.

In this same vein, the church should equip its members to lead exemplary lives in the marketplace, particularly in today's scandal-ridden corporate environment. Ethics training should be a prime task of the church. For one thing, if we fail to do this, we produce members who follow the world's standards rather than the Bible's, and the results will detract from our witness at large, as we mentioned in chapter 18.

But the larger call for the church to be the guiding voice for sound morality in culture comes because the church has the unique authority to do so. Sound ethical principles result from a binding moral law, the very thing society has rejected as it has driven absolute standards based on Judeo-Christian revelation from modern life. As we argued earlier, postmodern academicians, thinkers, writers, and value-free educators have embraced a dogmatic relativism and therefore have no unchanging standard by which to determine whether any particular business, biomedical, political, or personal choice is good or evil. So business schools may say they are teaching ethics, but in reality, they are not. They cannot.

The University of Michigan's curriculum for a business school class called "Ethics of Corporate Management" admits as much. "This course is not concerned with personal moral issues of honesty and truthfulness . . . it is assumed that the students of this university have already formed their own standards on these issues."[10] So each student's perceptions of "honesty and truthfulness" are based on what is right in his or her own eyes. This is not ethics.

Similarly, according to a 2002 poll, three-quarters of college students surveyed said that professors taught them that what is right and wrong depends on differences in individual values and cultural diversity. Only 25 percent were taught that there is a clear standard of right and wrong. When asked to rank which business practice was most important, 38 percent of students chose "recruiting a diverse work force in which women and minorities are advanced and promoted." Only 23 percent chose "providing clear and accurate business statements to stockholders and creditors."[11]

Churches must equip their members with an understanding of ethics based on enduring moral truths that are binding on all people at all times. One ministry designed to assist congregations in this area is the Executive Leadership Foundation, a resource center that teaches Christians how to apply absolute values in tough, realistic scenarios. The goal? That Christians "would have an impact" in their sphere of influence, whatever that is.[12]

The church must also equip its members to build strong marriages and families. The family, the most basic unit of civilized society, is the institution that may well be under the greatest attack in society today. Unless we insist on counseling and training before marriage, and then provide a full range of services to build and strengthen the family thereafter, the church cannot say it is making disciples and fulfilling the Great Commission. This is why the ministry of Jim Dobson's Focus on the Family is so critical, and every church can profit from it.[13]

For more than sixty years the Catholic Church has sought to strengthen marriages by requiring couples who wish to marry in the church to participate in PreCana, which focuses on practical and theological teachings about marriage and exposes young couples to mentoring relationships with older couples.

Similarly, as Mike McManus has contended so well in his book, *Marriage Savers,* couples with solid, seasoned marriages provide a great resource within the church for strengthening other marriages and preventing divorce.[14] Young couples greatly increase their chances of staying married if they are mentored by those who can draw on years of experience in how to best resolve conflicts, improve communication, and cherish one another.

This kind of mentoring speaks to Paul's principle in Titus, that older women are to "train the younger women to love their husbands and children." In the early church, the older generation was expected to mentor the younger one.

Mike McManus's Marriage Savers has also instituted an even more ambitious idea: Community Marriage Policies, a uniform requirement that all the local churches—Catholic and Protestant, liberal and conservative, black and white—adopt together, in order to radically reduce a given community's divorce rate. Typically, clergy agree to require engaged couples to undergo four months of marriage preparation, including a premarital inventory to evaluate the maturity of the relationship, and mentoring from older couples.

Community Marriage Policies are now in place in hundreds of cities, with dramatic results. In Modesto, California, the first city to adopt a Community Marriage Policy more than twenty years ago, divorce rates plunged 47 percent.[15]

"Clearly," says McManus, thinking big, "we hold in our hands the answer to America's divorce rate."

However, the troubling question is, Will we accept the challenge? W. Bradford Wilcox, a researcher on religion at Yale University, writes that America's houses of worship are "traditionally the most important custodians of marriage in the nation." And yet, he concludes, they "have been unable and unwilling to foster the beliefs and virtues that make for a strong marriage culture."[16]

What an indictment! But it is one we can—and must—answer.

In the same way that churches should be the training ground for healthy marriages, they need to equip their members to "train up their children in the way they should go." It is every Christian parent's responsibility to raise his or her children in the fear and admonition of the Lord—and it is every church body's responsibility to help them do that. Part of that training means equipping parents to be discerning in educational issues. Vigilance is the essential watchword for families whose children attend public schools.

When the Fairfax, Virginia, County School Board proposed a "value-free" curriculum designed for kindergarten through twelfth grade, parents at McLean Presbyterian Church examined the program and discovered that it undermined biblical moral values. So they organized an "information night" to alert parents to the issues involved, and then encouraged parents to make their voices heard at school board meetings. While they did not get the curriculum changed, Christian parents did build relationships with the staffs at the schools in question, and they were also able to change a few components of the program. And, having been educated in the curriculum material, many who otherwise would not have been aware opted to take their children out of the offensive classes. `

Sometimes the church needs to help children who have been forced to grow old before their time. In designing their program to work with children of divorced parents, the First Evangelical Free Church of Fullerton, California found a good model in the Catholic Church's "Rainbows for All God's Children." So fifteen people from First Evangelical were trained by a group of nuns in a nearby parish, who seemed to particularly delight in anointing their Protestant brothers and sisters with oil and ashes at the dedication service.

Fifty children were part of the first group at Fullerton, and church volunteers taught them Bible memory verses to help comfort and strengthen them in times of need as well as helping them learn how to express their feelings and work through their emotions.

At Faithful Central Missionary Baptist Church in South Central Los Angeles, Christian Education Minister LaVerne Tolbert and her volunteers provide Christian education in a real combat zone. The neighborhood is overrun by gangs and drugs, and teen pregnancy is commonplace. There, through role plays, frank Friday night discussions, and Bible study, the church equips kids not only to say no, but to call on the power of the Holy Spirit to enable them to do so.[17]

The church should equip its members to fulfill their various vocations. In the Reformation era, helping believers find their vocation was considered a key step of discipleship. Since our work is to bring glory to God, the church needs to teach a high view of labor and the Christian character traits of diligence, thrift, creativity, and excellence. If the church doesn't teach a healthy work ethic, who will?[18]

The church is also the natural place to provide vocational counseling. To do this, a number of congregations across the country use "gifts analysis inventories," which not only highlight an individual's spiritual gifts, but also focus on his or her strengths and aptitudes.

In Los Angeles, Victory Outreach, which evangelizes and disciples heroin addicts, provides an outstanding example of the church equipping believers with a healthy work ethic. Once clean of drugs, the participants spend nine months in intensive Bible study and training, breaking the old patterns of the streets and establishing basic Christian character and behavior. After that, they enter a nine-month reentry phase, during which they develop their work skills.

The church should equip its people to be good stewards of financial resources. The Presbyterian Church in America regularly offers seminars at individual churches to help believers manage their resources and determine how to maximize their charitable giving. Ron Blue of Atlanta is well-known in evangelical circles for his expertise in financial planning, investment management services, and estate and tax planning. Blue's books, including the *Personal Financial Planning Guide,* and his six-part videotape series, "Master Your Money," are excellent tools for church groups seeking to be good stewards.

Another great resource is Crown Financial Ministries. In it, two strong ministries, Larry Burkett's Christian Financial Concepts and Howard Dayton's Crown Ministries, took the unusual step of merging. It made sense: Crown was doing a great job equipping Christians with a biblical view of stewardship with small study groups in many local churches. Meanwhile Burkett's Christian Financial Concepts was running seminars for businesspeople on how to manage their companies, based on Christian principles, seminars for married couples on how to budget, as well as financial management training sessions for laity. Burkett was reaching individual people all over the world, but he wanted to root his ministry in the local church. So the two stewardship ministries combined forces, with the goal of reaching and training three hundred million people over the next fifteen years![19]

All believers are called to be witnesses, both in word and in deed. Thus, the church needs to train laypeople to identify their own evangelistic gifts and use them effectively in the marketplace. Willow Creek Community Church in South Barrington, Illinois, offers a seminar called "Network," designed to help members of that huge congregation identify spiritual gifts. Those with the gift of evangelism are directed into a training seminar where the first lesson "is called 'Being Yourself.' We want people to understand that they don't have to be Billy Graham in order to be salt and light," says the program's founder. "They can be themselves and reach people that Billy Graham can't."

Another well-known and powerful ministry is Evangelism Explosion (EE), which started in the Coral Ridge Presbyterian Church in Fort Lauderdale, Florida. EE has spread across the country, training laypeople to share their faith comfortably and effectively. But, as Dr. James Kennedy, pastor of Coral Ridge, emphasizes, evangelism is not an end in itself. Rather it exists in the context of loving discipleship relationships. So EE includes three levels of discipleship: trainer and trainee, EE participants and other members of the church, and new believers and their spiritual parents. The program consists of sixteen units of class instruction, home-work assignments, and on-the-job training.

When Ellen was in Cuba recently, she met pastors who have been trained in Evangelism Explosion's principles and are using them in their home churches. One such church in a fishing village near Havana has grown from one hundred to four hundred members in five years, and the members have also planted four daughter churches during that time. (Ellen's Cuban government-supplied tour guide, unfamiliar with evangel-ical terms, had no clue how to translate "Evangelism Explosion." He kept muttering about *la bomba!*)

And finally, the church must equip its people with specialized training that enables them to reach out to those in particular types of physical and spiritual need. A particular church's ministry will vary depending on location, cultural context, and the unique vision and burdens of its members. A church in a Cuban fishing village may well focus on different needs than a suburban church outside Boston. Whatever the particular needs, however, compassion ministries are tough, front-line work, and many churches have developed great programs for training believers to do them well.

One great outside resource is the Stephen Ministry, begun in the late 1970s by a Missouri Synod Lutheran pastor, Dr. Kenneth Haugk. This inter-denominational effort equips Christians with caregiving skills for people in crisis situations. Those who seek training must pay a fee for the fifty-hour core course, during which they develop counseling and other practical skills. Upon graduation, "Stephen ministers" work in every arena of need.

One key ministry field for believers is among prisoners, ex-prisoners, and their families. In Prison Fellowship's work with churches across the country, we've clearly seen the importance of solid training. Loving Christians can, with the noblest of motives, make a mess of prison ministry. They may buttonhole prisoners with tracts, respond naively to prisoners' requests, or promise things they can't deliver, which amounts to just another "rejection" in the prisoner's life. Training is critical. So PF requires laypeople to complete twenty hours of training courses in order to be certified as volunteers.[20]

As the church equips its people to minister to the living, it needs to train them as well to deal with death and disease. Many churches have done this with special ministries like "Bridges," a cancer support and Bible study group at Elmbrook Church. Members pray together, help one another with practical concerns, and shepherd each other through the rough times that affect both the individual sufferer and the family. They also seek to discern the spiritual opportunities that come through suffering.

Another vital ministry in our society is outreach to homosexuals. "Harvest" is just such a ministry in urban Philadelphia.

Tenth Presbyterian Church is located in the middle of a downtown neighborhood that caters to gay bars and homosexual meeting areas. Recognizing the need and the mission field in its own backyard, in 1984 the church began a Bible study for anyone interested in being freed from homosexuality; they began running a two-line advertisement in the *Philadelphia Inquirer*, "Homosexuals and Lesbians Can Change," followed by the Harvest phone number. Crank calls aside, Harvest heard from hundreds of people who had almost lost hope, and the ad now garners thousands of calls every year. Hundreds of men and women who felt trapped in homosexual lifestyles have been freed.

Hope, a companion ministry, seeks to help those who have contracted AIDS, tenderly offering them real help and spiritual healing. Ministries like this sensitize and equip the church to articulate a godly response to one of the great needs of our day.

Harvest's full-time director, John Freeman, understands the church's role: "It is within the church that healing, fellowship, growth, and maturing in Christ are to take place. It is therefore one of our goals to transfer dependence of an individual from Harvest to a caring local church as soon as we can.

"Speaking the truth in love," he adds, "this ministry brings the resources of the church to bear on the problem of homosexuality. It is an important part of any effort to reach modern America for Christ."[21]

As a local ministry, Harvest is a member of Exodus, an interdenominational ministry offering resources to help Christians, their loved ones, and others find freedom from homosexuality. Exodus includes 135 local Christian ministries in seventeen nations.[22]

This, of course, is only a sample of the tremendous churches and ministries that are effectively equipping believers to be the Body in the world today. But all such ministries share one singular characteristic: They focus on the Head of the Body, Christ Himself. As human beings, we can focus on ourselves, doing all the right things to meet spiritual, physical, and emotional needs . . . but if we do so with the wrong attitude, and in our own strength, all our good works are for naught. This is why the church's primary focus must always be on developing the Christlike character of its people.

When members of the church at Corinth were squabbling about their various gifts, the apostle Paul told them that the greatest gift—that which characterized their Lord—was love. So as we serve one another in the Body and reach to those beyond, we are to do so with the same loving, humble attitude as Jesus Himself. We must think more of others than of ourselves, caring most for "the least of these."

Nothing could be more at odds with the way of the world. Today's celebrity-mad culture is impressed and obsessed with power and position, fame and influence, not selfless service.

23

LET THIS MIND BE IN YOU . . .

We have too many people who have plenty of medals and no scars.

—WARREN WIERSBE

I WAS ALMOST TRAMPLED by the madding crowd.

It was a gray London morning, and I was stepping out of the doorway of Claridges, the British hotel that is a tradition unto itself in a country steeped in tradition. In the land of Chaucer, Shakespeare, and Keats, the city of Churchill, Gladstone, and Wilberforce, the very air of Claridges carries the weight of history, great literature, and the triumph of civilization in a barbarian world. Patty and I were in London to attend the ceremony at Buckingham Palace, at which Prince Phillip would award me the Templeton Prize for Progress in Religion, and friends had treated us to this delightful stay at Claridges.[1]

As we crossed the marble-floored lobby, the manager, resplendent in long tails, bowed to us. At the grand doors, the doorman snapped to attention. Then we stepped out onto the sidewalk . . . and were nearly trampled by a stampeding mob. It was a riot of reporters and photographers in pursuit of what we could only see as a swirl of blonde hair in the distance. Pressed against the doors, we heard the thunder of dozens of feet, the snapping of clicking cameras, shouts, and muffled curses. A young photographer fell down, his camera crashing to the pavement. A colleague stopped to help. "No, leave him!" shouted someone. "Can't wait. Hurry! She's getting away!"

Patty and I hurried to see who or what had caused the commotion.

It was, of course, Princess Diana.

A few years later when I heard the news and circumstances of Diana's death, I thought of that day at Claridges. How terrible to be hounded to the very moment of her death by packs of paparazzi!

And why the chase? Because Diana was unfortunate enough to be famous for being famous. When she became engaged to Prince Charles, she was a rather sheltered eighteen-year-old, plucked from an obscure, if wealthy, lifestyle and placed on the pinnacle of public display. From then on, every comment, action, hairstyle, or outfit received international media scrutiny. And though at times she used her celebrity for her own purposes, including causes for the needy, for the most part it was a bother and a burden to her. She complained that the adulation had more to do with how she looked than who she was.

On the day of her death, and for weeks thereafter, Diana dominated world news.

Ironically, in the same week that Diana died so tragically, the world lost another person of world renown—but a person whose public persona could not have been more different. Mother Teresa.

Afterward many said that perhaps Mother Teresa had somehow planned it that way. While the world's attention was focused on the fairy-tale princess who did not live happily ever after, and who, by her own accounts, was often miserable, self-destructive, and preoccupied with fashion, accessories, and the pursuit of love, the elderly nun who had spent her life giving to others, who had chosen to live with the poorest of the poor and devote her life to serve Jesus by helping suffering people die with dignity, secure in the knowledge of the love of God, quietly slipped away.

Hundreds of thousands of every faith and background lined Mother Teresa's funeral procession route, aware that she represented Someone far greater than herself.

Millions, of course, also watched Diana's last procession. And in the months and years to follow she filled the pages of magazines, just as did

John F. Kennedy Jr., our American version of dashing young royalty, after his tragic plane crash.

Diana, J.F.K. Jr., and their living counterparts reached the pinnacle of the cult of celebrity worship, a multibillion-dollar industry devoted largely to voyeurism. Entire newspapers, magazines, and television shows are devoted to clandestine photos of celebrities: celebrities caught with their clothes off, celebrities with other people's spouses, celebrities at the fat farm, the rehab center, the plastic surgeon, and wherever else a well-known person is unfortunate enough to be caught on film.

CELEBRITY SYNDROME AND THE PEDESTAL COMPLEX

People used to become celebrities because they were admired for accomplishing something unusual. By this we mean unusually brave or noble, not unusual as in eating a record number of slugs. People admired those who made the first solo flight across the Atlantic, broke the color barrier in baseball, and found cures for terrible diseases. They honored Olympic competitors who, through discipline and hard work, pushed their bodies to break records. They honored brave men and women who stood, against all odds, for the courage of their convictions.

But today, people are celebrities simply because they receive attention. As one commentator put it, people are well-known for being well-known. Fame has little to do with worth or character or achievement. It has to do with photographing well. So Princess Diana receives far more attention than Mother Teresa; celebrated adulterers are in the spotlight, while scientists who discover life-saving medicines are not.

Television and movies are the perfect media to fan this obsession. By elevating image over ideas and appearance over substance, the screen confers status. And audiences are so mesmerized that it matters little what one says or does.

Because of this uncritical acceptance, rappers and rockers wield inordinate influence as childhood heroes. Because of advertising and marketing tie-ins, Britney Spears becomes the role model for ten-year-old girls. And those screen and music idols who become victims of their own excesses are even more glorified in death. So musicians like Tupac Shakur and Curt

Cobain become heroic figures, even though their lifestyles killed them years ago. And then we have Elvis, a man who had become a parody of himself and died from his own sad self-indulgence. Yet a quarter century after his death, hundreds of thousands of devotees still make the pilgrimage to Graceland.

Christians can get caught up in the celebrity syndrome. I could not help but notice this after I guest-hosted a television talk show for two weeks. Everywhere I went, people stopped me, excited to tell me they had seen me on television.

"What was I talking about?" I would ask, curious about which segment they had seen and what they thought of it. But not one person could tell me what had been said on the program. I could have been selling bongo drums or preaching some perverted gospel. All that mattered was that I was "famous"; they had seen me on the tube. (By contrast, I find that when people listen to our BreakPoint radio program, they almost invariably remember what I've talked about. Radio, devoid of images that titillate and distract, requires people to listen to the meaning of the words and consider the ideas.)

The fact that a television show or a network is "Christian" doesn't alter its fundamental character. And for many Christians, watching our "stars" on television has become a substitute for participation in the local church. Why roll up our sleeves and get involved with all those troublesome people down on the corner when we can just sit in our family room and listen to smooth preaching and wonderful music, all within range of the remote control? So millions of able-bodied believers remove themselves from the fellowship of the Body and begin living their spiritual lives vicariously, through the religious celebrities they venerate.

Hence the blind devotion of thousands of Christians who continue sending their hard-earned ten- and twenty-dollar checks to televangelists who wear Rolex watches and live in palatial ministry-provided homes.

These larger-than-life figures do more than entertain. The fact that "our" person can be right up there with secular network stars also eases the insecurity of many Christians. Because we want to be like the world, we create our own celebrities, our own superstars—our Christian musicians, honey-tongued preachers, World Series heroes, converted rock stars, and sometimes even former White House aides.

All the blame can't be put on television, of course; it only plays to our human tendencies. Remember the ancient Israelites? Not satisfied with Yahweh as their king, they demanded a human leader. Even when warned of the consequences, they insisted.[2] They wanted to be like other nations. They wanted someone in the flesh they could follow.

Today this mentality translates into what we call the pedestal complex, and it's rampant throughout the church. Too many clergy and parachurch organizers see themselves as leaders, not servants, and their parishioners and followers eagerly reinforce that attitude. Thus we have the pastor who announces with a great sweep of his arm—like Charlton Heston parting the Red Sea—that God (pronounced "Gawd") has told him to preach on this verse. A hush falls over the congregation. And after the service the people give him just a slightly wider berth as he passes in the corridor. Everyone calls him "Doctor," even when his degree is an honorary one from West Overboot Bible School.

This pedestal complex carries over to leadership posts throughout the church—even to the Sunday school teacher who, filled with his or her own importance, patronizes those lesser souls who sit silently in their chairs.

CONSEQUENCES FOR THE CHURCH

It is unfair to generalize, of course, for many Christian leaders indeed exhibit the qualities of servanthood. But if we are honest, we have to admit that the pedestal complex has embedded itself firmly in the church—and it can have disastrous consequences. Consider the most obvious.

First, *exalting leaders encourages spiritual Lone Rangers.* Though extreme, Jim and Tammy Bakker's case years ago makes the point. When their excesses were exposed, everyone asked, "How could they do that?" But few asked, "Why did the PTL board of directors allow them to do it?" Where was the accountability?

The sad fact is, Jim Bakker's closest advisers not only allowed the excess, they approved and encouraged it. Apparently they were glad to see their leader getting the same fame and reward as his secular counterparts—which also, by association, filtered down to them. I remember once meeting a PTL board member on a plane flight long before the Bakkers' scandal brought them down. He bragged that the board had just given Jim a huge salary. My expression must have betrayed my feelings, because the man quickly added, "Well, look, do you know what he'd be making if he were running NBC?"

But PTL wasn't NBC.

The celebrity syndrome destroys accountability. "God told me to build this," announces the visionary leader. "Just look at all the stations God has put this program on," respond the loyal followers. Who can argue with that? And once the enterprise is launched, jobs depend upon it and the spreading of the gospel supposedly hangs in the balance. So we'd better do whatever the leader wants.

The strong leader who builds a large and successful church is often not held to strict account either. For this reason, more and more pastors seem to be falling into temptation. One, a man I had often cited as a model pastor, suddenly revealed that for eight years he had been carrying on an adulterous relationship. Eight years! It's almost inconceivable. Not only his hypocrisy in leading the congregation while continuing in his sin, but the apparent blindness—or unwillingness to confront—of his elders and deacons.

Many of these moral failures are the result of burnout, the second consequence of the pedestal complex. We expect the pastor to be a shrink in the pulpit, a CEO in the office, and flawless in every area of his life, says theologian Os Guinness. Unfortunately, the conscientious pastor who tries to live up to such unrealistic expectations can be swallowed up in his own frustrations, threatened by exhaustion, burnout, and the temptations of secret immorality. A 2001 *Leadership Journal* survey found that four in ten pastors on-line have visited a pornographic Web site—with more than one-third having done so in the past year.[3] One poll showed that nearly 40 percent of the pastors polled had had an extramarital affair since beginning their ministries.[4] And the divorce rate among clergy is increasing faster than in any other profession. The statistics show that the divorce rate among the Protestant clergy in the United States is higher than the national rate—65 percent as compared with 50 percent.[5] One friend who operates a ministry for pastors with burnout told me he cannot keep up with the demand for help.

Third, *the celebrity syndrome leads to a distorted view of people's worth.*

The late Max Cadenhead, when he was pastor of First Baptist Church in Naples, Florida, riveted his congregation one day with a bold confession.

"My message today is on the parable of the Good Samaritan," Max announced. "Let me start with an illustration.

"Remember last year when the Browns came forward to join the church?" he asked. Everyone nodded; the Browns were a very influential family. "Well, the same day a young man came forward and gave his life to Christ. I could tell he needed help—and we counseled him." No one nodded; no one remembered.

"We worked with the Browns, got them onto committees. They've been wonderful folks," Cadenhead said to muffled amens. "And the young man . . . well, we lost track.

"Until yesterday, that is, as I was preparing today's message on the Good Samaritan. I picked up the paper, and there was that young man's picture. He had shot and killed an elderly woman."

Chins dropped throughout the congregation, mine included, as the pastor continued. "I never followed up on that young man, so I'm the priest who saw the man in trouble and crossed to the other side of the road. I am a hypocrite."

More of that kind of sober honesty in the church would be very healthy. For God's kingdom is just the opposite of ours. We go after the rich or the influential, thinking if we can just bag this one or that one, we'll have a real catch for the kingdom. Like the folks profiled by the apostle James, we offer our head tables to the wealthy and well dressed and reserve the back seats for those we consider unimportant.[6]

We forget that it was an ordinary Sunday school teacher who dropped into a shoe store one day and began a process that changed the world. Few remember the name of the teacher who witnessed to the young shoe clerk that day—it was Edward Kimball—but they surely do remember the shoe clerk, Dwight L. Moody, who went on to evangelize two continents and shake nineteenth-century America to its roots.

Fourth, *the celebrity syndrome skews the theology of the church.* Adulation feeds on itself, as most politicians discover. It's addictive; once people taste it, they crave more. The pastor or Christian leader who is constantly the object of adoring crowds soon can't live without it and, often unconsciously, begins to shape his message to assure continued adulation. No more prophetic messages or challenges to the congregation.

The fifth, and in some ways most destructive, consequence of the pedestal complex is that it lets everyone else off the hook. We pay our leaders to do our spiritual service for us. They are like performers—and the better they perform, the more we pay.

Part of my responsibility at Prison Fellowship has involved visiting PF ministries abroad. I do this less than I used to because Mike Timmis has succeeded me as chairman of Prison Fellowship International, enabling me to concentrate on PF in the U.S. and BreakPoint. But I miss the travel abroad. Not because I enjoy overseas flights or accommodations in far-off places, but because I always returned home from visiting our partners in Third World nations invigorated, revived, and encouraged. I would often find more exciting, growing, church vitality in places like Sri Lanka or Papua New Guinea or Peru than in comfortable churches at home.

In many nations, the church is a tiny, embattled minority—and it has no superstars. So when the church wants to evangelize, for example, it can't depend on a celebrity or bring in Billy Graham for a crusade. The people do the work themselves. Which means the church functions as the church—not a bunch of observers watching someone else perform.

When we sit passively in our pews, paying some charismatic leader to entertain us and other staff people to do ministry, we do much more than miss the living dynamic of how Jesus intends His church to work in the world. When we mimic the culture around us with our pedestal complex, we offend a holy, all-powerful God—the most grievous consequence of all.

Of course we should respect those who are invested with spiritual authority. That's biblical. But there's a difference between respect and adulation. With the latter, we are always in danger of stepping over the line, giving glory to man rather than God.

THE BIBLICAL MODEL

It's easy to see how the world's fascination with fame has snuck into our tents and sapped our effectiveness. Yet this attitude runs absolutely contrary to that which Christ modeled when He, the King of the universe, came to live among us as a suffering servant.

Jesus said that the rulers of this world may lord it over their subjects, but if His followers wish to become truly great, they must be servants. Embodying this, the Messiah Himself washed His followers' feet.

The leader serves.[7] The mandate could not be clearer. We are to serve—and to reach out to the "least of these" to do it. That lesson first hit me while I was in prison.

During my early days as a federal prisoner, I experienced my share of self-pity. It had been a steep fall from an office next to the president of the United States to a prison cell, and I had been a very self-righteous man—one of the deadliest sins. And even though I was now a Christian, I still felt I was better than the car thieves, dope dealers, and murderers who shared my incarceration.

It was as a young Christian, sitting in a dreary prison day room studying a Navigators' discipleship Bible study, that I read the words of Hebrews 2 for the first time: "But we do see Him who has been made . . . lower than the angels, namely, Jesus . . . that by the grace of God He might taste death for everyone . . . for which reason He is not ashamed to call them [us] brethren."[8]

The God of the universe was made like us, undeserving sinners that we are, so He could save us! And He wasn't ashamed to call us His brothers?

As I wrote in *Born Again*, this was a life-changing moment. Suddenly the men around me looked entirely different. I was no better, nor more important, nor less deserving of punishment. They were my brothers.

Years later I would read Warren Wiersbe's comment that heads this chapter—"We have too many people who have plenty of medals and no scars"—and realize that described me perfectly. I had been so proud of my accomplishments, bedecked with all the "medals" the world could offer: education, power, influence. Now I began to see, in the light of eternity, how hollow those things really were. And at that point, God started tenderizing me, allowing me to develop some scars, making me malleable for His purposes, in preparation for the call He had for my future.

The humbling process is not a one-shot thing, of course. Our natural disposition will always tempt us right back into the mind-set of finding any way we can to advance and glorify ourselves. We must stay rooted in God's Word if we are to maintain the right perspective, constantly open to the urging of His Holy Spirit; and ready, too, to hear the truth about ourselves from Christian brothers and sisters.

One chapter of Scripture particularly convicts me, and I often find myself repeating the words over and over like a hymn. They were written by the apostle Paul from his own jail cell: "Let this mind be in you, which was also in Christ Jesus: Who, being in the form of God, thought it not robbery to be equal with God: But made himself of no reputation, and took upon him the form of a servant, and was made in the likeness of men: And being found in fashion as a man, he humbled himself, and became obedient unto death, even the death of the cross."[9]

But hard as we try to live out what we know to be the truth, our old selves often reemerge. It's a particular problem for someone like me, by nature assertive, strong-willed, and prideful. So God has to overcome my will, my pride, and sometimes my fear—as He did one time years ago, when AIDS was a strange, new medical phenomenon.

It was Christmas 1985, and I was scheduled to preach in several prisons in Raleigh, North Carolina. Arriving late on Christmas Eve, I checked into a hotel and, while preparing for bed, flipped on CNN to catch the late news. On the screen was Mother Teresa. The little nun with the love-lined face had her arms around two emaciated young men, advanced AIDS sufferers who had been released that very day from a New York state prison to enter a home established by Mother Teresa's order.

When a reporter demanded to know "why we should care about criminals with AIDS," Mother Teresa explained that these young men had been created in God's image and deserved to know of His love.

I sat on the side of the bed staring at the picture on the screen. How could she do it? Embrace those men who were dying of that deadly virus? I had to admit to myself that I wouldn't have the courage to do what this little ninety-pound nun was doing.

I went to sleep that night thinking about Mother Teresa, and at the same time thanking God that I didn't have to deal with AIDS patients.

The next morning I preached to several hundred women prisoners. As I was getting ready to leave, the warden asked if I would visit Bessie Shipp.

"Who is Bessie Shipp?" I asked.

"Bessie has AIDS," said the warden. "She's in an isolation cell. It's Christmas and nobody has visited her."

I reacted instinctively with, "I'm running late for the men's prison." *Besides,* I thought to myself, *I don't want to take the chance.* Much less was known then about how the virus was transmitted, and, frankly, I was nervous and unsure. Then the face of Mother Teresa flashed before me, and I heard her words: *These boys deserve to know of God's love. . . . Have this mind in you. . . .*

"Well, all right," I said, "take me to Bessie Shipp."

As the chaplain escorted me through two secured areas, he explained that a petition had been presented to the governor for Bessie's release, that it hadn't been acted upon, and that she was feeling particularly depressed. After all, it was Christmas, and the doctors had given her only a few weeks to live.

A chill came over me as we swung open the gate to the isolation cell, where a petite young woman sat bundled up in a bathrobe, reading a Bible. She looked up, and her eyes brightened as the chaplain said, "I promised I'd bring you a Christmas present, Bessie."

We chatted for a few moments, and since there wasn't much time for either of us, I decided I had better get to the point.

"Bessie, do you know Jesus?" I asked.

"No," she said. "I try to. I read this book. I want to know Him, but I haven't been able to find Him."

"We can settle it right now," I said, taking her hand. The chaplain took her other hand, and together we led Bessie in prayer. When we finished, she looked at us with tears flowing down her cheeks. It was a life-changing moment for Bessie—and for me.

Outside the prison, television crews were waiting to cover the "Christmas in Prison" story. Instead of my planned words, I made a plea for the governor to release Bessie Shipp, and that night on the plane flying back to Washington, I dictated a long letter to him. But the letter never had to be mailed. Two days later, Governor Jim Martin released Bessie, and she went home to Winston-Salem.

There Bessie studied her Bible, was baptized into a local church, and was visited regularly by Al Lawrence, our Prison Fellowship area director at the time. She told Al that those were the happiest days of her life because she knew that God loved her and God's people loved her as well.

Three weeks after her release, Bessie joined the Savior she had so recently come to know.

I shuddered later when I thought how close I had come to avoiding that visit. And since that day I have never hesitated to walk into an AIDS ward and embrace dying men and women. No heroics or courage on my part—just obedience. And in this case, through Mother Teresa's example, He took away the unholy fear that had gripped me.

The attitude Christ modeled for us is one that should typify every Christian, whether in pulpit or pew, whether leader of a vast organization or solitary prayer warrior. Not puffed up with self-importance, but poured out for others.

Speaking to a fractured German church in the post-Hitler era, the great pastor Helmut Thielicke eloquently put it into perspective: "The church must be a mother to all who are weary and heavy laden, to all who have strayed and gone wrong, even to those who have forsaken their mother in the last decade and fallen victim to strange ideas. And therefore its task is not to look to the great and powerful, to the Americans or the English, but rather to visit the prisoners and preach the gospel to those who cannot help the church because they have no privileges to bestow."[10]

SERVANT LEADERSHIP

How do we tear down the pedestals? How do we vigorously assert the biblical mind-set of servant leadership, so radically at odds with the celebrity-crazed culture in which we live?

Like everything else, it begins with each of us coming under the conviction of God's truth. All of us—pastors and lay leaders and parishioners—need to take a hard look at ourselves.

First, we must reassess our objectives. Is our goal to be the biggest and most powerful church in town? Is it to get on television and influence the community? Those things may happen, but they should be the fruit of faithful service, not the overarching goal.

The church, as a witness to the kingdom of God, is to be a community that worships God and equips men and women to be disciples, growing in holiness and service. How can the church fulfill these functions if it is not a servant church—from pulpit to pew? And this being the case, the principal job of the pastor is to serve: to equip others to serve.

Though I'm not a pastor, my own experience as a Christian leader has shown me how difficult it is to keep the focus on serving others. Particularly in the early years of Prison Fellowship's ministry, I found that I enjoyed the praise, focus, media exposure, and importance that came with my role. By a process of repentance, self-discipline, and perhaps age and some spiritual maturity, I've come to the point where I am now very uncomfortable with these things.

Of course I love to hear how God has used my life to touch others. There's nothing more thrilling than to hear the testimony of a man who was in prison, his family falling apart, and now he's out, working, part of a church, helping other inmates, his family restored. I am blessed to hear those stories; they are God's fruit of Prison Fellowship's ministry.

But the excited adulation that can come with my role feels more and more distasteful as the years go by. When someone gushes over me, I want to say, "If you had any ideas of the thoughts that go through my head, or things I've had to deal with in my life, you wouldn't say those things." I think Christian leaders in every arena, and at every level, must soberly assess themselves and fight against the natural inclination to glory in praise and adulation—as hard as they fight against any temptation in their lives.

Our second task, therefore, is to consciously strive to avoid the snares of celebrity. This is not easy. Temptations surround us every day—both our natural inclinations and the world's style of glitzy, gilded leadership. But there are ways to protect ourselves.

Bob Russell can attest to this. Pastor of one of the fastest-growing and most successful churches in America, Southeast Christian in Louisville, Kentucky, Bob has by all accounts been unaffected by success. But it hasn't been without real effort.

For one thing, Bob chose and trained an associate, a capable, bright, young preacher named Dave Stone, who takes the pulpit one Sunday out of four. ("Name" preachers in major churches do not readily share their pulpits. I know of one who brags he's done it only twice in thirty-five years.) This mentoring process both lessens the risk of the personality cult and trains a successor.

Bob delegates as well. For example, he took a gifts test and discovered, as many pastors eventually do, that he was a poor administrator; so Bob and his governing board appointed a business manager and have given him almost free rein.

Finally, Bob does little things to remind himself of his role as well as signal it to others. For example, Southeast outgrew its parking lot and had to use a satellite area a mile away for the overflow. Instead of reserving a "senior pastor" parking slot next to the church, Bob parked in the overflow lot and took the shuttle bus.

Another pastor who understood the need not to lord it over others was Mihai Gongola in Arad, Romania. When freedom came to Eastern Europe, Westerners poured in, showering money on pastors who had lived on next to nothing for so long. Some of them gratefully accepted new silk ties, luxury cars, and other gifts. But when Mihai Gongola was offered a new Mercedes, he refused. His people drove old cars or took trams, and he would not elevate himself above them.[11]

Vaclav Maly, the young Czech priest who played such a key role in the fall of Communism in his country, showed a similar humble spirit. He had heard crowds of nearly a million people shouting his name in the streets: "Maly! Maly!" Pretty intoxicating. After the revolution, power and position were his for the taking. Vaclav Havel, the new president of Czechoslovakia, offered him any post in government. Maly declined.

When I visited him in his simple, one-bedroom apartment in Prague, I told him he was a great hero to many of us in the West.

"Oh, no," Maly replied. "I am no hero. A hero is someone who does something he doesn't have to. I was just doing my duty."

Change in government was important, he said, and Vaclav Havel was doing vital work. But the work to which he, Maly, had been called, was the work of changing hearts. He must continue in that call, preaching the gospel and living among the people he served. Like his role in the revolution, it was not a matter of choice. He was simply doing his duty. And he did not want to get diverted from his duty by the seductions of power.

For sometimes it is the trappings of power that trap us.

Years ago, as we mentioned, I agreed to fill in for a Christian television talk show host. During my stint, a driver arrived every morning to take me to the studio; in the car were papers to read before the morning program (all reminiscent of White House days). When I arrived at the studio I was greeted by the makeup artist, the wardrobe person ready to press my jacket, more briefing papers, coffee, anything I wanted. Everyone showed deference to the "star."

I found the old adrenaline surging. And I found, worst of all, that I was beginning to enjoy it. The attention. The excitement of the countdown to broadcast. After I finished my commitment, I fled the studio. I knew I could never do that kind of thing again—and I haven't. I know some of my own weaknesses, and I don't trust myself.

Some can handle television and its power perks quite beautifully. But there are more who cannot.

That doesn't mean we shrink from responsibility. God calls each of us to a particular task. But when the temptation of pride comes knocking . . . as it will . . . we must lock the door against it—whatever that takes.

But the toughest question is: How do we know? Because usually the knock is faint, and we aren't listening for it. The best protection I have discovered is accountability. Since we all have blind spots, we must submit ourselves to those who can see the logs floating in our eyes.

How often does your church governing body review 1 Peter 5:2 with the pastor and elders: "Shepherd the flock of God among you, . . . not under compulsion, but voluntarily, according to the will of God; and not for sordid gain, but with eagerness"? Or Paul's first letter to Timothy? We must constantly check each other on how well we are measuring up to the clear biblical requirements of leadership.

In addition to the biblical passages, I have found one book especially useful for Christian leaders and workers: *Spiritual Leadership* by J. Oswald Sanders. I give it to every colleague, particularly for the twenty-two questions Sanders poses for every Christian's self-examination.[12]

As we develop the characteristics of biblical leadership, we begin to fulfill the third task, which is to identify with those to whom we minister. Missionaries soon learn this is vital for compassionate, intimate ministry. Like the

Baptist missionary couple who went to Sri Lanka a few years ago, taking with them four rooms of furniture. When they set up their home in Sri Lanka, it looked just like the one they had left in America, including a deep freezer, television, and microwave. After two years and many urgent appeals for funds from the faithful in the States, they had two or three converts. Disillusioned, they shipped themselves and their possessions home.

William Booth, founder and first general of the Salvation Army, sent a command to all of his missionaries in India: "Go to the Indian as a brother, which indeed you are, and show the love which none can doubt you feel . . . eat and drink and dress and live by his side. Speak his language, share his sorrow."[13]

A friend and I did this the best we could in a Russian prison years ago.

When Mikhail Gorbachev was loosening restraints within the Soviet Union, Jack Eckerd and I were invited to accompany a U.S. government delegation to visit Soviet prisons. It was an absolutely incredible experience to tour some of the world's most notorious gulags, including the infamous Perm Camp 35 in the foothills of the Ural Mountains.

Another was a women's prison about 120 miles from Moscow. All the inmates wore threadbare babushkas and ragged long dresses. The cellblocks were freezing and full of mud. We were able to talk with many inmates—to our surprise, a good number spoke English. But the whole time, we were herded by the prison officials and KGB officers, all wearing long, olive drab coats with red epaulets and hats with heavy black visors.

When we arrived at the mess hall, with its long rows of wooden tables and its dirty floor, none of the inmates looked up. They had been trained to keep their eyes down.

Our handlers were pointing out something to us, trying to keep our attention, but then Jack Eckerd did something they hadn't planned on. Jack is a tall, lanky, irrepressible lion of a man who loves Christ and is not intimidated by anybody. He was there to see prisoners, not to hear some government-sponsored sales job. So he walked over to where inmates were ladling out the food. It was a grayish-green stew dumped over a scoop of rice. It smelled dreadful.

Jack leaned down, smiled broadly, and asked the server, "So! How's the food in here?"

Oh, no, I thought. *She's going to offer us some. And we're going to have to eat it.* My doctor had told me to avoid foods of unknown origins on this trip. And this prison gruel was definitely unknown. The chunks sticking out of it looked like no animal I was acquainted with.

The next thing I knew, my fears came true. The woman heaped a huge serving onto a plate for Jack . . . and then smiled and ladled an even bigger portion for me. I did the only thing any of us would have done in those circumstances. I thanked her. Then Jack and I walked over to one of the wooden tables and joined the inmates there. (The government officials all stood back, stunned. None of them touched the food.) Jack and I bowed our heads and prayed—you can be sure that was the most fervent grace I have ever uttered in my life as I asked God to sanctify that food and save me from every microbe lurking within it.

The moment we started to eat, the atmosphere in that dismal prison dining hall was transformed. Inmates got up from other tables and joined us. People laughed and spoke with us. Some of the women showed us the crosses that they wore around their necks. Even the ones who did not speak English knew that because we were eating their food, breaking bread with them, we were one with them.

Almost three hundred years ago, Count Zinzendorf, the great reformer, sent missionaries around the world equipped with the same principle: Do not lord it over the unbelievers but simply live among them; preach not theology, but the crucified Christ.[14]

Those are good instructions for all of us. For in a post-Christian culture, the church in America is not unlike a missionary outpost.

As Dietrich Bonhoeffer put it: "The church is herself only when she exists for humanity. . . . She must take her part in the social life of the world, not lording it over men, but helping and serving them. She must tell men, whatever their calling, what it means to live in Christ, to exist for others."[15]

If the church can only be the church when it exists for others, then the Christian can only be truly Christian when he or she is willing to be emptied out for others. There are no harder words in all of Scripture than Jesus' commandment that we love one another as He loved us—which means love that lays down its life for another.

Sometimes that is a commandment we must take literally.

24

WHO ARE YOU?

Have you been to auschwitz?

From Warsaw, take the early train south to Krakow. A few blocks from that city's central square, find the small bus terminal and buy a ticket to Oswiecim, the Polish name for the pleasant town the Nazis turned into a horror. An hour and a half later, you disembark at Oswiecim's even smaller bus station and cross the street to catch a tram, which takes you to the camp.

On the tram you meet tourists. Two backpackers from Finland. A handful of university students from New Zealand. A retired couple from Detroit. You enjoy chatting together. But then, as the tram nears the camp entrance, you are all suddenly bound by a common curiosity and a common dread.

It is autumn, and dead leaves skitter across the long path to the entrance. You cannot quite believe you are here in this notorious place. The double rows of barbed-wire fencing, the railroad tracks that transported millions to their deaths, the famous iron-arched gate with its ironic motto spelled out in foot-high letters: ARBEIT MACHT FREI. *Work makes freedom.*

The camp is silent now, its brick barracks a museum, with rooms full of the ordinary items people brought to their imprisonment: a huge case of eyeglasses, another of shaving brushes and bowls; stacks of suitcases; and a giant case piled with thousands of shoes, heaped on top of one another.

The shoes alone tell the tales of millions of lives. Like that pair of black high heels over there, now fifty years old but still festive. Purchased for a special occasion, rarely worn, they happened to be on the feet of their owner the day the Gestapo rounded up her family.

You imagine her—call her Anna—getting off the train in Auschwitz, on edge because of the brutal discomfort of her journey in the cattle car yet not fully aware of what is happening. The knock on the door had come suddenly during dinnertime on the Sabbath; they, like other Jewish families, were to be resettled, the German officer said. But first they would spend some time in a work camp; after all, a war was raging, and the government needed laborers.

They had given Anna time to pack only a small bag: some clothes, the baby's medicine, a toy for her little boy, the prized, silver-framed photograph of her husband's parents. The soldiers also told them to bring their valuables, so she had her mother's gold necklace around her neck and her own wedding ring on her long, pale hand.

Now, as she stumbled off the train holding little Wiktor's hand, watching her husband Jan jump down with the baby, Biruta, in his arms, she laughed a little to herself. Here she was, detained away from home for who knew how long, and she was wearing her good shoes. In the fear and flurry of departure, she had forgotten to change. It would be a funny story to tell when the war was over—how she came to the work camp wobbling in high heels. Perhaps they would issue her a pair of work shoes.

But as you stand before the glass case fifty years later, you know what happened to Anna and her shoes.

As they came off the train, the Jews were divided into two groups, one large, the other small. Auschwitz was already crowded with non-Jewish prisoners—Poles who had displeased their Nazi rulers. No need to make room for Jews, except for the strongest of potential workers. Women and children were sent to one side, as were all but the most vigorous-looking men.[1]

Then the large group was herded along, clutching their suitcases, to another section of the camp. Here they found a scene both soothing and perplexing: a small orchestra of young women, each with her hair tied back with a bright ribbon, clothed in white blouses and navy blue skirts. They were playing a light, cheerful tune.

As the music continued, a camp matron made a general announcement: Because of the threat of disease, delousing showers would be necessary. The Jews were shown where to put their belongings for retrieval later. They carefully folded their clothing and left it with the family suitcase on a table.

Then, exposed and shivering, they walked toward the large, low building with a sign reading "BATHS." It was dug into a hill, and above its roof were plots of grass and tidy flower borders.

As the last of the large group—as many as two thousand—entered the shower rooms, the doors slid shut with a metallic click. Then, through mushroom-shaped vents hidden in the grass and flowers on top of the building, Nazi orderlies dropped a cache of blue crystals into the sealed rooms below. Perforations in the ceilings began to exude a deadly mist: Zyklon B, a potent poison produced by a German firm called Deutsche Gesellschaft zur Schädlingsbekämpfung—the "German Society for Combating Pests."

The crystals of hydrogen cyanide made quick work of those in the showers. The panicked victims vomited, suffocated, and emptied their bowels on the concrete floor. Within twenty-three minutes, workers wearing gas masks and rubber boots opened the door and begin unloading the corpses, a grim tangle of arms and legs.

Workers shaved the heads of the female corpses, snipped off long braids, then transported the bodies to large brick ovens, where they were fed to flames so intense that they would emerge as ash within the hour, to be sprinkled on the flower beds or dumped into the river Sola.

This was the fate of the owner of those high-heeled shoes you see in the case before you. Multiply her suffering by that represented by the small red shoes with the broken strap, the gentlemen's shoes with the dark brown laces, the old-fashioned boots, the soft baby booties—and multiply those by thousands, then millions of souls, and you begin to sense the horror of the camps.

At another exhibit you see ordinary bolts of cloth standing on end—a linenlike fabric in a neutral brown color. Look closer: there are braids of human hair wound over the bolts, hair that was found in Auschwitz storage rooms by Allied troops after the war. Eight tons of it. Forensic scientists found that the hair was full of cyanide. These ordinary bolts of tailor's lining were made from human hair.

You have stared long and hard at Anna's shoes; no reason not to believe you are now looking at her hair.

Touring the rest of the camp, you visit the prisoners' quarters where many non-Jewish inmates somehow survived in spite of crowding, disease, and starvation; the Wall of Death, where twenty thousand political prisoners were shot; the square where roll call was held each day; the gallows where insubordinate prisoners were hanged; the barracks where perverse medical experiments were carried out on children and pregnant women; and the gas chambers themselves, the crematorium, where the ovens are now cold, save for a single flame of remembrance.

What was it like then? you wonder. It's unimaginable to us, this surreal concentration of evil. How could anyone here have held on to hope of any sort? Could good ever overcome evil in a place of such cruel despair? Were there any flickers of faith in this darkness?

FATHER MAXIMILIAN KOLBE was forty-five years old in the early autumn of 1939 when the Nazis invaded his homeland. He was a Polish monk who had founded the Knights of the Immaculate, a Franciscan order whose headquarters was in Niepokalanow, a village near Warsaw. There 762 priests and lay brothers lived in the largest friary in the world. Father Kolbe presided over Niepokalanow with a combination of industry, joy, love, and humor that made him beloved by his plain-spoken brethren.

Maximilian Kolbe had a global vision for evangelism, and he saw the budding technology of his day as powerful potentials to be harnessed in his work. Radio, publishing, mass media—he dreamed of having the resources to use them all, without limit, to spread the good news. Whereas St. Francis, his predecessor, had loved all living things, exclaiming his delight in "Brother Son" and "Sister Moon," Kolbe roamed through his friary print shop reveling in the ministry made possible by what he called "Brother Motor" and "Sister Press."

In his simple room at Niepokalanow he sat each morning at a pigeon-hole desk, a large globe before him, praying over the world and focusing on the many opportunities for the gospel seed to be sown. He did so tortured by the fact that a far different seed was being spread in those dark days of the late 1930s.

A pale man with arresting blue eyes and a terrifying power of manipulation had whipped the people of Germany into a frenzy. Whole nations had already fallen to Adolf Hitler and his Nazis. Storm troops were already marching in the streets of Austria and Czechoslovakia.

"An atrocious conflict is brewing," Father Kolbe told a group of friars one day after he had finished his prayers.

"We do not know yet what will develop. In our beloved Poland we must expect the worst. During the first three centuries, the Church was persecuted. The blood of martyrs watered the seeds of Christianity. Later, when the persecutions ceased, one of the Fathers of the Church deplored the lukewarmness of Christians. He rejoiced when persecution returned. In the same way, we must rejoice in what will happen, for in the midst of trials our zeal will become more ardent."[2]

Father Kolbe was right. Poland was next. His zeal did become more ardent. On the last Sunday in August 1939, he preached an impassioned homily on the three stages of life: preparation, activity, and suffering.

As a young boy, Kolbe told the brothers, he'd had a dream in which he was offered a choice between two crowns: one white to symbolize purity, the other red for martyrdom. He had chosen both. All of his life he had practiced purity; perhaps the Nazis would now provide the opportunity for him to receive the second crown.

Were that to be the case, he said, one thing was sure: *Greater love hath no man than this, that he lay down his life for his friends.* He smiled as he said the words, and those in the small church would carry that phrase to their graves, their zeal for ministry inflamed by the boldness of this bearded, unassuming brother in his rope-belted black robe.

On September 1, 1939, the Nazi blitzkrieg broke over Poland. The skies above Niepokalanow were filled with bombers on their way east toward Warsaw.

Soon, however, Niepokalanow itself was a target. As flames roared in the night and glass shattered, the brothers in the friary prayed. When the skies cleared temporarily, Father Kolbe sent many of them home to their families; he encouraged others to join the Polish Red Cross. Thirty-six of the number remained with Kolbe at the friary, which now became a hospital and haven for refugees.

But not for long.

On September 19, a group of Germans arrived at Niepokalanow on motorcycles and arrested Father Kolbe and all but two of his friars. The monks were loaded into trucks, then into livestock wagons, and two days later arrived at Amtitz, a prison camp.

Conditions were horrible, but not horrific. Prisoners were hungry, but no one died of starvation. One day the camp administrator's wife, touched by Father Kolbe's grace in suffering, sent him a cake; he gathered all the brothers together and each received a thin slice.

The monks slept on prickly beds of straw in barracks overrun by rats. One night a brother named Juraszek woke from his troubled sleep, aware that someone was touching him. In the dim light he saw that it was Father Kolbe, tenderly tucking his feet into the dirty rag that served as his blanket. Kolbe smiled at Juraszek, then moved on through the barracks, praying over each brother, sharing a quiet word with those who could not sleep.

Oddly enough, within a few weeks the brothers were released from prison. Back at the friary, they found the buildings vandalized and the Nazis in control, using the facility as a deportation camp for political prisoners, refugees, and Jews.

The situation was a tremendous opportunity for ministry, and Father Kolbe took full advantage of it, helping the sick, comforting the fearful, and even publishing his magazine, which he now had to deliver by hand.

Sensing the anxiety of some of the brothers, he gathered a group of them before a chalkboard.

"I insist that you become saints," Kolbe said with a smile, "and great saints! Does that surprise you? But remember, my children, that holiness is not a luxury, but a simple duty. It is Jesus who told us to be perfect as our Father in heaven is perfect. So do not think it is such a difficult thing. Actually, it is a very simple mathematical problem."

On the blackboard he wrote "w = W," grinning widely as he did so.

"A very clear formula, don't you agree? The little 'w' stands for my will, the capital 'W' for the will of God. When the two wills run counter to each other, you have the cross. Do you want to get rid of the cross? Then let your will be identified with the will of God, who wants you to be saints. Isn't that simple? Now all you must do is obey!"[3]

While the monks used their time for such lessons, the Nazis used theirs to decide just how to impose their will on the rest of Europe. Their goal was clear: a Nazi-ruled Europe whose people would be slaves of the German master race and whose "undesirable elements" would be exterminated.[4] In their drive to achieve that goal, they lit a conflagration that would decimate cities, destroy cultures, and kill forty-five million people.

To the Nazis, the Jews and Slavic peoples were the *Untermenschen* (subhumans). Their cultures and cities were to be erased and their industry appropriated for Germany. On October 2, while Father Kolbe prayed for his nation, Adolf Hitler outlined a secret memorandum to Hans Frank, the Governor General of Poland. In a few phrases he determined the grim outcome for millions:

> The [ordinary] Poles are especially born for low labor . . . the Polish gentry must cease to exist . . . all representatives of the Polish intelligentsia are to be exterminated. . . . There should be one master only for the Poles, the German.
>
> As for Poland's hundreds of thousands of priests, spiritual leaders in a land nearly 100 percent Catholic?
>
> They will preach what we want them to preach. If any priest acts differently, we shall make short work of him. The task of the priest is to keep the Poles quiet, stupid and dull-witted.[5]

Maximilian Kolbe was clearly a priest who "acted differently" from the Nazis' designs.

In early February 1941, the Polish underground smuggled word to Kolbe that his name was on a Gestapo list. He was about to be arrested. Kolbe knew what happened to those who tried to elude the Nazis' grasp; their friends and colleagues and families were taken instead. He had no wife or children; his church was his family. And he could not risk the loss of any of his brothers in Christ. So he stayed at Niepokalanow.

At nine o'clock on the morning of February 17, Father Kolbe was sitting at his pigeonhole desk, his eyes and prayers on the globe before him, when he heard the sound of heavy vehicles outside the thick panes of his green-painted windows. He knew it was the Nazis, but he remained at his desk. He would wait for them to come to him.[6]

After being held in Nazi prisons for several months, Father Kolbe was found guilty of the crime of publishing unapproved materials and sentenced to Auschwitz. Upon his arrival at the camp in May 1941, an SS officer informed him that the life expectancy of priests there was about a month.

Kolbe was assigned the timber detail; he was to carry felled tree trunks from one place to another. Guards stood by to ensure that the exhausted prisoners did so at a quick trot.

Years of slim rations and overwork at Niepokalanow had already weakened Kolbe. Now, under the load of wood, he staggered and collapsed. Officers converged on him, kicking him with their shiny leather boots and beating him with whips. He was stretched out on a pile of wood, dealt fifty lashes, then shoved into a ditch, covered with branches, and left for dead.

Later, having been picked up by some brave prisoners, he awoke in a camp hospital bed alongside several other near-dead inmates. There, miraculously, he revived.

"No need to waste gas or a bullet on that one," chuckled one SS officer to another. "He'll be dead soon."

Kolbe was switched to other work and transferred to Barracks 14, where he continued to minister to his fellow prisoners, hearing their confessions, praying with them, comforting them. His eyes ringed by weary shadows, he would hug thin shoulders beneath gray striped uniforms and nod his understanding as men poured out their hearts. Then he would raise his emaciated arm and make the sign of the cross in the foul air of the packed barracks.

The cross, he thought. *Christ's cross has triumphed over its enemies in every age. I believe, in the end, even in these darkest days in Poland, the cross will triumph over the swastika. I pray I can be faithful to that end.*

Then priest and penitents lay down on their pallets, bone-tired yet so tortured by hunger they could not sleep.

By the end of July 1941, Auschwitz was a well-organized killing machine, and the Nazis congratulated themselves on their efficiency. At first, they admitted, there had been some doubt that they could find a utilitarian way to dispose of the undesirables. Early methods of execution—mass shootings, gas dispersed in vans, lethal injections—all made it too difficult to effectively dispose of the corpses or dispatched people in too-small quantities.

But Auschwitz—ah, it was going well. The camp's five chimneys never stopped smoking. The stench was terrible, but the results were excellent: Eight thousand Jews could be stripped, their possessions appropriated by the Reich, gassed, and cremated—all in twenty-four hours. Every twenty-four hours.

About the only problem was the occasional prisoner from the work side of the camp who would figure out a way to escape. When these escapees were caught, as they usually were, they would be hung with special nooses that slowly choked out their miserable lives—a grave warning to others who might be tempted to try.

Then one July night as the frogs and insects in the marshy land surrounding the camp began their evening chorus, the air was suddenly filled with the baying of dogs, the curses of soldiers, and the roar of motorcycles. A man had escaped from Barracks 14.

The next morning there was a peculiar tension as the ranks of phantom-thin prisoners lined up for morning roll call in the central square, their eyes on the large gallows before them. But there was no condemned man standing there, his hands bound behind him, his face bloodied from blows and dog bites. That meant the prisoner had made it out of Auschwitz. And that meant death for some of those who remained.

After the roll call, Camp Commandant Fritsch ordered the dismissal of all but Barracks 14. While the rest of the camp went about its duties, the prisoners from Barracks 14 stood motionless in line. They waited. Hours passed. The summer sun beat down. Some fainted and were dragged away. Some swayed in place but held on; those the SS officers beat with the butts of their guns. Father Kolbe, by some miracle, stayed on his feet, his posture as straight as his resolve.

By evening roll call the commandant was ready to levy sentence. The other prisoners had returned from their day of slave labor; now he could make a lesson out of the fate of this miserable barracks.

Fritsch began to speak, the veins in his thick neck standing out with rage. "The fugitive has not been found," he screamed. "Ten of you will die for him in the starvation bunker. Next time, twenty will be condemned."

The rows of exhausted prisoners began to sway as they heard the sentence. The guards let them; terror was part of their punishment.

The starvation bunker! Anything was better—death on the gallows, a bullet in the head at the Wall of Death, or even the gas in the chambers. All those were quick, even humane, compared to Nazi starvation, for they denied you water as well as food.

The prisoners had heard the stories from the starvation bunker in the basement of Barracks 11. They said the condemned didn't even look like human beings after a day or two. They frightened even the guards. Their throats turned to paper, their brains turned to fire, their intestines dried and shriveled like desiccated worms.

Commandant Fritsch walked the rows of prisoners. When he stopped before a man, he would command in bad Polish, "Open your mouth! Put out your tongue! Show your teeth!" And so he went, choosing victims like horses.

His dreary assistant, Palitsch, followed behind. As Fritsch chose a man, Palitsch noted the number stamped on the prisoner's filthy shirt. The Nazis, as always, were methodical. Soon there were ten men—ten numbers neatly listed on the death roll.

The chosen groaned, sweating with fear. "My poor wife!" one man cried. "My poor children! What will they do?"

"Take off your shoes!" the commandant barked at the ten men. This was one of his rituals; they must march to their deaths barefoot. A pile of twenty wooden clogs made a small heap at the front of the grassy square.

Suddenly there was a commotion in the ranks. A prisoner had broken out of line, calling for the commandant. It was unheard-of to leave the ranks, let alone address a Nazi officer; it was cause for execution.

Fritsch had his hand on his revolver, as did the officers behind him. But he broke precedent. Instead of shooting the prisoner, he shouted at him.

"Halt! What does this Polish pig want of me?"

The prisoners gasped. It was their beloved Father Kolbe, the priest who shared his last crust, who comforted the dying, who heard their confessions and nourished their souls. Not Father Kolbe!

The frail priest spoke softly, even calmly, to the Nazi butcher. "I would like to die in place of one of the men you condemned."

Fritsch stared at the prisoner. #16670. He never considered them as individuals; they were just a gray blur. But he looked now. #16670 didn't appear to be insane.

"Why?" snapped the commandant.

Father Kolbe sensed the need for exacting diplomacy. The Nazi never reversed an order; so he must not seem to be asking him to do so. Kolbe knew the Nazi dictum of destruction: the weak and the elderly first. He would play on this well-ingrained principle.

"I am an old man, sir, and good for nothing. My life will serve no purpose."

His ploy triggered the response Kolbe wanted. "In whose place do you want to die?" asked Fritsch.

"For that one," Kolbe responded, pointing to the weeping prisoner who had bemoaned his wife and children.

Fritsch glanced at the weeping prisoner. He did look stronger than this tattered #16670 before him.

For the first and last time, the commandant looked Kolbe in the eye. "Who are you?" he asked.

The prisoner looked back at him, a strange fire in his dark eyes. "I am a Catholic priest."

"Ein pfaffe!" the commandant snorted. He looked at his assistant and nodded. Palitsch drew a line through #5659 and wrote down #16670. Kolbe's place on the death ledger was set.

Father Kolbe bent down to take off his clogs, then joined the group to be marched to Barracks 11. As he did so, #5659 passed by him at a distance—the soldiers wouldn't let them come near one another—and on the man's face was an expression so astonished that it had not yet become gratitude.

But Kolbe wasn't looking for gratitude. If he was to lay down his life for another, the fulfillment had to be in the act of obedience itself. The joy must be found in submitting his small will to the Will of One more grand.

As the condemned men entered Barracks 11, guards roughly pushed them down the stairs to the basement.

"Remove your clothes!" shouted an officer.

Christ died on the cross naked, Father Kolbe thought as he took off his pants and thin shirt. *It is only fitting that I suffer as He suffered to gain the glory He gained.*

In the basement the ten men were herded into a dark, windowless cell.

"You will dry up like tulips," sneered one of their jailers. Then he swung the heavy door shut.

As the hours and days passed, however, the camp became aware of something extraordinary happening in the death cell. Past prisoners had spent their dying days howling, attacking one another, clawing the walls in a frenzy of despair.

But now, coming from the death box, those outside heard the faint sounds of singing. For this time the prisoners had a shepherd to gently lead them through the shadows of the valley of death, pointing them to the Great Shepherd. And perhaps for that reason Father Kolbe was the last to die.

A prisoner named Brono Borgowiec, who survived Auschwitz, served as attendant to the death cells. Each day he had to remove the corpses of those who had withered away. He also was supposed to empty the waste bucket, but each day the bucket was dry. The inmates had drunk its contents in a futile effort to slake their thirst.

On August 14, 1941, there were four prisoners still alive in the bunker, and it was needed for new occupants. A German doctor named Boch descended the steps of Barracks 11, four syringes in his hand. Several SS troopers and Brono Borgowiec were with him—the former to observe and the latter to carry out the bodies.

When they swung the bunker door open, there, in the light of their flashlight, they saw Father Maximilian Kolbe, a living skeleton, propped against one wall. His head was inclined a bit to the left. He had the ghost of a smile on his lips and his eyes wide open, fixed on some faraway vision. He did not move.

The other three prisoners were on the floor, unconscious but alive. The doctor took care of them first: a jab of the needle into the bony left arm, the push of the piston in the syringe. It seemed a waste of the drug, but he had his orders. Then he approached #16670 and repeated the action.

In a moment, Father Kolbe was dead.

HAVE YOU BEEN TO AUSCHWITZ?

If so, you know there *is* a flame of hope burning in that place of death and despair.

You see it when you descend the basement stairs of Barracks 11 and make your way to the cell at the end of the dim hallway, where countless men died. There on the floor next to a large spray of fresh flowers burns a steady flame. Like the candle in the crematorium, it is a flame of remembrance, commemorating the strange truth that ordinary men and women *can* become great saints, demonstrating, in the greatest of horrors, the greatest of loves.

25

BEING HIS WITNESSES

*The goal of evangelism is to persuade men and women to become disciples of
Jesus Christ and to serve Him in the fellowship of His Church.*

—LAUSANNE COMMITTEE ON EVANGELISM

WHAT WENT THROUGH MAXIMILIAN KOLBE'S MIND when he
volunteered to die for prisoner #5659?

No one knows. But we do know from those who were there that his
decision was instantaneous—a choice that was the natural consequence of
a character shaped by a lifelong commitment to Christ.

Few of us will find ourselves in such a situation. But the core principle
of Father Kolbe's story applies to every believer: *What you do emerges from
who you are. Being precedes doing.*

Maximilian Kolbe didn't have to witness to the guards who marched him
to the death chamber. He *was* a witness, which is exactly what Jesus calls us
to be. Just before His ascension, Christ told His disciples: "You will receive
power when the Holy Spirit comes on you; and *you will be my witnesses* in
Jerusalem, and in all Judea and Samaria, and to the ends of the earth."[1]

Many Christians have interpreted those words as *to* witness, rather
than *be* a witness. They see Christ's commission as an activity rather than
a description of our core identity. This is particularly true among some
evangelicals who regard "witnessing" as a task to be performed—and a
source of enormous pressure and guilt when they fail.

But telling others about how God has rescued us is not a task, a job to be done. Instead, it is a witness that flows naturally from a heart overwhelmed with gratitude by the miracle of deliverance.

For example, if you had been the prisoner for whom Father Kolbe died, what would you have done? Returned home after the war and lived quietly, perhaps occasionally, motivated only by pressure and guilt, telling people what Kolbe had done for you? Or would you have done what Franciszek Gajowniczek did?

Franciszek Gajowniczek was Prisoner #5659. He survived Auschwitz. And for fifty-three years—until his death at age ninety-five—he joyously told everyone he could about the man who had died in his place. His children, grandchildren, and their children honored the memory of Father Kolbe and in turn told others what he had done. During a trip to America in 1994, Gajowniczek told his translator that "as long as he ha[d] breath in his lungs, he would consider it his duty to tell people about the heroic act of love by Maximilian Kolbe."[2]

Why do we evangelize?

Like Gajowniczek, we tell the story of our rescue out of gratitude to the One who saved us! If we even begin to realize the horrors that Christ bore in our place, we can't help but love Him, thank Him, and tell everyone what He's done for us. And we honor Him not only with our words, but by living in a way that points others to Him. We not only witness, we are to *be* His witnesses, individually and collectively as the community of faith. Remember Francis of Assisi's challenge: "Preach the gospel all the time; if necessary, use words."

St. Francis lived both sides of his equation. His life itself served as testimony to the love of God, even as he was also a great evangelist and preacher who boldly articulated gospel truth.

Our first calling is to *be* a witness. That is our very nature, our character as people saved and made holy by God. But included within that calling is the duty to *proclaim* a witness of who God is and what He has done. And because the gospel is propositional, proclaiming the good news is a primary task of the church.

TO PROCLAIM THE GOOD NEWS

The word *evangelism* comes from the Greek noun *euangelion*—meaning "good news"—and the verb *euangelizomai,* "to announce or proclaim or bear good news."

Every believer is called to evangelize—to bear the good news of God's saving love for men and women. But not all are called to be evangelists. The latter is a specific office commissioned for the good of the church as a whole and filled by those called and gifted by God for that task. This was clear in the beginning when Timothy was called an evangelist and when Philip was given that specific charge.[3] The book of Acts is full of the evangelistic fervor of the early church, including the trials, travels, and travails of the greatest evangelist of them all, the apostle Paul.

One of the most remarkable evangelists in the history of the church was a man whose memory is associated more with green beer and leprechauns than the proclamation of the gospel—Patrick of Ireland.

Kidnapped by pirates as a teenager, Patrick was taken from his well-to-do home in Roman Britain in A.D. 405, transported to Ireland, sold to a farmer, and given responsibility for the man's sheep.

Patrick had grown up in a Christian home; his father was a deacon in the church, his grandfather an elder. But the faith had not been real to him until one day, tending sheep in the barren hills of Ireland, he encountered the Great Shepherd and purposed to follow Him.

Eventually Patrick escaped from slavery and returned to Britain, where he became a priest. Then in a dream he heard an Irish voice pleading with him: "Holy boy, we are asking you to come home and walk among us again."

Return to the land of his servitude? An unlikely mission. But Patrick was a slave to Christ now, and the Lord gave him a sense of compassion for the Irish. "I was struck to the heart," he wrote later.

Patrick returned to primarily pagan Ireland, determined to bring the gospel to people enslaved by superstition and Druid worship. Traveling throughout the land, he baptized thousands of new converts and discipled new believers, trained church leaders, ordained pastors, exerted discipline on unrepentant church members, and commissioned more evangelists. He started scores of churches and witnessed to kings and their courts, farmers and peasants. He also forcefully protested injustices against the common people. By the time he died, about A.D. 461, he had started a movement of the church that transformed ancient Ireland.

Through the centuries God has raised up many uniquely gifted evangelists to proclaim the truth to a lost world. That the calling of evangelist is a specific gift conferred by God has never been more evident than in the life of an upstate New York lawyer named Charles Finney. Converted to Christ in 1821 when he was twenty-nine years old, Finney left his successful law practice to become a Presbyterian minister. He told his family and friends that he now had but one client, with "a retainer from the Lord Jesus Christ to plead His cause."[4]

After Finney began preaching among settlers in upstate New York during the spring of 1824, a series of revivals broke out in that area and around the state, spreading to Rochester, New York City, Philadelphia, and Boston. And later in the century, one of the greatest evangelists of them all, Dwight L. Moody, set two continents aflame with his preaching, as well as profoundly influencing ministry to the needy of his day.

The greatest evangelist of our times—perhaps the greatest since Paul—is Billy Graham, who has fervently, yet humbly, preached the gospel to hundreds of millions of people in eighty-four countries. What accounts for his astonishing influence? Like Patrick, Finney, Moody, and others, it is the anointing of the Spirit and his single-minded devotion to his call from God.

Decades ago, I was among the friends who urged Billy to give up strenuous crusades and spend more time writing and perhaps teaching. It's the only time I have seen the man agitated.

"No," he said. "My call is to preach the gospel, and I will do that as long as God gives me the breath to preach."

Graham has been equally unswerving in his commitment to the church, both to the unity of the whole body (he's taken plenty of criticism, but invariably includes all traditions on the platforms of his crusades) and to the local confessing congregations.

There are also men and women in the body of Christ who may not be called to full-time evangelism, but who are gifted in winning others to Christ. The late Arthur DeMoss, insurance company founder, was surely one.

When Art and his family traveled by air, they often did not sit together. Scattered through the plane, the children would witness to their seatmates. Art himself would engage anyone and everyone in conversation, and before long he would have shared his own testimony, often leading the people to Christ.

At Art's memorial service many years ago—one of the greatest celebrations I've ever witnessed—the pastor asked those who had come to Christ through Art's ministry to stand. Throughout that packed congregation, men and women rose to their feet. What a legacy!

Another close friend, Dave Cauwels, a businessman and a colleague on Prison Fellowship's board of directors, has a similar calling. Dave has a gentle, sensitive heart for Christ and an innate sense of how to lovingly share Him with others.

Once Dave and I were traveling together, visiting Prison Fellowship International's ministries in the Far East. After ten arduous days on the road, we were resting in the lounge at the Singapore airport, awaiting our flight home. I was exhausted, my stomach in knots from too many exotic foods; all I wanted to do was slump in the corner, drink a Coke, and dream about home. I didn't want to talk to anyone, not even myself.

But Dave and another businessman traveling with us, Jim Zanios, noticed a fellow sitting despondently at the bar. Without exchanging a word, Dave and Jim moved across the lounge, sat near the man, and engaged him in conversation. Within minutes, they were telling him about Jesus Christ.

But what about the rest of us who don't have a special gift and boldness for sharing the faith? The good news is that God can use us even when we are not aware of what He is doing!

Some years ago I was in a very long line in the Jakarta airport. I was with some ministry colleagues, and we had been traveling all night. It was early morning and already steamy and quite hot inside the terminal. Passport in my sticky hand, I was exhausted and exasperated at the long, inefficient line snaking ahead of us. I was worried we would miss our next flight and the ministry friends who were waiting for us. But I was also determined not to let my frustration get the better of me. I talked with my friends; we laughed and made the best of the situation.

Two years later, I got a letter from a businessman who lived in Singapore. He told me he was a follower of Confucius, but that he had sent his children to a Presbyterian church so they could get some moral training in Sunday school. When he picked up his children one Sunday, he happened to hear the end of the sermon. A visiting missionary held up a copy of a book called *Born Again,* and on the cover the businessman saw a picture of Chuck Colson.

Then, a few months later, he was stuck in a long line in the steaming Jakarta airport. He looked over into the next line and saw the same face he had seen on the cover of *Born Again.* He was so impressed by my calm demeanor and cheerfulness, the man wrote, that when he went back to Singapore, he got the book *Born Again,* read it—and committed his life to Christ!

I was not doing anything special that day in the Jakarta airport. Nor was I "witnessing," per se. But evidently, simply by allowing the Holy Spirit to keep me at peace, God used my witness that hot day to draw someone to Himself.

God often uses people in just such surprising ways. For example, though I always tell people how Tom Phillips told me about Christ, it was only fairly recently that I discovered what was going through Tom's mind at the time.

Tom Phillips is a shrewd executive and a strong Christian. He also is the type of person who feels awkward and uncomfortable creating a scenario solely for the purpose of sharing his faith. So it was unusual that he set his sights on me. Actually, he didn't want to. God just wouldn't let him off the hook.

At the time, the spring of 1973, Tom was president of Raytheon, one of the largest and most successful companies in America. I had recently left the White House and was planning to return to Raytheon as legal advisor, but Tom was nervous about meeting with me. It was the early days of Watergate, and I was in the midst of the controversy, which could hurt the company. Besides, since he had become a Christian, Tom had changed a lot. We had known one another before on altogether different terms.

So, as he tells it, he prayed the night before our scheduled meeting, "God, make Chuck Colson go away!" And the Lord seemed to say to him, "No, you tell Chuck about Me. He needs a friend."

Tom didn't want to tell me about Christ. But he was the one the Holy Spirit had tagged—and empowered—for that particular task. He was the one chosen to break through my resistance and tell me about Jesus.

Tom was miserable. I was miserable. Yet it was God's appointed hour—and how eternally grateful I am for Tom Phillips's obedience.

The Great Commission itself gives us two of the key hallmarks of our witness. The first has to do with *when* we witness. The verb tense of the Great Commission is literally, *"as you are going,* make disciples." *As you go.* All the time. That means evangelism is not a set of formulas, techniques, or memorized scenarios. Evangelism is a consequence of holy living, of our own personal passion for Christ, and naturally flows out of our everyday activities, as we are going about them.

And second, we are to be witnesses *in the context of the church.* "As you are going," Jesus tells us in Matthew 28:19–20, "make disciples of all nations, baptizing them in the name of the Father and of the Son and of the Holy Spirit, and teaching them to obey everything I have commanded you." Baptism, teaching of the Word, and disciple making are functions of the local church. It is in this context that healthy evangelism takes place.

Evangelicals have often fallen short on this score, though there are encouraging signs that we're changing. In the past it seems that we've focused on organizing highly publicized campaigns to win people to Christ. We pick up some catchy name, "mission this or mission that," raise money on the promise of a new Great Awakening, barrage some area or group, count the hands raised—which, particularly overseas, may be nothing more than a polite response—and then boast about the number of conversions. Unfortunately, many of these evangelical efforts become a kind of hit-and-run extravaganza. And when they do, they are often little more than a hyped fundraiser for some enterprise or an ego trip for the charismatic leader.

I've been in this kind of meeting. For every hundred decisions that the promoter trumpets, two individuals may show up for the follow-up. In fact, I've become so dismayed with this kind of scalp hunting that I will not give an invitation unless I know in advance there is a follow-up mechanism in place. It is a gross disservice to unsaved people—as well as an impediment to the cause of Christ—to get them excited, lead them into some emotional response, and then dump them on the doorstep. Unless evangelism brings converts into the visible body of Christ, it is like assisting at a baby's birth and then leaving the infant out in the cold. We must bring people into the Body.

A friend told us how he was driven—literally—into the church.

Bill O'Neill is a distinguished superior court judge and a tremendous influence for Christ in his home state of Arizona and in the criminal justice system at large. Decades ago, when Bill was in high school in Arizona, he had a teacher named Ben Day. Ben invited Bill to his Baptist church; Bill began attending regularly, though he didn't receive Christ. Ben kept in contact when Bill went away to college—even, at one point, strongly influencing him to stay in school rather than quit.

When Bill was in law school in St. Petersburg, Florida, in the early 1970s, he was adrift, careening off any rational course, his life a mess. Then, the week before Easter, his old high school teacher, Ben Day, unexpectedly arrived in Florida. He had driven nonstop from Arizona, he said, and he had to turn around in exactly two hours in order to make it back in time for class on Monday morning. As they visited together, Bill confessed that his life was spinning out of control. Ben listened and gave some words of gentle counsel. Then, all too soon, it was time for Ben to go, and his counsel became a little less gentle.

Ben was seated in his car with the window down. Bill stood at the driver's side, leaning down a little and bidding him farewell. He was wearing a tie, as was required for class attendance at the time.

"Where are you going to church, Bill?" Ben asked.

Bill shrugged. "Nowhere," he said. "There's no church nearby."

Ben sighed and stared into the distance for a few moments. Then he slowly shook his head and raised the car window. Bill's tie was caught in it like a vise.

Ben put the car in gear and started driving away. Bill ran alongside sideways, like a crab. "Hey! My tie's caught! Stop the car! Stop!"

Ben kept driving.

"Stop!" yelled Bill. He had already gone one block, running along in the grip of the tie that binds. To his immense relief, the window lowered a few inches—but Ben now held the end of his tie in a firm grasp.

"See that church ahead of us?" he shouted to Ben, driving with one hand. "You'd better pray that it's not Baptist!"

Still running sideways, Bill peered into the distance. The closer they got, the more he could see of the sign . . . B - A - P - T - I - S - T. Now they were right in front of the church, and Bill wasn't sure he'd ever be able to hold his head up in that town again. Literally.

Ben stopped the car and turned off the engine. Bill stood, gasping hard and rubbing his neck. "Son," said Ben. "I drove all the way here from Arizona—plus these two blocks with your tie stuck in my window—for one reason. I am concerned for your soul. Promise me you will attend this church on Sunday."

Terrified of another tie run, Bill agreed. Ben closed the window and headed back to Arizona.

"I kept my promise," Judge Bill O'Neill says today. "I went to that church, time and time again. And weeks later, I asked Christ into my heart. Christ has made all the difference in the world in my life. But He used one teacher, my friend Ben Day, who was willing to give his time and drive across the country to make a great sacrifice for my soul."

Ben Day's tie-in-the-window approach might be slightly unconventional, but it emphasizes the point that evangelistic efforts must be integrated with the local church. The Great Commission involves baptism and disciple making, and this can only be done in the context of a local confessing congregation. So while individuals certainly—and rightly—introduce people to Christ, or people come to Him alone in a prison cell or in areas where the church is banned, the normative practice has to be to evangelize and then immediately bring the new convert from the church universal into the fellowship and discipline of the church particular.

This is why the fourth-century Patristic Fathers went out to proclaim the gospel in small groups, rather than as individuals. As people responded to their message and became believers, the monks could act as the church, baptize them, and get them started in community and discipleship.

J. C. Harris, pastor of a Baptist church as well as chaplain in a North Carolina prison, has taken pains to do the same. In the prison he is constantly seeking to bring inmates to Christ. But when a prisoner does make a profession of faith, J. C. counsels the new convert about choosing and joining a local church in his hometown, even though he's still in prison.

"We don't baptize people," he says. "Baptism is an ordinance of the church. We want our men baptized into the fellowship of a church in their hometown, and then to become a long-distance part of that particular congregation, just as if they were away in the army or something. Then, when they get out, they go back home and their church families are waiting for them, ready to help with clothes, food, a job—and accountability."

Similarly, when Ellen has traveled in Cuba, she's observed that many Cuban pastors who are seeing huge growth in their churches are not content to count up new sheep and leave it at that. They are very disciplined about discipleship.

Some statistics show that 70 percent of the people joining churches in Cuba are under the age of thirty. They have grown up in an aggressively secular culture. But they long for more. So they are coming to Christ by the thousands. But before these new believers join the church, they spend a year in Bible study, mentoring, and discipleship. So they are not just converts, but disciples who are firmly rooted in the Word and can in turn draw others to Christ.

This discipleship focus on the local church has been one of the great hallmarks of Billy Graham's crusades. They are always held at the request of local churches, are meticulously planned in cooperation with those churches, and are designed so those who make decisions at a crusade are then integrated into a local church where they can be discipled and grow in Christian maturity.[5] As one of Graham's biographers has put it:

> The fundamental objective of Graham's follow-up program was not merely to get a person to come forward . . . but to help solidify that decision and insure that the individual became an integral part of a local congregation. . . . . Recognition must be paid to Graham's early discernment that the true object of evangelism, in the context of the Great Commission, is discipleship.[6]

Important words: *The true object of evangelism, in the context of the Great*

Commission, is discipleship. And that discipleship takes place in the church particular.

THE MISSIONAL CHURCH

One pastor who can speak to this norm far better than we can is Tim Keller. Earlier in the book, we mentioned Tim's church, Redeemer Presbyterian in Manhattan, several times, although as a church body, Redeemer is not particularly anxious to be in the spotlight. By design its goal is to give itself away, to divide and start new churches rather than swell as a megachurch in Manhattan.[7] Yet we cannot help but focus on another key to Redeemer's tremendous ministry and growth: In terms of evangelism and everything else, Redeemer views itself as a missional body of believers.

Tim Keller describes this mind-set in terms of missionaries living in foreign cultures. He cites the British missionary, Leslie Newbiggin, who went to India around 1950 and gradually established a church there that lived "in mission" in a distinctly non-Christian culture. When Newbiggin returned to England thirty years later, he found that churches at home were now living in a non-Christian culture as well. The Christian veneer had been gradually stripped away over the decades, but the church had not adapted to its new situation. Christians were still communicating their faith as if nonbelievers shared their same basic assumptions about life.

Keller says that for the evangelical church in the U.S. to reach a post-Christian culture, we must live in mission, much like a church in a non-Christian culture. We must adapt and reformulate everything we do in worship, discipleship, community, and service if we are to engage the non-Christian society around us. We must translate gospel truth so people can understand it.

A missional church must discourse in the vernacular. The missional church uses biblical language, but explains it for those with no biblical knowledge.

As we have already said, in the midpoint of the last century there was little difference between the language inside and outside the church. In fact, biblically based language used to be the common currency of communication in Western civilization. For example, during World War II, after

Hitler blitzkrieged his way across France, demanding the unconditional surrender of the Allied forces in the European theater, thousands of British and French troops dug in along the coast of northern France in a last-ditch effort to hold off the German forces. Trapped on the beaches of Dunkirk, they knew they would soon be obliterated by the Nazis.

During that agonizing period, it is said that the British soldiers broadcast a terse message across the English Channel. Just three words: "And if not."

"And if not"? Was it code?

No. It was a reference to the Old Testament episode when Shadrach, Meshach, and Abednego stood before King Nebuchadnezzar's fiery furnace. "Our God is able to save us, and He will save us," the young men had said, *"and if not,* we will remain faithful to Him anyway."

And, as astonishing as it seems today, the oblique message was immediately understood by the British people. In the days that followed, a ragtag flotilla of fishing boats, pleasure cruisers, yachts, and rowboats set out from the shores of England, managing to rescue 338,000 Allied troops.

If the same message came to America today, it would be greeted with blank stares—even from many Christians. The shared familiarity with the Bible that informed daily discourse and understanding is gone. The closest our fragmented culture comes today to a common language would be the communications that flow from our television sets. So phrases like "Just do it" and the ubiquitous "whatever" become the words by which we live.

Expressions Christians have used for decades, like "God loves you and has a wonderful plan for your life," no longer connect with most Americans. Christians understand them; older generations who grew up in a biblically informed culture, or those still influenced by the Bible belt, can relate; but most people today—and the great majority of people under thirty-five—are absolutely clueless when it comes to such phrases. We may as well be speaking Latin.

This is why the missional church avoids "tribal" language: pious evangelical jargon and inspirational catchall phrases. It avoids a "we-they" approach that disdains those who are unlike us. It speaks as if the whole neighborhood was present, not just Christians.

And, concludes Tim, unless these principles of discourse are "the outflow of a truly gospel-changed heart, it is all just marketing and 'spin.'"

The missional church enters and retells the culture's stories with the gospel. We must enter into the stories of the surrounding culture, which takes real listening. This means we build relationships with people who don't believe, and we connect with the literature, music, theater, arts, and issues that express the existing culture's hopes, dreams, and fears. This builds a bridge by which we can show how the gospel can enter and transform those stories.

As we discussed earlier, the prevailing world-view denies the existence of absolute truth. The existential, not the historical, conditions the American view of life. So when the Christian message, which is essentially historical and propositional, is proclaimed, modern listeners hear what they interpret as simply one person's preference—another autonomous human's choice of lifestyle or belief. Thus, sharing your personal testimony may or may not be convicting to your listener, who may well think, *If Christianity works for you, that's great. But it doesn't mean anything to me.*

I discovered this during a conversation with an acquaintance who happens to be a prominent journalist. He had told me he was intrigued by my commitment to Jesus Christ, and we met for dinner to discuss it further.

I was armed with all sorts of arguments, ready to tell him about my own experiences. But when I started talking about what Christ had done in my life, he cut me off.

"It's wonderful that you've found peace and fulfillment through Jesus," he said in effect, "but I don't believe in Jesus." He told me he had friends in the New Age movement who had found spirituality too; it had worked for them as well as Christ had "worked" for me.

So I shifted gears and began to talk about eternal life. This man had had some health problems in the past; surely he had done some thinking about his own mortality.

Again he cut me off. Death was simply the end, he said. When we die we are just like a tree or an animal: We return to the dust. No such thing as an afterlife.

I talked about the Bible. He put his hand up, palm outward. "All legends," he said firmly.

What could I say? He didn't care about God's plan for his life, getting into heaven, or what the Bible said.

Perhaps it's when we are caught short—when our canned answers don't work—that God uses us most effectively. For even as I was fumbling with my fork and my facts, an idea popped into my head.

"Have you seen Woody Allen's *Crimes and Misdemeanors?*" I asked.

He had, and we talked about it for a few minutes. Then, catching him off guard, I asked, "Are you Judah Rosenthal?"*

He laughed, but it was a nervous laugh.

"You may think this life is all there is," I said, "but if so, then there is still an issue at hand—how do you live with yourself while you're here? I know you have a conscience. So how do you deal with that when you know you do wrong?"

He picked at his food and told me that very issue gave him a lot of problems. Then somehow we moved into a discussion of Leo Tolstoy's novel, *War and Peace,* in which Pierre, the central character, cries out, "Why is it that I know what is right but do what is wrong?" That in turn led us to C. S. Lewis's concept of the natural law ingrained in all of us, and then to the central point of Romans 1: We all are imbued with a conscience, run from it though we might, and that conscience itself points to questions that can only be answered outside of ourselves.

I don't know what's going to happen to this friend. It's been years since we had that conversation, and we still get together now and then. I think he's eventually going to come to Christ, because I believe the Holy Spirit is hounding him. But I know one thing: Without Woody Allen, Leo Tolstoy, and C. S. Lewis, I wouldn't have found a common ground and language with which to discuss the spiritual realm with him.

This does not mean that we must all run out to the video store and rent *Crimes and Misdemeanors* or slog through *War and Peace,* though both are worthwhile. But it does mean that to evangelize today we must address the human condition at its point of real need—conscience, guilt, dealing with others, finding a purpose for staying alive and the real source of the freedom modern men and women crave. We must be familiar enough with the prevailing world-view to look for points of contact and discern points of disagreement.

This is what the apostle Paul did in the events described in Acts 17. When he addressed the Greeks on Mars Hill, he framed the gospel in a context they could understand, quoting their own poets. And he did not begin with the message of salvation. He began with a common starting point, creation: "The God who made the world and everything in it is the Lord of heaven and earth" (Acts 17:24). Paul argued that even the Greeks, though unschooled in Scripture, ought to know that God is no golden idol. Since He created us, He must be a personal being—and thus someone to whom we are personally accountable. Only after establishing who God is did Paul preach about the resurrection.

This is the approach we must take in our modern Athens. Before we tell people what the Bible says, we may need to give sound evidence that the Bible is reliable and authoritative. (There's a great case to be made too, and we don't need to be theologians or debate champs or lawyers to make it.[8]) Our Christian apologetic flows from the reality of Christ in our own lives, but it doesn't stop there. We can make the case for Christ in a way that strikes a chord with our unbelieving friends and neighbors, gently challenging their own views of reality and touching their own experiences.

Odessa Moore, a Prison Fellowship volunteer and member of the Faithful Central Missionary Baptist Church in South Central Los Angeles, gives us a great example of how to do this.

Years ago when Odessa was visiting a juvenile jail, she met a teenager waiting to be tried as an adult for first-degree murder. His eyes chilled her, they were so full of hate and anger.

"I don't care about anything," he said defiantly. "I don't feel no shame."

A familiar story emerged as they talked. His father was a drug user, his mother an alcoholic, and both parents abusive. They would beat the boy and tie him up in the closet for hours. All of his life he had been told he was nothing. No one cared about him. But that was all right, he said. "I don't care about nobody."

"There is Someone who loves you," Odessa told him.

"No way," he responded. "Nobody."

"You're in here for murder, right?" asked Odessa.

"Yes, and I'd do it again," he said.

"How would you like it if Someone came in here tonight and said, 'I know you committed the murder, and they are going to give you the death penalty, but I am going to take your place for you'? How would you like that?"

For the first time the boy showed a spark of life. "Are you kidding? That would be great!"

Odessa went on to tell him about Jesus, the Prisoner who did take his place, who had already paid the price for his wrongdoing. Using word pictures the young man could understand, she walked him through the steps to a growing understanding of sin, repentance, forgiveness, and free-dom—true freedom—in Christ.

By the end of the evening the teenager's hard heart had softened. He wept tears of repentance and committed his life to Christ that night.

I have experienced the same thing many times. Christianity seems remote to prisoners, but when I talk about the real person, Jesus, who was abandoned by His friends and executed for a crime He didn't commit, their eyes light up. Because of their own stories, they connect to the historical Jesus.

The missional church theologically trains laypeople for public life and vocation. Tim Keller makes the point that lay people need to know how to think Christianly about all of life—both public and private—and how to work with Christian distinctiveness. This means being well equipped to exercise a truly Christian approach to our work, to business, art, the use of commu-nity resources, race relations, politics, ethics, and every other endeavor.

The missional church creates Christian community that is countercultural and counterintuitive. A missional church is a community that shows the world how radically different Christian society is with regard to sex, money, and power. It must be more deeply and practically committed to deeds of compassion and social justice than traditional liberal churches, and more deeply and practically committed to evangelism and conversion than traditional fundamentalist churches. This is counterintuitive to American observers, because it defies the stereotypes by which so many perceive Christians. The countercultural congregation breaks observers' ability to categorize a church as liberal or conservative and thereby dismiss it if it doesn't fit in their particular box.

The missional church practices Christian unity on the local level. This, too, is radically different from the unity of the world around us, which is based on likeness or common affinities. Unity in the church thrives even amid diversity, for it is based on common commitment to Christ.

At Redeemer, this unity is demonstrated most visibly through fellowship groups—small communities of six to twelve people meeting in homes throughout the city during the week. They are the setting in which church members apply the gospel to their everyday lives, caring for one another and demonstrating unity and love. The groups are led by trained lay leaders and receive shepherding care from elders.

As Redeemer's guidelines put it, these groups are more than just Bible studies. "They include prayer, worship, fellowship, sharing of what God is doing in our lives, spiritual nurturing, accountability, and opportunities for service. While some churches have small groups on the side, Redeemer is centered around our Fellowship Groups. They are the church."[9]

Gatherings like this—whether they are called fellowship groups, small groups, cell groups, or community groups—are the key means by which the Body is demonstrated, experienced, and grows in today's culture. Many, many large churches like Redeemer use this model, as does one of the most dramatic examples we've seen of the church growing and changing the culture around it.

In India, an extensive network of cell churches, organized by the Harvest Network, is growing organically. In two northern Indian provinces which have historically been areas of political unrest, terrorism, and general upheaval, twelve thousand house churches have been planted in the past five years. The goal is to plant *one million* house churches by 2012. That's incredible—and probable, the way things are going.

The reproducible beauty of these cell groups is that they get right into local neighborhoods and serve as salt and light. They directly influence the kids, families, and neighbors around them. They look outward, not inward—and as a result, people are constantly coming to Christ, joining the groups, and then dividing and spreading in an organic way.[10]

HOW THE CHURCH REACHES THE CULTURE

The best-known example of a church that has helped to make the gospel accessible to postmodern people is Willow Creek Community Church in South Barrington, Illinois.

Almost thirty years ago a youth pastor named Bill Hybels and a couple of his buddies conducted a door-to-door survey throughout the west Chicago suburbs. They simply asked, "Do you regularly attend a local church?" If the answer was yes, they thanked the respondent and moved on. If it was no, they asked the follow-up question, "Why not?"

They got an earful. But essentially there were four reasons people had no interest in attending church: (1) churches are always asking for money; (2) church services are boring and predictable; (3) church is irrelevant to real life; and (4) pastors make people feel ignorant and guilty.

Eventually Hybels and his colleagues began a church that would, while faithfully preaching the gospel, address these four objections. The new local body, meeting in a movie theater, began to grow and eventually became a congregation of thousands, who eventually funded an immense, campuslike facility that hosts activities throughout the week, from the weekend "seeker services" on Saturday evenings and Sunday mornings, designed to draw in unbelievers, to the midweek worship services on Wednesday and Thursday evenings, designed for believers to grow deeper in their faith.

Lee Strobel is a great example of the type of person this approach has reached. Lee was legal affairs editor of the *Chicago Tribune*. As a child, he had been confirmed in a mainline church; but as an adult, he felt no need for God. He called himself an atheist.

Then Lee's wife, Leslie, became friends with a neighbor who was a Christian. Gradually the neighbor began to talk about Christ and invited Leslie to come to Willow Creek. There Leslie was comfortable but also confronted, and she committed her life to Christ.

Oh, isn't that cute, thought Lee. "If that's good for you, if you want to believe it, that's okay," he told his wife. "I'm certainly not going to get involved with it."

But Leslie kept urging Lee to come to Willow Creek. "You'll like the music," she said. "Just come and check it out."

Lee finally gave in. The music *was* great. He felt comfortable, not like he had landed in a foreign culture. The pastor didn't wear robes and preach from a lofty pulpit. He wore khakis, stood at a lectern, and used an overhead projector during his message. He talked about grace. Lee had heard about grace back in the dim religious mist of his childhood, but this seemed new.

It pulled at him. *What if it's true?* he thought. *But of course it's not.*

With his legal and journalistic background, it was natural for Lee to investigate the case fully. For almost two years he researched other religions, read the Bible critically, and continued to attend Willow Creek. Then Lee realized he had run out of questions. He surrendered to Christ.[11]

Willow Creek isn't for everyone, nor does it claim to be. And, like all churches, it has its warts. It's been accused by some of bending the gospel and being too market-oriented. But, says Lee Strobel, who served on Willow Creek's pastoral staff for years, "we're not using entertainment to pacify people, helping them to have fun. We are taking contemporary art forms—music, drama, dance, multimedia, video—to communicate Christ. We take the historic Christian message and translate it into language [modern] Americans understand; in that way, a suburbanite like me, a cynic, can come in and be hit right in the heart with the gospel."[12]

How do we retain biblical faithfulness and yet speak in a way that can woo today's nonbelievers to Jesus? Over the past decade, perhaps as a result of Willow Creek's high profile, evangelicals have begun to wrestle with this important issue. And as a result, many smaller churches across the country are doing solid biblical ministry, evangelism, and discipleship in new ways, and they are bringing in vast numbers of new believers into the kingdom.

Can any local church perfectly and constantly practice all the characteristics of being Christ's witnesses? No. But it is safe to say that just a few decades from now, when the Christianized veneer is totally expunged from American culture, it is the churches with a missional mind-set that will be drawing men and women to Christ. Traditional congregations, talking only to themselves, will be like the Shakers of the last century. Since they did not reproduce, they died off.

The church has been entrusted with the truth in an age when so many people proclaim that truth does not exist. Yet such skeptics secretly long for the paradoxical liberty of absolutes. The church has been entrusted with a message of hope in a culture that has put its hope in temporal toys and human achievement—and has seen just how temporal those things can be.

Believers of the first-century church, when told to cease proclaiming the good news by the authorities of the day, burst out, "We cannot stop talking about what we have seen and heard!"[13] In the same way, modern-day evangelism must exuberantly flow from our character as a worshiping, godly community; it must be done in the context of the corporate body; and it must articulate the gospel in language and ways that twenty-first century men and women can understand, as well as demonstrate it in the timeless language of love.

For, as we said at the outset of this chapter, we will not always *proclaim* the gospel in words. Usually, in order to be heard, we must first be *seen*. We must *be* his witnesses, right where we live.

26

BEING SALT

Every Christian mind is a seed of change so long as it is a living mind, not enervated by custom or ossified by prejudice. A Christian has only to be in order to change the world, for in that act of being, there is contained all the mystery of supernatural life. It is the function of the church to sow this Divine seed, to produce not merely good men, but spiritual men—that is to say, super men. In so far as the church fulfills this function it transmits to the world a continuous stream of spiritual energy. If the salt itself loses its savor, then indeed the world sinks back into disorder and death.

—CHRISTOPHER DAWSON

IN HIS MOST PLAIN-SPOKEN yet most enigmatic sermon, Jesus told His followers what we are to be. "You are the salt of the earth," He said. Then came the blunt warning: "But if the salt loses its saltiness, how can it be made salty again? It is no longer good for anything, except to be thrown out and trampled by men.

"You are the light of the world," He continued. "A city on a hill cannot be hidden. Neither do people light a lamp and put it under a bowl. Instead they put it on its stand, and it gives light to everyone in the house. In the same way, let your light shine before men, that they may see your good deeds and praise your Father in heaven."[1]

These metaphors are so familiar that we often overlook their deeper meaning. Many Christians lump the two images together to describe good works, such as "salt and light ministries." But salt and light are not projects we undertake; they are descriptions of the character of the people of God living in biblical faithfulness. We *are* salt; we *are* light. Yet Jesus clearly differentiated between the two.

Light is visible. Thus, wherever the people of God bear visible witness in a darkened world, their light "cannot be hidden," and it glorifies God. In the next chapter, we'll consider one of the most dramatic stories we've ever heard about the power of the light to triumph over the forces of darkness.

First, though, let's focus on what Jesus meant when He called us salt. Salt is not as immediately obvious as light. In fact, when used properly it isn't visible at all—at least not in the same sense.

In the ancient world salt was a vital staple, both as a seasoning and as a preservative. When it comes to the first function of salt, seasoning, penetration is essential. If salt is to flavor food, it can't stay in the shaker. It has to be *in* the beef, or the potatoes, or the broccoli. So, too, Christians must flavor our culture, bringing good taste, if you will, to every arena of the world in which we live.

The second function of salt was particularly critical in ancient times, since it was the only preservative available. Farmers would slaughter animals, carve the meat, and then rub raw mineral salt into it until the flesh was penetrated and the salt was dissolved. This prevented the meat from decaying.

Just as meat exposed to the natural elements of air and sun will decay, so society, exposed as it is to the natural elements of the evils in this world, will decay. It is an inevitable natural process, *unless* Christians are part of culture, penetrating and preserving its expressions—like the arts—and its institutions—like government.

Often Christians are so busy building our own visible institutions—buildings and retreat centers and places for fellowship—that we are in danger of becoming pillars of salt. But the object isn't for the world to see how glorious our organizations are. Instead, nonbelievers should benefit from our pervasive presence in their midst.

The church as salt is particularly crucial today. The heyday of religious political activism certainly demonstrated that direct confrontation seldom works. Besides, direct assaults mobilize the opposition. Start an organized campaign against pornography, and before long the ACLU and the pornographers will marshal a better-funded defense. They've often bragged that they can tie that kind of legislation up in courts for an indefinite time—and they've done so.

We are outnumbered on most social and moral issues. And we live in a culture in which the primary influencers—the gatekeepers of television, radio, newspaper, and other public forums—are unsympathetic if not hostile to a Christian perspective.[2] Frequently we can't even get a hearing.

Some years ago Cal Thomas, the well-known Christian columnist and commentator, discovered this when he was scheduled to appear on a morning network show. During the preliminary interview, when it appeared that he might quote Scripture on the air, Thomas was politely told that would not be acceptable and was subsequently scrubbed from the show.

I've encountered the same reaction many times. Over and over in public debate, we are told that religious issues are private matters. Those who dare mention their faith are mocked, or at the very least their motives and reliability are suspect.

These obstacles do not mean that we should never confront. Christians need to stand courageously against evil, proclaiming the Word and presenting a world-view informed by Judeo-Christian truth. Protests against immoral laws and practices—like partial-birth abortion—are one example of this; fighting against repressive laws are another, as in religious liberty cases. And we must debate ethical issues, as in the growing arena of biomedical research.

But as a general *strategy,* we will be more effective when we penetrate *behind* the lines, influencing the culture from within. Which, by the way, does not mean we lose our character. As we wrote in chapter 18, when the church accommodates the world's values in a desperate attempt to be relevant, we lose our saltiness. Then we end up being "trampled by men," as Jesus put it: scorned and used by the very forces we've tried so hard to please. Salt, as a preservative and as a seasoning, does not become *like* the food it preserves or seasons. It does not lose its saltiness.

So how does an army fight behind enemy lines? Well, it certainly doesn't move its forces en masse; it can't. Rather, it infiltrates small units to disrupt the enemy's communication and attack strategic targets. And that's exactly what Christians must do in a post-Christian culture.

One important note: Though we are using military word pictures to get a strategic idea across here, we must never forget that non-Christians are not the enemy. Satan is the enemy. We must love those who do not share our views, even as we seek to loosen their stranglehold on culture.

FROM THE INSIDE OUT

There are thousands of ways we can infiltrate the camps of those who are hostile to Christian truth, thousands of ways we can bring a Christian perspective to the public arena. Sometimes that means infiltrating a command post by gaining a position of influence.

A Christian friend of ours, for example, works as an assistant producer for a network news program. When appropriate, she arranges for articulate Christians to appear on the show, assuring that a biblical world-view is represented in a medium that often screens out biblically informed perspectives. We are aware of believers salted away in network news positions on and off camera, in mainstream radio and journalism, and in key speechwriting positions, where they can craft persuasive public communications based on a Judeo-Christian view of life, truth, and conduct.

Although people outside Washington often deride it as a haven of power-crazed excess and godlessness, many believers work in the halls of Congress, in government agencies, and in the White House. Bright young Christian men and women influence lawmakers through staff positions on Capitol Hill; Christian attorneys in the Justice Department wrestle with the tough issues of drugs, crime, and pornography; key aides in the Department of Education influence educational policy. (So if you think Washington is bad now, just think how much further decayed it would be if the preserving "salty" influence of these people were not present!)

Christians have also infiltrated the government arena in every state. One of our favorite examples comes from North Carolina.

Years ago, when then North Carolina Governor James Martin asked Aaron Johnson to join his state government team, he said that he wanted this Secretary of Correction to be different from those who had preceded him. Governor Martin got what he was looking for.

Aaron Johnson was the first African-American to be appointed to the position in North Carolina, and the only ordained minister in the nation to hold such a job. And from his first day in office, he made God's presence felt.

When he arrived at his new post, Aaron Johnson walked into his large office, stared at the huge desk, the official insignia, the trappings of power, and dropped to his knees. *Lord,* he prayed, *here I am. Use me however You want to.* Then he got up and called in his chief legal adviser.

"Tell me," said Johnson, "how much power does a secretary of correction have?"

"As much as you want," responded his legal adviser.

"I mean from a statutory standpoint, how much authority do I have?"

The adviser looked him in the eye. "Mr. Secretary," he said, "you can do what you want in these prisons."

"Well, then," responded Johnson, "I want to stop the cursing in them, taking the Lord's name in vain. The profanity in these places is horrible."

"Are you serious, Mr. Secretary?"

"I am dead serious. I want the very first order I send out to be an anti-cursing ordinance. You find a way to do it."

The man left, shaking his head. He returned a few hours later, dust from old law books covering his sleeves. "I found it, Mr. Secretary!" he said. "There's a statute against cursing in public, and we can use it to issue your order!"

And thus profanity was prohibited within the North Carolina prison system.

Soon after that, Aaron Johnson discovered that soft-core pornography magazines were being bought at state expense for inmates. He called in his legal counsel.

"How much authority do I have?" he asked.

By now his legal adviser was ready for anything. "What do you want to do?" he asked.

"I want to stop *Playboy* magazines from coming into the prisons," said Johnson. "Can I do that?"

"You're the secretary!"

And so, by official order, *Playboy* magazines were barred from North Carolina prisons.

Now this doesn't mean that never a foul word nor a lascivious thought exited the mouths or entered the minds of North Carolina inmates while Aaron Johnson was in office. But it does show that Christians can take advantage of their positions to be a direct, righteous influence on their environments.

State and federal governments need the preserving effect of Christian influence. So does every level of the business world and corporate America, particularly since scandals and excesses have ripped through Wall Street and corporate headquarters across the country.

Over the years I've known many able Christian businessmen and women, but none more committed Tom Phillips, who I told you earlier led me to Christ.

For twenty years Tom was CEO of Raytheon, the large electronics firm best known for its defense missiles and systems. One of the many ways Tom brought Christian influence into the marketplace was by creating an ethics office that reviewed company policies and offered guidance to managers and employees on a confidential, case-by-case basis. Employees were encouraged to consult the office about their own decisions, ask questions, and report any violations they witnessed. Since the ethics officer reported only to Tom, they were assured total confidentiality and no recrimination.

The standard was "absolute integrity," Tom said bluntly in a message to all employees. "Even if you think you are serving your company by bending the rules, let me be absolutely clear: Don't do it. Don't even think about doing it." Competitive pressures were great, he acknowledged, but more important than winning was playing by the rules. Tough rules. Submit honest bids, nothing inflated; charge honest hours to the right job; don't pad any figures for any purpose; never pay except for services performed; never give or receive a favor.

To what extent was this motivated by Tom's faith? "Virtue is a natural consequence of one's faith," he says, citing 2 Peter 1:5. He has always seen it as part of his witness to not only seek to be righteous, but to encourage virtue in those around him.[3]

No large company like Raytheon, with tens of thousands of employees, can totally avoid conflicts and ethical failures within its ranks. But during Tom's tenure the company enjoyed a remarkably clean record, something observed even by outsiders. He was cited by *Time* magazine for his spiritually dynamic leadership, along with a list of other chief executives and businessmen known for their Christian commitment. "Flocks of businessmen are born-again Christians, and many run their companies according to biblical principles. Putting service to the Lord in first place gives them peace of mind but doesn't stop them from racking up some glorious earnings."[4]

The corporate scandals of 2002 put less-ethical business practices on the front pages: CEOs who padded their own pockets while hiding liabilities from stockholders, books cooked, insider tips so friends could sell their stock just before it plummeted, phony partnerships set up to hide liabilities. Secular critics are always sensitive about Christians attempting, as they say, to "impose" our view on others. But with people losing fortunes in their 401Ks because of lack of moral character on the part of CEOs, I'm wondering how many people would really resent up-front Christian executives like Tom Phillips. When Christians live their faith, they don't repress people; instead, they provide the kind of integrity that a free society demands. Capitalism doesn't work without conscience; and consciences cannot be informed apart from absolute moral truth, which comes from biblical revelation.

We can't all be CEOs. But any of us can be a salty influence in an area of even more lasting influence: our children's schools.

A friend we'll call Amy is one of those serious, dedicated believers who has taken time to read up on issues from a Christian world-view perspective. One day when her twelve-year-old daughter, Becca, came home from school, a piece of paper dropped out of her notebook. When Amy picked it up for her, she saw it was a test on the topic, "How did the universe come into existence?"

Becca had given the answer the teacher expected, which was at odds with what Becca had been learning at home and at church.

"Why'd you put that, honey?" Amy asked. "You know that we believe that God created the universe. It didn't just come to be out of nothing."

Becca burst into tears. "I know, Mom," she said. "But if I had answered that way I would have failed the test."

Amy consoled her daughter, and then she made an appointment with the teacher in question. In a nonconfrontative way, she explained at some length, from a scientific perspective, what their family believed and laid out the evidence of why they believed it.

The teacher put her off, not really listening. (Perhaps she automatically pigeonholed Amy as some wacked-out religious fundamentalist.)

Not intimidated, Amy made an appointment with the principal. In that meeting she laid out her case again, not on biblical grounds, which the principal may or may not have agreed with, but on the grounds of scientific evidence and logical deduction.

The principal listened carefully, and then called in the teacher. "I think you've made a mistake in the classroom," she said. "You need to explain to the kids that the origins of the universe as you are teaching them are in fact a *theory,* and not meant to contradict anything they're learning at home. I think you need to apologize to them."

The teacher agreed to do so.

The principal then turned back to Amy. "You seem to know quite a lot about these issues," she said. "Would you have any interest in serving on the curriculum committee here?"

Amy served on the curriculum committee and was able to bring a biblically informed world-view influence to that public school.

Amy would call herself just an ordinary soccer mom, a faithful churchgoer, not a scientific expert. But because she is using her mind and isn't afraid to stand up for what she believes, she's been able to make an important difference in her child's school. Any of us can do the same.

SHAKING THE SALT

Being salt demands an understanding of our cultural environment and the use of innovative strategies for infiltration and influence. Writers have been doing this for centuries, with the result that much of the classic literature of the past three hundred years contains Christian truth. The great Russian works of Dostoevsky, Tolstoy, and Pushkin, for example, with the Christian message salted in their pages in such a way that the Communists forgot to ban them, were the books that led Irina Ratushinskaya toward Christ.

In many ways, literature has the most lasting power to shape ideas. Great books are read, reread, passed around, discussed, debated, and then passed on to succeeding generations.

Today, many writers reveal in their work the incoherence, shattered logic, and relativistic chaos that mark a culture that has lost its understanding of order and truth. So when a writer who is a Christian crafts words and stories that spring from a world-view informed by truth, he or she is salting modern culture.

C. S. Lewis did this brilliantly, his cogent, tough-minded logic riding on wings of lucid prose. The Oxford don crafted the compelling didactic arguments in his superb *Mere Christianity* (a book instrumental in my conversion and thousands of others). He also chose more whimsical forms, such as *The Screwtape Letters,* described as "the wittiest piece of writing the twentieth century has yet produced to stimulate the ordinary man to godliness."[5] And his children's stories, *The Chronicles of Narnia,* which present the history of redemption, have been read and reread and enjoyed by millions of children and adults.[6]

Years ago a British film company produced the Narnia stories in a faithful interpretation of Lewis's books, and I was delighted when I discovered them in the U.S. on video. I gave them to my grandchildren, who have watched them over and over. Charlie took them to his class, where they were shown to all the students. (This was in the public school system, mind you, where the children can't pray publicly or, in some schools, say "Merry Christmas" to one another.)

Lewis's friend and spiritual mentor, J. R. R. Tolkien, has infiltrated culture in the same way. Enthusiastic readers have bought more than *fifty million copies* of his *Lord of the Rings* trilogy. And since the release of the New Line film versions, the trilogy has captured a new generation of fans. Tolkien believed that human stories could reflect the noble truths of God's divine story. So his work is filled with the great themes of good, evil, sacrifice, resurrection, obedience, and faithfulness. With the success of the books and the films, they are right there on the cultural table, ready for discussion.

As Focus on the Family vice president Kurt Bruner and coauthor Jim Ware say in *Finding God in The Lord of the Rings:* "Many hard-line believers have been hesitant to embrace a creative work that includes mythic figures, magic rings, and supernatural themes. This is unfortunate because the transcendent truths of Christianity bubble up throughout this story, baptizing our imaginations with realities better experienced than studied. Like the works of C. S. Lewis, Tolkien's myth and fantasy can open the heart's back door when the front door is locked. . . . The result has been that millions, many of whom reject formal religion, have encountered realities that flourish in the unexplored regions of Christian belief."[7]

Other salty modern Christian writers—some orthodox, some not so orthodox—include Flannery O'Connor, Walter Wangerin, Dorothy Sayers, Frederick Buechner, Annie Dillard, and Katherine Paterson, to mention just a few. Writing for general audiences rather than just for Christian readers, many of these authors evoke truth subtly, rather than in overt, explicit ways.

Paterson, whose books for young people have won wide critical acclaim, has said about this process: "Really good books . . . pull together for us a world that is falling apart. They are the words that integrate us, stretch us, judge us, comfort and heal us. They are the words that mirror the Word of creation, bringing order out of chaos. . . . I believe we must try . . . to give our children these words. . . . We must try as best we are able to give our children words that will shape their minds so they can make those miraculous leaps of imagination that no sinless computer will ever be able to rival—those connections in science, in art, in the living of this life that will reveal the little truths. For it is these little truths that point to the awesome . . . Truth, which holds us together and makes us members one of another.[8]

Another writer who pointed to the truth was Walker Percy, without platitudinous Christianese or push-button rhetoric. Percy's critically acclaimed works, like *The Thanatos Syndrome,* a novel that sketched the horrors of abortion and euthanasia on a canvas of America in the late 1990s, have been digested by thousands of secular readers who wouldn't go near a religious publisher or a Christian bookstore.

The modern novelist, Percy said, "should be a nag . . . a proclaimer of banal atrocities. People get desensitized. . . . True legalized abortion—a million and a half fetuses flushed down the Disposal every year in this country—is yet another banal atrocity in a century where atrocities have become commonplace."[9]

Percy captured the imaginations of secular readers in a way that Christians who write for Christians have not. Because he was a master at surrounding his barbs with elegant prose and superb stories, reviewers applauded Percy enthusiastically even as he was assaulting their most cherished opinions.[10]

On a popular level, no writer infiltrates more widely than John Grisham—lawyer, husband, father, Little League coach, Baptist, and one of the most commercially successful writers in our time. In best-selling novels like *The Chamber* and *The Testament* he depicts scenes of Christian conversion without sentiment, jargon, or manipulation. They flow out of his stories. He presents the reality of sin and the power of grace better than some pastors—and, like Walker Percy, though to a different audience, he is doing so for millions of readers who would never think of picking up an overtly "Christian" novel.

In *The Testament*, the protagonist is a lawyer named Nate O'Riley. He is a recovering alcoholic and drug addict, has two broken marriages, and is in trouble with the IRS. Through his contact with a gutsy missionary who lives her faith among needy villagers in Brazil, he realizes his need for God. And, if you can imagine it in a book that dominated the *New York Times* bestseller list, he admits his many sins and repents: "He repeated the list, mumbling softly every weakness and flaw and affliction and evil that plagued him. He confessed them all. In one long glorious acknowledgement of failure, he laid himself bare before God. He held nothing back."[11]

Salty language.

Jan Karon does the same thing in a very different style. Her warm and winsome Mitford series, which has sold millions and millions of copies, features characters whose Christian faith shapes their character and makes them salt and light in the midst of the real-life struggles in a small town. Christians must penetrate Hollywood as well. TV and film producer David McFadzean is one of "at least 73 openly Christian executive producers or key producers in television, reports the *Chicago Tribune*.[12] His production credits include a number of hit TV shows and movies.

At best, says McFadzean, Hollywood sees Christians as dull-witted and out of touch. At worst, Hollywood sees them as the enemy, with a dangerous right-wing political agenda.

"They don't know who [Christians] are," McFadzean recently told a group of Christian college students. "The reason you're depicted on the screen the way you are is because you're here, and they're there.

"You need to be in Hollywood changing Hollywood, not lobbing stones from the outside. . . . There is no great conspiracy against Christianity. I think most of Hollywood is apathetic toward any spiritual point of view."

Instead of avoiding show business, Christians should become part of it, McFadzean says. Even a minority of Christian production assistants, leading by example, could change Hollywood.

That isn't something you hear every day in Christian circles. But it is sound strategy and the essence of what it means to be salt in a decaying culture. And if we are wise, we'll equip our young people to do just that.

Few of us can reach the literary heights of a Tolkien or a Lewis. Few of us will ever be CEOs of multibillion-dollar companies like Raytheon, or write books that consistently top the bestseller lists like John Grisham. Not all of us are called to work in Hollywood like David McFadzean. And not many of us are Aaron Johnsons, placed in a position of authority where we can issue an order that fifteen thousand employees and twenty thousand prisoners must obey.

But all of us—like our friend Amy the soccer mom—can be, and *must* be—salt, wherever we find ourselves.

Each of us must see ourselves as ministers of the gospel. We don't simply attend church, consuming a religious product. Rather, our whole understanding of ourselves as members of the Body is directed toward being equipped to serve effectively in our vocation and our community—wherever God places us.

Many Christians have a bifurcated view of life: Faith is over here in this compartment, and the rest of life—work, family, leisure time, and everything else—is over there.

Like the young woman who stopped me in an airport. "Mr. Colson, I so admire the work that Prison Fellowship is doing," she said. "I'm a believer; I wish that I could be in full-time Christian service like you."

"What is it you do?" I asked.

"Well, I'm still in school," she said. "I'm finishing up my doctoral work in molecular biology. I had planned to teach full-time. I love it. But lately I've realized I should do more for the Lord. My parents were missionaries. I'm thinking of going to Brazil as a missionary."

"You are in a tremendous position to be a missionary right where you are!" I said adamantly. "How many Christians are there who are molecular biologists? The university needs people like you!"

She looked relieved, even excited, as it sank in: She was a missionary right where she was.

Thousands of Christians suffer from this same kind of false understanding of the glory of vocation and a parallel misunderstanding of how God places particular people in particular places in every arena to be salt and accomplish His preserving, flavoring purposes.

We must be willing to be uncomfortable. Living in a post-Christian culture means that our Christian faith will be ridiculed. We'll sometimes be seen as strange. But if we love the approval of Christ more than the approval of our peers, we'll be willing to be perceived as odd now and then!

And we must learn how to support and encourage one another. If we are to be the agents behind enemy lines, then it is critical that we establish a network whereby Christians can pass information back and forth to one another. We can learn a lot about the world from *Time* and *Newsweek,* but we must also equip one another with Christian perspectives on critical issues. And we need to exchange information. That's what we've tried to do on BreakPoint Radio, and through our Wilberforce Forum Web site, for years.

What Christians must do in a post-Christian age can be likened to the way the underground operated in Europe during the Nazi occupation in World War II. The underground had its own elaborate network of signals, method of communication, maps, charts, and its own command structure. The parallel is a bit extreme perhaps, but useful as Christians determine how they will network with one another in a culture hostile to the open expression of Christian truth.

In seventeenth-century London, as Reformation thinking about the church's influence in society was making itself felt in the city, someone painted a billboard with a picture of a tailor, a cook, a porter, a blacksmith, and a saddle-maker. The inscription read: "These tradesmen are preachers in the city of London, 1647."

Who are the preachers of America in the late twentieth century?

Each of us, as we infiltrate the arena in which God has placed us.

We begin, like Aaron Johnson, by falling on our knees in our workplace, our kitchen, our classroom, our neighborhood and praying those simple words, "Lord, here I am. Use me however You want to."

Sometimes God will use us in ways we never could dream. Sometimes that prayer unleashes the power to actually begin to change not just our neighborhood, but our nation at large. That is, in fact, what happened to ordinary believers in one of the most dramatic historic events of the twentieth century.

27

LIGHTING THE NIGHT

TIMISOARA sits next to the Bega River, and for decades life there has been as drab as its gray waters.

Founded in medieval times, Timisoara was part of the kingdom of Hungary. After World War I, along with the rest of Transylvania, it was annexed by Romania. After World War II, Romania was seized by the Soviet Union. Since then, the university town of Timisoara had grown more and more dreary, until its shops were full of nothing and its faces were full of fear.

In the center of downtown lies a long, rectangular paved mall studded with statues, plots of grass, and beds of flowers. In one of the grassy areas stands a wooden cross surrounded by candles, flowers, and black-and-white photos. It is a shrine to the martyrs of Timisoara, the men and women who died here in December 1989.

The brown, turreted Orthodox cathedral stands at one end of the rectangle. At the other end rises the white, balconied opera house. Buildings with apartments on their upper levels and shops on their first floors line the long sides of the rectangle.

A few blocks from this central square, on a corner across from a tram stop, sits a massive, ugly building. An optician occupies the ground floor on one side of the building; the other side is occupied by the Hungarian Reformed Church. On its gray stone wall two simple wreaths hang next to small plaques proclaiming in four languages: "Here began the revolution that felled a dictator."

Visit Timisoara today and you will notice all this, for Timisoara is no ordinary town. This is where the Romanian revolution began . . . with just a few candles in the darkness.

WHEN THE SOVIETS overran Romania in August 1944, there were only 750 Communists in the entire country. I told you about one of them earlier, a short, fleshy-lipped shoemaker named Nicolae Ceausescu, who had just been released from prison, where he had spent much of World War II. He was rewarded for his foresight by being named secretary general of the Union of Communist Youth.

Under young leaders like Ceausescu, Romania's nightmare began. Multiplying like cockroaches, the Communists eliminated the light of opposition any way they could. Students and peasants, pastors and priests—over the years, millions were thrown into prison. Many died there.

Meanwhile, Ceausescu climbed through the party ranks, dreaming of the day Romania would be his. By the early 1970s his dream had come true. He was president of the country, with the party and the army firmly behind him.

Ceausescu's leadership was marked by his manipulation of Western leaders.[1] To capitalize on the West's Cold War attitudes toward Moscow, he distanced himself from the Soviet Union. But Ceausescu was no moderate Communist leader. Ruling from a kitschy Versailles-style palace in Bucharest, he brutally plundered Romania and reshaped it in his own sick image.

Romania's soil has been called the most fertile in Eastern Europe, yet the Ceausescu government starved its people. While citizens shivered in long lines to buy bread laced with sawdust, the government shipped most of Romania's food abroad. Meat, butter, sugar, oil, and flour were strictly rationed. Vegetables were scarce, citrus fruits nonexistent.

While their people competed for bony chickens and occasional pork knuckles, the Ceausescus and top party officials had difficulty keeping their cholesterol levels in check. A menu from a birthday dinner for Elena Ceausescu makes Marie Antoinette seem frugal: three kinds of caviar, pâté de foie gras, filet mignon, roast beef, baby pork, pork chops and pork loin, venison, roast turkey, cornish game hens, pheasant, lobster, frogs' legs, smoked salmon, and three kinds of trout.[2]

When he wasn't choosing which type of caviar to consume, Ceausescu was promoting his pet program of "systematization," which razed thousands of rural villages and transferred their citizens to apartment blocks in designated urban-industrial centers. Raw concrete and exposed joints pockmarked these midrise flats that were a warren of dark, tiny rooms and flimsy walls, smelling of sewage and old garbage. Heated by a central system controlled by some sadistic state functionary, the blocks were maintained at about fifty degrees during the winter. Many families had hot water only once a week, and electricity was rationed as well. Forty-watt bulbs were the highest wattage allowed in homes that had current only certain hours a day, and bulbs were removed from the streetlights. At night the roads were utterly black, flanked by worthless steel stalks.

Seeking to fortify his labor force, Ceausescu demanded that all good Romanian families produce five children. "The fetus is the property of the entire society," he decreed. "Anyone who avoids having children is a deserter who abandons the laws of national continuity."[3]

Birthrates increased with his regime, as did infant mortality. Unable to feed their babies, many parents were forced to abandon them. Eventually more than two hundred state-run orphanages dotted Romania, miserable monuments to Ceausescu's most helpless citizens.

Meanwhile the Securitate, a spidery network of secret police that webbed the country, enforced the wretched status quo. An estimated one in four citizens informed for the secret police, who harassed and imprisoned anyone who didn't salute the regime.

But Ceausescu's greatest repressive fervor was reserved for Christians.

He began by gaining control of many in the Romanian Orthodox Church. Deciding that compromise was a reasonable price to pay for existence, many priests and bishops entered the Communist fold. These church officials cleared all activities with the Department of Religious Affairs and reported the names of all who attended services. Priests were required to relate the confidences of their parishioners. Church publications sang the praises of the regime and reprinted words of wisdom from its leaders. Prayers were said for the health and prosperity of the Communist government. The apostle Paul's admonition to the Romans—"be in subjection to the government authorities"—was a favorite verse cited by those in charge.[4]

Over the years, Catholics were suppressed and their churches coopted by the Orthodox majority. Baptists, Adventists, Pentecostals, and other Protestant groups formed a tiny minority among Romania's twenty-three million people; yet the authorities sought to seduce Protestant church leaders as well, assuming that if they could manipulate the shepherd, they could gain control of the flock. Some pastors compromised with the state; others did not. One who did not was a young Reformed pastor named Laszlo Tokes.

LASZLO TOKES, a large, handsome man with a deep, compelling voice, had become pastor of the Hungarian Reformed Church in the center of Timisoara in 1987. His predecessor, Leo Peuker, had pastored the congregation for years and was well known as a government collaborator. Peuker had even worn the red star of Communism on his clerical vestments.

Under Peuker's unsavory blend of church and state, the membership had shrunk to fewer than fifty parishioners. Services had been reduced to ritual. With no catechism, no confirmation class, and no Bible studies, the only time people gathered together was for Sunday morning services or for funeral rites when one of their dwindling number died.

Then early in 1987, while conducting one of those funerals, Peuker himself had a fatal heart attack, and Tokes became "probationary" pastor of the Hungarian Reformed Church. He quickly gained immense popularity, not only with the elderly in his congregation, but also with students from the university.

While the Communists weren't particularly concerned about the old people, they did care about the students. Religion should have been irrelevant to this generation coming of age in the last decade of the century of Lenin.

Tokes's superior didn't care for him either. For years Bishop Laszlo Papp had compromised with the authorities, and he didn't appreciate the threat of this young pastor's nonconformity. So Bishop Papp kept a wary eye on Tokes. In spite of this surveillance, however, the young minister would not allow the travesty of a church in name only to continue.

Tokes mourned for his town and his country. The secularism of the atheistic regime had bitten deep into the hearts of the people. Still, he knew the church could help set those hearts on fire. His Reformed faith had given Tokes eyes to see what could happen when the church understood its identity, when the people stopped thinking of their faith as just a Sunday morning ritual and understood that the church was the community of the people of God that could infiltrate the world.[5]

"Now we can start a new phase," Tokes announced to his small congregation. "To do that we need the help of every member of the presbytery and every parishioner. It is not a matter of my being in charge. I am not the only pastor here; we must all be pastors to each other."[6]

Tokes reorganized the church and requested more hymn books, more Bibles. Young people were prepared for confirmation. Catechisms were restored. Revitalized worship services celebrated the great festivals of the church calendar.

The authorities were scandalized by his initiatives, but Tokes was actually within the bounds of the Romanian constitution, which officially guaranteed freedom of religion. In practice, of course, the authorities violated that freedom all the time.

In Peuker's old files Tokes found dusty baptismal records of families who had once been part of the church but had dropped away because of the collaborator's empty rites. Tokes invited them back. New converts were baptized. New tithes came in. The celebration of Communion took on new meaning as parishioners remembered the body and blood of Christ and realized that, indeed, the risen Christ was among them.

Within two years, the membership rolls of the Timisoara Hungarian Reformed Church had swelled to five thousand. But the growth was more than numbers; people were being discipled.

As the church body grew, Tokes began to attend to the building itself. The dark old sanctuary echoed with the sounds of hammers and saws as carpenters constructed a new balcony. Growing crowds of worshipers soon tested its strength. People arrived by the tramload, their voices ringing in joyous celebration, singing the great hymns of the faith.

Listening from near and far, both the Securitate and the ecclesiastical superiors knew they could not allow the church to continue like this. Tokes's booming voice proclaiming the Word of God from the pulpit echoed in their minds like a bad dream. There was no place for this passionate Christian faith in Ceausescu's Romania.

Tokes further complicated his case by granting an interview in August 1989 to a Hungarian television station. During the interview he criticized Ceausescu's "systematization" plan. Some fifty thousand citizens of Hungarian descent would be affected, Tokes charged, and this was just another chapter in the Romanian government's repression of Hungarians.

Tokes's statements were broadcast on a Hungarian program called *Panorama*, which made its way to Radio Free Europe, the BBC, and other Western radio stations. They, in turn, transmitted the clandestine interview back into Romania. Ceausescu's government was not pleased.

Earlier that year Bishop Papp had accused Tokes of "violating the laws of both church and state" and officially suspended him from ministry. Yet Tokes kept preaching the truth and exposing the lies of the Ceausescu government—and his stubborn congregation kept growing. Worst of all, this sanctimonious upstart was breaking down the walls between churches that the Communists had so carefully erected for their own purposes.

In a spirit of unity, Tokes told his elders, "I want to invite each church to visit us. Not just its priests or clergy, but the whole congregation as well. We will have a Communion festival together. I will preach and so will the visiting priest. There will be hymn singing from both traditions, and we will invite the believers to take part with songs and poems."[7]

For their first such festival, the Hungarian Reformed Church invited the members of the local Catholic parish. Tokes figured that since the Reformed Church had emerged from the Catholic Church, it was only natural that they hold this festival on October 31, the day Martin Luther had launched his Reformation. Both sides of that centuries-old divide would extend their hands to one another.

Immediately after that celebration of unity, the authorities increased their pressure. The secret police had encountered types like Tokes before. Intimidation and repression would take care of the problem.

The methods of the Securitate were anything but subtle. They threatened members of Tokes's church, and parishioners had to run a gauntlet of secret police just to enter the building each Sunday. Once the service began, agents would stand in front of the church cradling machine guns in their arms or dangling handcuffs in front of them. Merely attending church services became a silent act of protest.

Meanwhile, Tokes was denied his ration book; without it he was unable to buy bread, fuel, or meat. Parishioners, who by now had learned the real meaning of fellowship, shared from their own slim resources, smuggling firewood and food to the pastor and his family.

Tokes was also barred from meeting with friends or relatives. Friends used children or old women to carry their messages to Tokes; others were searched by the secret police. His phone was shut off, except for incoming abusive and threatening phone calls for which the secret police then charged him long-distance rates. Afraid for their four-year-old son, Mate, Tokes and his wife, Edith, sent the child to live with relatives.[8]

Their fears were well founded. The Securitate contacted one of Tokes's friends, an architect who had worked on the church balcony construction project, and ordered him to comply with their campaign against the pastor. The architect refused. A few days later his body was found in a Timisoara park. The police termed his death a suicide.

Then Tokes himself was attacked. Four men, their faces concealed behind ski masks, burst into the pastor's small apartment in the church building. Laszlo and Edith happened to have visitors that evening, who helped them fight off the attackers with chairs. The assailants ran away, leaving Tokes bleeding from a knife wound in the face.

Soon after that the secret police must have concluded that killing Tokes would simply make him a martyr. Instead, they would render him ineffective by exiling him to a small, remote village outside of Timisoara. A court ordered his eviction from his home and church, setting the date for December 15, 1989.

ON SUNDAY, DECEMBER 10, Laszlo Tokes looked out over the upturned faces of his congregation. These Christians had paid a high price to worship, each of them braving the gauntlet of secret police in order to enter the church building, their names noted on the Securitate's endless lists, and their physical lives made more and more miserable by their stand, even as their souls grew more and more prosperous.

"Dear brothers and sisters in Christ," Tokes announced, "I have been issued a summons of eviction. I will not accept it, so I will be taken from you by force next Friday. They want to do this in secret because they have no right to do it. Please, come next Friday and be witnesses of what will happen. Come, be peaceful, but be witnesses."[9]

Tokes could see the pain on the faces of the faithful and the smooth, inscrutable looks of the informers sprinkled throughout the congregation.

Five days later, on December 15, 1989, the secret police came to take Laszlo and Edith. They brought a moving van for the Tokeses' belongings, but they never got to load the truck. For massed protectively around the entrance to the church building stood a human shield. Heeding their pastor's call, members of the congregation had come to protest his removal.

Residents of Romania were used to friends and loved ones disappearing in the night, hauled off to prison or interrogation at the whim of the secret police. But on this day a flame of hope sprang up within the crowd. Perhaps they really could prevent their pastor's departure. Perhaps this time they could make a difference.

The brick-and-concrete home of the Hungarian Reformed Church sat directly across from a tram stop. Each time the crowded cars unloaded, passengers could see the people gathered outside the church building.

"What is going on?" they asked. When they learned what was happening, many joined the group. Some were from other churches; some were just curious or supportive onlookers.

Meanwhile, Lajos Varga, a friend of Tokes, began making telephone calls, rallying believers from all over Timisoara—Baptists, Adventists, Pentecostals, Orthodox, and Catholics. And later that day when Tokes opened the window of his flat to talk with the people, he experienced what he called "the turning point in my life."

"These were not only my parishioners, with a few Baptists and Adventists, but Orthodox priests and some of their Romanian flocks. I was very moved," he said, "and it changed what I now see as my old prejudices—that we cannot make common cause, cannot fight side by side. Now that I have seen Romanians, Germans, Catholics, and Orthodox defending me, I know that I have to work for reconciliation between the nationalities and creeds in this country."[10]

He called out in Hungarian and then in Romanian: "We are one in Christ. We speak different languages, but we have the same Bible and the same God. We are one."[11]

Below, the people looked at one another, struck by the truth of his statement. Though hungry and cold, they continued to stand shoulder to shoulder in a semicircle around the church entrance.

Darkness fell, and Timisoara's Communist mayor, Peter Mot, visited Tokes. He could stay on at the church, the mayor said, if the crowd dispersed.

When Tokes shouted this news to the people, someone shouted back, "We don't trust them, Father!"[12]

Then Mayor Mot appeared at the window. "You Romanians, go home," he said, attempting to play on ethnic divisions. "Let the Hungarians be rebellious and stay here!"[13] But his divide-and-conquer strategy did not work.

Adina Jinaru, a Romanian Orthodox believer who lived nearby, looked around her at the great diversity of people joined together to support the Hungarian pastor. The crowd was infiltrated by Securitate agents as well; she could tell by looking into their eyes.

A burly, hearty Baptist pastor named Peter Dugulescu was also part of the crowd, as was Daniel Gavra, a student from Dugulescu's congregation. Gavra made his way through the people toward Dugulescu.

"Look, Pastor," he said, opening his jacket surreptitiously because of the Securitate agents.

The way things were escalating, Dugulescu half expected to see some sort of weapon. But the lump in Gavra's jacket was a paper packet filled with dozens of candle stubs.

IT WAS PAST ONE O'CLOCK in the morning when Tokes opened the window of his apartment a final time before he went to bed. He couldn't believe his eyes. Light from hundreds of candles pierced the darkness. Hands, cupped close to the people's hearts, sheltered the flickering flames, and the flames lighted their faces with a warm glow.

I do not know where I will be tomorrow or the next day, Tokes thought. *I know only this moment. And I know that the Spirit of God Himself is with us.*

The extraordinary demonstration continued throughout that night and into the following day. Then, late in the afternoon, the people took the protest a step further than a show of solidarity for Laszlo Tokes. For the first time in their lives, Romanians shouted their secret dreams aloud: "Liberty! Freedom!"[14]

Students began singing a patriotic song that the Communists had banned years before: "Awake, Romania!" And much later, as night fell on December 16, someone began shouting: "Down with Ceausescu! Down with Communism!" Part of the crowd headed downtown to the city square, while the remainder kept guard at Tokes's church.[15]

Before dawn on December 17 the secret police finally made their move and broke through the people. As they did so, Laszlo and Edith took refuge in the church sanctuary near the Communion table. Tokes wrapped himself in his heavy clerical robe and picked up a Bible, holding it like a weapon.

The bolted church door gave way with a splintering crash, and the police swarmed into the building. They beat Tokes until his face was bloody. Then they took him and Edith away into the night.

WITH THEIR PASTOR GONE, the crowds moved from the Hungarian Reformed Church to the central square of Timisoara. By now armed troops, shields, dogs, and tanks filled the streets. But even with the army in place, the people did not retreat. For this had become a full-scale protest against the intrusion of the state. There was no turning back. The people of Timisoara massed in the city square, shouting and singing. Daniel Gavra and many others distributed candles. And when darkness fell, the people lighted their flames against the night.

The Communists responded with the brute force they had always employed when threatened by freedom seekers. They ordered their troops to open fire on the protesters.

Daniel Gavra and a number of other believers marched into the square carrying the new flag of the revolution: Romania's tricolor with its Communist emblem scissored out of the middle. As they marched, Gavra linked arms with a young Pentecostal girl.

The soldiers opened fire, and the girl slipped from his arm. She was dead by the time she hit the pavement. Daniel barely had time to comprehend what had happened when there was another explosion and he fell, his left leg blown away by a barrage of bullets.

In the confusion of the crowd and the darkness, the savage gunfire claimed hundreds of victims, but the people of Timisoara stood strong. Though shocked at the cost of their stand, they knew there was no middle ground. They had decided to stand for truth against lies, and stand they would.

By Christmas 1989, the world reeled with the results of that stand: Romania was free and Ceausescu was gone. The people of Timisoara rejoiced. Churches filled with worshipers praising God.

A few days after Christmas, Pastor Peter Dugulescu opened the door of the hospital ward where Daniel Gavra had been taken after he was shot. The boy was still recuperating, his wounds bandaged and a stump where his left leg had been. But Daniel's spirit had not been shattered.

"Pastor," he said, "I don't mind so much the loss of my leg. After all, it was I who lit the first candle." [16]

28

Go Light Your Candle

Before its revolution, Communist Romania was dark. There were no streetlights. The nights were dense and full of fear. Packs of wild dogs roamed the roads; secret police rapped on doors and made their midnight arrests. In a locked land that hustled away its heroes on moonless nights, there was no hope for change.

What if the Christians in Romania had believed their eyes? What if they had fallen prey to the fears surrounding them? What if they had given in to the dark despair that said a candle stub could do no good?

But they did not. A kid from a church youth group lit the first candle. His friend lit the next. Soon the fires of the community of faith were ablaze in the night . . . and Christians equipped only with gospel armor took their stand against the killing columns of heavy tanks.

If a boy with a candle can light the night and stir a nation to freedom, what then can we do? Does God not give us such stories to show us His truth and strengthen our own resolve?

We, too, live in a darkening land. No, we don't suffer the overt repression of the old Romania. The bright lights of Vanity Fair still blaze. But the long shadows creep from within and without. War and its rumors fill the air . . . random shootings, in schools and on the streets . . . economic uncertainties . . . disdainful voices scorn God . . . the forces of terror lurking in any seemingly ordinary situation.

And amid it all, Satan spins his snares of weariness and fear, dejection and despair. He tempts God's people to feel trapped, impotent, helpless.

But what does the risen Lord of the church tell His people 366 times throughout the Scriptures?

Fear not!

Fear not!

Fear not!

His perfect love casts out all fear.

Satan's sin of despair denies God's sovereign truth and the way He chooses to work in this broken world. God acts through His people, His Body. Just like Daniel Gavra, each of us can make a difference as we unite with the family of faith. Christ has told us that we are the light of the world. Even as we step forth with our smallest flames of love and truth, Christ's great light will blaze and dispel the darkness . . . for the darkness cannot overcome it.

So we need not despair. The simple truth is our greatest hope. As we live as His Body on earth, God *will* use us for His purposes. As we exhibit the characteristics of His church throughout the ages, consuming the Word of God, celebrating the sacraments, loving one another in holy purity, the world around us will be changed.

If faith is at war with fear, if catastrophe can turn from death to resurrection, if hope can triumph over despair . . . if there was ever a time for the church to *be* the church, it is *now*.

Go light your candle!

ENDNOTES

PROLOGUE

1. Quoted in Paul Heyer, *Architects on Architecture: New Directions in America* (New York: Van Nostrand Reinhold, 1993), 194–95. Yamasaki's humanism also contains an inherent hubris, as one can hear in these reflections about his creation [also from Heyer's book, page 186, emphasis added]:

> There are a few very influential architects who sincerely believe that all buildings must be "strong." The word "strong" in this context seems to connote "powerful"-that is, each building should be a monument to the virility of our society. These architects look with derision upon attempts to build a friendly, more gentle kind of building. . . . Although it is inevitable for architects who admire [the] great monumental buildings of Europe *to strive for the quality most evident in them-grandeur, the elements of mysticism and power, basic to cathedrals and palaces, are also incongruous today, because the buildings we build for our times are for a totally different purpose.*

2. This information regarding the towers' design is taken from Dennis Smith, *Report from Ground Zero* (New York: Viking Penguin, 2002), 186–89.

3. John is a composite character. His experiences are those of actual individuals whose names have not been included in order to protect their privacy.

CHAPTER I

1. Cited in Malcolm Muggeridge, *The End of Christendom* (Grand Rapids, Mich.: Eerdmans, 1980), 22.

2. Islam's early history offers a fascinating comparison with the birth of Christianity. Jesus, the suffering servant, told His followers that their numbers would grow through love and service rather than seeking to conquer the political structures of their day. For more thorough studies on Islam and Christianity than we can offer here, see Timothy George, *Is the Father of Jesus the God of Mohammed?: Understanding the Differences between Christianity and Islam* (Grand Rapids, Mich.: Zondervan, 2002); Bernard Lewis, *What Went Wrong? Western Impact and Middle Eastern Response* (New York: Oxford University Press, 2001); and Bernard Lewis, *The Middle East: A Brief History of the Last 2,000 Years* (New York: Scribner, 1996).

ENDNOTES

3. There is only one Christian country in the world that could raise the suggestion of theocracy, and that is Tonga, a small island republic in the South Pacific where the king, a Methodist, enforces church law.

4. "Americans Struggle with Religion's Role at Home and Abroad," *Pew Forum on Religion and Public Life,* 20 March 2002.

5. Delinda C. Hanley, "President Bush Holds Ittar Dinner at White House," *Ethnic News Watch* 21, no. 1 (February 28, 2002): 82.

6. "Americans Struggle with Religion's Role at Home and Abroad," *Pew Forum on Religion and Public Life,* 20 March 2002.

7. See Charles Colson, *Loving God* (Grand Rapids, Mich.: Zondervan, 1983), chap. 6: "Watergate and the Resurrection."

8. See John 15:1–8.

9. 2 Timothy 3:14–7.

CHAPTER 2

1. Al Dobras, "Liberal Churches See Drop in Attendance; 'Lack of Relevance' Cited in Decline," Concerned Women for America Culture and Family Institute, May 2002.

2. "Americans Are Most Likely to Base Truth on Feelings," survey conducted by Barna Research Online, 12 February 2002.

3. George Barna, "Rechurching the Unchurched," cited in *Washington Times,* 11 April 2002.

4. *Hedge Hog Review* 4, no. 1 (Spring 2002): 18. Published by The Institute for Advanced Studies in Culture at the University of Virginia.

5. Robert Bellah, *Habits of the Heart* (New York: Harper & Row, 1985).

6. Ibid., emphasis added.

7. "A Vision for a Renewed City," publication of Redeemer Presbyterian Church, 1998.

8. George Gallup, Jr., cited in Felicia R. Lee, "The Secular Society Gets Religion," *New York Times,* 24 August 2002: 7B. See also George Barna and George Gallup, Jr., "It All Adds Up: Religion Surveys Find Us More Spiritual, Less Faithful," *Dallas Morning News,* 26 December 1998: 1G.

9. Kenneth L. Woodward, et al., "A Time to Seek," *Newsweek,* 17 December 1990, 17 (emphasis added).

10. Terry Mattingly, "9/11: Spirituality Up, Doctrine Down," 11 September 2002.

11. Woodward, "A Time to Seek," 11.

12. Eli Lilly-funded study cited in Martha Sawyer, "Protestants Take Aim at Baby Boomers," *Naples Daily News.*

13. John Dart, "It's Not all in a Name for Some Churches," *Los Angeles Times,* 22 December 1990: 1S.

14. Woodward, "A Time to Seek," 17.

15. Constance Casey, "Gimme That New Age Religion," review in "Book World," *Washington Post,* 2 February 1991, 2–4.

16. American religious identification survey, Graduate Center of City University of New York, 2001. (See Kathy Grossman, "Charting the Unchurched in America," *USA Today,* 7 March 2002.)

17. Ibid.

18. Lisa Richardson, "Proportion of Americans Claiming No Religion in the 1990s," *New York Times,* 18 May 2002.

19. George Barna, "State of the Church 2002," Issachar Resources, Barna Research Group, Ventura, Calif.

20. John 17:21.

21. Woodward, "A Time to Seek," 13.

22. Rich Gilbert, "Corporate Worship," *Modern Reformation* (September-October 1991).

23. See Dale Buss, "Peddling God," *VNU Business Media Sales and Marketing Management,* March 2002.

24. Acts 2:47.

25. Richard John Neuhaus, *Freedom for Ministry* (New York: Harper & Row, 1979), 89.

Endnotes

CHAPTER 3

1. John 1:12–13.

CHAPTER 4

1. Matthew 16:19; 18:18.

2. Because "church" in the New Testament refers also to the entire body of believers in a given community, the individual "house churches" made diligent efforts to maintain their common identity. They came together regularly for worship, shared resources throughout the community (not just within their particular congregation), and joined in acts of discipline and ordination, as well as evangelism. In that way the individual churches of early believers affirmed their oneness with their sister churches-a practice we do well to emulate today.

3. Richard Avery and Donald Marsh, *We Are the Church* (Pasadena, Calif.: Hope, 1972).

4. 1 Corinthians 12; 1 Peter 2:9. See also Carl F. H. Henry, "Churches and Christian Fellowship," pt. 5, teaching sessions and internal study prepared for Prison Fellowship.

5. Acts 20:28.

6. Acts 20:28; Ephesians 5:25.

7. The pastor's name has been changed.

8. Hebrews 12:23; Romans 16:5; Acts 15:22.

9. The word *catholic* here is a contraction from the Greek *kata*, "according to," and *holos,* "the whole."

10. Acts 2:37–39.

11. Acts 2:42.

12. As Calvin argued so powerfully, it is this—the communion of the saints—that is the true expression of our invisible essence, not the mere ritual or routine participation in external forms (see John Calvin, *Institutes of the Christian Religion*, ed. J. T. McNeill, 2 vols. (Philadelphia: Westminster, 1960), 4.1.9–12).

13. Acts 2.

14. Hebrews 10:19–25.

15. J. Pelikan and H. Lehmann, ed., *Luther's Works,* 55 vols. (Reprint, St. Louis: Concordia, 1955), 21:127.

16. Calvin, *Institutes of the Christian Religion*, 2:1012.

17. Warren Wiersbe, *The Integrity Crisis* (Nashville: Thomas Nelson, 1988), 130.

18. Richard Neuhaus, *Freedom for Ministry* (New York: Harper & Row, 1979), 53.

19. C. S. Lewis, *The Screwtape Letters* (Reprint, New York: Macmillan, 1977), 12.

20. Ibid., 44; see also H. Richard Niebuhr, *The Purpose of the Church and Its Ministry* (New York: Harper & Row, 1956); also, references in Vatican Council II to the fact that many elements of sanctification of truth can be found outside of "her visible structure," as well as the powerful writings of eminent Catholic theologian Fr. Avery Dulles, S.J.

CHAPTER 5

1. Irina Ratushinskaya, interviews with Ellen Vaughn, San Jose, Costa Rica, July 1989.

2. Irina Ratushinskaya, *In the Beginning,* trans. Alyona Kojevnikov (London: Hodder & Stoughton, 1990), 46.

3. Irina would not read the writings of British author C. S. Lewis until much later in her life, when as an adult she was exiled from her Russia into the West. But she had already found what Lewis called the Rule of Right and Wrong in his book *Mere Christianity.* "This Rule of Right and Wrong, or Law of Human Nature, or whatever you call it, must somehow or other be a real thing—a thing that is really there, not made up by ourselves. . . . It begins to look as if we shall have to admit that there is more than one kind of reality; that, in this particular case, there is something above and beyond the ordinary facts of men's behavior, and yet quite definitely real—a real law, which none of us made, but which we find pressing on us" (C. S. Lewis, *Mere Christianity* [New York: Macmillan, 1960], 30).

4. Ratushinskaya, *In the Beginning,* 46.

5. Ibid., 71.

6. Ibid., 106–7.

ENDNOTES

CHAPTER 6

1. John 3:8

2. For anyone questioning Mother Teresa's Christian commitment, I would recommend reading Malcolm Muggeridge's *Confessions of a Twentieth-Century Pilgrim* (New York: Harper & Row, 1988), esp. 138-39. Reprinted here for edification is one of Mother Teresa's letters to Malcolm Muggeridge:

> I think, dear friend . . . I understand you better now. I'm afraid I could not answer your deep suffering. I don't know why, but you are to me like Nicodemus (who came to Jesus under cover of night), and I'm sure the answer is the same. "Unless you become a little child."
>
> I'm sure you will understand beautifully everything—if you'd only become a little child in God's hands. Your longing for God is so deep and yet He keeps Himself away from you. He must be forcing Himself to do so because He loves you so much as to give Jesus to die for you and for me. Christ is longing to be your food. Surrounded with fullness of living Food, you allow yourself to starve.
>
> The personal love Christ has for you is infinite—the small difficulty you have regarding the church is finite. Overcome the finite with the infinite. Christ has created you because He wanted you. I know what you feel—terrible longing with dark emptiness—and yet He is the one in love with you. I do not know if you have seen these few lines before, but they fill and empty me:

> *My God, my God what is a heart*
> *That Thou shouldst so eye and woo*
> *Pouring upon it all Thy heart*
> *As if Thou hadst nothing else to do.*

3. For example, in cases of moral impropriety (1 Corinthians 5; Galatians 5:19–32; Jude 4); in cases of defiling the Lord's Supper (1 Corinthians 11:17–34); in cases of profaning worship (1 Corinthians 11:2–16); in cases of doctrinal deviance (Galatians 1:6–9; 3:1–14; 5:1–12; 1 Timothy 1:3–7; 5:1; 2 Timothy 4:2–3; 2 Peter 2:1–3; 3:17; Jude 3; 1 John 4:1–2); miscellaneous (Galatians 2:11–14; 6:1; Ephesians 4:25; 1 Thessalonians 5:21; 2 Thessalonians 3:11–12; 1 Timothy 5:19; 2 Timothy 2:14, 25; 4:2, 14; Titus 1:10–14; 2:15; 3:10; Jude 23; Revelation 2–3).

4. Matthew 7:15–23, 12:33–37; Luke 6:43–45.

CHAPTER 7

1. "Christian Soldiers: A church goes to war over bingo, accusations of theft, and threats of excommunication," *Cleveland Scene,* 7 February 2002.

2. Study by Jerrien Gunnink, cited by Frank Martin, *War in the Pews* (Downer's Grove, Ill.: InterVarsity, 1995), 25.

3. Ibid.

4. Ibid.

5. Paul Tournier, *The Whole Person in a Broken World* (New York: Harper & Row, 1964), 34.

6. John 13:35

7. Ephesians 4:5

CHAPTER 8

1. John 17:21.

2. As Francis Schaeffer pleaded: "Let us raise a testimony that may still turn both the churches and society around—for the salvation of souls, the building of God's people, and at least the slowing down of the slide toward a totally humanistic society and an authoritarian suppressive state" (Schaeffer, *The Great Evangelical Disaster* [Westchester, Ill.: Crossway, 1984], 91).

3. A leading Roman Catholic cardinal convened a meeting at Regensburg, Germany, with a delegation of Reformation leaders headed by Philip Melanchthon. John Calvin was a young aide during this meeting,

which actually showed great promise that the participants would in fact resolve their dispute over the issue of justification. Calvin wrote to William Farel, "You will marvel when you read the copy [of the article on justification] . . . that our adversaries have conceded so much. For they have committed themselves to the essentials of what is our true teaching. Nothing is to be found in it which does not stand in our writings. I know that you would prefer a more explicit exposition and in this you are at one with myself. But if you consider with what sort of men we have to deal, you will acknowledge that a great deal has been achieved" (Peter Matheson, *Cardinal Contarini at Regensburg* (New York: Oxford University Press, 1972), 109.

4. Abraham Kuyper, *Lectures on Calvinism* (Reprint, Grand Rapids, Mich.: Eerdmans, 1981), 183.

5. Henry Drummond, "Mr. Moody: Some Impressions and Facts," *McClure's* 4, no. 1 (December 1894): 189.

6. Machen wrote, "Far more serious still is the division between the Church of Rome and Evangelical Protestantism in all its forms. Yet how great is the common heritage which unites the Roman Catholic with its maintenance of the authority of Holy Scripture and with its acceptance of the great early creeds, to devout Protestants today! We would not indeed obscure the difference which divides us from Rome. The gulf is indeed profound. But profound as it is it seems almost trifling compared to the abyss which stands between us and many ministers of our own church."

7. "The Gift of Salvation," *First Things* 79 (January 1998): 20–23. The full quotation from the passage cited is as follows:

Justification is central to the scriptural account of salvation, and its meaning has been much debated between Protestants and Catholics. We agree that justification is not earned by any good works or merits of our own; it is entirely God's gift, conferred through the Father's sheer graciousness, out of the love that he bears us in his Son, who suffered on our behalf and rose from the dead for our justification. Jesus was "put to death for our trespasses and raised for our justification" (Romans 4:25). In justification, God, on the basis of Christ's righteousness alone, declares us to be no longer his rebellious enemies but his forgiven friends, and by virtue of his declaration it is so.

The New Testament makes it clear that the gift of justification is received through faith. "By grace you have been saved through faith; and this is not your own doing, it is the gift of God" (Ephesians 2:8). By faith, which is also the gift of God, we repent of our sins and freely adhere to the gospel, the good news of God's saving work for us in Christ. By our response of faith to Christ, we enter into the blessings promised by the gospel. Faith is not merely intellectual assent but an act of the whole person, involving the mind, the will, and the affections, issuing in a changed life. We understand that what we here affirm is in agreement with what the Reformation traditions have meant by justification by faith alone (*sola fide*).

In justification we receive the gift of the Holy Spirit, through whom the love of God is poured forth into our hearts (Romans 5:5). The grace of Christ and the gift of the Spirit received through faith (Galatians 3:14) are experienced and expressed in diverse ways by different Christians and in different Christian traditions, but God's gift is never dependent upon our human experiences or our ways of expressing that experience.

8. C. S. Lewis, *Mere Christianity* (New York: Macmillan, 1952), 148.

9. Theologian R. C. Sproul says that the Christian puts himself in grave danger when he attempts to probe the hidden counsel of God. And Catholic theologian Father Tom Weinandy makes an interesting distinction: "There is a difference between striving for doctrinal purity and rationalistically probing the mysteries of the gospel. The true theologian or church body wishes to know ever more clearly the mysteries of the faith so that . . . we know better what the mystery is, not that we comprehend the mystery and so deprive it of its mystery. The Trinity is three persons in one God. Jesus is the one person of the Son existing as God and man. This is doctrinal purity, but the mystery survives, and actually with the clarity comes more mystery-more awe and reverence. Now the rationalistic approach does not want to clarify the mysteries of our faith but to solve them, making them completely understandable to the human mind. This can never be done" (letter from Father Weinandy to Charles Colson, 18 June 1992).

10. Kuyper, *Lectures on Calvinism,* 184.

11. W. H. Lewis, ed., *The Letters of C. S. Lewis* (New York: Harcourt Brace Jovanovich, 1966), 224 (7 December 1950).

12. See Kefa Sempangi, *A Distant Grief* (Glendale, Calif.: Regal, 1979).

13. 1 Corinthians 13:12; Richard Neuhaus, *Freedom for Ministry* (New York: Harper & Row, 1979), 87. For a development of his thought, see 86–91.

14. John Calvin to William Farel, from Strasbourg, 24 October 1538, in H. Beveridge and J. Bonnet, eds., *Selected Books of John Calvin: Tracts and Letters,* vol. 4, trans. D. Constable (Grand Rapids, Mich.: Baker, 1983), 101–2.

15. Helmut Thielicke, *Trouble with the Church* (Grand Rapids, Mich.: Baker, 1965), 104–5; note particularly Thielicke's candid discussion of changing differences between Protestants and Catholics.

16. J. Stevenson, ed., *A New Eusebius* (London: SPCK, 1957, 1987), 111–13.

17. Vatican Council II specifically repudiates this view, though many Catholics are unaware of the fact.

18. For a Roman Catholic perspective on this witness of healthy ecumenism, see Kenneth Craycraft, "Our Kind of Ecumenism: Why Catholics Need to Be More Evangelical and Vice Versa," *Crisis* (October 1991): 30–33.

19. Edward E. Plowman and J. L. Grady, eds., *National and International Religion Report,* 29 July 1991, 2.

20. EP News Service, 21 June 1991.

21. John Aker, *Lengthen Your Stride* (Old Tappan, N.J.: Revell, 1988), 190–92.

22. Steve Brown, *Key Life* (May–June 1990):4.

23. Schaeffer, *The Great Evangelical Disaster,* 160.

24. These organizations were involved as of November 2002.

25. Acts 1:4; 2:44, 46.

CHAPTER 9

1. Iain H. Murray, *Jonathan Edwards: A New Biography* (Carlisle, Pa.: Banner of Truth, 1987).

2. Following Enfield, there arose an antirevival movement that caused a number of Hampshire County pastors to band together to offer joint testimony in the year 1743 to the effect that "to the glory of God's grace . . . there has been a happy revival of religion in the congregations." The pastoral letter continues, "abiding manifestations of a serious . . . and humble spirit, and a conscientious care and watchfulness in their behavior towards God and man [have] validated the sincerity of these professions" (C. C. Goen, ed., *The Works of Jonathan Edwards,* vol. 4: The Great Awakening [New Haven: Yale University Press, 1972], 543). See also F. O. Allen, *The History of Enfield, Connecticut* (Hartford: n.p., 1900); Benjamin Trumbull, *A Complete History of Connecticut,* 2 vols. (New Haven: Maltby, Goldsmith and Co.; Samuel Wadsworth, 1818), vol. 2; E. H. Davidson, *Jonathan Edwards: The Narrative of a Puritan Mind* (Cambridge, Mass.: Harvard University Press, 1968); and Murray, *Jonathan Edwards.*

3. Matthew 28:19–20 NIV (emphasis added).

4. *Papal Encyclical on Evangelism,* January 1991; for the text, see John Paul II, "Redemptoris Missio," *Origins* 20, no. 34 (January 1991).

5. Ephesians 4.

6. Acts 20:28.

7. Lectures on the church given by Dr. Carl F. H. Henry to Prison Fellowship staff, December 1990.

8. It is important for the pastor and congregation to have a clear understanding of their respective responsibilities and expectations. One of the best such covenants we have encountered was written by Dr. Hayes Wicker upon his call to the First Baptist Church of Naples, Florida. Note also the insightful way this defines the character of the church.

COVENANT UNDERSTANDING BETWEEN PASTOR AND PEOPLE

1. We must discover the activity of God and adjust to it. It will be unique to First Baptist Naples.

2. Undergird everything with prayer.

3. We must walk by faith. Think big not small. ("With God nothing is impossible.")

4. The bottom line is not "can we afford it?" but "is it God's will?" (Where He guides He provides.)

5. Everything should be done in the light of this mission statement, "To know Christ and to make Him known." (We glorify God by reaching people.)

6. All matters should be subjected to the Scriptures. (The issue is truth not tradition or convenience.)

7. The church is a hospital for sinners not a country club for saints.

8. Problems will be dealt with, not ignored.

9. Hard work is necessary. (William Carey said, "Expect great things from God, attempt great things for God.")

10. Strive for week-long and year-long ministry (not just Sunday or the season).

11. There must be constant adjustment for growth. We cannot get overly comfortable. We must create new Bible study units, new ministries, and constantly improve the quality of education.

12. Recognizing that most people have limited time for church, then we must maximize time and do the most important.

13. Ministry is more important than meeting (committees, etc.).

14. Each Christian should discover his/her gift, passion and ministry.

15. We must seek to understand our cultural context and minister to it (baby-boomers, Florida leisure lifestyle, etc.).

16. We should strive for quality and excellence in every area (appearance, music, publication, etc.)

17. The Pastor and staff should be allowed to initiate and lead with trust, support and prayers of the church.

18. Criticism, murmuring and slander must not be allowed to disrupt the fellowship. The Deacons act as peacemakers.

19. We must recognize the need for additional staff to equip believers. (Rarely does a church have too many staff. They pay their way.) This involves more ministers and support personnel.

20. The family must be strengthened not undermined.

21. Outreach must be the priority.

22. We must be vitally concerned with meeting needs and healing hurts through ministries and developing relationships.

23. Biblical doctrine is nonnegotiable; methods are open to evaluation.

24. Since all sin and make mistakes, an attitude and atmosphere of grace must abound.

25. We must seek to develop a lighthouse ministry to all of Southwest Florida. (Drafted by Dr. Wicker and reprinted with his permission.)

9. Warren Wiersbe, *The Integrity Crisis* (Nashville: Thomas Nelson, 1988).

10. Martin Kahler, *Theologe und Christ,* cited in Helmut Thielicke, *The Trouble with the Church* (Grand Rapids, Mich.: Baker, 1965).

11. Acts 20:28.

12. 1 Corinthians 2:3.

13. Iain H. Murray, *The Forgotten Spurgeon* (Carlisle, Pa.: Banner of Truth, 1966), 45.

14. Helmut Thielicke, *The Trouble with the Church* (Grand Rapids, Mich.: Baker, 1965), 108–10. Whatever Thielicke's occasional theological deficiencies, it must be noted that after the Nazi era, university students crowded the Hamburg cathedral to hear Thielicke's sermons because of his bold resistance of Hitler; they were convinced that if a Word of God did exist, it might be found when this man spoke.

15. Ibid., 107–8.

16. Ibid.

17. Charles Finney, *Power from on High* (Fort Washington, Pa.: Christian Literature Crusade, n.d.), 108.

18. Richard Alderson, *No Holiness, No Heaven* (Carlisle, Pa.: Banner of Truth, 1986), 33.

19. *People,* 29 April 1991, last page.

20. Hosea 4:6.

CHAPTER 10

1. Louis Berkhof, *Systematic Theology* (Grand Rapids, Mich.: Eerdmans, 1978), 357.

2. Romans 14:17.

3. 1 John 1:3.

4. Cited in David Bercott, *Will the Real Heretics Please Stand Up?* (Henderson, Tex.: Scroll, 1989), 28.

5. See Berkhoff, *Systematic Theology,* 576.

6. "Abortion Rights Win Follows Bishop's Rebuke," *Washington Post,* 6 December 1989.

7. "Cardinal in Peru may excommunicate pro-choice pols," *Americans United for Separation of Church and State* 54, no. 11 (1 December 2001): 20.

8. Peter Charlton, "Via the Pope, by George," Nationwide News Pty Limited, Courier Mail, 15 May 2001: 9.

9. Merritt was just getting warmed up. Holding up his Bible, he exhorted Baptists to preach, promote, and "practice this book; and any time this word is diluted, denied, or debased we ought to defend it with pride. That is a battle worth fighting. We will go against the tide of personal opinion and political correctness. But that's all right because we are twice-born men in a once-born world, and we should never stoop to go with the flow."

But Merritt's remarks were not made in a "we-they" spirit. His greatest challenge was to his church: "Twenty years ago, our battle was against live liberalism," he concluded. "But today I candidly tell you that my greatest fear for the Southern Baptist Convention is no live liberalism, it is dead orthodoxy. I fear becoming a denomination that is straight as a gun barrel theologically, but dry as a gun barrel spiritually" ("SBC president urges biblical morality," *Biblical Recorder,* 15 June 2001).

10. For a more complete account, see Charles Colson and Ellen Vaughn, *Kingdoms in Conflict* (Grand Rapids, Mich.: Zondervan, 1987), chap. 14.

11. Greg Bahnsen, "The Challenge and Duty of Church Discipline," *Antithesis* (May–June 1990): 28.

12. Romans 12:1.

13. For the Catholic Church the seven sacraments are baptism, confirmation, Eucharist, matrimony, penance, anointing the sick, and holy orders; for the Reformers and a majority of Protestant traditions, the sacraments are baptism and communion.

14. Prison Fellowship Seminar Report, Luther Luckett Prison, LaGrange, Kentucky, 26 May 1985.

15. Matt. 26:26, 28 NIV.

16. Leviticus 10:1ff. NIV.

17. 2 Samuel 6:6.

18. 1 Corinthians 11:17–18.

19. 1 Corinthians 11:27, 29 NIV.

20. Acts 1:14.

21. Acts 1:14; 2:42–43; 4:21–31; 12:5; 16:25.

22. Acts 6:4; 13:34; 14:23.

23. William Temple, *Readings in St. John's Gospel* (New York: Macmillan, 1939), 68.

24. Charles G. Finney, *Power from on High* (Fort Washington, Pa.: Christian Literature Crusade, n.d.), 41–51. See also Psalm 66:18 NIV.

25. Psalm 66:18.

26. Healing, growth, and renewal may, of course, result from fervent prayer. Revivals in particular clearly move on the wings of prayer.

27. Richard Neuhaus, *Freedom for Ministry* (New York: Harper & Row, 1979), 126.

28. Ellen Vaughn visited the leper church in 2001. The building is completed, its cross rising into the sky above that rocky hill. And the leper fellowship is complete as well, since their church now has a pastor-a healthy young man who converted to Christ after hearing about Jesus from a leper he met on the street! For more about that church and Dois Rosser's tremendous ministry of building churches in developing nations around the world, often where governments are hostile to Christianity, we recommend Dois Rosser and Ellen Vaughn, *The God Who Hung on the Cross* (Grand Rapids, Mich.: Zondervan, 2003).

29. Although the U.S. national average for recidivism is that nearly 70 percent of ex-prisoners are re-arrested within three years of their release from prison, Prison Fellowship's Christian prison programs are showing reincarceration statistics of between 6 and 18 percent for offenders who participated in InnerChange Freedom programs for sixteen months or more before their release.

CHAPTER 11

1. Acts 5:11–14.

2. Acts 9:31.

CHAPTER 12

1. Bob McAlister, interviews with Ellen Vaughn, Columbia, S.C., August 1991.

2. 1 Corinthians 1:27, Bob's paraphrase.

3. Wardell Patterson was eventually resentenced to life in prison.

4. Bob McAlister, "Countdown to Paradise," *Jubilee* (July 1990): 4.

5. Margaret N. O'Shea, "Death Issue Difficult," *The State,* 14 June 1989, 1A.

6. Names changed.

7. Isaiah 53:5.

8. John 11:25.

9. This conversation was reconstructed from detailed notes Bob made during the Easter Sunday meeting between Rusty and Lee.

10. Later, when the birds had flown, Warden George Martin got the bird's nest as a memento for Bob McAlister. Today it sits in the den in Bob's home.

11. Warden George Martin determined that carrying out the state's sentence would be done in the most professional and dignified way possible. He told Rusty that he would do everything in his power to try to help him get through it with as little difficulty as one could expect. "Don't worry 'bout me," Rusty told the warden. "I am not going to cause you any trouble."

But George Martin was deeply troubled. He had never hidden his distaste for the death penalty from the staff or the inmates or the officials within the corrections administration, but at this point it was a matter of carrying out the official duty. The execution of another human being was an excruciating process for everyone involved, especially one as well liked by the staff as Rusty. George arranged for personal counseling to be available for any officers or staff members who felt they needed it. Quite a few did (George Martin, interview with Ellen Vaughn, Columbia, S. C., August 1991).

12. Matthew 10:19.

CHAPTER 14

1. John 18:37.

2. For a much more thorough discussion of this and related arguments about cosmology, see Charles Colson and Nancy Pearcey, *How Now Shall We Live?* (Wheaton, Ill.: Tyndale, 1999).

3. John 8:58.

4. John 1:14.

5. Immanuel Kant (1724–1804) held that the only things one could know for sure were the phenomenological. Everything else had to be accepted by faith. The well-known chair example originated with George Berkeley, the eighteenth-century Irish philosopher who postulated *esse est percippi* ("to be is to be perceived"). David Hume (1711–76), one of the Enlightenment's most influential philosophers, denied all that is supernatural and miraculous because it could not be scientifically—empirically—verified. Likewise the logical positivists (such as A. J. Ayer, in his *Language, Truth and Logic*) of this century. The result of all this was to perceive God as only a personal subjective experience and to separate Him from all other verifiable disciplines of life.

6. Wolfhart Pannenberg, "The Present and Future Church," *First Things* (November 1991): 51.

7. Colossians 1:15–17; Hebrews 1:1–3.

8. Loren Eiseley, *Darwin's Century* (New York: Doubleday, 1961), 62.

9. Another science historian states that the idea of "laws" in nature comes from the "Hebraic and Christian belief in a deity who was at once Creator and Lawgiver" (A. R. Hall, *The Scientific Revolution, 1500–1800* [Boston: Beacon, 1954] 171–72). And sociologist R. K. Merton, in his famous thesis, says that modern science owes its very existence to the Christian notion of moral obligation. Since God made the world, it is not to be despised; it is to be used for the benefit of mankind (R. K. Merton, "Puritanism, Pietism, and Science," *Sociological Review* 28, no. 1 [1936]: 37–68).

10. See Norman Podhoretz, *Breaking Ranks* (New York: Harper & Row, 1979); and Charles H. Malik, *A Christian Critique of the University* (Downers Grove, Ill.: InterVarsity, 1982).

11. Schaeffer, *The Church at the End of the Twentieth Century,* 2nd ed. (Westchester, Ill.: Crossway, 1985), 24.

12. Herbert Schlossberg, *Idols for Destruction: Christian Faith and Its Confrontation with American Society* (Nashville: Thomas Nelson, 1983), 222–27; and Donald Bloesch, *Crumbling Foundations* (Grand Rapids, Mich.: Zondervan, 1984).

13. John 17:17.

14. John 18:37.

CHAPTER 15

1. LaTonya Taylor, "The Church of O," *Christianity Today,* 1 April 2002.

2. Ibid.

3. Marc Peyser, "Paging Dr. Phil," *Newsweek,* 2 September 2002.

4. Andrew Sullivan, *New York Times,* 7 October 2001, Magazine section.

5. Ibid.

6. See columns cited in *World,* May to June 2002 special issue entitled "Osama bin Ashcroft."

7. Charles Austin, "Colson's Call to Convert Muslims is Dangerous," *The Record,* 14 February 2002: L7.

8. Charles Colson, speech to Vision New England, January 2002.

9. Nicholas Kristof, "Bigotry in Islam and Here," *New York Times,* 9 July 2002.

10. Allan Bloom, *The Closing of the American Mind* (New York: Simon & Schuster, 1987), 25.

11. From Arthur Schlesinger's speech at Brown University, in *Brown Alumni Monthly* (May 1989): 18, 22.

12. Dinesh D'Souza, *Illiberal Education: The Politics of Race and Sex on Campus* (New York: Free Press, 1991). For universities that are teaching a traditional view of truth and of the history of Western Civilization, see Charles Sykes and Brad Miner, eds., *National Review College Guide* (New York: National Review, 1991). This publication lists schools according to the criteria of intellectual environment, faculty accessibility, and credentials and curricula offered.

13. Dinesh D'Souza, "Illiberal Education," *Atlantic Monthly* (March 1991): 58.

14. *Compassion in Dying v. Washington,* 79F 3d, 790 (9th Circuit, 1996).

15. *Romer v. Evans,* 517 US 620 (1996).

16. For more in-depth material regarding world-view, see Charles Colson and Nancy Pearcey, *How Now Shall We Live?* (Wheaton, Ill.: Tyndale, 1999). Stimulated in part by the first edition of *The Body,* this volume probes the causes and effects of today's reigning world-view in far more detail. Our purposes here are simply to give an overview of worldviews and their consequences, so as to equip the Body of Christ to live and serve strategically in today's cultural climate.

17. *City Slickers,* Columbia Pictures, 1991, directed by Ron Underwood; produced by Irby Smith and Billy Crystal.

18. Caroline raised these objections with her teachers. The issue went to the principal, and for this and other reasons the book was removed from the course.

19. Richard Grenier, *Washington Times,* "'Scarlet Letter' sin is really no sin at all," 24 October 1995.

20. "The 'Animal Rights' War on Medicine," *Reader's Digest* (June 1990): 70-76.

21. Stephanie Mills, *Whatever Happened to Ecology?* (San Francisco: Sierra Club, 1999).

22. Princeton philosopher Peter Singer takes this belief system regarding human origins to its logical consequence. "On the basis of evolution," he says, ". . . there is no clear dividing line between humans and animals." [*Animal Liberation* [Warsaw, Poland: Ecco, 2002]. In Germany voters passed a law "obliging the state to respect and protect the dignity" of animals, just as it does humans. Meanwhile the Swiss are changing their laws to move animals from the realm of "things" to the realm of "beings." And in Florida, voters passed a constitutional amendment that outlaws keeping pregnant pigs from being housed in too-small stalls. As Christians, of course we want to treat pregnant pigs humanely. Not because animals are equal to humans, but because a sovereign God has given us dominion over creation and commands us to treat it with compassion and excellent stewardship.

23. Paul Johnson, "Is Totalitarianism Dead? New Temptations for Today's Intellectuals," *Crisis* (February 1989), 9–16.

24. John Taylor, "Don't Blame Me," *New York Magazine,* 3 June 1991.

25. Lou Carlozom, "The fine art of slinging mud; add the dim-bulb strategy to the list of far-fetched defenses," *Chicago Tribune,* 3 December 2001.

26. Ibid.

27. R. C. Sproul, *Lifeviews: Understanding the Ideas That Shape Society Today* (Old Tappan, N.J.: Revell, 1986), 89.

28. Oliver Wendell Holmes, Jr., quoted by Lawrence H. Summers, president of Harvard University, in his Harvard commencement address, 6 June 2002.

29. Walker Percy, *Lost in the Cosmos: The Last Self-Help Book* (New York: Washington Square, 1983).

CHAPTER 16

1. 1 Timothy 3:15.

2. John 8:32.

3. "Evangelical Beliefs on Decline, Pollster Says; Barna Research Group," *Christian Century* 111, no. 36 (14 December 1994): 1185.

4. J. Budziszewski, *The Revenge of Conscience: Politics and the Fall of Man* (Dallas: Spece, 1999).

5. Edward Rothstein, "Moral Relativity Is a Hot Topic? True. Absolutely," *New York Times* (14 July 2002).

6. For a more thorough discussion of *The Fundamentals* and the fundamentalist movement of the early twentieth century, see Ned B. Stonehouse, J. Gresham Machen: *A Biographical Memoir* (Carlisle, Pa.: Banner of Truth, 1987), 335–39; also, E. R. Sandeen, *The Roots of Fundamentalism: British and American Millenarianism, 1800–1930* (Chicago: University of Chicago Press, 1970).

7. Cal Thomas, "Guess Who's There for TV Dinner," *Washington Times,* 6 June 1991.

8. Mark 7:15, 23.

9. From transcript of *60 Minutes* 15, no. 21, as broadcast over the CBS television network, 6 February 1983.

10. Francis Schaeffer, *The Great Evangelical Disaster* (Westchester, Ill.: Crossway, 1984), 81, 102.

11. Walker Percy, *The Second Coming* (New York: Farrar, Straus & Giroux, 1980).

12. Kenneth Hunger, "When Nice People Do Bad Theology," *First Things* (April 1991): 12–15.

13. *The New Book of Christian Quotations* (Westchester, Ill.: Crossway, 1984), 226.

14. Malachi 2:2–17; Amos 2:6–8; 5:10–13; Isaiah 1:10–15, 21–23.

15. Psalm 78:1–8.

16. Micah 4:1–5.

17. 2 Corinthians 10:5.

18. Matthew 13:33.

19. Matthew 25:14–30.

20. Jesus did not intend to reform the immediate structures of His day. His mission was greater than that, and He did not succumb to Satan's attempts to sidetrack Him. Yet Christ in no way changed God's mandate that we exercise dominion over the earth. To the contrary, He taught His followers in imagery and metaphors based on the most comprehensive world-view of all: the kingdom of God.

21. Romans 12:2; Colossians 2:8; 1 Peter 1:16; 2 Corinthians 10:5.

22. Harry Blamires, *The Christian Mind: How Should a Christian Think?* (Ann Arbor, Mich.: Servant, 1978), 3–4.

23. Abraham Kuyper, *Lectures on Calvinism* (Reprint, Grand Rapids, Mich.: Eerdmans, 1981), 52.

24. Kuyper, *Lectures on Calvinism,* iii.

25. To be consistent with the Christian world-view, the church may need to engage in peaceful civil resistance. For a more in-depth discussion of this complex issue, see Chuck Colson and Ellen Vaughn, *Kingdoms in Conflict* (Grand Rapids, Mich.: Zondervan, 1989), 246-51.

26. 1 Peter 3:15.

27. How to determine consent is an interesting question, but Singer does not shrink from it. You can tell the animal's willingness, he says, by the way it behaves. The less said at this point, the better.

28. Adriel Bettelheim, "Emotionally Charged Cloning Debate Pits Advocates of Total Human Ban Against Backers of Biomedical Research," *Congressional Quarterly Weekly* (5 April 2002).

ENDNOTES

29. Anthony Dragani, "How Many?" EWTN Faith: Catholic Q & A. r=264518 and Kathleen Lavey, "World Religions Are As Varied As Its People," *Lansing State Journal* (31 March 2002): 8, and Jay Tokasz, "A Fragile Easter Unity," *Rochester Democrat and Chronicle,* 15 April 2001: 1A, and "At Least 600 Expected to Attend WEF Meet in KL," *New Straits Time,* 2 February 2001: 4.

30. There are projections, which we choose to believe, which state that Christianity will grow faster than Islam, largely because of the growth of the faith in Africa and Asia. For instance, in 1900, there were approximately 10 million Christians in Africa. In 2000, there were 360 million. By 2025, conservative estimates see that number rising to 633 million. Those same estimates put the number of Christians in Latin America in 2025 at 640 million and in Asia at 460 million. (BreakPoint)

According to Philip Jenkins, the percentage of the world's population that is, at least by name, Christian will be roughly the same in 2050 as it was in 1900. By the middle of this century there will be 3 billion Christians in the world-one and a half times the number of Muslims. In fact, by 2050 there will be nearly as many Pentecostal Christians in the world as there are Muslims today. (Philip Jenkins, *The Next Christendom: The Coming of Global Christianity* (New York: Oxford University Press, 2002).

CHAPTER 17

1. The material in this chapter is based on interviews conducted by Ellen Vaughn in Romania, Hungary, and Poland in September 1990, and by Chuck Colson in Russia, Hungary, and Czechoslovakia; we have also drawn on a wide variety of news reports, books, and articles.

2. Matthew 16:18 KJV.

3. Dr. Joseph Tson, interview with Ellen Vaughn, Oradea, Romania, 12 September 1990.

4. Paul Johnson, *Pope John Paul II and the Catholic Restoration* (Ann Arbor, Mich.: Servant, 1981), 19–20.

5. Bob Omstead, "People," *National Catholic Register,* 4 March 1990; see also Sister Nijole, *A Radiance in the Gulag* (Manassas, Va.: Trinity, n.d.).

6. William Echikson, *Lighting the Night: Revolution in Eastern Europe* (New York: William Morrow, 1990), 134.

7. Johnson, *Pope John Paul II and the Catholic Restoration,* 47.

8. Father Jan Sikorski, interview with Ellen Vaughn, Warsaw, Poland, 27 September 1990.

9. These descriptions are based on extended interviews conducted by Ellen Vaughn with priests and citizens in Krakow, Poland, 25–26 September 1990.

10. John Fox, "Murder of a Polish Priest," *Reader's Digest* (December 1985): 65, 248.

11. Grazyna Sikorskia, Jerzy Popieluszko, *A Martyr for the Truth* (Grand Rapids, Mich.: Eerdmans, n.d.), 56, 57, 58. Father Jerzy was preaching true "liberation theology." What we need to be liberated from is ego and fear, and that comes through submission to Christ. Whether under the Communist yoke in the East or materialistic bondage in the West, people need the message he delivered, made all the more poignant by his willingness to live out his commitment to the kingdom of God by refusing to knuckle under to the kingdom of man-and paying the price of death.

12. Father Antoni Lewek, *New Sanctuary of Poles* (Warsaw: n.p., 1986).

13. Peter Dugulescu, interview with Ellen Vaughn, Timosoara, Romania, 17 September 1990.

14. Echikson, *Lighting the Night,* 22.

15. Roddy Ray, "A Triumph of Spirit: Church Plays Role in Tearing Down Communism," *Orange County Register,* 2 September 1990, Knight-Ridder Newspapers, from Leipzig, East Germany; see also Lance Dickie, "Keepers of the Faith: The Lutheran Church Played a Crucial but Little-Known Role in East Germany's Peaceful Revolution," *Seattle Times,* 4 November 1990.

16. Ibid.

17. Ibid.

18. Mihai Gongola, interview with Ellen Vaughn, Arad, Romania, 14 September 1990.

19. Doru Popa, interview with Ellen Vaughn, Arad, Romania, 15 September 1990.

20. Ray, "A Triumph of Spirit."

21. Correspondents of the *New York Times, The Collapse of Communism,* ed. Bernard Gwertzman and Michael T. Kaufman (New York: New York Times Co., 1990), 237.

22. Ibid., 292.

23. Ibid., 291.

24. Ibid., 311.

25. Gelu Paul, interview with Ellen Vaughn, Timisoara, Romania, 18 September 1990.

26. Robert Cullen, "Report from Romania: Down with the Tyrant," *New Yorker,* 2 April 1990: 101.

27. Marius Miron, interview with Ellen Vaughn, Timisoara, Romania, 17 September 1990.

28. Adina Jinaru, interview with Ellen Vaughn, Timisoara, Romania, 16 September 1990.

29. Nellie Iovin, interview with Ellen Vaughn, Arad, Romania, 15 September 1990.

30. Cullen, Report from Romania, 102.

31. Ibid.

32. Many Ellen Vaughn interviewed reported this. One Romanian journalist said that Milea killed himself out of guilt because he had given the order to fire on protestors in Timisoara. The truth may never be known, but today a street in Arad, once named for Lenin, now bears the name of General Milea.

33. Bruce W. Nelan, "The Year of the People," *Time,* 1 January 1990: 46.

34. The press was not alone. U.S. embassy officials in Moscow were oblivious to the spiritual forces at work, as Colson discovered during his visit in 1990. A consular officer asked him to quiet a protest of "Baptists" wanting to emigrate; they turned out to be Pentecostals. The embassy official didn't know the difference and seemed not to care or even recognize the persecution they had suffered. In Hungary, newly elected anti-Communist politicians told Colson that the Western officials they had met had had no inkling what was coming, let alone any information about the persecuted churches.

35. From Valav Havel's New Year's Address to the Nation (LD0101133190), Prague Television Service, 1 January 1990.

CHAPTER 18

1. These quotes from Sudanese church leaders were recorded by Herb McMullan, an Episcopal priest in a Washington, D.C. suburb who traveled to Sudan on a fact-finding mission in 2001 (Herb McMullan, "Living on Faith in East Africa," American Anglican Council, *God Changes Lives for Good,* Spring 2001). In her book *In the Lion's Den,* author and international human-rights lawyer Nina Shea wrote: "Millions of American Christians pray in their churches each week, oblivious to the fact that Christians in many parts of the world suffer brutal torture, arrest, imprisonment and even death. . . . The shocking untold story of our times is that more Christians have died this century, simply for being Christian, than in the first nineteen centuries after the birth of Christ. They have been persecuted and martyred before an unknowing, indifferent world and a largely silent Christian community."

2. The oil regions have become killing fields as government forces have battled rebels for their control. A Canadian oil company, Talisman Energy, which owns 25 percent of Sudan's Greater Nile Oil Project in the Blue Nile region, has materially aided the Khartoum government's war effort. And the China National Petroleum Corporation, which owns a 40 percent stake of the same oil project, hopes to raise $5 to $7 billion to finance it through the New York Stock Exchange with help from investment bankers Goldman Sachs International. The U.S. Treasury Department has imposed sanctions on Sudan's oil companies. But they have not blocked business with Talisman or China National—which, according to Congressman Frank Wolf, is like letting a Nazi-affiliated company raise money on Wall Street.

3. Paul Campos, "Can being gay excuse infidelity?" *Rocky Mountain News,* 15 January 2002.

4. Virginia Culver, "Pastor 'outs' self; church cheers," *Denver Post,* 14 January 2002, 1A.

5. Data collected from Barna Research Institute, Ventura, Calif., 6 August 2001.

6. *Atlanta Journal Constitution,* cited in Christianity Today.com, 22 May 2000.

7. "Pro-'Gay' Mainline Church Caucus Groups Rally," Institute of Religion and Democracy Web site, 5 February 2001.

8. Ibid.

9. Ibid.

10. Ibid.

11. "Keeping Body and Soul Together: Sexuality, Spirituality, and Social Justice," authored by a seventeen-member task force on sexuality, presented to the 203rd General Assembly of the Presbyterian Church (USA) meeting in Baltimore, Maryland, 1991.

12. Ken Garfield, "Presbyterians in Stalemate over Homosexual Ordination," *Christianity Today,* 10 August 1998.

13. "God, Markets, Merges and Money," *Ottawa Citizen,* 1 August 2002.

14. From Allen O. Morris, "The Church in Bondage: Problems and Trends in the United Methodist Church" [final emphasis added].

15. John D. Levinson, "Theological Liberalism Aborting Itself," *Christian Century* 12 February 1992, 139.

16. "The Church and World Religions," *Contact,* Summer 2002.

17. Peter Kreeft, *Fundamentals of the Faith: Essays in Christian Apologetics* (San Francisco: Ignatius, 1998), 93.

18. "The Archdruid of Canterbury?", *World,* August 3, 2002

19. Mark Tooley, "World Council of Churches Leaders Oppose War on Terrorism," IRD online, 8 March 2002.

20. Ibid.

21. Mark Tooley, "Latin Bishop Denounces Capitalism at UM Meeting," IRD online, 1 April 2002.

22. Uwe Siemon-Netto, "Martyrs with Padlocked Lips," Institute on Religion and Democracy online, 5 April 2001.

23. Years ago we wrote a book on these issues. It's called *Kingdoms in Conflict,* and it is still being read by Christians in politics around the world (Wheaton, Ill.: Tyndale, 1989). When I was in the former Soviet Union the year that the Iron Curtain fell, a luncheon was hosted for me with members of the Russian Parliament. Many of them brought their copies of *Kingdoms in Conflict* for me to sign.

24. George Gallup, Jr. and D. Michael Lindsay, *Surveying the Religious Landscape: Trends in U.S. Beliefs* (Harrisburg, Ps.: Morehouse, 1999), 40.

25. Wade Clark Roof, *Spiritual Marketplace: Baby Boomers and the Remaking of American Religion* (Princeton, N.J.: Princeton University Press, 1999).

26. "TBN Gives Platform to Prominent New Age Advocate," CRI Report, May 2002.

27. See Isaiah 6.

28. Numbers 3:4.

29. Luke 18:9, 11–12.

30. Luke 18:14.

CHAPTER 19

1. We are deeply indebted to Roland Bainton for his landmark 1950 biography of Martin Luther, *Here I Stand: A Life of Martin Luther,* which was of tremendous help in crafting this chapter. For readers who would like to further explore Luther's colorful life and thought, we recommend the following works: Roland Bainton, *Here I Stand: A Life of Martin Luther* (New York: Abingdon-Cokesbury, 1950); R. H. Fife, *The Revolt of Martin Luther* (New York: Columbia University Press, 1957), a more standard work; Eric W. Gritsch, *Martin—God's Court Jester: Luther in Retrospect* (Philadelphia: Fortress, 1985), a very readable work combining biography and some theological reflection; E. G. Schwiebert, *Luther and His Times: The Reformation from a New Perspective* (Saint Louis: Concordia, 1950), a historical biography; P. Smith, *The Life and Letters of Martin Luther* (New York: Barnes and Noble, 1968); Martin Brecht, *Martin Luther: His Road to Reformation, 1483–1521,* trans. J. L. Schaff (Philadelphia: Fortress, 1985), the first in a threefold division of Luther's life; Heinrich Bornkamm, *Luther in Mid-Career, 1521–1530* (Philadelphia: Fortress, 1983), the second of a series of three (the third part of this trilogy, written in 1983, awaits translation into English). The Brecht and Bornkamm works, though written on a more scholarly level, constitute perhaps the most thorough biographical study yet attempted on Luther and would satisfy the needs of any Luther student. With regard to works written by Luther himself, we refer readers to Jaroslav Pelikan and H. T. Lehmann, eds., *Luther's Works,* 55 vols. (Philadelphia: Fortress; Saint Louis: Concordia, 1955). Between 1516 and 1546 Luther published 93 forewords, 13 lectures, 64 open letters, 29 expositions of Scripture, 22 disputations, 178 sermons, and 130 treatises.

2. Bainton, *Here I Stand,* 21–22.

3. Based on Luther's quote in Ibid., 44.

4. Ibid.

5. Ibid., 50.

ENDNOTES

6. Ibid.

7. Ibid., 59–60

8. Pelikan and Lehmann, "Introduction to the Theses," *Luther's Works*, 31.

9. Albrecht did not attain his archbishopric by means of his piety or commitment to Christ. Rather, he had paid Rome the equivalent of $250,000 to become archbishop. The bulk of these funds were recouped through the sale of indulgences.

10. Bainton, *Here I Stand*, 65.

11. Ibid., 77.

12. Ibid., 117.

13. Ibid.

14. Ibid., 140.

15. Ibid., 143.

CHAPTER 20

1. Roland H. Bainton, *Here I Stand: A Life of Martin Luther* (New York: Abingdon, 1977), 145.

2. People further the confusion by defining justice in secular terms-everyone getting his or her due-then politicizing that interpretation depending on their partisan leanings. Conservatives often suppose that justice means punishing wrongdoers, while liberals assert that it means everyone getting a fair share of society's benefits. Both are embraced within, but fall far short of, the full biblical meaning.

3. Martin Luther, *The Babylonian Captivity*, in *Luther's Works*, 55 vols, ed. H. T. Lehmann and A. R. Wentz, (Philadelphia: Fortress, 1959), 36:54.

4. In this, radical though it sounded at the time, Luther was simply restoring the teaching of the early church fathers that work had dignity and was a Christian virtue and duty, an act of service to God as master.

5. Sadly, as Francis Schaeffer points out, the church at large did little to actually guide the tide of increased wealth during the Industrial Revolution. While there were individual attempts to do so, for the most part the church ignored biblical principles regarding the use of wealth. This lack of Christian compassion was partially responsible for the abuses of the day: the slums in industrial towns, the exploitation of children and women in particular, the vast gulf between the wealth of the few and the misery of the many, and the growth of the slave trade. Reform-minded Christians eventually woke up and addressed these abuses (Francis Schaeffer, *How Shall We Then Live? The Rise and Decline of Western Thought and Culture* [Old Tappan, N.J.: Revell, 1976]).

6. Pope John Paul II, "Centesimus Annus ('The 100th Year')," *Origins* 21, no. 1 (16 May 1991): 1–23.

7. Some zealous Reformers were known to destroy invaluable works that they saw as graven images, so the Reformation gained a reputation among some as being anti-art. What is not known-or at least not stated-is that the destruction was often carried out by those who had donated the art to the churches in the first place, and the smashing, say of an image of a saint, was not done to denigrate its beauty or the saint per se, but was a statement by the donor that donations to the church could not buy salvation-and that no other gods came before the holy Lord.

8. Schaeffer points out that Rembrandt's work shows the tensions and balances of the Reformation spirit: He neither idealized nature nor demeaned it. As he portrayed both man's potential for greatness and his proclivity to evil, Rembrandt's world-view encompassed both man's sin and God's grace.

9. J. Pelikan and H. T. Lehmann, eds., *Luther's Works*, 55 vols. (Philadelphia: Fortress; St. Louis: Concordia, 1955), 53:323.

10. For Luther, Christians, of all people, should be in tune with God's creation, using their hearts and minds and bodies for the fullest for His glory. Part of this entailed "recovery of the external world," which had been obscured as a result of the Fall. E. W. Gritsch, author of *Martin-God's Court Jester: Luther in Perspective* (Philadelphia: Fortress, 1983) argues that Luther's sense of wonder at God's creation is sorely needed among Christians who are often blinded by the forces of anxiety, guilt, and self-righteousness. Luther helped later generations embrace a holistic view of life contrary to the bifurcated view of theological and philosophical anthropologies dominated by dualistic separations of mind/body and flesh/spirit."

11. Pope John Paul II, "Cristifideles Laici ('Apostolic Exhortation on the Vocation and Mission of the Lay Faithful in the Church and in the World')," *Origins* 18, no. 35 (9 February 1989).

ENDNOTES

12. *L'osservatore Romano,* weekly edition in English, 14 October 1991, 7–8.

13. Joey Veenker, "Lutherans and Catholics Sign Declaration on Justification," *Christianity Today* (25 October 1999).

14. Joseph Cardinal Ratzinger, *Introduction to Christianity* (San Francisco: Ignatius, 1990), 57.

CHAPTER 21

1. John 14:12.

2. John 14:16–17.

3. John 17:20.

4. While there are exceptions-like prisoners who come to Christ in solitary confinement but are not able to become part of a church particular, even though they are part of the church universal-it is normative for believers to gather together, and some in hostile circumstances do so under great hardship. For example, former hostage Terry Anderson wrote movingly of his fellowship with his Catholic and Protestant brethren—the Church of the Locked Door—during his captivity in Lebanon (see "How They Survived," *Newsweek,* 16 December 1991, 34–37).

CHAPTER 22

1. Matthew 28:18–20.

2. Ephesians 4:11–16.

3. See 2 Peter 1:16 and 2 Corinthians 10:5.

4. For reference to numerical growth, see Acts 2:46–47; for qualitative growth see also Hebrews 5:11–6:3. The delineation and definition of these seven points taken from T. M. Moore, *Teaching in the Spirit: A Workbook and Training Program for Christian Education in the Church* (Ellicott City, Md.: Chesapeake Publications, 1989), 51–53.

5. Ephesians 4:11–12.

6. Jacques Ellul, *Presence of the Kingdom* (New York: Seabury, 1948), 19.

7. Para-local church ministries, or what we often call parachurch organizations, are ministries and movements that come alongside the local church to equip members with specialized skills for ministry. Prison Fellowship, for example, exists to "exhort and assist the church in its ministry" to those affected by crime, seeking to equip believers with expertise and resources for ministry to prisoners, ex-prisoners, victims of crime, and their families that local churches would not ordinarily have at their disposal. Dozens of ministries do the same thing in a variety of different arenas of need.

8. 1 Peter 3:15.

9. For more information about world-view coursework, check out our Web site at www.wilberforce.org. Also, the *How Now Shall We Live?* film series produced by LifeWay is an excellent resource not only for ethics, but for full-spectrum world-view teaching.

10. "Quotables," *World,* 17, no. 24 (2 October 2002).

11. April 2002 poll of 401 randomly selected college seniors at public and private four-year institutions, conducted by Zogby International and the National Association of Scholars as reported in the *Chronicle of Higher Education,* 3 July 2002.

12. ELF, established in 1986 by twelve Christian business executives, trains people to think through situations like these: You're a young career person ranking in the top 10 percent of your company's sales. In order to boost sales in a depressed economy, the company has asked you to engage in questionable tactics. What do you do? You are a high school teacher. One of your students is under extreme pressure from home to make good grades and is abused verbally, and possibly physically, when she makes anything lower than a B. She has worked hard, but her average in math turns out to be three points short of a B. What do you do? Other resources include Gordon College in Wenham, Mass., which conducts ethics seminars and offers course material. So do Biola University in La Mirada, Calif., Ligonier Ministries in Orlando, Fla., and the C. S. Lewis Institute in Washington, D. C.

13. See also Keith Fournier, *Bringing Christ's Presence into Your Home: Your Family as a Domestic Church* (Nashville: Thomas Nelson, 1992), which deals with the themes of the family as domestic church and the church as family.

14. Mike McManus, *Marriage Savers*, (Grand Rapids, Mich.: Zondervan, 1995).

15. Patrick E. Fagan, "Encouraging Marriage and Discouraging Divorce," *Heritage Foundation Report*, no. 1421 (26 March 2001): 1.

16. W. Bradford Wilcox, "Recapturing the Theological Voice," *What Next for the Marriage Movement: A Strategic Discussion* (New York: Center of the American Experiment, Coalition of Marriage, Family and Couples Education, 2002): 7.

17. At Fullerton's Evangelical Free Church, kids confront similar temptations and problems in a very different environment. They see their parents' expensive lifestyles and the peer pressure and temptations are all around them. So in equipping these kids to avoid the attitudes of the world, Youth Pastor Eric Heard focuses on the antidote to materialism: service. "We offer a lot of service ministries to show them that there's something bigger in life than making a buck," says Eric. Over the past eight years the youth group has built an orphanage in Mexico and in the process established a strong relationship with the children. They put up a small house for a woman and her two children who were living in a shack beyond description. The kids also visit convalescent homes and minister to the inner-city homeless at the L.A. Mission. "We are committed to helping kids see that they don't have to buy into what the culture is saying," says Eric. "It's tough, but it's definitely worthwhile."

18. For a more detailed discussion of the work ethic and its loss in America, see Chuck Colson and Jack Eckerd, *Why America Doesn't Work* (Dallas: Word, 1991).

19. See www.crown.org.

20. For more about Prison Fellowship, see www.pfm.org.

21. Harvest staff and volunteers speak to adult Sunday school classes, Sunday evening services, youth groups, annual missions conferences, and seminarians regarding issues of homosexuality and AIDS. All their training is intended to equip believers to better understand sexual brokenness and the specific means of healing God offers through the power of His Holy Spirit. Regeneration, a ministry of a number of churches in the Baltimore, Maryland, and Northern Virginia areas, fosters support groups for prayer, discipleship, and reorientation.

Regeneration also sponsors a twenty-one week, intensive discipleship program called New Directions, to help those struggling with homosexual temptations and to challenge them to become an integral part of a local church.

New Beginnings, a ministry of Whittier Area Baptist Fellowship, is designed for gays and lesbians who want to go straight and live under the lordship of Christ. One member of the group was a pastor from a nearby church. He was struggling with bisexuality, but rather than firing him, his church put him under discipline and told him that if he would deal with the issue, they would consider keeping him on. The pastor agreed and attended the New Beginnings group for a year. At the end of that time he had made so much progress that the church brought him back as their pastor. "It was a story of remarkable spiritual and personal breakthrough," says Whittier Baptist Fellowship Pastor Lee Eliason.

22. See www.exodusnorthamerica.org.

CHAPTER 23

1. The Templeton Prize awards the world's largest cash prize, over one million dollars. Chuck did not accept the money personally, but directed that it be given to the ministry of Prison Fellowship.

2. 1 Samuel 8:4–22; 10:19; 12:19.

3. *Christianity Today International/Leadership Journal* 22, no. 1 (Winter 2001), 89.

4. Shiloh Place Ministries, 2000.

5. Why Divorce is Increasing," *The Gleaner*, Global News Wire, 19 May 2002.

6. James 2:1–9.

7. Matthew 20:26; Mark 9:35; 10:41–45; Luke 22:24–27.

8. Hebrews 2:9–11.

9. Philippians 2:5–8.

10. "Deliver Us from Evil," *Christianity Today*, 9 November 1984, 35.

11. Mihai has finished the race. He continued to minister in Romania, pouring himself out for the sake of Christ and his fellow Romanians. Several years ago he was driving home after preaching at a poor coun-

try church one Sunday night. Exhausted, he fell asleep at the wheel—and was killed when his car smashed into a tree.

12. J. Oswald Sanders, *Spiritual Leadership* (Chicago: Moody, 1967, 1980).

13. F. Booth Tucker, *Muktifanj, or Forty Years with the Salvation Army in India and Ceylon* (London: Marshall Brothers, n.d.).

14. William P. Showalter, "Zinzendorf, That Remarkable Man of God," *Crosspoint* (Summer 1991): 25.

15. Dietrich Bonhoeffer, *Letters and Papers from Prison,* ed. Eberhard Bethge (New York: Macmillan, 1967), 11–12.

CHAPTER 24

1. Details in these descriptions come from James A. Michener, *Poland* (New York: Random House, 1983), 514; and from William L. Shirer, *The Rise and Fall of the Third Reich: A History of Nazi Germany* (New York: Touchstone, 1959), 967–74. This chapter is based on interviews in Warsaw, Auschwitz, and Niepokalanow in Poland, conducted by Ellen Vaughn in September 1990.

2. Maria Winowska, *Our Lady's Fool* (Westminster, Md.: Newman, 1952), 138–39.

3. Sergius C. Lorit, *The Last Days of Maximilian Kolbe* (New York: New City, 1968), 142.

4. Shirer, *Rise and Fall of the Third Reich,* 937.

5. Ibid., 938.

6. Some biographers say Kolbe went to meet the Nazis. Father George at Niepokalanow told Ellen Vaughn that Kolbe was arrested in his room.

CHAPTER 25

1. Acts 1:8.

2. Chaplain Thaddeus Horbowy, quoted in "Maximilian Kolbe," Jewish Virtual Library Web site, www.us-israel.org

3. 2 Timothy 4:5; Acts 8:29; 21:8.

4. Garth Rosell, "Charles Gradison Finney," in *Great Leaders of the Christian Church,* ed. John D. Woodbridge (Chicago: Moody, 1988), 318.

5. For a detailed analysis of Billy Graham's discipleship-centered crusades, see Sterling W. Huston, *Crusade Evangelism and the Local Church* (Minneapolis: World Wide Publications, 1984).

6. Waldron Scott, "Discipleship Evangelism," in *Evangelism: The Next Ten Years,* ed. Sherwood Eliot Wirt (Waco, Tex.: Word, 1978), 106.

7. We cannot recommend Tim Keller's writings and tapes highly enough. The ideas we are summarizing here are just the tip of a mammoth iceberg of thoughtful writings whose ideas are not just academic, but have been lived out in the reality of Redeemer's life in New York. See "The Missional Church," by Tim Keller, November 2001, one of a number of papers available through Redeemer's excellent Web site, www.redeemer.com. One more note: In keeping with Redeemer's missional mind-set, when you're in New York, don't visit Redeemer! They need the seats for people from their neighborhoods who don't yet know Christ.

8. The "Why I Believe" tape series, available on the Wilberforce Forum Web site, is a helpful tool toward this end.

9. See Redeemer's Web site, www.redeemer.org, "Fellowship Groups."

10. Due to cultural, religious, and political sensitivities in India, it is not appropriate for us to include more specific data and details here. But for related information on the model of these kind of culture-changing cell churches, please see Dr. Robert M. Lewis and Rob Wilkins, *The Church of Irresistible Influence* (Grand Rapids, Mich.: Zondervan, 2001).

11. Lee's bestselling books that chronicle his own spiritual journey and clear apologetics for Christian faith include Gold Medallion winners *The Case for Christ* and *The Case for Faith.*

12. From Ellen Vaughn interview with Lee Strobel, 24 August 1991.

13. Acts 4:20.

CHAPTER 26

1. Matthew 5:13–16.

2. Job 6:6. Salt was also used to season incense (Exodus 30:35); all offerings were to be salted (Leviticus 2:13; Ezekiel 43:24); salt was a symbol for the covenant (Leviticus 2:13; 2 Kings 2:20; 2 Chronicles 13:5).

3. Tom Phillips, phone interview with Chuck Colson, November 1991.

4. E. C. Baig, "Profiting with Help from Above," *Time*, 27 April 1987, 37.

5. From jacket blurb of the 1968 Macmillan paperback edition.

6. Lewis's science fiction trilogy—*Out of the Silent Planet, Perelandra*, and *That Hideous Strength*—evoke elements of the gospel story in a different way for adults.

7. Kurt Bruner and Jim Ware, *Finding God in the Lord of the Rings* (Wheaton, Ill.: Tyndale, 2001), x.

8. Katherine Paterson, *Gates of Excellence* (New York: E. P. Dutton, 1981), 18.

9. Walker Percy, "A View of Abortion, With Something to Offend Everybody," in *Signposts in a Strange Land* (New York: Farrar, Straus and Giroux, 1991), 340.

10. Percy used language and illustrations that may offend some Christians, even as they pound home Christian truth to secularly minded readers.

11. John Grisham, *The Testament* (New York: Doubleday, 1999).

12. *Chicago Tribune*, 12 April 2002: Metro section, 8.

CHAPTER 27

1. Chuck visited Ceausescu in Romania in 1973, and the two talked for more than an hour. He was a charming rogue. President Richard Nixon and Ceausescu were fast friends because each could use the other-and did.

2. Hannah Pakula, "Elena Ceausescu: The Shaping of an Ogress," *Vanity Fair* (August 1990): 166.

3. Cited in *Programs of Compassionate Intervention for Romanian Orphans* (Monrovia, Calif.: World Vision, 1992).

4. Marius Moon, interview with Ellen Vaughn, Timisoara, Romania, 17 September 1990.

5. See Laszlo Tokes and David Porter, *The Fall of Tyrants* (Westchester, Ill.: Crossway, 1991).

6. Ibid., 95.

7. Ibid., 104.

8. Lajos Varga, interview with Ellen Vaughn, Budapest, Hungary, 19 September 1990; see also Robert Cullen, "Report from Romania," *New Yorker*, 2 April 1990, 94–112.

9. Tokes and Porter, *The Fall of Tyrants*, 3–4.

10. Jack Friedman and Traudl Lessing, "Laszlo Tokes, The Pastor Who Helped to Free Romania, Is Home," *People*, 5 February 1990, 63ff.

11. Tokes and Porter, *The Fall of Tyrants*, 11.

12. Cullen, "Report from Romania," 96.

13. Peter Dugulescu, interview with Ellen Vaughn, Timosoara, Romania, 17 September 1990.

14. Adina Jinaru, interview with Ellen Vaughn, Timosoara, Romania, 16 September 1990.

15. Unfortunately, as Tokes makes clear in his account, the character of the crowd by this time was not entirely peaceful or Christian. Some became violent and headed downtown, where they tangled with the Securitate and started setting government-only shops on fire.

16. Peter Dugulescu, interview with Ellen Vaughn, Timisoara, Romania, 17 September 1990.

RECOMMENDED READING

We could not presume to list the wealth of great books written through the centuries on the character and mission of the church. Nor have we cataloged here an exhaustive list of theological and doctrinal resources. But many of the following books and articles have been helpful in the preparation of this book. We recommend them for readers who would like to dig a bit deeper into the historical mandate of the church.

Aker, John D. *Lengthen Your Stride.* Old Tappan, N.J.: Revell, 1988.

Anderson, Leith. *A Church for the 21st Century.* Minneapolis: Bethany House, 1992.

Atkins, Stanley, and Theodore McConnell, eds. *Churches on the Wrong Road.* Chicago: Regnery Gateway, 1986.

Augustine. *City of God.* Translated by J. Healey. New York: E. P. Dutton and Co., 1956.

———. *On Christian Doctrine.* Translated by D. W. Robertson. New York: Bobbs–Merrill Co., 1958.

Bainton, Roland. *The Age of the Reformation.* Coronado, Calif.: D. Van Nostrand, 1956.

———. *Here I Stand: A Life of Martin Luther.* New York: Abingdon/Cokesbury, 1950.

———. *The Horizon History of Christianity.* New York: Avon, 1966.

———. *The Reformation of the Sixteenth Century*. Boston: Beacon, 1952.

Banister, Doug. *The Word and Power Church*. Grand Rapids, Mich.: Zondervan, 1999.

Bannerman, D. Douglas. *The Scriptural Doctrine of the Church*. Grand Rapids, Mich.: Eerdmans, 1955.

Barna, George. *The Frog in the Kettle*. Glendale, Calif.: Regal, 1990.

———. *The Power of Vision*. Ventura, Calif.: Regal, 1992.

———. *Turning Vision into Action*. Ventura, Calif.: Regal, 1996.

———. *User Friendly Churches*. Glendale, Calif.: Regal, 1991.

Barrett, C. K. *Church, Ministry, and Sacraments in the New Testament*. Grand Rapids, Mich.: Eerdmans, 1985.

Basden, Paul, and David S. Dockery, eds. *The People of God: Essays on the Believers' Church*. Nashville: Broadman, 1990.

Baxter, Ern. "What Makes God Angry?" *New Wine* (January 1978): 4–15.

Berger, Peter. *The Noise of Solemn Assemblies: Christian Commitment and the Religious Establishment in America*. New York: Doubleday, 1961.

———., and Richard John Neuhaus, eds. *Against the World for the World*. New York: Seabury, 1976.

Bettenson, H., ed. *Documents of the Christian Church*. New York: Oxford University, 1970.

———. *Early Christian Fathers*. New York: Oxford University, 1956.

Billingsley, K. L. *From Mainline to Sideline: The Social Witness of the National Council of Churches*. Washington, D.C.: Ethics and Public Policy Center, 1990.

Blamires, Harry. *The Christian Mind: How Should a Christian Think?* Reprint, Ann Arbor, Mich.: Servant, 1978.

————. *The Faith and Modern Error: An Essay on the Christian Message in the Twentieth Century.* New York: Macmillan, 1956.

————. *Where Do We Stand?: An Examination of the Christian's Position in the Modern World.* Ann Arbor, Mich.: Servant, 1980.

Blattner, John C. "One-to-One Pastoral Care." *Faith & Renewal,* 13 February 1988, 3–11.

————. *Leading Christians to Maturity.* Altamonte Springs, Fla.: Creation House, 1987.

———— et al., eds. *Center for Pastoral Renewal Series.* Ann Arbor, Mich.: Servant, n.d.

Bloesch, Donald G. *The Church.* Downer's Grove, Ill.: InterVarsity, 2002.

————. *The Christian Witness in a Secular Age.* Minneapolis: Augsburg, 1968.

————. *Essentials of Evangelical Theology.* 2 vols. Reprint, New York: Harper & Row, 1982.

————. *The Evangelical Renaissance.* Grand Rapids, Mich.: Eerdmans, 1973.

————. "The Finality of Christ and Religious Pluralism." *Touchstone,* 3 April 1991, 4–9.

————. *The Future of Evangelical Christianity: A Call for Unity Amid Diversity.* New York: Doubleday, 1983.

————. *The Reform of the Church.* Grand Rapids, Mich.: Eerdmans, 1970.

————, and Robert Webber, eds. *The Orthodox Evangelicals.* Nashville: Thomas Nelson, 1978.

Boice, James M., ed. *Transforming Our World: A Call to Action.* Portland, Oreg.: Multnomah, 1988.

Braaten, Carl. *Mother Church.* Grand Rapids, Mich.: Eerdmans, 1998.

RECOMMENDED READING

Calvin, John. *Institutes of the Christian Religion*. Edited by J. T. McNeill and F. L. Battles. 2 vols. Philadelphia: Westminster, 1960.

Campenhausen, Hans von. *Ecclesiastical Authority and Spiritual Power*. Palo Alto, Calif.: Stanford University, 1969.

Chadwick, Henry. *The Early Church*. New York: Penguin, 1967.

Chadwick, O. *The Reformation*. London: SCM, 1964.

Charles, J. Daryl. "Pomp, Circumstance and Capitulation." *Faith & Renewal* 17, no. 3 (1992): 26–27.

Clowney, Edmund P. *The Biblical Doctrine of the Church*. Philadelphia: Westminster Theological Seminary, 1979.

———. *The Church*. Downer's Grove, Ill.: Intervarsity, 1995.

Cochrane, Charles N. *Christianity and Classical Culture: A Study of Thought and Action from Augustus to Constantine*. New York and London: Clarendon, 1940.

Coleman, Richard J. *Issues of Theological Conflict*. Grand Rapids, Mich.: Eerdmans, 1972.

Cook, Harold. "Who Really Sent the First Missionaries?" *Evangelical Missions Quarterly* 12 (1975): 233–39.

Craycraft, Kenneth R. "Our Kind of Ecumenism: Why Catholics Need to Be More Evangelical and Vice Versa." *Crisis* (October 1991): 30–33.

Davis, John Jefferson. *Foundations of Evangelical Theology*. Grand Rapids, Mich.: Baker, 1984.

Dawson, Christopher. *Christianity and the New Age*. Manchester, N.H.: Sophia Institute, 1985.

Demarest, Bruce, and Gordon Lewis. *Integrative Theology*. Grand Rapids, Mich.: Zondervan, 1987, 1990.

Dever, Mark E. *Nine Marks of a Healthy Church*. Westchester, Ill.: Crossway, 2000.

Dulles, Avery. *Models of the Church*. New York: Doubleday, 1974.

Edge, Findley B. *A Quest for Vitality in Religion*. Nashville: Broadman, 1963.

Edwards, David L., and John Stott. *Evangelical Essentials: A Liberal–Evangelical Dialogue*. Downers Grove, Ill.: InterVarsity, 1988.

Edwards, Jonathan. *The Works of Jonathan Edwards*. 2 vols. Carlisle, Pa.: Banner of Truth, 1984.

Ellul, Jacques. *The Presence of the Kingdom*. New York: Seabury, 1948, 1967.

———. *The Subversion of Christianity*. Reprint, Grand Rapids, Mich.: Eerdmans, 1988.

Engel, James F. and William A. Dyrness, *Changing the Mind of Missions: Where Have We Gone Wrong*. Downers Grove, Ill.: Intervarsity, 2000.

Erickson, Millard J. *Christian Theology*. 3 vols. Grand Rapids, Mich.: Baker, 1983–85.

Eusebius. *The History of the Church from Christ to Constantine*. Translated by G. A. Williamson. Minneapolis: Augsburg, 1965.

The Faith of the Early Fathers. Translated by W. A. Jurgens. Collegeville, Minn.: Liturgical, 1970.

Finney, Charles G. *Power from on High*. Philadelphia: Christian Literature Crusade, n.d.

———. *Revivals of Religion*. London: Oliphant, 1928.

Fournier, Keith A. *Bringing Christ's Presence into Your Home: Your Family as a Domestic Church*. Nashville: Thomas Nelson, 1992.

———. *Evangelical Catholics*. Nashville: Thomas Nelson, 1990.

Frame, John M. *Evangelical Reunion: Denominations and the Body of Christ*. Grand Rapids, Mich.: Baker, 1991.

Frazee, Randy. *The Connecting Church.* Grand Rapids, Mich.: Zondervan, 2001.

Gallup, George, Jr., and Jim Castelli. *The People's Religion.* New York: Macmillan, 1989.

————, and Timothy K. Jones. *The Saints Among Us.* Ridgefield, Conn.: Morehouse, 1992.

Gibbs, Eddie. *Church Next: Quantum Changes in How We Do Ministry.* Downers Grove, Ill.: Intervarsity, 2000.

Goerge, Timothy, ed., *John Calvin and the Church: A Prism of Reform.* Westminster: John Knox Press, 1990.

Green, Michael. *Called to Serve.* London: Hodder & Stoughton, 1978.

————. *Evangelism and the Early Church.* Grand Rapids, Mich.: Eerdmans, 1976.

————. *Evangelism Then and Now.* Downers Grove, Ill.: InterVarsity, 1979.

Greene, Colin. "Spirit–Led Evangelism." *Renewal* (June 1991): 37–39.

Gritsch, Eric W. *Martin—God's Court Jester: Luther in Retrospect.* Philadelphia: Fortress, 1983.

Guiness, Os. *The American Hour: A Time of Reckoning and the Once and Future Role of Faith.* New York: Free Press, 1992.

Hall, Douglas John. *The End of Christendom and the Future of Christianity.* Harrisburg: Trinity, 1997.

Harper, Michael. *Let My People Grow!* London: Hodder & Stoughton, 1977.

Hastings, Adrian. *A Concise Guide to the Documents of the Second Vatican.* Greenwood, S.C.: Darton, Longman and Todd, 1968.

Hauerwas, Stanley, and William Willimon. *Resident Aliens.* Nashville: Abingdon, 1989.

Henry, Carl F. H., ed. *Basic Christian Doctrines.* New York: Holt, Rinehart & Winston, 1962.

———. *Christian Countermoves in a Decadent Culture.* Portland, Oreg.: Multnomah, 1986.

———. *Evangelicals in Search of Identity.* Waco, Tex.: Word, 1976.

———. *God, Revelation and Authority.* 6 vols. Waco, Tex.: Word, 1976–83.

———, ed. *Revelation and the Bible: Contemporary Evangelical Thought.* Grand Rapids, Mich.: Baker, 1958.

———. *Toward a Recovery of Christian Belief.* Westchester, Ill.: Crossway, 1990.

Heppe, Heinrich. *Reformed Dogmatics.* Translated by G. T. Thomson. New York: George Allen and Unwin, 1950.

Hillerbrand, H. J. *Christendom Divided.* New York: Theological Resources, 1971.

———. *The World of the Reformation.* London: Hodder & Stoughton, 1975.

Horton, Michael S. *The Agony of Deceit.* Chicago: Moody, 1990.

———. "Members Only." *Modern Reformation* (July/August 1991): 1–3.

Hughes, Kent, and Barbara Hughes. *Liberating Ministry from the Success Syndrome.* Wheaton, Ill.: Tyndale, 1987.

Hunsberger, George R. and Craig Van Gelder, eds. *The Church Between Gospel and Culture.* Grand Rapids, Mich.: Eerdmans, 1996.

Hunter, James Davison. *American Evangelicalism: Conservative Religion and the Quandary of Modernity.* New Brunswick, N.J.: Rutgers University Press, 1983.

———. "The Evangelical Worldview Since 1890." In *Piety and Politics: Evangelicals Confront the World.* Edited by Richard John Neuhaus and Michael Cromartie. Washington, D.C.: Ethics and Public Policy Center, 1987, 19–53.

———. *Evangelicals: The Coming Generation*. Chicago: University of Chicago, 1987.

Hunter, Kenneth E. "When Nice People Do Bad Theology." *First Things* (April 1991): 12–15.

Huston, Sterling. *Crusade Evangelism and the Local Church*. Minneapolis: Worldwide Publications, 1984.

John Paul II. "Cristifideles Laici." *Origins* 18, no. 35 (February 1989).

———. *The Lay Members of Christ's Faithful People*. Boston: Daughters of St. Paul, n.d.

———. "Redemptoris Missio." *Origins* 20, no. 34 (January 1991).

Karkkainen, Veli–Matti. *An Introduction to Ecclesiology*. Downer's Grove, Ill.: Intervarsity, 2002.

Kelly, George A. *The Battle for the American Church*. New York: Doubleday, 1979.

Kelly, J. N. D. *Early Christian Creeds*. London: Longmans, Green & Co., 1950.

Kimel, Alvin F., Jr. "The God Who Likes His Name." *Interpretation* 45 (1991): 147–58.

Kreeft, Peter. "The Good War." *Christianity Today,* 17 December 1990, 29–31.

Kuyper, Abraham. *Lectures on Calvinism*. Grand Rapids, Mich.: Eerdmans, Reprint, 1981.

Ladd, George E. *Jesus and the Kingdom*. New York: Harper & Row, 1964.

Latourette, Kenneth Scott. *A History of the Expansion of Christianity*. 7 vols. Grand Rapids, Mich.: Zondervan, 1970.

LeBlanc, Doug. "The Catholic Temptation: An Evangelical's Second Thoughts." *Crisis* (March 1991): 30–32.

Leith, John L., ed. *Creeds of the Churches*. Atlanta, Ga.: John Knox, 1979.

Little, Joyce A. "Naming Good and Evil." *First Things* (May 1992): 23–30.

Lovelace, Richard F. *Dynamics of Spiritual Life: An Evangelical Theology of Renewal.* Downers Grove, Ill.: InterVarsity, 1979.

Luther, Martin. *Selected Writings of Martin Luther.* Translated by T. G. Tappert. 4 vols. Philadelphia: Fortress, 1967.

Malphurs, Aubrey. *Developing Vision for Ministry in the 21st Century.* Grand Rapids: Baker, 1999.

Marsden, George. *Fundamentalism and American Culture.* New York: Oxford University, 1980.

Martin, Ralph. *A Crisis of Truth.* Ann Arbor, Mich.: Servant, 1982.

McGrath, Alister E. "Doctrine and Ethics." *Journal of the Evangelical Theological Society* 34, no. 2 (1991): 145–56.

McLaren, Brian D. *The Church on the Other Side.* Grand Rapids: Zondervan, 2000.

Miller, Donald E. *Reinventing American Protestantism: Christianity in the New Millennium.* Berkeley: University of California Press, 1997.

Mills, David. "The Creed of Our Salvation." *Mission and Ministry* (Spring 1992): 1–7.

Minear, Paul. *Images of the Church in the New Testament.* Philadelphia: Westminster, 1960.

Moore, T. M. *Teaching in the Spirit: A Workbook and Training Program for Christian Education in the Church.* Ellicott City, Md.: Chesapeake Publications, 1989.

Muggeridge, Malcolm. *The Third Testament.* Boston: Little, Brown and Co., 1976.

Murray, Iain H. *Jonathan Edwards: A New Biography.* Carlisle, Pa.: Banner of Truth, 1984.

Neuhaus, Richard John. *The Catholic Moment.* New York: Harper & Row, 1987.

———. *Freedom for Ministry.* New York: Harper & Row, 1979.

———. *The Naked Public Square: Religion and Democracy in America.* Grand Rapids, Mich.: Eerdmans, 1984.

———. "The Protestant Mainline." *Faith & Renewal* (July/August 1990): 4–6.

———, ed. *The Ratzinger Conference on Bible and Church.* Grand Rapids, Mich.: Eerdmans, 1988.

Niebuhr, H. Richard. *The Purpose of the Church and Its Ministry.* New York: Harper & Row, 1956.

Noll, Mark A., and David Wells, eds. *Christian Faith and Practice in the Modern World.* Grand Rapids, Mich.: Eerdmans, 1988.

Noll, Mark A., et al. *The Search for Christian America.* Colorado Springs: Helmers & Howard, 1989.

Oberman, Heiko. *Forerunners of the Reformation.* Reprint, Philadelphia: Fortress, 1981.

———. *The Harvest of Medieval Theology.* Grand Rapids, Mich.: Eerdmans, 1967.

Oden, Thomas C. *After Modernity . . . What? Agenda for Theology.* New York: Akademie, 1990.

———. "The Long Journey Home." *Journal of the Evangelical Theological Society* 34, no. 1 (1991): 77–92.

———. "Then and Now: The Recovery of Patristic Wisdom." *Christian Century,* 12 December 1990, 1164–68.

Packer, J. I. *A Quest for Godliness: The Puritan Vision of the Christian Life.* Westchester, Ill.: Crossway, 1990.

———. *Evangelism and the Sovereignty of God.* Downers Grove, Ill.: InterVarsity, 1961.

———. *"Fundamentalism" and the Word of God.* Reprint, Grand Rapids, Mich.: Eerdmans, 1990.

———. *Hot Tub Religion.* Wheaton, Ill.: Tyndale, 1987.

———. "Shepherds after God's Own Heart." *Faith & Renewal* 15, no. 3 (1990): 12–17.

Pannenberg, Wolfhart. "The Present and Future Church." *First Things* (November 1991): 47–51.

Patterson, Robert. "In Search of the Visible Church." *Christianity Today,* 11 March 1991, 36–40.

Pauck, W. *The Heritage of the Reformation.* New York: Oxford University, 1961.

Perotta, Kevin. "Who Pastors the Pastors?" *Faith & Renewal* 15, no. 3 (1990): 3–11.

Petersen, Jim. *Church Without Walls.* Colorado Springs: NavPress, 1992.

———. *Living Proof.* Colorado Springs: NavPress, 1989.

Peterson, Eugene H. *Working the Angles: The Shape of Pastoral Integrity.* Grand Rapids: Eerdmans, 1993.

Piercy, H. R. *The Meaning of the Church in the Thought of Calvin.* Chicago: University of Chicago, 1941.

Pope, Randy. *The Prevailing Church.* Chicago: Moody, 2002.

Quebedeaux, Richard. *The Worldly Evangelicals.* New York: Harper & Row, 1978.

Quinn, John R. "Orthodoxy—as Opposed to Fundamentalism, Theological Liberalism, and Integralism." *New Oxford Review* (May 1991): 15–23.

Radmacher, Earl D. *The Nature of the Church.* Portland, Oreg.: Western Baptist Press, 1972.

Ratzinger, Joseph Cardinal. *Church, Ecumenism and Politics.* New York: Crossroad, 1988.

———. *Introduction to Christianity.* San Francisco: Ignatius, 1990.

Rayburn, Robert G. *O Come, Let us Worship: Corporate Worship in the Evangelical Church.* Grand Rapids, Mich.: Baker, 1980.

Reardon, Bernard M. G. *Religious Thought in the Reformation.* White Plains, N.Y.: Longman, 1981.

Riddlebarger, Kim. "Thy Kingdom Come." *Modern Reformation* (March/April 1992): 7–9.

Roberts, Richard Owen. *Revival.* Wheaton, Ill.: Tyndale, 1982.

Roof, Wade C., and William McKinney. *American Mainline Religion: Its Changing Shape and Future.* New Brunswick, N.J.: Rutgers University Press, 1987.

Ryken, Leland. *Worldly Saints: The Puritans As They Really Were.* Grand Rapids, Mich.: Zondervan, 1986.

Sanders, J. Oswald. *Spiritual Leadership.* Chicago: Moody, 1967, 1980.

Sayers, Dorothy. *Christian Letters to a Post-Christian World.* Grand Rapids, Mich.: Eerdmans, 1969.

———. *Creed or Chaos.* New York: Harcourt Brace, 1949.

Schaeffer, Francis A. *The Church at the End of the Twentieth Century.* Westchester, Ill.: Crossway, 1985.

———. *The Great Evangelical Disaster.* Westchester, Ill.: Crossway, 1984, 1987.

Schlossberg, Herbert. *Idols for Destruction: Christian Faith and Its Confrontation with American Society.* Nashville: Thomas Nelson, 1983.

————, and Marvin Olasky. "Piety and Pietism." In *Turning Point: A Christian Worldview Declaration*. Westchester, Ill.: Crossway, 1987, 25–41.

Shenk, Wilbert R. *Write the Vision: The Church Renewed*. Harrisburg: Trinity Press, 1995.

Sider, Ronald J., Philip N. Olson, Heidi Rolland Unruh. *Churches That Make a Difference*. Grand Rapids: Baker, 2002.

Simpson, Charles. *The Challenge to Care*. Ann Arbor, Mich.: Servant, 1986.

Smith, Glenn C. *Evangelizing Adults*. Wheaton, Ill.: Tyndale, 1985.

Smith, Timothy L. *Revivalism and Social Reform*. New York: Harper & Row, 1965.

Snyder, Howard A. and Daniel V. Runyon, *Decoding the Church*. Grand Rapids, Mich.: Baker, 2002.

Sproul, R. C. *Chosen by God*. Wheaton, Ill.: Tyndale, 1986.

————. *The Holiness of God*. Wheaton, Ill.: Tyndale, 1985.

————. *Lifeviews: Understanding the Ideas that Shape Society Today*. Old Tappan, N.J.: Revell, 1986.

Stephenson, J., ed. *Creeds, Councils and Controversies: Documents Illustrative of the History of the Church A.D. 337–461*. Nashville: Abingdon, 1988.

Thielicke, Helmut. *The Trouble with the Church*. Grand Rapids, Mich.: Baker, 1965.

Til, Cornelius Van. *Essays on Christian Education*. Nutley, N.J.: Presbyterian and Reformed, 1977.

Todd, J. M. *Luther: A Life*. New York: Crossroad, 1982.

Walker, Andrew. "We Believe." *Christianity Today*, 29 April 1991, 25–27.

Walker, William, et al. *A History of the Christian Church*. Reprint, New York: Charles Scribner's Sons, 1985.

Watson, David. *I Believe in the Church.* Reprint, Grand Rapids, Mich.: Eerdmans, 1982.

Webber, Robert E. *Ancient-Future Faith: Rethinking Evangelicalism for a Postmodern World.* Grand Rapids, Mich.: Baker, 2000.

Webber, Robert. *The Church in the World.* Grand Rapids, Mich.: Zondervan, 1986.

————., and Rodney Clapp. *People of the Truth.* New York: Harper & Row, 1988.

Wells, David F. "Conversion: Our Work or God's?" *Action* (January/February 1991): 4–7.

Wesley, John. *The Works of John Wesley.* Edited by F. Baker. 9 vols. Nashville: Abingdon, 1975.

White, Jerry. *The Church and the Parachurch: An Uneasy Marriage.* Portland, Oreg.: Multnomah, 1983.

Wiersbe, Warren. *The Integrity Crisis.* Nashville: Oliver Nelson, 1988.

————. *Real Worship.* Nashville: Oliver Nelson, 1986.

Wilkes, Paul. "The Hands That Would Shape Our Souls." *Atlantic Monthly* (December 1990): 59–88.

Winter, Ralph D. "The Two Structures of God's Redemptive Mission." *Missiology* 2 (1974): 121–39.

————. "Protestant Mission Societies: The American Experience." *Missiology* 7 (1979): 139–78.

Wolf, Miroslav. *After Our Likeness: The Church as the Image of the Trinity.* Grand Rapids, Mich.: Eerdmans, 1998.

Wuthnnow, Robert. *Christianity in the 21st Century: Reflections on the Challenges Ahead.* Oxford: Oxford University Press, 1993.

INDEX

INDEX

INDEX

World–view, 185.
 See also Christian world–view
Worship, 106, 274–76
Woytyla, Karol, 226–27.
 See also John Paul II
Wright, Earldean, 137

—X/Y/Z—

Yamasaki, Minoru, xiv

Yaweh, 171–72
Yeltsin, Boris, 239
Youth Direct Ministries, 88
Zanios, Jim, 363
Zinzendorf, Count, 343

STUDY GUIDE

BY T. M. MOORE

*Pastor of Teaching Ministries, Cedar Springs Presbyterian Church,
and theological consultant to the Wilberforce Forum*

INTRODUCTION

This study guide is designed to lead you through an exploration of the content, biblical foundations, and practical implications of Chuck Colson and Ellen Vaughn's, *Being the Body*. In each of the thirteen lessons in this series you will do the following:

Get the Point

You will be asked to read a section of *Being the Body*, usually two or three chapters, and then to answer a few brief questions reflecting on the argument of that section. By reading the questions in the study guide in advance, you will be better able to follow the primary points in the discussion of each section, so that you can get the most out of your reading.

Reflect

Next you will be led through an investigation of various passages of Scripture underlying the argument of the section you have read. In this section you will study the biblical teaching about the church, her character and mission, and the role each of us must play in being the Body of Christ.

Apply

The questions in this section will lead you to consider how God would have you respond to what you have read and studied. Try to make your applications as clear and personal as you can, and make plans to implement what you are learning.

Pray

Finally, you will be asked to list items for prayer relative to the material you have read and studied, and to commit to praying for these items as part of your regular time of prayer. Being the Body of Christ must begin before the throne of grace, where alone we can find the wisdom and strength we need to help us in every way.

There has never been a more important time for us to revisit the biblical teaching on the church and to consider the opportunities for being the Body that are before us. As Christians we need to work for a better understanding of the church—the Body of Christ—and to consider how we might join together as one in actually *being* that Body in these rapidly changing and uncertain times. Our prayer is that you will find these lessons informative, challenging, and helpful in leading you to discover God's will for your life in the high calling of *Being the Body*.

1
CONCEPTIONS & MISCONCEPTIONS

As September 11 should remind us forever, we are to be the Body—the manifestation of God's hope—in the blood, dirt, dust, and tears of the battlefields of this world.

Get the Point

Read *Being the Body*, Prologue and chapters 1–3.

1. How did John's experience in Redeemer Presbyterian Church help him to come to a saving knowledge of Jesus Christ?

2. In what ways does the world-view of Islam differ from that of Christianity?

3. Summarize the four caveats the authors put forth in chapter 1. Do you anticipate having a problem with any of these? Why or why not?

4. What is the role of individualism and relativism in today's society? Why does the church need to be aware of this?

5. Summarize each of the following *mis*conceptions of the church:
   - the church as a building:
   - the church as therapy:
   - the church for growth's sake:

6. In chapter 3, summarize the four key characteristics essential for being the church in the world today.

Reflect

Read 1 Peter 2:1–10.

7. What is suggested by each of the following images of the church in this passage?
   - the church as spiritual house:
   - the church as chosen people:
   - the church as royal priesthood:
   - the church as holy nation:
   - the church as God's own possession:

8. According to Peter, what is the mission of the church in the world (v. 9)?

9. As Peter puts it in v. 10, what is our *motivation* for mission?

10. Look back at the various images of the church you considered in question 7. What does each of these imply for an individual church member? What, for example, does it mean for a church member to be a "living stone"? A "priest" in God's house?

Apply

11. Review the images of the church from question 7. Which of these images best characterizes your church at this time? In which of these does your church seem to fall short? Why?

12. Consider the ways you are presently involved in your church. Compare your involvement in your church with the implications for individual believers you summarized in question 10. In which of these areas of implications would you like to see more progress in

your own life as a member of the church? What opportunities does your church afford for you to begin to do this?

Pray

Pray that, as you grow through this study, you and your church will begin to understand more of what it means to *be* the Body of Christ. What other items come to mind for prayer from this lesson? List them below, and make sure to pray for them each day.

2
GOD'S CHURCH

When the church is the church, the people of God moved by the Spirit of God do the work of God, and evil cannot stand against them.

Get the Point

Read chapters 4–6 of *Being the Body*.

1. Summarize each of the following points about the nature of the church from chapter 4:
   - the church is not a building:
   - the church is a new community:
   - the church belongs to God:
   - the church will triumph:

2. What are some of the differences between the church universal and the church particular? Why is it important that we consider ourselves members of each?

3. In chapter 6, explain the difference the authors insist on between a "decision" for Christ and true conversion. Why is this an important distinction?

4. Why is it wrong to consider any one formula or method for salvation to be the only true and reliable one?

Reflect

Read Hebrews 12:18–28.

5. What words does the writer use to instruct us that, as believers in Jesus Christ, we have become members of the church universal (v. 23)?

6. As members of the Body of Christ we are also part of an "unshakable Kingdom" (v. 28). How does this idea relate to the authors' claim that the church will ultimately triumph? How should this guide us in thinking about the various challenges and struggles that face our particular churches in today's world?

7. As members of the church—and of particular churches—and citizens in an unshakable kingdom, we have certain obligations. That is, certain kinds of *practice* ought to characterize us as we go about being the Body of Christ. Explain these as they are listed in the following verses:
   • v. 25:
   • v. 27:
   • v. 28a:
   • v. 28b:

8. The writer says that we have become one with "the spirits of the righteous made perfect" (v. 23). To whom does this refer? What does this imply about our own ultimate destiny as members of the church?

Apply

9. How does your church express the fact that it is also part of the universal church? How do you practice that fact?

10. In what ways is it apparent that God's "unshakable Kingdom" is working in and through your church? In and through your own life?

11. Review the practices listed in question 7. Which of these do you find to be most consistently present in your own life? In what ways? Of which of these would you like to see greater evidence in your life?

12. Our ultimate destination is to join those whose spirits have already been made perfect. How should you expect the practices examined in question 7 to help you make progress toward that state in this life? What can keep you from realizing this progress?

Pray

Pray for a greater vision of the church universal, and for yourself as a member of that church. What other items for prayer come to mind as a result of your studies in this lesson? List them below, and begin praying about them right away.

3
THAT THEY MAY BE ONE

Non-Christians aren't looking so much at our tracts and rallies and
telecasts and books as they are looking at us and how we behave.
When they fail to see the unity of Jesus' followers—the church—
they fail to see the validation that Christ is indeed the Son of God.

Get the Point

Read *Being the Body,* chapters 7 and 8.

1. From your reading of these chapters, what kinds of things threaten the unity we are called to have in the Body of Christ?

2. What three critical reasons for unity do the authors list in chapter 8?

3. What are the characteristics of true unity?

4. Why is "diversity within the Body" an important part of the unity of the church? What "healthy corrective" does this provide?

5. The authors list four ways of working for greater unity within the Body of Christ. In which of these ways is your church currently active? How?

Reflect

Read John 17:9–23.

6. For whom is Jesus praying in these verses (v. 20)? In one word, what does He seem to want most of all for them (v. 21)?

7. According to the following verses, what characteristics do all true Christians have in common that should serve to help them achieve greater unity?
   • v. 9c:
   • v. 10:
   • v. 11a:
   • v. 13:
   • vv. 14, 17:
   • vv. 14, 15:
   • v. 18:
   • v. 23 (recall our ultimate destination as believers from the last lesson):

8. In this passages several things might be seen as working against our achieving greater unity. How does each of the following get in the way of this objective?
   • self-interest (v. 12):
   • lack of attention to the Word of God (vv. 14, 17):
   • the world (v. 15):
   • the devil (v. 15):
   • neglect of our mission (v. 18):

9. According to verse 21, what does the Lord promise if His people can achieve visible unity in some ways?

Apply

10. How conscious are you of the forces working against unity in the churches in your community? How can you see this opposition to unity at work?

11. How would you apply the promise of verse 21 to your community, if the churches in your community could begin to discover ways of achieving greater unity? What would you expect to see happen?

12. Review the characteristics of true unity that we examined in question 7. Which of these seem to be most lacking in your church? In your own life? How might you begin to work toward nurturing more of these characteristics in yourself? Your church?

Pray

Pray that God will begin to bring greater unity to your church, and to the churches in your community. What other items for prayer come to mind from this lesson? Write them below, and be faithful to pray about them daily.

4

NO OTHER FOUNDATION

The church is to be one—living in unity. It is to be holy—its members living righteous lives. It is catholic—that is, universal in its compass, not confined to one denomination or culture. It is apostolic—rooted in and proclaiming the apostles' teaching.

Get the Point

Read *Being the Body*, chapters 9 and 10.

1. How was Jonathan Edwards's sermon at Enfield a demonstration of the power of God's Word?

2. What is required of those called to preach the Word?

3. Whose responsibility is it to ensure that the Word is being taught in churches?

4. Where the Word is faithfully preached and taught, a *communio sanctorum arises*—a new community in Christ. Briefly explain each of the following characteristics of that new community:
    *   fellowship:
    *   accountability and discipline:
    *   the sacraments:
    *   prayer and worship:
    *   witness:

5. Why is each of the sacraments of baptism and the Lord's Supper so important to our identity as the Body of Christ? How can churches keep these from being a source of division rather than unity?

Reflect

Read 1 Corinthians 3:10–16.

6. Who has the responsibility for building the church (v. 10)? What must be their general attitude toward this calling?

7. A building always arises according to the shape of its "footprint"— its foundation. Since Christ is the foundation of the Church, what does this imply for individual churches (v. 11)? For all the churches in a given community?

8. We all bring certain "building material" to the task of building the church. Can you give some examples of what each of the following "building materials" might be in your church?
   • gold, silver, precious stones:
   • wood, hay, stubble:

9. What promise does Paul make about our works, that is, our use of these building materials in constructing the Body of Christ (vv. 13-15)? How should that motivate us in choosing our materials and using them wisely?

10. According to verse 16, what common source do we have to draw on for building the Body of Christ together? How should we expect that to help us?

Apply

11. What kind of "building materials" are you presently bringing to the task of building the church? In your particular church? In the larger church in your community?

12. Suggest some ways that the churches in your community might come together, in the power of the Spirit, to join hands in building the church in your community. How might you help this to come about?

Pray

Pray for your fellow church members, that they will be more conscious of being called to work together in building the church. Below, list any additional items for prayer that arise from this lesson, and be sure to pray for them daily.

5

THE BEGINNING OF WISDOM

*We need to know the fear of the Lord: the overwhelming, compelling awe
and reverence of a holy God. The Proverbs tell us that the fear of the Lord
is the beginning of wisdom. Why?*

Get the Point

Read *Being the Body*, chapters 11 and 12.

1. What advantages come to us from learning the fear of the Lord?

2. What do the authors mean by the phrase, *coram deo?*

3. How did Rusty Woomer grow in the fear of the Lord? In what ways
   did this help him?

4. What can we learn from the life of Rusty Woomer about the importance of cultivating the fear of the Lord?

Reflect

Read 1 Timothy 3:14–16.

5. How does Paul describe the church in this passage? What does each
   of these phrases mean?

6. What is the basic confession of all those who truly fear the Lord (v. 16)?

7. Paul calls this confession "the mystery of godliness." If by "mystery" we understand the idea of "revelation," what should we expect to happen in our churches if we can nurture the fear of God and practice this confession more consistently?

8. What is Paul's basic reason for writing this letter and this passage (vv. 14, 15)? What does it suggest about us, and about our church, if we are not practicing the fear of the Lord like this?

Apply

9. In what ways does your church consciously work to nurture the fear of the Lord in its members?

10. How do you experience the fear of the Lord? How do you express it?

11. In what ways does your experience of fearing the Lord parallel that of Rusty Woomer? In what ways is it different?

12. Can you think of some ways that the churches in your community might work together to practice the fear of the Lord? What is keeping them from doing this? How might you help your church, and the churches in your community, to practice more of the *coram deo?*

Pray

Pray that your church might grow in the fear of the Lord. What other items for prayer are suggested by this lesson? List them below, and pray for them daily.

6

THE CORNERSTONE

*Christianity itself rests on the astonishing claim that
Jesus rose bodily from the dead and ascended into heaven.
But of all these claims, the most remarkable
is His bold statement: I am the truth.*

Get the Point

Read *Being the Body*, chapters 13 and 14.

1. How did Pilate respond to Jesus' statement about truth? What did he conclude?

2. How do the authors define truth in chapter 14? How does this definition apply to Jesus' claim to *be* the truth?

3. Because Jesus is truth, His teaching—Christianity—is also truth. Does this mean that there is a conflict between faith and reason? Why or why not?

4. What does it mean for Christians to be the "people of the truth" in a day when so many new world-views are proliferating?

Reflect

Read Ephesians 2:18–22.

5. What does this passage teach about how people come to know God as Father (v. 18)?

6. How does coming to the knowledge of God affect people from all kinds of different backgrounds (v. 19)?

7. The cornerstone is the first stone laid in constructing a building. It provides both horizontal and vertical direction for the rest of the construction. What is the significance of this for thinking of Jesus as the Cornerstone of the church?

8. Since the church is built on "the foundation of the apostles and the prophets," what place should the Word of God have in all our undertakings as the Body of Christ? Are you confident that all the undertakings of your church have this foundation? Why or why not?

9. According to verses 21 and 22, how can we tell when a particular church is being properly built on the foundation of truth? What does that look like? What would we expect it to look like in a community of churches?

Apply

10. How much time do you presently spend each week being built up on the foundation of truth? In what kinds of settings? How would you describe the quality of time you spend in each of those settings?

11. Can you think of any areas in which it seems clear that your church is not building on the *whole* truth of God's Word? What might you do to help get that construction going?

12. Do any people in your church feel more like "strangers and aliens" than "members of God's household"? Why do you think that is? What can you do to help alleviate this problem?

Pray

Pray that, more and more, your church will grow to become a temple of the living God. What other items for prayer arise from this lesson? List them below, and begin praying for them daily.

7

A WAR OF WORLDVIEWS

*The Christian concept of truth—that ultimate reality
is found in Jesus Christ—is held today by a small minority.*

Get the Point

Read *Being the Body*, chapters 14 and 15.

1. What do the authors mean by a "world-view"?

2. Briefly explain each of the following aspects of today's unbelieving "world-view":
   - the Donahueites:
   - Oprahfication:
   - the Goodmanites:
   - Relative relativism:

3. Briefly summarize each of the following aspects of the prevailing worldview today:
   - secularism:
   - antihistoricism:
   - naturalism:
   - utopianism:
   - pragmatism and utilitarianism:

4. What are the important aspects of truth to which Christians must pay increasing attention in order to assert the biblical world-view in these postmodern times?

5. What challenges confront us, and to what tasks are we called, in asserting the biblical world-view?

Reflect

Read 1 Corinthians 3:18–22.

6. How does Paul say we should regard the "wisdom of this age" (vv. 19, 20)? How should this warn us?

7. What does Paul mean by saying that those who regard themselves as wise according to the world-views of this age should become fools (v. 18; cf. 1:26-31)?

8. All things are ours, according to Paul (vv. 21, 22). What does this include?

9. Given that we belong to Christ—and Christ belongs to God—what should we be seeking to do with this "all things" (vv. 22, 23)?

Apply

10. Following are some of the "all things" that make up our lives. In each of these areas, how are you working to use these things as one who belongs to Christ?
    • your work:
    • your free time:
    • your family life:
    • your daily conversations:
    • your involvement in church:

- your life in your neighborhood:
- your wealth and possessions:

11. Where might a believer expect to encounter the "wisdom of this age"? How would you counsel a new believer to prepare himself or herself so as not to be ensnared by the futile thinking that comes from these sources?

12. Does your church equip its members to recognize and resist unbelieving world-views? In what ways? How does your church try to equip its members to take their place in asserting the biblical world-view? To what extent do you feel personally equipped to take up that challenge?

Pray

Pray that your church might become increasingly aware of the unbelieving world-views prevalent in your community, and of its calling to assert the biblical world-view. What additional matters for prayer arise from this study? List them below, and begin praying about them daily.

8

CAPTIVE?

Christ is risen indeed. And regardless of the prevailing political powers,
be they the reign of the Caesars or the Communists or the cultures of moral
decay, He will build His church. And the gates of hell
will not prevail against it.

Get the Point

Read *Being the Body*, chapters 17 and 18.

1. How did the believers in Romania help to hasten the fall of the Communist regime?

2. In what ways do the authors suggest that the church today is in captivity?

3. How does the prevailing culture threaten the life and mission of the church?

4. How would you be able to tell when your church was being a pawn in the game of contemporary culture? When it was serving as a prophet?

5. What is repentance, and why is it so important?

Reflect

Read Ephesians 4:17–24.

6. How does Paul describe the mind-set of unbelief? What is the cause of this (v. 18)?

7. How might someone be able to tell that you had indeed "learned Christ" (v. 20)?

8. What is the role of the renewal of the mind in authenticating faith in Christ? Of repentance (vv. 21–23)?

9. What does it mean to "put on the new man" (v. 24)? To what disciplines must a person submit if he or she wants to put on the new man?

Apply

10. In what ways do you find that the unbelieving ideas and habits of the "old man" yet linger in your life? In your church?

11. What are you doing to achieve the "renewing of the mind"? In what ways have you seen your mind being renewed in recent months?

12. How can Christians help one another to "put on the new man"? What opportunities does your church provide for Christians to practice this? How can you begin to be more helpful to your fellow Christians in this important calling?

Pray

Pray that a spirit of repentance would pervade your church. Below, list any additional thoughts, concerns, or other matters that arise from this study, and begin to pray for them daily.

9

THE CALL FOR JUSTICE

*How desperately the modern church needs to recapture the full biblical
vision of justice! And we need also to take hold of Luther's third great
contribution to the church: the unity of biblical truth and
its relevance to all of life.*

Get the Point

Read *Being the Body,* chapters 19 and 20.

1. Outline the steps that resulted in Martin Luther's coming to trial
   before the emperor.

2. How do the authors define "justice" in chapter 20? How is it evident
   that the contemporary church has failed to understand this idea?

3. Suggest some ways that biblical truth applies to each of the following areas:
   • politics and government:
   • vocation:
   • economics:
   • education:
   • science:
   • art:
   • the church:

Reflect

Read Genesis 12:1–3.

4. As we saw in our study of Hebrews 12:22–28, believers have come to the new covenant, which is really the fulfillment of the covenant God spoke to Abraham. In Genesis 12:1–3, how would you explain each of the following promises God made to Abraham?

    • a great nation:

    • bless you:

    • make your name great:

    • make you a blessing:

    • bless those who bless, curse those who curse:

    • bless all families of the earth:

5. How can you see that these various blessings and promises relate to the idea of justice (righteousness)?

6. How did God expect Abraham to show that he believed God and was willing to receive these promises (v. 1)? What might this imply for believers today?

7. Think of what you know about the rest of Abraham's life. In what ways did he begin to realize all the promises God had made to him?

8. Read Romans 4:4–14. To whom are the promises God made to Abraham available today?

Apply

9. The basic promise made to Abraham is that God would bless him— that is, would establish him in a right relationship with God, in which he could hear what God required, receive what God promised, and go forth to serve Him. How would someone be able to tell that a believer today had been "blessed" in this kind of way?

10. Who are the people you see most often week by week? List their names below:

11. In what ways should you expect that the justice and righteousness of God—His blessings—would extend through you to these people? In other words, how do you expect to "be a blessing" to these people in the week ahead?

12. Suggest some ways that your church might begin to make more of the promises of God to Abraham the common possession of all its members. How might your church begin to work together with other churches in your community to "be a blessing" to all the families in your community?

Pray

Pray that your church will become increasingly committed to the idea of being blessed to be a blessing. What other items for prayer are suggested by your study in this lesson? List them below, and begin to pray for them daily.

10

FOR THE WORK OF THE MINISTRY

Since a biblical world-view involves all of life, the Church must equip its members for all of life. Like the military, this begins with the basics and moves on to building the mature character of the seasoned warrior.

Get the Point

Read *Being the Body*, chapters 21 and 22.

1. What is the essential charge of the Great Commission? How does this sometimes become confused?

2. In chapter 22 the authors describe eight basic ways local churches must begin equipping their members for ministry. List these below:

3. Why is it important that church members begin learning how to minister to the "outcasts" of society—prisoners, the dying, homosexuals, and so forth?

4. Why is it important to focus first of all on building the character of God's people?

Reflect

Read Ephesians 4:12–16.

5. According to Paul, why have pastors and teachers (among others) been given to local churches? In what should this result?

6. What would be some examples of "works of ministry?" Think of the life of the Lord Jesus Christ in your answer:

7. As equipped believers do works of ministry the local church is built up, so that "we all"—all church members together—begin to arrive at a certain condition of maturity and health. How would you explain the following marks of a church that was growing together like Paul suggests?
   • unity of the faith and of the knowledge of the Son of God:
   • no longer children with respect to false teachings:
   • speaking the truth in love:
   • every joint supplying:
   • the body makes increase of itself in love:

8. On a scale of 1 to 10, with 10 being the highest rating, how would you assess the state of your church in each of the above categories of health? In the margin to the left of the items mentioned in question 7, place a number, 1 to 10, to indicate your assessment.

9. If pastors and teachers are given to the church "for the equipping of the saints," how might we be able to tell if they are doing their job well? What is the responsibility of "the saints" in this matter?

Apply

10. What opportunities for equipping the saints for ministry does your church presently offer? In which of these are you active? What evidence—in terms of "works of ministry"—have you seen to indicate that you are, in fact, being adequately equipped?

11. In which areas of a healthy, growing church (question 7) did you indicate some need for improvement in your church? Why? Can you suggest some ways that your church might begin to address this need?

12. What is your responsibility toward those whom God has given to your church for the equipping of the saints? How might you support or encourage them better? What can you do to help make their work more effective in building up the Body of Christ?

Pray

Pray that God will work in your church to equip more of His saints for the work of ministry, and that your church will grow healthier as a result. What other items for prayer come to mind as a result of your study of this lesson? List them below, and begin praying for them daily.

11
LET THIS MIND BE IN YOU

*Because we want to be like the world, we create our own celebrities,
our own superstars—our Christian musicians, honey-tongued preachers,
World Series heroes, converted rock stars, and sometimes even former
White House aides.*

Get the Point

Read *Being the Body,* chapter 23.

1. What do the authors mean by the "celebrity syndrome"?

2. In what ways does this manifest itself in the church today?

3. What problems arise in the church from tolerating this celebrity syndrome?

4. What model does the Bible give in opposition to the celebrity syndrome?

Reflect

Read John 13:1–15.

5. What did Jesus know going into this situation (vv. 1, 3)? If this had been you, and you had known this to be true of yourself, how might you have been tempted?

6. The first challenge to a true servant is to be able to identify the need. What need did Jesus identify in this situation? Why would we *not* expect Him to have to meet this need? What does it say to us that He determined to do so?

7. The second challenge is to prepare for meeting the need. How did Jesus do this?

8. The third challenge is to see the need through to completion. What obstacles did Jesus confront as He went about to meet this need? How did He respond?

9. Jesus taught His disciples how they should regard what He had just done (vv. 12–15). How should we interpret His teaching about this situation for our churches today?

Apply

10. Do you see any evidence that the celebrity syndrome has taken hold in your church? Have you contributed to this in any way?

11. Can you identify any needs in your church that, at this time, are not being met?

12. How would you apply the example and teaching of Jesus to yourself in the face of these unmet needs in your church?

Pray

Pray that the Lord will raise up true servant leaders for your church. What other items for prayer come to mind as a result of this lesson? List them below, and begin praying for them daily.

12

TO THE WHOLE WORLD

Telling others about how God has rescued us is not a task,
a job to be done. Instead, it is a witness that flows naturally from a heart
overwhelmed with gratitude by the miracle of deliverance.

Get the Point

Read *Being the Body*, chapters 24–26.

1. What gave Father Kolbe the courage to offer to die for another prisoner?

2. Are we called first to "do witnessing" or to "be witnesses"? Explain your answer.

3. What are the two key hallmarks of our witness as Christians?

4. Summarize the characteristics of a "missional church."

5. Why is the idea of "salt" a good way of thinking about our witness for Christ?

Reflect

Read Acts 1:1–8.

6. What did Jesus spend forty days doing prior to His ascension? Why do you suppose He spent so much time on this one subject?

7. What did Jesus promise was going to happen to His followers (v. 5)? What would this bring into their lives, and how would it affect them (v. 8)?

8. What did Jesus *explicitly* discourage His disciples from spending time doing (v. 7)? Why?

9. How would you explain the significance for your church of the "Jerusalem, Judea, Samaria, and uttermost parts" sequence of the mandate in verse 8?

Apply

10. Have you received the Holy Spirit? What evidence of His power at work in you have you seen? Do you regularly see the evidence Jesus promised in verse 8? Why or why not?

11. Does your church have a "Jerusalem, Judea, Samaria, uttermost parts" strategy for being witnesses? In what part of that strategy are you involved? Does that strategy need improving in any areas? Which?

12. Why do you think so many believers spend so much time—and money—reading and studying and talking about the very thing Jesus discouraged His disciples from devoting themselves to (v. 7)? What should we be devoting our time, energy, and resources to instead?

Prayer

Pray that the Lord would begin to give you power to be His witness each day. What additional items for prayer come to mind as a result of this study? List them below, and begin praying for them daily.

13

LET YOUR LIGHT SHINE

*If a boy with a candle can light the night and stir a nation to freedom,
then what can we do? Does God not give us such stories to show us His truth
and strengthen our own resolve?*

Get the Point

Read *Being the Body,* chapters 27 and 28.

1. What is the significance of the candles in the story in chapter 27? How does this relate to the challenges facing the church in our post-modern times?

2. What do the Scriptures tell us *366 times?* Why is this an important word for us to hear in these times?

3. Why must we not give in to despair over the hard road that lies ahead?

Reflect

Read Matthew 5:13–16 and 1 Corinthians 12:4–11.

4. In what ways is it true that each believer is like the candles in Romania?

5. In Matthew 5:13–16, what does God promise if we let our lights shine before the watching world? What would this look like in your community, if your church were more consistent in this?

6. In 1 Corinthians 12:4–11 Paul begins a discussion of spiritual gifts. How would you explain the concept of spiritual gifts to a new believer? What are they? What are they for?

7. Should we expect every believer to possess every gift? Who determines who will receive which gifts? Should we expect to find in a local congregation a healthy mix of many of the spiritual gifts? Why? What might that look like?

8. The gifts of the Spirit are given "for the common good" (v. 7). How might we be able to tell when spiritual gifts were not being used for that purpose, or when they were being misused?

9. Gifts of the Spirit are "empowered" by the Spirit. They work rather like our witness for Christ. We may not sense that we can *do* this— whether bear witness or exercise some spiritual gift—because we don't *feel* that *we* have this ability. Why is this not a good way to think about spiritual gifts? How would a person who was living by faith think about spiritual gifts?

Apply

10. Think back to lesson 11 and the list of needs you discerned in question 11. Which spiritual gifts would seem to be required in beginning to meet these needs? Since these gifts come from the Spirit of God and are not ours inherently (by nature, that is), how would someone acting in faith show that he or she was eager to possess and use the gifts these needs require?

11. What are your spiritual gifts? How are you using them to light a candle of good works for the Lord?

12. Which spiritual gifts would you like to possess? How can you see that God might use these in your life as a candle for Him? How might you begin to go about seeking, acquiring, and developing these gifts? What would you expect to result (v. 7) from your using these gifts properly?

Pray

Pray that God's Spirit would move and stir among the members of your church to bring forth more of His gifts for ministry. What other matters for prayer come to mind from your study of this lesson? List them below, and begin to pray for them daily.